JOURNAL OF GLASS STUDIES

Roundel, Joab Murdering Abner, *enameled and silver-stained. North Holland (Amster-dam?), about 1515. D. 21.5 cm.* The Cloisters, The Metropolitan Museum of Art (*1984.206*).

JOURNAL

OF GLASS

STUDIES

VOLUME 27 · 1985

THE CORNING MUSEUM OF GLASS

CORNING, NEW YORK

14831

Members of the Advisory Board serve for three-year renewable terms. Term expiration dates are listed for each advisor.

The *Journal of Glass Studies* is published by The Corning Museum of Glass, Thomas S. Buechner, President; William C. Ughetta, Secretary; James L. Flynn, Treasurer.

Subscriptions for the *Journal* should be sent to The Corning Museum of Glass, Corning, New York 14831. The subscription price of the *Journal* is $20.00 a number plus postage and handling; one number is issued each year. The price of the *Index* to the *Journal of Glass Studies*, Vols. 1–15, 1959–1973, is $8.00 plus postage and handling.

THE JOURNAL OF GLASS STUDIES

has been conceived to meet the need for the recording of those discoveries, interpretations, acquisitions, and publications which affect the understanding of the art and history of glassmaking. Articles of a scholarly nature are meant to include contributions of archeological and of early scientific-technical nature as well as of art historical accounts. The "Recent Important Acquisitions" section includes a selection of noted acquisitions during the previous year by museums and private collections. The "Check List of Recently Published Articles and Books on Glass" records those items added to the Rakow Library of The Corning Museum of Glass since the last publication of this listing. The Museum Librarians welcome a notice from readers of any lacunae in the "Check List."

Although the final content of each issue is the responsibility of the editors, it is largely determined by the number, nature, and quality of contributions and illustrations received. No articles are commissioned, and unsolicited manuscripts are always welcome. Additional information for prospective authors may be found at the end of the "Notes" section.

The success and ultimate value of the *Journal of Glass Studies* are dependent on its contributors.

The Leonard S. and Juliette K. Rakow Awards

THE Leonard S. and Juliette K. Rakow Awards for Excellence in the History of Glass and for Excellence in the Art of Glass annually recognize significant individual accomplishments in the fields of glassmaking, glass decorating, and glass scholarship. Those who have won the Award, and the juries selecting the winners, are listed below.

WINNERS OF THE HISTORY AWARD

1983   Dr. Donald B. Harden

Jury: Robert J. Charleston
Sidney M. Goldstein
Dwight P. Lanmon
Ada M. Polak
Axel von Saldern

1984   Dr. David F. Grose
Dr. Danièle Foy

Jury: Thomas S. Buechner
Robert J. Charleston
Donald B. Harden
Dwight P. Lanmon
David B. Whitehouse

WINNERS OF THE ART AWARD

1984   Stanislav Libenský and Jaroslava Brychtová

Jury: Thomas S. Buechner
Robert J. Charleston
Dale Chihuly
Dwight P. Lanmon
Bertil Vallien

JOURNAL OF GLASS STUDIES

Contents

VOLUME 27 · 1985

Articles in the *Journal of Glass Studies* are arranged chronologically by historical period.

* Co-winner of the 1984 Leonard S. and Juliette K. Rakow Award for Excellence in the History of Glass.

A NEW ROMAN RELIEF-CUT
VESSEL FROM CAERWENT

GEORGE C. BOON

THIS ACCOUNT is of a new find which parallels a vessel discovered at Caerwent in 1855 and mentioned in a Ravenna paper (*Journées Internationales du Verre, Annales 1967*) in terms of some puzzlement.[1] There have been extensive excavations at this little Romano-British town on the southern seaboard of Wales, and the glass was published in 1973 (including the same vessel; a rim fragment has come to light meanwhile, Fig. 7, though fresh analyses suggest that a different vessel is involved).[2] That there is now "new" glass results from a National Museum of Wales research project under the direction of R. J. Brewer, which has as its object the recovery of the history of *Venta Silurum* as seen in its remains.

The fragments now to be discussed (Fig. 1–6) were found in Insula I, House 1, in 1983–1984. They lay with fragments of a colorless snake-thread vessel in soil brought in to level up a court-yard toward the year 300; but pottery from the same deposit was of late second to mid third-century date, and the snake-thread would be of that period. Accordingly, there is no reason to think that the relief-cut cup is later. The point is not without importance, for the 1855 vessel lacks context, and a third cup of the same kind, represented by a basal fragment (Fig. 9), came from disturbed levels at Exeter.[3] That piece, however, was assimilated by the late Dorothy Charlesworth to another Exeter fragment (from a fourth-century pit), which belonged to a relief-cut *skyphos* bearing the first letter of a motto ΠΙΕ ΖΗCΑΙC or the like.[4] It would by no means be the only

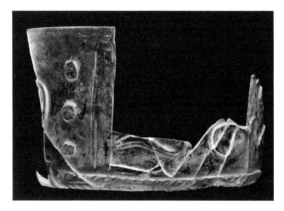

FIG. 1.

relief-cut *skyphos* of late Roman date; in particular, it may be compared with the recent discovery in a tomb at Zülpich, datable dendrochronologically after about 356. This vessel is inscribed ΚΑΛѠC ΖΗCΑΙC (or ΖΗCΑΙC ΚΑΛѠC) which, as we shall see, is the inscription on the

---

Ed. Note: This article is dedicated to Dr. Clasina Isings, who retired from the University of Utrecht in 1984 after a distinguished career.

1. *Annales du 4ᵉ Congrès des Journées Internationales du Verre, 1967*, pp. 100–102.

2. *Monmouthshire Antiquary* iii.2, 1972–1973, pp. 111–123, no. 22.

3. D. Charlesworth in P. T. Bidwell, *The Legionary Bath-House...at Exeter*, 1979, p. 222, Fig. 70, 2, drawn upside-down.

4. *Ibid.*, Fig. 70, 1. Not so identified by Miss Charlesworth, but I have seen the piece, and there is no doubt of the *pi*.

11

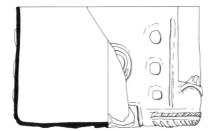

FIG. 2.

FIG. 5.

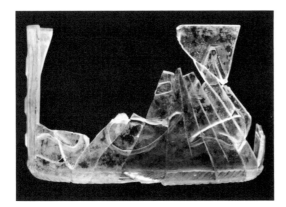

FIG. 3.

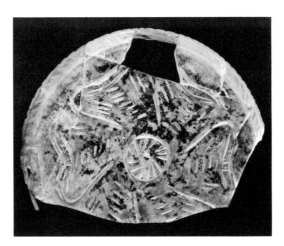

FIG. 4.

new Caerwent find.[5] Far from being the type-fossil of the early imperial period which it is some-times supposed to be, the cut glass *skyphos* enjoyed an almost antiquarian vogue later on.

The four cups (analyses, p. 16) are all of which I can find record. They must emanate from the same workshop; as the general parallels in decor-ation come from the Rhineland, they serve to lo-cate its whereabouts. The metal is colorless, with pinhead bubbles and the shiny inner surface that betrays a mold-blown blank. The whole outer surface is cut. The plain cylindrical shape, with simple ground rim but without a base ring, is not easy to match, particularly since the decoration of the new find shows that there cannot have been any handles. The few published cylindrical cups of similar proportions are not close;[6] but given the versatility of the Rhenish glasshouses, which could *inter alia* invent the pyramidal relief-cut

5. U. Heimberg, *Das Rhein. Landesmuseum Bonn:Ber. aus der Arbeit* 3/80, pp. 34–37, illus. top of 37. The position of the adverb depends on whether one reads it first or last; there is no grammatical point.

6. Among the few parallels listed is the mold-blown first-century "Sidonian" beaker in New York from Constantine (A. Kisa, *Das Glas im Altertume*, 1908, Abb. 260–260a) with its double wreath at the carination. More of the date of ours, but plain and thick, a small cup, K. Goethert-Polaschek, *Kat. röm. Gläser des Rhein. Landesmuseum Trier*, 1977, Type 47b, cf. 47a, with base ring. May not our cups have been designed *en suite* with a mold-blown *stamnium* bottle?

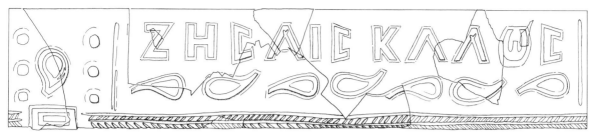

Fɪɢ. 6.

mug with transverse pierced handles at Trier,[7] this absence of close parallels as to shape seems unimportant. The design, in any case, required the whole field of the base; and like the Seksárd cage cup with the relief-cut fish and snails on its exposed base,[8] our little series may have been set out with their bottoms up.

On the base of the new find, and on that from Exeter, there is a central, rayed roundel; we may note something similar on the base of the much finer relief-cut *skyphos* from a Köln grave of the late third century.[9] On the Caerwent piece, six leaves converge on the roundel, but their tips have been chamfered away the better to set it off; the workmanship is rather hasty, and better on the Exeter piece, where the one surviving leaf and a feature next to it are arranged circumferentially. The internal detail of the leaves in both cases reappears on the tall, footed beaker in Vienna from Bršljin (Berslin), Slovenia, but there they are all engraved.[10] Despite the differences in technique, however, we may not be wrong in claiming this kind of detail as the "signature" of an ancient craftsman.

Enough remains of the wall of the new find to permit its decorative scheme to be reconstructed (Fig. 6). About three-quarters of the 310 mm periphery is occupied by an inscribed band, of which the bottom sloping bar of a *sigma* and an unbarred *alpha* next to it are joined to the main fragment, and part of another *alpha*, and a complete *lambda*, are preserved on a loose piece. On this basis we may certainly restore ZHCAIC KAΛωC, *zēsais kalōs*, "mayest thou live well";[11] and one tiny scrap from the *zeta* is recognizable.

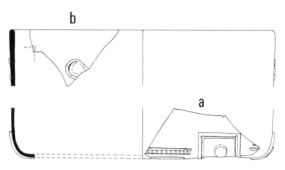

Fɪɢ. 7a, 7b

7. Goethert-Polaschek, *op. cit.*, Taf, 15, 170, at last provides a really good drawing of this famous vessel, including a view of the base.

8. D. B. Harden, *Archaeologia* cxvii, 1959, p. 204, A.4, pl. lxviia-c.

9. P. La Baume, *Kölner Jahrbuch* xii, 1971, pp. 80, 92, Abb. 4, 16.

10. D. B. Harden, *Kölner Jahrbuch* ix, 1967–1968, p. 44, no. 2; with foot restored T. Knez, *Razprave* [Ljubljana] vi, 1969, pp. 117–119, fig. ?

11. Ζήσαις or ζήσειας is the 2nd. person singular, aorist optative, of *ζάω (I live). Note also the shallow dish or lid from Köln lost in the last war, F. Fremersdorf, *Die röm. Glaser mit Schliff. . . aus Köln*, 1967, Taf. 28, upper, with ZHCAIN, the same, 3rd. person plural ("may they live"). Similar aorist optatives occur, for example, in the *New Testament* (e.g., 2 *Timothy* 1:16 and 18, and 1 *Peter* 1:2—respectively 2nd aorist optative and aorist optative passive). This use of the aorist is difficult for moderns. Indeed the Byzantine lexicographer Suidas (see under ’αμνοτι) could render it only as present subjunctive in Latin, ζήσειας-*vivas*. The aorist tense is unlimited (*a-oriston*), in its reference onward from a single completed action; hence it is suitably used for the unlimited continuance of the effect of wishes. We, like the Romans, have to make do with the present tense.

On the left, a small vertical cut is doubtless a guideline, there being no room for further ornament; another occurs above, and in the position of the absent crossbar of the first *alpha*. Below, plain leaves (without indented base or internal detail) are arranged in a band of four back-to-back pairs. The rest of the periphery is occupied by a geometrical figure of which the surviving part, a vertical bar with a row of three buttons to one side and a central device which seems again to have been a leaf, may be restored symmetrically; the best parallel to the buttons occurs on a fragment of unknown but presumably local provenance in the Tarragona Museum (Fig.10), with part of a leaf-scroll and a cross-hatched tendril or bud to the right.[12] This panel seems to have no purpose other than as a space-filler, and it is interesting that the motto was not expanded to include ΠΙΕ, *piè*, "drink!" at one end and perhaps ΑΕΙ, *aei* "always," at the other, for which there would be just the right space.[13]

At the carination, there is a stout double wreath with a rectangular jewel, set centrally with regard to the space-filling panel; inside was an oblong shape. Such a wreath, without the jewel, is seen on the small globular bottle from Köln in the British Museum[14] and on the Soria cage cup in Madrid.[15] The 1855 Caerwent basal fragment exhibits a jewel in high relief, but it is square rather than rectangular, and contains a circular button. Little can be said of other features of the 1855 pieces: the linear relief to the left and right of the jewel (Figs. 7a, 8) is not the same as on the new find, and not enough is left to be sure of its character. The curved relief on the rim fragment from another vessel is probably part of a tendril or leaf, not a letter: the curve comes too far down to suit an S (Fig.7b).

Relief-cut glass is rare in Britain. Only two small pieces of cage cups have been found, for example. There is accordingly a natural inclination to call such things luxurious or sumptuous— i.e., costly—and it is important, therefore, to remind ourselves that even the finest polychrome cage cup, with a Greek inscription, appears to

FIG. 8.

have been within the means of the proprietor of quite a small farmstead on the outskirts of Köln. Indeed, the example recovered from the little cemetery of the house was not the only important glass found there.[16] In this light, our cups corresponded to a very modest outlay, though the costs of carriage and frequent breakages *en route* no doubt inflated their price in the distant markets of western Britain.

The significance of the mottoes, similar to yet different from those on pottery,[17] is, at a superficial level, not in doubt. Kisa quotes from the Epitome of Cassius Dio's *Roman History* (but without reference or context)[18] warrant for claiming ζήσαις as a toast. The occasion concerned the Emperor Commodus, who, having dispatched an excessive number of beasts in the arena, sank

---

12. It is mentioned in Dr. Jennifer Price's doctoral thesis, University of Wales, 1981, ii, 414. I am grateful to her for providing me with her photograph of it, and for her permission to use it here.

13. ΠΙΕ ΖΗΣΑΙΣ ΚΑΛωΣ occurs on both the Köln cage cups with Greek inscription (Harden, *loc. cit.*, note 8, p. 208, B. 1; and the 1960 find mentioned below, note 16, both from the same workshop). ΑΕΙ, a useful filler-word, comes in the legend ΠΙΕ ΖΗΣΑΙΣ ΑΕΙ ΕΝ ΑΓΑΘΟΙΣ on the British Museum globular bottle from Köln (Harden, *ibid.*, 211 C. 5; Fremersdorf, *op. cit.* note 11, Taf. 28, lower).

14. *Loc. cit.*, last note.

15. Harden, *loc. cit.*, last note, 210 B. 11, pl. lxxid.

16. O. Doppelfeld, *Kölner Jahrbuch* v, 1960–1961, pp. 7–35. Other glasses of distinction from other graves were the engraved circus dish and the gold glass bowl with Biblical subjects.

17. *Pie zeses* and *calo* on Rhenish pottery, S. Loeschcke, *Kölner Jahrbuch* vii, 1932, p. 47, etc. A long list of beaker mottoes is given by G. Hagenow, *Aus dem Weingarten der Antike*, 1982, p. 135ff.

18. Dio, lxxiii, 18.2, cf. Kisa, 862, who gives a longer form not printed in the Loeb text.

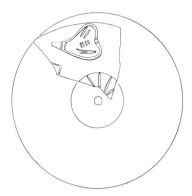

FIG. 9.

FIG. 10.

back exhausted and drained at a gulp a tall beaker of cooled wine. Thereupon, the audience gave spontaneous vent to what the historian called "this customary expression at *symposia*." This quotation has never settled matters, and, as Doppelfeld pointed out, attempts have been made to claim the *Diatretgläser* (of which a few have mottoes with ζήσαις) as Christian, though without gaining approval.[19] Though the acclamation is always in Greek on relief-cut glass, which tells us more of the origins of the glass-worker than of the purchaser, *piè zēses* appears in that Latin guise on engraved glasses and *fondi d'oro*. Indeed, so popular was it in the common tongue that it came to be abbreviated down to P.Z., and eventually lost its meaning, being tacked on to Latin mottoes with *bibe* and *vivas*. However, much of this material falls later than the period of our cups.[20]

The past is a foreign country, and it is strange to us moderns that what are apparently no more than mottoes for a drinking party should have been carved with such labor out of solid glass. It is interesting, therefore, to find two vessels and one cage cup which depart from the norm. It is diffi-cult to see what part the shallow dish and lid with ZHCAIN, "may they live,"[21] could have played in *symposia*, or what could have been the contents of the globular bottle with very narrow neck, holding well under a third of a liter, inscribed ΠΙΕ ΖΗCAIC ΑΕΙ ΕΝ ΑΓΑΘΟΙC, *piè*

zēsais aei en agathois, 'drink, mayest thou live for ever among the good [the blessed],' which is ac-cepted as a motto of Christian significance.[22] The cage cup is the Seksárd example from a Christian grave and reads ΛΕΙΒ[Ε Ѡ Π]ΟΙΜΕΝΙ ΠΙΕ ΖΗ[CAIC], *leibe O Poimeni piè zēsais*, "libate, O Shepherd, drink, mayest thou live."[23] E. B. Thomas has recently emphasized the cultic and Christian implication of this legend.[24] Dear or not so dear, delicate glassware—and no single cage cup has ever been found perfect, some part of the fretwork always being missing—would have been a hostage to fortune at any ordinary drinking party. Perhaps the restraint and solemnities of the weekly Christian *agape* offered by the well-to-do

19. Doppelfeld, *loc. cit.*, p. 23.

20. For *fondi d'oro* see the useful summary by F. Zanchi Roppo, *Vetri paleo-cristiani a figure d'oro* (Istituto di Antichità rav. e biz., Ravenna, *Quaderno* no. 8, 1967), *passim*, and table, pp. 57–59. Harden's Wint Hill group of engraved glasses, *Journal of Glass Studies*, II, 1960, pp. 45–81, esp. 78, is late third and fourth century.

21. See note 11.

22. See note 13, and O. M. Dalton, *Cat. Early Christian Antiq-uities*, British Museum, 1901, p. 131, no. 653.

23. Harden, *loc. cit.*, note 8.

24. E. B. Thomas in A. Lengyel and G. T. B. Radan (eds.), *The Archaeology of Roman Pannonia*, 1980, p. 199.

to their poorer brethren would have been a more suitable occasion for its use. The Zülpich *skyphos* (p. 11) was found in the grave of a Christian lady and may likewise have served in the *agape*; not much can be made of the absence of ΠΙΕ in its motto, and not much in the Caerwent case either: the standard acclamation recorded by Cassius Dio omits it too.

There is no reason to believe that the Caerwent cup and its fellows, with their sensible flat bottoms, were set aside for Christian use. But that use cannot be excluded. There is at Caerwent what I believe to have been a house converted to a church in an outlying part of the town, and in another house a sealed set of vessels used in the *agape* was found;[25] but the one is undated and requires re-excavation, and the other is well over a century later than our cups. Exeter likewise has yielded a trace of Romano-British Christianity, but again from a period long after the Peace of the Church.[26] How deep were the roots of these typically urban Christian communities? It is worth recalling that among the protomartyrs of Britain, two, Julius and Aaron, are believed to have suffered at Caerleon, only a few miles from Caerwent, probably under Decius or Valerian in the middle of the third century.[27] Who is to say, therefore, that the ζήσαις καλῶς on the Caerwent cup found in 1983–1984 was *never* meant to be understood . . . ἐν Θεῷ *en Theō*, "in God"?

ANALYSES

The analyses detailed below were carried out for the National Museum of Wales by C. J. Salter, of the Department of Metallurgy and Science of Materials of the University of Oxford, through the intermediacy of Dr. J. P. Northover. They concern samples of the relief-cut vessel with Greek inscription described in the preceding pages, found at Caerwent in 1983–1984 (OX284); a sample of a vessel of similar kind from Caerwent, 1855 (OX285); a sample of what had hitherto been regarded as a rim fragment from the same vessel (OX286); a sample of a flat handle as from a *trulleus* (*Monmouthshire Antiquary* iii.2, 1972–1973, 123, no. 51, Fig. 5) (OX287) and a sample of a colorless beaker with ground spiral furrowed decoration from Caerleon (*Archaeologia Cambrensis* lxxxvii, 1932, 87, no. 53, Fig. 35, dated Flavian-Hadrianic) (OX288), the last two being included for comparative purposes. The 1855 find (OX285) had previously been analyzed by Corning (cf. *Annales du 4ᵉ Congrès des Journées Internationales du Verre, 1967*, 101), where an unusually high phosphorus content, given as 1.0% (cf. *Monmouthshire Antiquary, loc. cit.*, 119), was erroneously reported owing to a typewriting error. Otherwise the analyses of the 1855 vessel at Oxford and Corning are, as might be expected, well in balance; little manganese decolorant was reported in either, but the Oxford analysis did not pick up the 0.6% antimony oxide recorded in the Corning analysis of the same and similar colorless vessel glass, where it was used as a decolorant in preference to manganese. For the major elements cf. E. R. Caley, *Analyses of Ancient Glasses 1790–1957*, Corning, 1962, p. 98, Table cxxiii.

25. Suggested church, Insula V House 22N—not a new idea, cf. *Archaeologia* lxii, 1911, p. 412. Deposit, G. C. Boon, *Bulletin of the Board of Celtic Studies*, University of Wales xix, 1962, pp. 338–345.

26. Aileen Fox, *Roman Exeter*, 1952, p. 92.

27. C. Thomas, *Christianity in Roman Britain*, 1981, pp. 48–50. With other glasses of 2nd-3rd century date, one is in the same doubtful position as with the much later bowls of Harden's Wint Hill group (note 20), in that some are pagan and others as obviously Christian. I refer to the cups with fish, palms, etc., engraved on them, of which there are five or more in evidence from Britain, *inter alia* from Silchester and Caerleon. See N. Walke, *Das röm. Donaukastell Straubing-Sorviodurum*, 1965, p. 49, for a comment, and J. Price, in J. du Plat Taylor and H. Cleere (eds.), *Roman Shipping and Trade: Britain and the Rhine Provinces* (C.B.A. Research Report, no. 24, 1978), p. 75, fig. 58. There is, as far as I know, absolutely no object of unequivocally Christian character from Roman Britain which can be assigned to a period before the Peace of the Church.

Mr. Salter states that the analysis for elements Na, Mg, Al, Si, P, S, Cl, K, Ca, and Ti was carried out using a wavelength dispersive spectrometer and an accelerating voltage of 10kV, whereas the elements Mn and Fe were analysed at 20kV using the Kevex dispersive detector. All analyses represent the mean of 10 individual area measurements, each area covering 50 micron squares of the surface of the sample. The glasses lie toward the top end of the range of silica contents recorded for Roman glass, and would have had a comparatively high softening point.

TABLE

	Na_2O	MgO	Al_2O_3	SiO_2	P_2O_5	SO_3	Cl	K_2O	CaO	TiO_2	MnO	FeO
OX284	17.4	0.3	1.5	73.2	0.0	0.3	1.3	0.4	5.3	0.1	—	0.3
OX285	17.1	0.3	1.6	73.3	0.1	0.3	1.2	0.5	5.4	0.1	—	0.2
OX286	17.0	0.4	1.7	72.5	0.1	0.5	1.2	0.5	5.7	0.1	—	0.3
OX287	18.3	0.4	1.7	70.6	0.1	0.4	1.4	0.5	6.2	0.1	—	0.4
OX288	19.1	0.3	2.0	69.4	0.1	0.4	1.5	0.5	6.4	0.1	—	0.3

ESSAI DE TYPOLOGIE DES VERRES MEDIEVAUX D'APRES LES FOUILLES PROVENCALES ET LANGUEDOCIENNES

DANIÈLE FOY*

L'ESSAI de typologie présenté dans ces pages n'a pas d'autre prétention que de réunir une grande partie des verres médiévaux (XIIᵉ–XVᵉ siècles) exhumés sur les sites de la France méditerranéenne. Ce travail, tributaire de la documentation, est forcément inégal: les pièces du XIVᵉ siècle, relativement abondantes permettent de donner un répertoire varié de formes souvent complètes. En revanche la définition des verreries du XIIᵉ et XIIIᵉ siècle reste incomplète. Les rares verres découverts dans des niveaux de la fin du XIIᵉ siècle ne sont que des éléments de forme. Les verres du XIIIᵉ siècle, plus diversifiés ne sont pas toujours complets. Cette recherche sur le verre creux du moyen-âge est récente. Elle a débuté par des fouilles spécifiques: ateliers et habitats de verriers, et elle bénéficie de l'apport renouvelé des fouilles médiévales qui se multiplient depuis une quinzaine d'années dans le Midi méditerranéen.

Le matériel étudié provient d'une vingtaine de sites (Fig. 1). Les habitats dominent: ce sont les chateaux de Montségur, Collioure, Saint Roman, les *castra* de Rougiers, La Môle, Nans, et les dépotoirs urbains de Martigues et d'Avignon (ville dans laquelle il faut distinguer les fouilles de l'Hôtel J. de Brion, du Petit-Palais et de la rue Racine). Les verres déposés dans les tombes médiévales sont rares, mais leur état de conservation est souvent exceptionnel. Nous avons étudié les verreries de la nécropole de Sainte-Croix (Die), de Cancabeau (Châteauneuf-de-Gadagne) et Viviers. D'autres verres ont été exhumés au cours des fouilles de l'église de Psalmodi (Saint-Laurent d'Aigouzes), de la chapelle d'une commanderie des Templiers de la Bastide-des-Jourdans et de la cathédrale Saint-Sauveur d'Aix-en-Provence. Enfin les fouilles de quatre ateliers de verriers ont complété notre documentation et surtout ont permis d'assurer l'origine régionale de la plupart des verres utilisés dans les habitats. L'atelier de Planier (Signes, Var) qui dépendait d'une communauté religieuse, est daté par les textes et l'archéologie de l'extrême fin du XIIIᵉ siècle; les débris de verre y étaient malheureusement peu nombreux.[1] La verrerie languedocienne de la Seube (Claret, Hérault)[2] et l'atelier varois de Rougiers

*Co-winner of the 1984 Leonard S. and Juliette K. Rakow Award for Excellence in the History of Glass.

The editors have adjusted the footnotes in part to bring them into closer accord with normal *Journal* usage.

1. D. Foy, Premiers sondages sur la verrerie médiévale de Planier (Signes, Var) dans "Activités archéologiques du Centre de Documentation Archéologique du Var, Toulon, 1979," *Annales de la Société des Sciences Naturelles et d'Archéologie de Toulon et du Var*, nº 31, 1979, pp. 27–43, en part. p. 30.

2. N. Lambert, "La Seube: témoin de l'art du verre en France méridionale du Bas Empire à la fin du Moyen-Age," *Journal of Glass Studies*, XIV, 1972, pp. 77–116.

Fig. 1. *Localisation des sites d'où proviennent les verres étudiés.*

contemporains sont datés du second quart du XIVe siècle. Bien qu'aucun four n'ait été découvert sur le *castrum* de Rougiers, l'abondance des creusets vitrifiés, des scories et des déchets de verres ne laissent aucun doute sur la fixation d'artisans verriers.[3] Le matériel en verre provenant de cette fouille bien stratifiée est à la base de notre classification: les verres datés de la fin du XIIe au XVe viennent d'une part des productions de l'atelier du XIVe siècle et d'autre part de la vaisselle de table utilisée par les habitants installés antérieurement, en même temps, ou postérieurement à la fabrique.[4] Le dernier atelier fouillé au lieu dit Cadrix (Saint-Maximin-la-Sainte-Baume, Var) est immédiatement postérieur aux ateliers précédents, mais il est difficile de préciser combien d'années fonctionna le four au cours de la seconde moitié du XIVe siècle.[5] Enfin près de

l'abbaye de Pré-Bayon (Gigondas, Vaucluse), un atelier localisé au cours d'une prospection, mais non fouillé, est daté grossièrement XIVe–XVe siècles. Des analyses physicochimiques effectuées sur les déchets de cet atelier et des trois autres fabriques provençales, ainsi que sur chacune des formes de verre distinguées ici, font apparaître

3. G. Demians D'Archimbaud, *Les fouilles de Rougiers (Var). Contribution à l'archéologie de l'habitat rural médiéval en pays méditerranéen*, Paris-Valbonne, 1980. D. Foy, *Le verre médiéval et son artisanat en France méditerranéenne, état de la question*. Thèse de 3e cycle dactylographiée, 1981, Aix-en-Provence.

4. D. Foy, *Verre et verreries dans la Provence médiévale*, mémoire de maîtrise dactylographiée, Aix-en-Provence, 1973; *ib.*, "L'artisanat du verre creux en Provence médiévale," *Archéologie Médiévale*, V, 1975, pp. 103–139.

5. D. Foy, "Fouilles de la verrerie médiévale de Cadrix (Var)," *Annales du 8e Congrès de l'Association Internationale du Verre*, Londres, 1979 (1981), pp. 178–194.

19

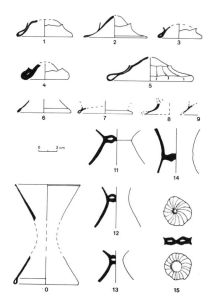

Fig. 2. *Pieds coniques, forme A1/1 à 6: Rougiers; 6 à 9: Planier. Verres bicontroniques, forme A3/10 à 13 et 15: Rougiers; 14: Psalmodi.*

diverses compositions et contribuent à l'établissement d'une classification qui, bien qu'incomplète et souvent imprécise, pose les premiers jalons d'une typologie.

A.
LES VERRES DU XIIe ET DU XIIIe SIECLE

De la gobeleterie des XIIe et XIIIe siècles, nous ne connaissons dans le midi méditerranéen pratiquement que des verres à boire. Jusqu'à présent aucun vase à embouchure étroite n'a été découvert; les premiers fragments de flacon ou de bouteille n'apparaissent qu'à la fin du XIIIe siècle. Ces verres individuels, même incomplètement définis, présentent néanmoins une grande variété dans leur forme, leur technique décorative et leur composition.[6]

I. Verres à Pied Conique, forme A1.

Les pieds coniques sont les seuls indices de l'existence et de l'utilisation de verres à boire dès la fin du XIIe siècle. La forme générale de ces

pièces, probablement très fines et fragiles, est inconnue. Les pieds sont obtenus par refoulement de la partie inférieure de la paraison jusqu'à l'étranglement séparant le corps du pied. Tout le verre est donc formé dans une seule paraison. Le pied possède ainsi deux épaisseurs de verre étroitement appliquées l'une contre l'autre sauf sur le pourtour de la base où subsiste un ourlet creux de quelques millimètres.

Les pieds, malgré leur technique de fabrication commune, présentent des variations dans leur matière et leur forme. Le verre, de teinte vert-jaunâtre, est irisé et parfois recouvert d'un feuillet brunâtre; quelques fragments plus altérés se délitent. Rares sont les objets dont l'épaisseur du verre dépasse 2 ou 3 mm (Fig. 2,4). Les diamètres des bases sont beaucoup moins constants; ils passent de 45 mm (Fig. 2,3) à 70 mm et atteignent exceptionnellement 96 mm (Fig. 2,5).

Les trente-deux pièces de ce type, mises au jour dans les fouilles de Rougiers, se concentrent dans les premiers temps de l'occupation du *castrum*, c'est-à-dire dès la fin du XIIe siècle et pendant tout le XIIIe siècle; ils disparaissent ensuite. Aucune autre fouille d'habitat n'a pu vérifier ces datations. On retrouve pourtant ces pieds coniques dans les productions de l'atelier de Planier, à la fin du XIIIe siècle (Fig. 2,7 à 9) et hors de notre zone géographique étudiée, en Apulie[7] et dans le château de Caen, où vingt-trois pieds intacts retrouvés, sont datés de la fin du XIIIe siècle;[8] leur décor côtelé rappelle le plus grand exemplaire exhumé à Rougiers. Nulle part la coupe supportée par le pied ne fut retrouvée ou déterminée: rien ne prouve alors la similitude des

6. Quelques verres étudiés ici ont été présenté à l'exposition *Aujourd'hui le Moyen-Age*, voir catalogue: *Aujourd'hui le Moyen-Age, archéologie et vie quotidienne en France méridionale*, Aix, 1981, en part. pp. 51–55 et 115.

7. D. B. Harden, "Some Glass Fragments Mainly of the 12th–13th Century A.D., from Northern Apulia," *Journal of Glass Studies*, VIII, 1966, pp. 70–79.

8. M. de Bouard, "Verres à boire du XIIIe siècle trouvés à Caen," *Annales de Normandie*, XIV, 1964, pp. 231–248.

Fig. 3. *Verre bitronconique, Châteauneuf de Gadagne (d'après S. Gagniere et J. Granier).*

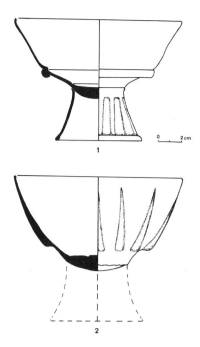

Fig. 4. *Calices forme A2 (Cancabeau, Châteauneuf de Gadagne).*

objets et l'on peut craindre à Rougiers même, des objets différents supportés par des pieds comparables.

Deux échantillons de pieds coniques trouvés à Rougiers, ont été analysés (annexe 1, VEM 40 et 41). Les variations sont relativement peu importantes dans la teneur de chacun des éléments. La présence d'un fondant sodique n'exclut pas une proportion toujours plus faible de potassium: le sodium est entre 2 fois et 2 fois et demi plus important que le potassium. Ces analyses, bien que réduites, suffisent à montrer l'emploi prédominant du fondant sodique dès la fin du XIIe siècle; technique originale par rapport aux productions contemporaines des pays septentrionaux qui utilisent un fondant presque exclusivement potassique, et par rapport aux verres antiques qui sont uniquement sodiques. Pourtant la teneur relativement importante des alcalins terreux (CaO+ MgO supérieurs à 15,50%) et le pourcentage de phosphore supérieur à 1,50% sont comparables aux verres potassiques.

II. Calices, forme A2.

Nous appelons calices les verres à large coupe reposant sur un pied relativement important et distinct dans son façonnement de la coupe. La fabrication des dits calices a donc nécessité d'abord le soufflage de la coupe et ensuite celui du pied; les deux parties étant ensuite raccordées.

Quatre calices ont été exhumés des sépultures du cimetière de Cancabeau à Châteauneuf-de-Gadagne dans le Vaucluse. Ces pièces ont en commun leur coupe évasée montée sur un pied tronconique. Il ne reste des deux exemplaires trouvés en 1919 qu'un mauvais croquis, cependant suffisant pour permettre un rapprochement évident avec les deux autres verres trouvés en 1965.[9] L'un de ceux-ci, complet, est d'une matière légèrement verdâtre, piquetée et attaquée par un début d'oxydation. Haute de 96 mm pour une largeur maximum de 140 mm, cette verrerie présente une belle forme équilibrée: le pied tronconique, au rebord ourlé vers l'intérieur, étant presque aussi haut que la coupe évasée. Un cordon de verre rapporté à la base de la coupe souligne la jonction des deux parties du vase. Un autre décor, à peine percepti-

9. S. Gagniere et J. Granier, "Le cimetière de Cancabeau," *Revue d'Etudes ligures XXVII, hommage à F. Benoit*, vol. V, 1971, pp. 178–184.

ble, consiste en de fines cannelures irrégulières sur le pied tronconique; ces stries ont sans doute été faites à la pointe d'un outil dans le verre chaud, encore malléable. L'élégance du profil et les proportions de cette belle pièce, sont légèrement affectés par le façonnement grossier de l'objet: une partie du rebord plus haute que le restant de l'ouverture rend le calice asymétrique (Fig. 5 et Fig. 4,1).

Le second exemplaire, trouvé dans une autre tombe du même cimetière, consiste en une coupe d'un calice très altéré. Le verre a perdu toute sa transparence et sa teinte d'origine: il est absolument opaque et très friable. Cette coupe appartenait à un calice de grande dimension, elle est richement ornée de 14 côtes en haut relief obtenues au moule. Le pied manque, il était vraisemblablement tronconique (Fig. 4,2).

Les verres ne sont pas les seuls objets découverts dans les tombes de Cancabeau; la présence de *pégau* sans bec, à bec, et à bec ponté, en pâte grise non glaçurée à l'exception d'un seul, et les données de la fouille permettent aux fouilleurs de dater les sépultures et leur dépôt du XIIe ou du XIIIe siècle.

Le lieu de fabrication et la fonction de ces objets restent difficiles à déterminer. Une origine régionale n'est pas exclure puisque des ateliers de verriers existaient dans le Vaucluse dès le XIIe siècle. De plus, des fragments de coupe côtelée appartenant à des formes indéterminées et découvertes sur l'atelier du XIIIe siècle de Planier, montrent que le décor de grosses côtes moulées était réalisé au moins au XIIIe siècle en Provence. Ces verres étaient-ils utilisés dans la vie quotidienne ou bien réservés à un usage précis, liturgique peut-être. La question reste sans réponse de notre part, mais M. Gagnière, l'inventeur des calices, suggère que le vase complet, découvert, non pas auprès de la tête mais sur la poitrine du squelette, soit un fac-similé d'un calice eucharistique rappelant la dignité de prêtre du défunt. Ces deux pièces restent exceptionnelles; mais des fragments de coupe évasée et côtelée ont été découverts aussi à Planier. Ces éléments n'appartiennent pas forcément à des verres similaires. Des bouteilles et des ampoules attribuées au XIIIe siècle et trouvées dans l'ouest de la France sont aussi côtelées. Le calice à côtes découvert dans l'autel de Saint-Christophe de Liège, attribué lui aussi au XIIIe siècle, est proche des calices décrits, malgré son rebord différent.[10] Tout aussi comparable est la pièce côtelée, trouvée en Italie méridionale dans les fouilles du château de Lucera, et dans un niveau de la fin du XIIIe siècle; son pied est cependant plus haut et plus cylindrique que celui que nous avons restitué.[11] Aucun fragment du type A2 n'a malheureusement pû être analysé.

III. Verres Bitronconiques, forme A3.

Mieux représentés et de provenance plus diversifiée que les calices, les verres bitronconiques sont probablement contemporains des pièces précédentes.

Ces verres sont toujours dans un très mauvais état de conservation. D'aspect noirâtre, la matière se délite facilement. Certains fragments semblent faits de la superposition de plusieurs feuillets de verre, aspect qui est simplement dû aux effets de l'oxydation.

La forme bitronconique fait la particularité de ces verres à boire. La coupe, en tronc de cône renversé, repose sur sa base la plus étroite contre le tronc de cône que constitue le pied. Un étranglement sépare ainsi nettement la coupe du pied. Bien que de même forme, ces deux parties ne sont pas symétriques: la coupe, généralement plus haute et plus évasée, se termine par un rebord arrondi, souligné parfois par une mouluration (Fig. 2,10). Le pourtour du pied est au contraire ourlé vers l'intérieur.

L'examen du noeud d'étranglement séparant

10. J. Barrelet, *La verrerie en France de l'époque gallo-romaine à nos jours*, Larousse 1953, fig. XX.

11. D. B. Whitehouse, "Ceramiche e vetri medioevali provenienti dal castello di Lucera," *Bolletino d'Arte*, LI, 1966, pp. 171–178 en part. p. 177 et fig. 31,5.

Fig. 5. Calice (cf. Fig. 4,1; photo C. Hussy).

la coupe du pied, permet de retrouver la technique de fabrication. Contrairement aux pièces précédentes les verres semblent avoir été soufflés dans une seule et même boule de verre. Le verrier, après avoir soufflé une paraison de forme allongée, a étranglé avec sa pince la partie centrale de la paraison. Ensuite le fond de la partie supérieure a été rabattu contre le haut de ce qui deviendra le pied. Entre les diverses soudures subsistent ainsi deux vides ovalisés. La canne est ensuite détachée et l'on fait claquer le fond de la pièce. Il ne reste plus qu'à terminer le pourtour des rebords de l'ouverture et du pied en tenant le verre par un pontil planté au centre du noeud médian. L'aspect plissé de ce noeud est peut-être dû à la rotation de l'objet tenu au bout de l'outil pendant que le verrier façonnait la base et le rebord (Fig. 2,15).

Des verres bitronconiques ont été trouvés dans des sépultures, sur des lieux de culte et sur des habitats.

Dans des tombes de Cancabeau deux verres, l'un intact (Fig. 3), l'autre ne possédant que sa coupe, étaient déposés à la droite de la tête du squelette.[12] La datation XIIe–XIIIe siècle donnée par la fouille de ce cimetière, est confirmée par les trouvailles de Rougiers. Vingt-quatre objets de ce type (comptabilisés par la présence de noeuds d'étranglement, pièces uniques pour chaque verre, constituant un élément de comptage sûr) étaient concentrés dans les strates datées du XIIIe siècle; l'abandon de ces pièces à la fin du XIIIe siècle est très net. D'autres éléments de ces mêmes verres, trouvés dans les fouilles de l'abbaye de Psalmodi (Saint-Laurent-d'Aigouze, Gard)[13] et dans celles du château de Beaucaire,[14] complètent ce groupe de verreries très homogène, malgré quelques différences notamment dans les dimensions. Le verre intact de Cancabeau a une hauteur de 124 mm; le pied étant nettement moins haut que la coupe. Le diamètre supérieur a 107 mm et la base 84 mm; le noeud d'étranglement possède 32 mm d'épaisseur. Bien qu'il ne reste que la coupe du second objet trouvé à Cancabeau, on peut restituer un verre nettement plus haut et plus mince, puisque le diamètre à l'étranglement n'a que 26 mm alors que la coupe seule a 110 mm de haut pour un diamètre à l'ouverture de 102 mm. Les fragments des verres bitronconiques de Rougiers laissent deviner un échelonnement des formes: les noeuds sont compris entre 15,5 mm et 32 mm.

Sur l'atelier de Planier n'apparaît pas le moindre fragment pouvant référer à ces formes. Sans doute sont-elles complètement abandonnées à la fin du XIIIe siècle, comme d'ailleurs le prouvent les trouvailles de Rougiers. Il n'est pas impossible non plus que ces verres soient importés.

L'iconographie nous fournit une représentation très fidèle du verre bitronconique; les vieillards de l'Apocalypse des fresques de la chapelle Saint-Martin de Fenollar en Roussillon, tiennent dans une main un verre bitronconique dont l'anneau médian est curieusement signifié. Malheureusement la matière de ces objets n'apparaît pas

12. S. Gagniere et J. Granier, *op. cit.*, pp. 182–183.

13. Fondé vers 780, Saint-Pierre de Psalmodi devint au XIe siècle abbaye bénédictine. Les fouilles dans l'église, conduites par les professeurs B. et W. Stoddart ont mis au jour de nombreux verres que nous avons pu étudier.

14. Les fouilles du château de Beaucaire sont dirigées par M. Contestin qui a bien voulu nous laisser examiner ses trouvailles en verre.

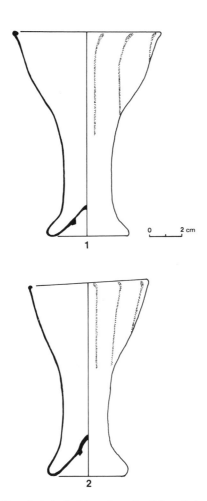

Fig. 6. *Verres à pied cylindrique, forme A4, Sainte-Croix.*

Fig. 7. *Vue d'une sépulture contenant un verre de type A4, Sainte-Croix (photo M. C. Bailly Maitre, M. Colardelle).*

dans ces peintures datées du début du XIIe siècle.

Nous avons effectué six analyses sur des fragments de verres bitronconiques (annexe n° 1); quatre échantillons proviennent de Rougiers, deux autres de Psalmodi et de Beaucaire. Une grande prudence s'impose dans l'analyse de ces résultats, le degré d'oxydation pouvant modifier sensiblement la teneur d'origine de chaque élément, comme le montrent les analyses VEM 8 et 9 d'un même fragment: la première analyse portant sur l'âme du verre, l'autre sur les parties extérieures les plus altérées. On remarque que ces dernières ont perdu tout leur fondant potassique ou sodique. Compte-tenu de ces réserves, nous pouvons observer des teneurs en potassium et sodium comparables, dans un seul cas le potassium est

plus de deux fois plus important que le sodium (VEM 8). Cette faiblesse en soude n'est peut-être due qu'aux effets de l'oxydation. Le graphique comparant les proportions de sodium et potassium des verres A1 et A3 (Fig. 20) montre des rapports comparables bien que de type A3 soit plus riche en potassium.

IV. Verres à Pied Cylindrique, forme A4.

Cette catégorie de verres est peu représentée géographiquement puisque jusqu'à présent nous ne l'avons rencontrée que dans les tombes à coffrage du cimetière de Saint-Giraud, à Sainte-Croix dans la Drôme et en Languedoc à Saint-Jean-de-Cas.[15] Les verreries constituent la plus

15. M. Colardelle, "Le cimetière médiéval de Sainte-Croix (Drôme)," *Cinq ans d'archéologie médiévale dans la région Rhône-Alpes*, plaquette de l'Association Lyonnaise de Sauvetage des

24

Fig. 8. *Verre de type A4 à ouverture quadrilobée, Sainte-Croix (photo M. Colardelle).*

grande partie du mobilier funéraire de la nécropole de la Drôme sise sur une terrasse dominant la vallée de la Sure. Ces verreries, seules, ou bien accompagnées d'un pégau globulaire, étaient déposées à la droite de la tête; dans un seul cas, le verre était sur la poitrine (Fig. 7).

La matière très fine, légèrement bleutée ou verdâtre, est souvent piquetée et par endroit opaque ou irisée. Deux formes, bien que relevant d'une même technique, peuvent être distinguées. La plus fréquente, celle d'un verre de 110 à 120 mm de haut, possède un pied cylindrique et haut dont la base conique est formée par refoulement de la pâte de verre vers l'intérieur; la coupe légèrement évasée est tronconique et parfois décorée de fines nervures moulées, à peine perceptibles au toucher (Fig. 6). Le rebord est simplement arrondi (Fig. 6,2), ou bien ourlé vers l'intérieur (Fig. 6,1). Un autre décor sous forme de bandes meulées est parallèle au rebord. Les diamètres à la base sont compris entre 45 et 55 mm. L'ouverture de la coupe, plus ou moins évasée, varie de 74 à 90 mm. Le façonnement de ces pièces est plus ou moins soigné; certaines, franchement asymétriques, sont plus hautes d'un côté que d'un autre, et toutes portent au centre de leur fond la marque proéminante du pontil qui n'a pas été "épluché." La fonction de ces verreries reste incertaine: s'agit-il de verres à boire ou de lampes? Leur profil est comparable à une pièce identifiée comme lampe et présentée au musée du Vatican.

Le second type de verre ne diffère du premier que par la coupe plus évasée, en forme de quadrilobe (Fig. 8).

Toutes les verreries se trouvaient dans les sépultures des niveaux supérieurs de la fouille, et peuvent être datées d'après les fouilles du XIIIe siècle. L'abondance de ces verreries (une pour huit tombes environ), la répétition d'une même forme parfois grossièrement exécutée et la découverte de plusieurs scories de verre à proximité du cimetière laissent deviner l'existence d'un atelier de verrier, dans une région où les textes attestent la présence de nombreuses verreries médiévales puis modernes.

V. Verres à Tige Creuse, forme A5.

Malgré la fragmentation rendant incertaine voire impossible, la reconnaissance de la structure générale des verres à tige, la présence de ces derniers est incontestable dès le XIIIe siècle au moins.

Nous connaissons parfaitement la partie inférieure de grands verres à tige creuse reposant sur un large pied circulaire plat ou légèrement conique. Sous la pellicule d'oxydation noirâtre qui recouvre ces verres, la teinte d'origine verdâtre est difficile à percevoir et dans bien des cas elle a complètement disparu, l'objet étant constitué d'une matière friable et opaque. De structure relativement massive, ces tiges rectilignes ou légèrement amincies en leur milieu (Fig. 9,5) ou à leur base (Fig. 7), ont des parois de 1,5 à 4 mm d'épaisseur selon leur hauteur. Les pieds, formés d'une double épaisseur de verre sauf sur leur pourtour fait d'un ourlet creux, ont un diamètre compris entre 70 et 92 mm, diamètre proportionnel à l'épaisseur de la tige et à la hauteur de la

Sites archéologiques Médiévaux et de la Société Alpine de Documentation et de Recherches en Archéologie historique, non daté, p. 9; M. C. Bailly-Maitre et M. Colardelle, "Le cimetière médiéval de Sainte-Croix (Drôme)," *Archéologie médiévale dans la région Rhône-Alpes*, 1977, pp. 21–22, même publication. M. Colardelle, *Sépulture et tradition funéraires du Vᵉ au XIIIᵉ siècle dans les Alpes françaises du Nord*, Grenoble, 1983, 466 pp. Le verre découvert à Saint-Jean de Cas n'est pas publié, fouille O. Taffanel.

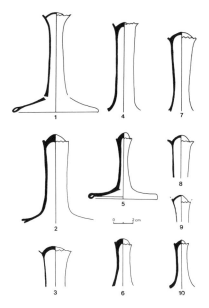

Fig. 9. *Verres à tige creuse, forme A5 (1 à 4, 7, 8, et 10: Psalmodi; 5 et 6: Saint-Roman; 9: Rougiers).*

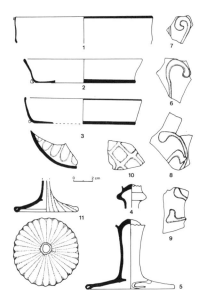

Fig. 10. *Verres à tige creuse, forme A5 (1 à 3, 5, 6, 8, 9 et 11: Psalmodi; 4, 7 et 10: Rougiers).*

partie inférieure de l'objet. Les plus petites pièces ont ainsi une épaisseur de tige de 7 à 10 mm pour une hauteur de 55 à 65 mm environ (Fig. 9,5, 6, 9, & 10) alors que les plus gros objets possèdent une tige large de 22 mm environ et une hauteur de 73 à 85 mm (Fig. 9,2 & 3 et Fig. 9,5). Quelques verres échappant à ces normes sont d'une structure plus fine et peuvent atteindre 95 à 100 mm de haut tout en conservant une épaisseur de tige moyenne de 15 à 17 mm (Fig. 9,1 & 4).

Peu nombreux à Rougiers (pièces attestées par un fond et deux fragments de tige: Fig. 9,9), ces verres sont courants à Psalmodi (quinze pièces) et représentés par quelques exemplaires au château de Beaucaire (Fig. 9,5 & 6). Des coupelles très basses, apparemment de même matière que les tiges pourraient constituer la partie supérieure. Ces coupelles, toutes trouvées à Psalmodi, ont des parois rectilignes (Fig. 10,1) ou très légèrement évasées (Fig. 10,2 & 3); leur hauteur constante ne varie que de 4 mm au plus et n'atteint jamais 30 mm; par contre le diamètre de l'ouverture passe de 126 à 149 mm.

Ces verres à tige étaient des pièces luxueuses,

parfois richement décorées de la coupe jusqu'au pied selon divers procédés ornementaux. Un décor de filet bleu couvre tantôt le rebord (Fig. 10,1), tantôt la base des coupelles (Fig. 10,3) et plus exceptionnellement à la fois l'ouverture et la base (Fig. 10,2). Une pièce est aussi décorée dans son fond de côtes moulées (Fig. 10,3); décor qui pouvait se prolonger sur la tige sous forme de spirales, et sur tout le pied (Fig. 10,11). Un décor rapporté, en verre incolore, se retrouve serpentant sur un pied (Fig. 10,5 et Fig. 11) et sur des fragments, encore non identifiés, qui pourraient appartenir, malgré leur finesse, à des coupes. Ces fragments sont couverts de filets de verre s'enroulant pour dessiner des feuillages souples (Fig. 10,6, 8, & 9). Nous avons rapproché de cette série deux pièces, de même matière, trouvées à Rougiers et portant un décor de quadrillages obtenu au moule ou un décor rapporté en forme de crosse (Fig. 10,7 & 10).

Les indices de datation de cette forme sont minces mais certains. Les rares fragments découverts à Rougiers se situent dans des niveaux antérieurs ou contemporains de ceux des verres

26

bitronconiques. Ce matériel est trop réduit pour que l'on puisse dire si les verres A5 connus dès la fin du XIIᵉ siècle ont été en usage principalement à cette époque-là ou dans le courant du XIIIᵉ siècle. Il semble que les verres A1, A3 et A5 que l'on ne retrouve pas sur l'atelier de Planier de la fin du XIIIᵉ siècle et sur les sites d'habitat riches en matériel de cette même époque (le château de Montségur et certaines zones de la fouille du Petit Palais à Avignon), aient été abandonnés à la fin du XIIIᵉ siècle. C'est ce que tend à prouver aussi la stratigraphie de Rougiers pour les verres A3 et A5. Nous pouvons donc émettre l'hypothèse que tous les verres cités ci-dessus ont été utilisés vers le milieu du XIIIᵉ siècle, les verres à pied conique et les verres à tiges creuses étant certainement les plus précoces (fin XIIᵉ–début XIIIᵉ ?).

Les analyses physico-chimiques réalisées sur des fragments de la forme A5 mettent en évidence une composition proche des verres A3. Les analyses 37 et 37′ portant sur le même fragment, montrent que la partie corrodée (analyse VEM 37′) a perdu ses fondants; résultats qui rejoignent ceux obtenus sur un verre bitronconique (VEM 8 & 9). Les verres A5 ont généralement moins de potassium que les verres A3 (cf. annexe nᵒ 1).

D'autres verres à tige de matière et de structure différentes sont sans doute plus tardifs.

B.
LES VERRES DE L'EXTREME FIN DU XIIIᵉ ET DU DEBUT DU XIVᵉ SIECLE

I. Verres à Tige Creuse, forme B1.

Plus fragiles et plus fins que les précédents, ces verres nous sont parvenus très fragmentés et leur forme générale reste incomplète. Il n'y a en fait que le principe de la tige creuse qui rapproche ces verres des précédents. Leur matière, leur forme et leurs décors sont tout à fait différents. Ces pièces beaucoup plus frêles sont probablement de taille inférieure au type A5, à en juger par l'évasement de la base des coupes (Fig. 12,1 à 4 & 7); seul un fond paraît relativement large (Fig. 12,8). Le

Fig. 11. *Verre à tige creuse décoré d'un fil de verre rapporté (cf. Fig. 10,5; photo D. Foy).*

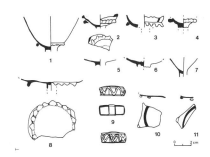

Fig. 12. *Verres à tige creuse et cordon pincé; forme B1 (1 et 9: Rougiers; 2, 3, 5, 6 et 7: Planier; 4: Fontvieille; 7 et 8: Petit Palais).*

verre incolore légèrement jaunâtre ou verdâtre est parfois irisé par endroits; il est très mince puisque les parois des tiges et des coupes n'atteint pas 2 mm; il s'épaissit uniquement à la base de la coupe. Les tiges étaient portées par des bases circulaires formant un disque de 70 mm de diamètre environ comme en témoignent des fragments découverts à Planier. Ces verres déjà précieux par leur matière fine et incolore, le sont aussi par leur décor: un cordon pincé souligne la base de la coupe souvent rehaussée par des filets de verre colorés en bleu foncé. Ce filet bleu, parfois parallèle au cordon pincé, est placé au-dessous de ce dernier (Fig. 12,10 & 11) ou bien au-dessus (Fig.

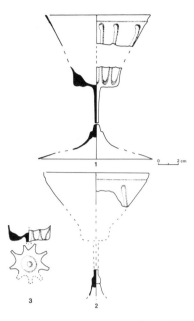

Fig. 13. *Verres à tige massive, forme B2 (1 et 2: Petit Palais; 3: Beaucaire).*

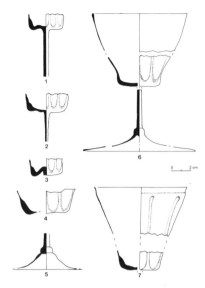

Fig. 14. *Verres à tige massive, forme B2, Petit Palais.*

12,3). Sur d'autres fragments le décor bleu forme une ligne, ou sans doute plusieurs lignes, perpendiculaires au cordon pincé (Fig. 12,2). Nous ne savons pas si les tiges étaient décorées: de petits anneaux formés d'un fil de verre bleu foncé ou incolore, lisse ou plissé, trouvés à Planier, laissent supposer que les tiges étaient baguées. Un très bel anneau, malheureusement très altéré, trouvé à Rougiers est constitué de deux lames de verre circulaires réunies par un fil déposé en onde et par un fragment de tige creuse au centre. Cet objet baguait certainement un verre à tige, antérieur à la série B1 et différent du type A5: en effet, le diamètre très étroit de cet anneau et son contexte archéologique qui tendrait à le dater de la fin du XIIe siècle, démontrent qu'il existe des verres à tige différents et antérieurs à ceux que nous présentons. Un fond de coupe découvert à Fontvieille (Bouches-du-Rhône) apparemment comparable aux autres verres à tige et décoré d'un cordon pincé, permet d'imaginer une variante du type B1: cette pièce semble en effet être portée par une tige massive, peut-être semblable à celle qui fut trouvée sur le même site (Fig. 16,2).

Bien que très partiellement définis, les verres B1 peuvent être assez bien datés: nous les trouvons fragmentés mais relativement nombreux sur le site de l'atelier de Planier, ce qui permet de les situer à la fin du XIIIe siècle et de certifier leur fabrication régionale. Ce type de verre est aussi représenté dans les fouilles du Petit Palais d'Avignon et à Rougiers où cette datation n'est pas rejetée.

II. Verres à Tige Massive et Coupe Côtelée, forme B2.

Divers types de verres à tige massive apparaissent à l'examen des nombreux fragments retrouvés sur plusieurs sites.

Les plus précoces de ces verres, dans le Midi méditerranéen, se caractérisent par une tige rectiligne, un pied le plus souvent en forme de disque presque plat, ou plus exceptionnellement troconique (Fig. 15) et une coupe en forme de tulipe portant un décor de côtes.

Le verre, fin, est de teinte légèrement verdâtre ou bleutée. La fragilité des parois de la coupe, n'excédant pas un millimètre d'épaisseur, est compensée par la massivité de la tige et le renforcement de la base de la coupe dû aux côtes du

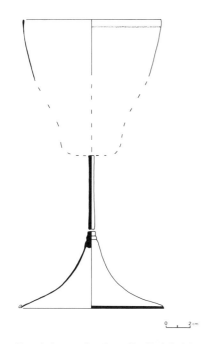

Fig. 15. *Verre à tige massive, forme B2, Petit Palais.*

décor en fort relief. Aucun verre ne nous est parvenu complet mais les nombreux éléments retrouvés permettent d'en connaître sa forme générale, ses dimensions et son décor. Ces objets devaient avoir environ 140 mm de haut. Contrairement à la forme A5, les tiges semblent relativement courtes (de l'ordre de 40 à 50 mm), et la coupe haute égale, d'après nos restitutions, à la moitié de la hauteur totale de l'objet. Le pied, fragile par la minceur de ses parois, pouvait grâce à son diamètre important (110 à 120 mm) assurer la bonne stabilité de ces verres.

Tous ne semblent pourtant pas avoir la même taille: les dimensions données ci-dessus correspondent à des verreries dont le diamètre à la base est de 45 mm environ (Fig. 13,1 et Fig. 14,4 & 6). D'autres, moins nombreux, étaient plus petits comme en témoignent les variations des diamètres des bases égaux à 32 mm (Fig. 14,3) ou 35 mm (Fig. 14,1). Un exemplaire apparaît nettement plus important à cause de son pied, tronconique qui rend le verre nettement plus haut (Fig. 15). Les coupes toujours évasées sont simplement

tronconiques (Fig. 13,1 et Fig. 14,7) ou en forme de tulipe, due à la gorge marquant la base du décor des côtes (Fig. 14,6). Les diamètres des rebords oscillent entre 100 et 105 mm, sauf pour l'objet de taille exceptionnellement importante déjà cité, où il atteint 115 mm.

Tous ces verres, de forme élégante, sont enrichis d'un décor de côtes au nombre de huit ou de neuf. Cette ornementation a été obtenue par soufflage dans un moule, mais les bases en fort relief ont sans doute été remodelées et étirées à la pince, car la partie saillante à la base aurait empêché l'extraction de la pièce du moule qui était sans doute d'un seul tenant: aucune marque de "jonction" de deux parties d'un moule n'ayant jamais été observée. Les côtes sur les parois sont à peine visibles et parfois même complètement effacées (Fig. 14,6). Quelques pieds portent aussi un décor de côtes moulées en spirale, pareille ornementation se retrouve sur des pièces de même type découvertes à Utrecht.[16] Sur une seule pièce, la plus grande, un filet de verre bleu entoure le pied soulignant le caractère luxueux de cet objet (Fig. 15).

Tous les verres B2 découverts dans le midi, proviennent de sites établis sur le Rhône: Beaucaire (Fig. 14,3) et surtout Avignon dont les fouilles du Petit Palais ont fourni une douzaine de pièces au moins;[17] d'autres exemplaires ont été mis au jour en Languedoc: plusieurs bases de coupes, ornées de neuf côtes, sont apparues dans les fouilles de Montségur,[18] et un seul fragment

---

16. C. Isings et H. F. Wijman, "Medieval Glass from Utrecht," *Journal of Glass Studies*, XIX, 1977, pp. 77–83, voir en part. fig. 1, p. 79, n° 13 à 19.

17. Sur les fouilles du Petit Palais voir *Lettre d'information du C.R.A., Archéologie du Midi Méditerranéen*, n° 9, 1983.

18. J. Tricoire et J. Mathieu, "La verrerie du Pog dans la recherche archéologique à Montségur," *Bulletin du Groupe de Recherches Archéologiques* de Montségur et de ses environs, 1974, n° 2, pp. 17–29, part. 20–21. Il faut aussi noter dans les collections du musée de Carcassonne une série de 5 tiges parfois munies d'un départ de coupe côtelée; leur origine, sans doute régionale, n'est cependant pas connue. F. Sarret, "Carcassonne, inventaire des collections médiévales du musée des Beaux-Arts," *Archéologie du Midi Médiéval*, I, 1983, Notes et Documents p. 125.

comprenant base côtelée et tige, a été découvert sur l'atelier de la Seube.[19] Cet unique fragment dans cet atelier peut-il prouver une production locale?

L'absence de ces verres dans les fouilles de village et d'atelier, en dehors du fragment cité plus haut, et surtout la présence de ces objets sur des sites importants comme Avignon et Montségur pouvaient laisser penser à un produit d'importation, d'autant plus que ces verreries sont bien représentées dans les pays septentrionaux. La plus connue d'entre elles est le verre trouvé muré dans l'église des Augustins de Rouen, construite à l'extrême fin du XIIIe siècle.[20] Ce vase haut de 180 mm ne se différencie des pièces méridionales que par sa coupe un peu moins évasée.[21] Sont beaucoup plus comparables au type B2, les trouvailles faites dans un dépotoir de la ville de Huy en Belgique[22] et faites à Utrecht.[23] Parmi ces deux dernières découvertes, se trouvent aussi des verres différents, uniquement par leur tige creuse. Encore en Hollande, dans les fossés du château de Nieuwendoorn, un verre côtelé mais à tige creuse, a pu être reconstitué.[24] Dans les fouilles de Saint-Denis apparaît un verre au décor comparable; la coupe très basse et la tige creuse diffèrent cependant.[25]

L'analyse physico-chimique réalisée sur quatre fragments de la forme B2, révèle une composition beaucoup plus riche en sodium que les verres cités antérieurement, et plus pauvre en potassium (annexe 2, VEM 131 à 134). Cette composition ainsi que le fragment de verre découvert à la Seube, sont les seuls éléments permettant d'avancer l'hypothèse d'une production locale. Les éléments de datation sont tout aussi minces. Nous proposons de situer la forme B2 à l'extrême fin du XIIIe siècle. En effet, si les dépotoirs du Petit Palais d'Avignon dans lesquels se trouvaient de nombreux verres de ce type ne peuvent encore être datés finement, il semble par contre que la majorité du matériel des fouilles de Montségur puisse être attribué à la fin du XIIIe ou au début du XIVe siècle. L'unique fragment découvert à la Seube, atelier de la première moitié du XIVe

siècle, ne peut contredire cette hypothèse de datation. La composition sodique de ces verres à la fin du XIIIe est un argument de plus en faveur d'une production régionale.

La forme B2 n'est pas le seul type de verre à tige médiéval et méditerranéen. Au début du XIVe siècle, nous connaissons les ateliers fabricant divers types de verres à tige, dont seule la tige, élément le plus solide de la pièce, nous est parvenue.

III. Autres Verres à Tige Massive, Type B3.

D'autres verres à tige massive étaient utilisés à la fin du XIIIe et au début du XIVe siècle. Nous ne connaissons d'eux que quelques fragments de tige et des anneaux (aussi cette série B3, peu homogène regroupe-t-elle divers fragments faisant probablement partie de différents types. La multiplication des découvertes permettra sans doute d'affiner plus tard ce regroupement qui n'est qu'un pis-aller). Les tiges retrouvées principalement à Rougiers, La Seube et dans les fouilles du Petit Palais, montrent rarement un profil rectiligne. La seule pièce droite provenant de Rougiers

19. N. Lambert, *op. cit.*, p. 91 et pl. VII,2.

20. R. Flavigny, "Condamnation et démolition des Augustins," *Bulletin des Amis des Monuments Rouennais*, 1964–1950, pp. 30–31.

21. Voir la représentation de ce verre dans J. Barrelet, *op. cit.*, pl. XXV.

22. M. Cognioul-Thiry, "Verres du XIVe siècle récemment découverts en Belgique." *Annales du 7e Congrès de l'Association Internationale du Verre*, Berlin-Leipzig, 1977, pp. 159–166; R. Chambon, "La verrerie entre Rhin et Loire au XIVe siècle," *Journal of Glass Studies*, XVII, 1975, pp. 151–156. Les verres ne sont pas datés par leur contexte archéologique.

23. C. Isings et H. Wijman, *op. cit.*

24. J. G. N. Renaud, "Middleeuwse glasfragmenten uit Maastricht," *Bulletin van de koninklijke Nederlandse Oudeidkundige Bond*, série 6, 1958, col 1–7; J. C. N. Renaud, "Un verre à boire du XIVe siècle," *7e Congrès International du Verre*, Bruxelles, 1965, Comptes-rendus II, communication 267.

25. O. Meyer, L. Bourgeau, D. J. Coxall et N. Meyer, *Archéologie urbaine à Saint-Denis*, publication de la maison des Jeunes et de la Culture de Saint-Denis, sept. 1969; O. et N. Meyer, L. Bourgeau et D. J. Coxall, "Archéologie urbaine à Saint-Denis, présentation d'une expérience en cours," *Archéologie Médiévale*, 1980, pp. 271–297. De nombreux autres verres provenant de Saint-Denis ont été étudiés par Nicole Le Tiec dans le cadre d'une maîtrise.

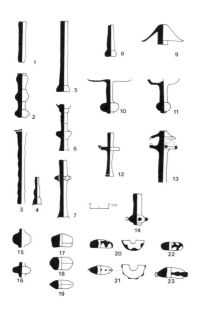

Fig. 16. *Verres à tige et anneaux; forme B3 (1: Planier; 2: Fontvieille; 3 et 4: Psalmodi; 5, 6, 10, 15 à 23: Rougiers; 7, 11, 13 et 14: Petit Palais; 8 et 9: Cadrix; 12: Avignon, Palais des Papes).*

(Fig. 16,5) est semblable aux tiges de la forme B2, mais l'absence de tout autre élément de ce dernier type nous a interdit de le rapprocher des verres B2.

Le plus souvent ce sont des tiges moulurées (Fig. 16,2 & 6) ou torsadées (Fig. 16,3 & 4). Les pièces ayant ce dernier décor pourraient en fait appartenir aux verreries B2. En effet des découvertes septentrionales indiquent que certaines coupes côtelées étaient supportées par des tiges torsadées.[26]

La plupart des tiges retrouvées sont munies, en leur milieu ou à leur extrémité, d'un bouton de préhension globulaire (Fig. 16,10, 11, 15, & 16). Ce bouton, à la fois décoratif et fonctionnel est quelquefois remplacé par un ou plusieurs petits disques plats et minces de teinte incolore sur lesquels on trouve un arrachement de fils bleus (Fig. 16,12 & 13). Sans doute faut-il imaginer autour de cette tige une ornementation complexe à l'image de la pièce récemment découverte lors de fouilles urbaines à Montauban (Tarn et Garonne).[27] Ce fragment présente tout autour de la

tige une résille savante faite de cordons de verre alternativement bleus ou incolores, tantôt droits, tantôt plissés. Trouvé dans une couche parfaitement datée de la première moitié du XIVe siècle, cet objet préfigure de façon étonnante la verrerie italienne post médiévale. Certains verres n'avaient peut-être qu'un seul disque plat coloré dans la masse en bleu foncé, tel celui retrouvé à la Seube; plus simplement un cordon plissé fait parfois office de bouton (Fig. 16,7).

Le décor bleu se retrouve sous forme de pointillés décorant un bouton de tige (Fig. 16,14) et sur d'autres anneaux retrouvés sans le moindre arrachement de tige. La fonction des nombreux anneaux de verres, uniquement découverts sur les sites producteurs (La Seube, Rougiers) reste incertaine. Trop lourds pour être suspendus aux anses d'une vaisselle, ces anneaux étaient peut-être utilisés comme perles. Ils étaient plus vraisemblablement situés au milieu des tiges comme le montre un exemplaire (Fig. 16,14). Sans doute faut-il considérer tous les autres anneaux découverts sans le moindre arrachement de tige comme des pièces encore inutilisées. D'après les fouilles de Rougiers et de la Seube, on peut dater ce matériel du début du XIVe siècle. Son existence semble brève puisque aucun anneau n'apparaît sur l'atelier de Cadrix daté de la seconde moitié du XIVe siècle.

De section triangulaire ou arrondie et en verre incolore légèrement teinté en verdâtre ou jaunâtre, ces anneaux ont un diamètre externe compris entre 25 et 30 mm. Le diamètre interne compris entre 6 et 10 mm est relativement important pour identifier ces pièces à des perles. Leurs faces sont plates (Fig. 16,18, 19, & 20) ou légèrement bombées (Fig. 16,21); très souvent l'une des faces

---

26. R. Chambon, *op. cit.*, 1975, pp. 151–157, fig. 1, B1 et B2.

27. De nombreux verres ont été découverts lors des fouilles de la place F. Roosevelt à Montauban en 1983 et 1984. Quelques pièces ont été publiées dans le catalogue de l'exposition: *Montauban, l'archéologie dans la ville, les fouilles de la place de la cathédrale*, 10 juillet–10 octobre 1984, Montauban, voir en particulier pp. 19–21, n° 80.

est plate comme destinée à être appliquée sur une surface, et l'autre bombée (Fig. 16,17, 20, & 23). Un seul anneau est formé de deux pièces accolées, de profil et d'épaisseur différents (Fig. 16,17). La plupart de ces objets sont décorés de fils bleus déposés sur la tranche sous forme de gouttelettes (Fig. 16,21), d'onde (Fig. 16,20), de feston (Fig. 16,22) ou d'un cordon pincé (Fig. 16,23).

Les échantillons analysés (annexe 2) montrent que les tiges et leur bouton ainsi que les anneaux isolés, ont une proportion de sodium et de potassium semblables. Comme on l'avait déjà remarqué pour les verres B2, la composition de la fin du XIIIe siècle, à dominante sodique, est en cela comparable à celle des productions du XIVe siècle.

A la fin du XIIIe siècle, les verreries à tige massive ne représentent qu'une part des verreries produites et/ou utilisées dans les régions méditerranéennes. Sur l'atelier de Planier les verres à tiges creuses sont assez bien représentés, alors qu'un seul fragment atteste la présence rare des verres à tige massive (Fig. 16,1).

Les éléments de tige massive provenant de Rougiers, sont concentrés dans les niveaux de la fin du XIIIe–début XIVe siècle et représentent un faible pourcentage des verreries de cette période dans laquelle le gobelet semble déjà fréquent. Le verre à tige dont la coupe est côtelée est par contre relativement important en Languedoc et Comtat. Il conviendrait pourtant de multiplier les recherches afin de confirmer ou non l'absence quasi totale de ces verres à l'est du Rhône[28] et de tenter de localiser la provenance de ces produits comparables aux découvertes septentrionales par leur décor côtelé, mais différents par leur tige toujours massive et leur coupe haute en forme de tulipe; la composition sodique de ces verres suggérerait d'ailleurs une production régionale peut-être limitée à quelques centres languedociens. En effet, nous ne connaissons pas dans le monde méditerranéen des verres semblables. En Italie, où les découvertes de verres médiévaux deviennent de plus en plus nombreuses, il est remarquable de noter l'absence de verre à coupe côtelée.

Dans le Midi méditerranéen français comme en Italie, le gobelet (aux formes et aux décors variés) est presque exclusivement utilisé comme verre à boire dès le second quart du XIVe siècle; il supplante le verre à tige dont l'usage, sans doute assez limité à la fin du XIIIe et au début du XIVe siècle, disparaît complètement ensuite. Sur l'atelier varois de Cadrix (deuxième moitié du XIVe siècle) seuls deux éléments de verre à tige ont été découverts parmi de nombreux gobelets. De même, on ne trouve pas un seul verre à tige parmi les milliers de pièces de verre qui composent l'admirable série récemment exhumée dans le comblement, de l'extrême fin du XIVe siècle, de trois silos à Tarquinia.[29]

Alors que les historiens du verre s'accordent pour dire que le verre à tige est le seul type de verre individuel en usage dans les terres continentales jusqu'à la fin du XIVe siècle, nous pouvons affirmer l'emploi du gobelet en Provence et Languedoc dès la fin du XIIIe siècle. Précocité que l'on devinait, avant même les découvertes archéologiques, dans la représentation iconographique de gobelets sur les peintures italiennes de la fin du XIIIe et du début du XIVe siècle. La vaisselle de table est souvent figurée dans des représentations de la Cène. L'une de ces miniatures, extraite d'un missel toulonnais exécuté entre 1334 et 1342, illustre bien l'emploi simultané du gobelet et du verre à tige côtelée au cours de la première moitié du XIVe siècle dans nos régions méditerranéennes.[30]

IV. Gobelets à Décor de Pastilles Rapportées, forme B4.

Nous avons rattaché à la forme B4 des gobelets dont on ignore la partie haute. En verre fin et incolore, souvent irisé, le gobelet, à sa base, est

---

28. La seule pièce appartenant à la forme B2 située à l'est du Rhône a été retrouvée lors des fouilles urbaines de Digne, non publié.

29. Nous tenons à remercier le Docteur D. Whitehouse qui nous a permis d'examiner l'important matériel en verre trouvé à Tarquinia.

30. Missale Tolonense, B.N., ms. latin 877 f° 293.

cylindrique; les parois s'évasent ensuite. Trois décors relevant du même procédé technique, caractérisent ces gobelets. Un décor rapporté et pincé entoure le pourtour de la base qui atteint entre 55 et 60 mm (Fig. 17,1). Les parois du gobelet sont décorées de petites pastilles de verre rapportées et parfois étirées à la pince. Nous pouvons tenter de restituer la disposition de ce décor à partir de pièces très fragmentaires. Deux verres trouvés dans les fouilles du jardin ouest du Petit Palais montrent des pastilles espacées de 15 mm environ, formant un alignement parallèle à la base et entourant le corps de l'objet. Nous ne pouvons savoir sur combien de rangs ces pastilles pouvaient être disposées. Ces gouttes de verre rapportées sont associées ici, comme sur des verres découverts à Planier, à des filets en verre bleu foncé. Filets qui peuvent séparer les rangs de pastilles (Fig. 17,1 & 2) ou bien les encadrer dans des carrés (Fig. 17,3) ou des losanges (Fig.17,5). Les filets bleus sont parfois doubles (Fig. 17,4); ils peuvent former les angles ou des triangles (Fig. 17,9 & 10) ou chevaucher la pastille de verre rapportée (Fig. 17,8).

Nombreux sont, à Planier, les fragments de verre portant ce décor de pastilles; quelques-uns furent retrouvés à Rougiers (Fig. 17,6 & 7) ainsi qu'au Petit Palais d'Avignon. Dans le Languedoc, des débris de verre portant des petites pastilles juxtaposées à des filets de verre, non pas bleu comme dans les trouvailles provençales, mais incolores comme le restant du verre, apparaissent à Montségur[31] et sur l'atelier de la Seube.[32] L'ensemble de ces trouvailles permet de dater le type B4 de la fin du XIIIe et du début du XIVe siècle. Les gobelets B4 sont sans doute contemporains des verres à tige B2. Deux fragments appartenant respectivement à chacun de ces types furent retrouvés dans une même strate au cours des fouilles urbaines effectuées en 1984 à Digne (Alpes-de-Haute-Provence). Cette découverte est un argument de plus pour croire en la concomittance de ces deux formes de verre; malheureusement aucun jalon chronologique (absence de tout matériel céramique bien connu) ne

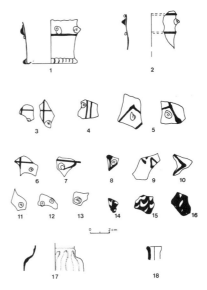

Fig. 17. *Gobelets à gouttes de verre rapportées, forme B4 (1 et 2: Petit Palais; 3 à 5: Planier; 6 et 7: Rougiers; 8 à 13: Planier). Verres à décor peint, forme E7 (14 et 15: Planier; 16: Petit Palais). Fioles, Planier.*

peut apporter une datation absolue.[33] Le seul fragment de gobelet B4 analysé (annexe 2, VEM 135) est comparable par sa composition aux verres B2 attribués à l'extrême fin du XIIIe siècle.

La technique décorative consistant à rapporter des gouttes de verre sur la coupe d'un gobelet est largement répandue: principalement en Italie,[34] Tchécoslovaquie, Pays des Balkans, Allemagne. Cette ornementation se retrouve ainsi sur des formes diverses, soufflées dans des matières différentes et datées tout aussi diversement du XIIe

31. J. Tricoire et J. Mathieu, *op. cit.*, p. 24.

32. N. Lambert, *op. cit.*, pl. VIII n° 7.

33. Renseignement communiqué par M. Bonifay, responsable de la fouille, (D.R.A.H. Provence-Alpes-Côte d'Azur).

34. Les découvertes de gobelets à gouttes rapportées augmentent en Italie au fur et à mesure de la multiplication des fouilles. En 1979, D. Whitehouse avait signalé 22 sites ayant fourni ce type de verre; en 1983 le même auteur en signale 29. D. Whitehouse, "Notes on Late Medieval Glass in Italy," *Annales du 8e Congrès de l'Association Internationale pour l'Histoire du Verre* (Londres-Liverpool sept. 1979), pp. 165–177. *Id.*, "Medieval Glass in Italy: Some Recent Developments," *Journal of Glass Studies*, XXV, 1983, pp. 115–120.

au début du XVIe siècle. L'iconographie confirme d'ailleurs la multiplicité des types utilisés sur plus de quatre siècles.[35]

En revanche cette décoration retrouvée sur quelques pièces provençales et languedociennes étonne par sa rareté et sa concentration dans une période relativement brève (fin XIIIe siècle-début XIVe); elle semble appartenir à un seul type que nous pouvons comparer avec les pièces les plus anciennes exhumées en Italie et à Corinthe: il faut probablement rechercher le prototype de cette technique en Europe orientale: les exemplaires les plus précoces furent découverts sur un atelier de verrier à Corinthe qui a fonctionné dès la première moitié du XIIe siècle:[36] deux formes de gobelets à gouttes rapportées proviennent de ce site: le type le plus fréquent, très probablement fabriqué sur le site même a un corps haut et étroit; le fond est entouré d'un cordon dentelé; le verre très fin est presque incolore; l'autre type, qui n'est peut-être pas produit par la verrerie de Corinthe, est beaucoup plus trapu; le fond est cette fois ci entouré par un cordon lisse, ce verre diffère aussi du premier par sa matière jaunâtre. Il est difficile de comparer les pièces que nous présentons ici avec les découvertes de Corinthe, puisque nos trouvailles, réduites à quelques tessons (fragments de panse et de fond), ne permettent aucune restitution du profil complet des objets. Nous savons seulement que les fonds entourés d'un cordon festonné s'évasent légèrement, aussi imagine-t-on des gobelets étroits comparables à la forme la plus courante de Corinthe; de plus la matière fine et incolore est semblable. Cependant l'originalité des verres de nos régions apparaît dans la décoration rapportée qui associe toujours gouttes de verre incolore et filets de verre bleu foncé.

La fouille de l'atelier de Planier atteste, de façon indiscutable, que les verres du Midi méditerranéen de la France, ont été fabriqués régionalement et sans doute dans plusieurs centres; en effet la fouille du site de Planier montre que la verrerie, peut-être itinérante, est modeste. Comme de nombreux historiens du verre, nous pensons que l'origine de ce type doit être recherchée en Orient. C'est sans doute par les ateliers du sud de l'Italie que s'est transmise cette technique d'ornementation.[37] Celle-ci ne semble pas avoir été vouée à un grand avenir dans le Midi de la France où elle n'a été adoptée qu'un temps restreint, limité, dans l'état actuel des recherches, à la fin du XIIIe et au début du XIVe siècle (très peu de fouilles ont été effectuées sur les sites du XIIIe siècle, aussi des travaux ultérieurs pourraient modifier l'apparition de ces gobelets en les situant plus tôt dans le temps; par contre leur disparition vers le deuxième quart du XIVe siècle est certaine). En revanche, cette ornementation a eu particulièrement la faveur des artisans verriers d'Italie, de Yougoslavie[38] et des pays voisins qui l'ont utilisé jusqu'au XVe siècle. A titre d'exemple, nous citerons les récentes découvertes de Tarquinia qui illustrent de façon éloquente l'importance de cette technique dans les productions de la fin du

35. De nombreux historiens du verre ont signalé des représentations de gobelets à gouttes rapportées, à titre d'exemple on peut citer M. Wenzel, "A Reconsideration of Bosnian Medieval Glass," *Journal of Glass Studies*, XIX, 1977, pp. 63–76 et D. Whitehouse 1979, *op. cit.*

36. G. Davidson, "A Medieval Glass Factory at Corinth," *American Journal of Archaeology XLIV*, I, 1940, pp. 297–324, en part. fig. 15,1 et 3; G. Davidson, "A Medieval Mystery: Byzantine Glass Production," *Journal of Glass Studies*, XVII, 1975, pp. 127–141, en part. fig. 16 à 20; et aussi D. B. Harden, "Ancient Glass III: Post-Roman," *Archaeological Journal*, CXXVIII, 1972, pp. 78–106, en part. p. 102.

37. Cette hypothèse a été émise par les historiens du verre et les archéologues qui ont vu des parentés entre les verres de Corinthe et les découvertes du sud de l'Italie. D. Harden, "Some Glass Fragments, Mainly of the 12th–13th Century A.D., from Northern Apulia," *Journal of Glass Studies*, VIII, 1966, pp. 70–79. D. Whitehouse, *op. cit.*, 1966, pp. 171–178.

38. De nombreux verres à gouttes rapportées ont été découverts dans des tombes et des habitats datés essentiellement du XIVe siècle: L. Kojic et M. Wenzel, "Medieval Glass Found in Yugoslavia," *Journal of Glass Studies*, VIII, 1967, pp. 76–93. V. Han, "The Origin and Style of Medieval Glass Found in the Central Balkans," *Journal of Glass Studies*, XVII, 1975, pp. 114–125. P. Andelic, "Un aperçu de la typologie du verre médiéval en Bosnie et en Herzegovine," *Verre médiéval aux Balkans* (Ve–XVe siècle), recueil des travaux, Conférence internationale Belgrade 24–26 avril 1974, Belgrade, 1975, pp. 167–176.

XIVe siècle.[39] L'intérêt principal de ce matériel dont l'étude en cours est effectuée par D. Whitehouse, est son abondance et son homogénéité chronologique donnant ainsi une sorte d'instantané de la vaisselle en usage dans une grande demeure seigneuriale du Latium; la richesse des verres autorisera des études typologiques précises faisant ressortir avec évidence les grandes catégories, de production vraisemblablement régionale; mais dès à présent, on peut affirmer que les verres à gouttes rapportées forment l'un des groupes les plus conséquents: groupe que l'on peut scinder en deux en fonction de la matière: la série la plus importante composée de formes très diverses (les profils sont globulaires, tronconiques, ou bien très hauts et étroits presque coniques ou cylindriques; le cordon qui entoure la base est dentelé ou lisse; les gouttes de verres plus ou moins grandes sont parfois proéminentes: très étirées à la pince elles peuvent être très effilées donnant un aspect de piquants aux verres hauts et cylindriques) a une matière jaunâtre relativement épaisse. Cette matière qui est comparable à celle de nombreuses autres pièces retrouvées sur le même lieu. Aussi est-il raisonnable d'imaginer une production locale. Le second groupe, plus restreint, se caractérise par la qualité de son verre plus fin que le précédent et de teinte incolore légèrement bleuté. Ces verres pourraient provenir d'un autre atelier (?). Ceci montrerait alors l'unité des productions de cette époque, unité qui n'exclue pas de très légères variantes d'un atelier à l'autre que ce soit dans le détail des formes ou dans la matière.

L'aboutissement de la technique décorative des gouttes rapportées peut se voir dans les verres de type *kraustrunk* dans l'Europe du nord-ouest en particulier en Germanie à l'extrême fin du moyen-âge.

Les verres B4 du Midi méditerranéen se rattachent donc à l'une des formes précoces reconnues à Corinthe; ils doivent être comparés, malgré une légère variante décorative due à l'adjonction d'un filet bleu aux pièces italiennes découvertes dans un contexte du XIIIe siècle en particulier en Sicile

(Palerme[40]), Apulie (Lucera[41] et Petrulla[42]), Basilicate (Monte Irsi[43]), et à Cividale del Friuli.[44]

Le décor de pastilles rapportées associées aux applications bleues et au cordon pincé encerclant la base est-il réservé uniquement aux gobelets? On peut en douter. En effet un récipient globulaire à large ouverture, découvert dans les fouilles du réfectoire du monastère dominicain de Boston (Lincolnshire), possède toute cette ornementation. La pièce, datée de la fin du XIIIe siècle, serait une importation méridionale.[45]

V. Gobelet à Cordon Lisse ou Pincé, forme B5.

Le gobelet à gouttes rapportées n'est pas le seul type de gobelet en usage à la fin du XIIIe siècle. D'autres fonds, trouvés dans des niveaux archéologiques de même période, ont appartenu à des verres apodes. Ils se caractérisent par leur forme cylindrique—du moins dans leur partie inférieure—et leur matière différente de celle de la forme B4. Le verre plus lourd, teinté en jaunâtre ou verdâtre, est souvent criblé de petites bulles.

La hauteur et le rebord des gobelets B5, très fragmentés, sont inconnus. Les fonds coniques, saillants à l'intérieur de la pièce, ont un diamètre compris entre 38 et 59 mm. Le pourtour du fond est cerclé par un cordon pincé ou lisse.

Nous ne pouvons pas dire si les fonds décorés d'un cordon pincé appartiennent à la forme B4 ou relèvent d'un autre type; trop fragmentées, ces pièces ne laissent pas deviner le décor de leur

39. R. Chambon, *op. cit.*, 1975, pp. 151–157, fig. 1, B1 et B2.

40. F. D'Angelo, "Produzione e consumo del vetro in Sicilia," *Archeologia Medievale*, 1976, pp. 379–389, en part. fig. 1.

41. D. Whitehouse, 1966, *op. cit.*

42. D. B. Harden, *op. cit.*, 1966, pp. 70–79, en part. p. 74.

43. J. F. Cherry, "A Trial Excavation at Monte d'Irsi Basilicate," *Papers of the British School at Rome*, XXXIX, 1971, pp. 138–170.

44. A. Gasparetto, "Matrici e aspetti della vetraria veneziana e veneta medievale," *Journal of Glass Studies*, XXI, 1979, pp. 76–95, en part. 18 et 19.

45. R. J. Charleston, "Glass," dans "Finds from Excavations in the Refectory at the Dominican Friary, Boston," *Lincolnshire History and Archaeology*, VII, 1972, pp. 45–48.

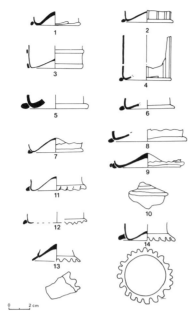

Fig. 18. *Gobelets à cordon rapporté, forme B5 (1 à 5, 13 et 14: Rougiers; 6 à 8, 10, 12: Planier; 9: Petit Palais, 11: Nans).*

paroi et leur forme générale. Les fonds à cordon pincé proviennent de Rougiers (Fig. 18,13 & 14), Planier (Fig. 18,12) et de sondages réalisés par G. Démians d'Archimbaud sur le *castrum* de Nans (Fig. 18,11). D'autres bases de gobelet cernées d'un cordon lisse attestent l'existence de gobelets différents du type B4. Sur ces pièces découvertes à Rougiers (Fig. 18,1 à 5), Planier (Fig. 18,6 à 8) et dans les fouilles du Petit Palais (Fig. 18,9), l'épaisseur du cordon varie de 2 mm à 5 mm. La jonction des deux extrémités du cordon est, sur certains fragments, bien visible.

A ce cordon sont parfois associés d'autres décors: ceux-ci peuvent relever du même procédé technique qui consiste à rapporter autour du corps de l'objet un second cordon, parallèle au premier (Fig. 18,3). Ornementation obtenue au moule et cordon rapporté sont parfois réunis sur un même gobelet. Les côtes fines et verticales sont les motifs moulés invariables de ce décor qui subsiste très estompé sous le fond de l'objet. A Rougiers, quatre fonds de ce type ont été retrouvés, dont deux assez complets pour pouvoir y compter

huit ou seize côtes plus ou moins espacées (Fig. 18,2 & 4). Ces pièces sont trop incomplètes pour être utilement comparées à d'autres trouvailles. Seul le gobelet provenant de l'atelier corinthien du XIIe siècle, pourrait être le prototype de ces fragments: ce verre cylindrique est décoré de côtes verticales s'élevant au-dessus du cordon lisse qui encercle la base de la pièce.[46]

Bien qu'excessivement fragmentés, ces verres témoignent de l'apparition de divers gobelets dans la seconde moitié du XIIIe siècle, gobelets qui sont de composition sodique, comme le révèlent quatre analyses effectuées sur des pièces provenant de Rougiers (annexe 2. VEM 21 à 24).

VI. Gobelets à Décor de Spirales, forme B6.

Les gobelets B6, dont la forme et la matière rappellent le type antérieur, apparaissent légèrement postérieurs aux premiers gobelets cités. Quoique absents des productions de l'atelier de Planier, les verres B6 comptent parmi les trouvailles exhumées dans les niveaux de la fin du XIIIe siècle à Rougiers. Ils sont cependant mieux représentés, toujours sur ce même site, dans les niveaux du XIVe siècle et n'ont certainement pas perduré longtemps car ils restent exceptionnels dans les fouilles de Cadrix (Fig. 19,9).

Bien qu'aucun profil n'ait été retrouvé complet, la forme de ces gobelets a pu être restituée à partir de plusieurs fragments; cette restitution reste bien sûr incertaine. Le gobelet est presque parfaitement cylindrique, seule la partie supérieure s'évase à peine: la différence entre les diamètres du fond et du rebord est inférieure à 15 mm; les fonds varient de 40 à 57 mm de diamètre. Le rebord est formé d'un fil bleu rapporté à l'extérieur; ce n'est pas l'unique ornementation de ce gobelet dont le décor moulé est très caractéristique (Fig. 19,1 & 7).

Sur le pourtour du fond, à partir de 15 à 20 mm du centre conique, rayonnent douze à seize côtes qui montent en forme de S très saillants et inclinés

46. G. Davidson, *op. cit.*, 1940, fig. 15,4.

à la base des parois. L'extrémité du S se prolonge
ensuite en se transformant en spirales plus fines et
de faible relief qui s'enroulent autour de l'objet
jusqu'au bandeau lisse de 4 à 6 mm de large,
annonçant le rebord. Différents moules furent
utilisés puisque le décor présente des variations
dans le nombre de spirales et dans l'orientation de
celles-ci: les deux tiers des fonds retrouvés à
Rougiers sont couverts de spirales adoptant un
mouvement orienté vers la droite. Le restant,
ainsi que les fragments découverts à Cadrix, sont
dotés d'un décor contraire. Le nombre de spirales, comptabilisées sur les fonds assez complets,
varie du simple au double: le diamètre des fonds
n'étant pas relatif au nombre de côtes; ainsi le
plus grand, qui atteint 57 mm de diamètre n'a que
douze côtes, le nombre minimum (Fig. 19,4 & 5),
alors qu'un fond de 45 mm de diamètre est orné
de 24 spirales (Fig. 19,6). Une des pièces du type
B6 retrouvée à Rougiers est particulière par son
verre épais et ses côtes verticales (Fig. 19,8). Les
neuf fonds complets ou restituables provenant de
Rougiers montrent que plusieurs matrices ont été
utilisées puisque six combinaisons apparaissent.
Les pièces dont le décor est orienté vers la droite
possédent douze, seize, ou vingt-quatre côtes (Fig.
19,1 & 3 à 6); les côtes s'enroulant sur la gauche
sont au nombre de douze ou quatorze; un seul
gobelet porte quatorze côtes verticales (Fig. 19,8).

Bien que très caractéristique de ces gobelets, le
décor de spirales ne suffit pas pour identifier tous
les gobelets dotés de ce décor au type B6. Certaines pièces en effet, par leur verre fin et incolore,
s'apparentent bien mieux aux grandes productions des gobelets moulés du XIVe siècle qu'à
cette série en fait peu représentée en dehors des
trouvailles de Rougiers. Un fragment de paroi de
gobelet, portant des spirales et un fil bleu sur le
rebord, provient des verreries trouvées rassemblées dans une chapelle dépendante d'un Commanderie des Templiers, à la Cavalerie de la
Limaye (La-Bastide-des-Jourdans, Vaucluse).
La finesse de son verre incolore le rapproche des
gobelets fréquents au XIVe siècle (Fig. 19,2).

De même, les nombreux verres décorés de spi-

Fig. 19. *Gobelets à spirales, forme B6 (1, 3 et 8: Rougiers; 2: La Bastide-des-Jourdans; 9: Cadrix).*

rales et représentés par l'iconographie, n'appartiennent pas forcément au type B6. Ces figura-
tions sont d'ailleurs tardives: dans deux oeuvres
de Nicolas Froment de la deuxième moitié du
XVe siècle, "le repas chez le pharisien" et "la
Résurrection de Lazare" apparaissent des gobelets à spirales. Les analyses physico-chimiques
réalisées sur deux fragments du type B6, montrent une composition semblable aux verres précédents (annexe 2, VEM 13 et 20).

VII. Verres Colorés et Peints, série B7.

La série B7 ne renvoie pas à une forme mais à
une technique décorative consistant particulièrement à peindre en blanc opaque des verres colorés
en bleu dans la masse.

Trois petits fragments découverts sur l'atelier
de Planier qui fonctionna à la fin du XIIIe siècle,
attestent l'existence, à cette époque, de verres
émaillés bleu et blanc. Sur le fond bleu apparaît
un décor de petites feuilles ou d'écailles serrées
blanches (Fig. 17,14 & 15). Malheureusement ces
pièces de très petite taille ne laissent pas deviner
la forme qui portait ce décor; il en est de même

37

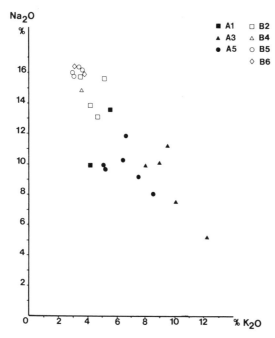

Fig. 20. *Pourcentage de la soude et de la potasse dans les verres des XIIe et XIIIe siècles (formes A1, A3, A5, B2, B4, B5, B6).*

pour le fragment découvert au Petit Palais (Fig. 17,16).

Dans la première moitié du XIVe siècle, cette technique a été poursuivie, du moins en Languedoc. Si ce décor est complètement absent à Rougiers à toute époque, il est assez bien représenté sur l'atelier de la Seube par des pièces diversifiées. Le verre bleu décoré de blanc est le plus fréquent: ainsi une perle cylindrique porte des applications blanches très comparables aux pièces trouvées à Planier.[47] Plusieurs fragments colorés d'un bleu plus clair sont rehaussés d'accolades imbriquées blanches; ils appartiennent à un objet au pied conique.[48] Des rubans blanc opaque décorent aussi des verres violets identifiés à des éléments de plat.[49] Les fonds sur lesquels sont disposés les applications blanches ont donc différentes couleurs, et les applications elles-mêmes peuvent varier dans les teintes blanches et rouges. Ces décors répétitifs apparaissent toujours sous forme de petites écailles ou accolades, ou bien encore sous forme de pointillés.

VIII. Composition des Verres de la Fin du XIIIe Siècle.

Un graphique illustrant la proportion de sodium et de potassium dans la composition des verres du XIIe et XIIIe siècle montre une progression de la quantité de sodium dans les verres les plus récents (Fig. 20). Trop peu d'analyses ont été effectuées sur des échantillons qui ne représentent d'ailleurs pas toutes les formes des séries A et B. On remarque pourtant que les verres A3 et A5 sont beaucoup moins riches en sodium que les autres. Il faut cependant s'étonner de la relative pauvreté en potassium des verres A1, considérés comme les plus anciens. (Nous avons volontairement omis de représenter dans nos graphiques la série B3, très hétéroclite comprenant des pièces du XIIIe au XIVe siècle.) La comparaison entre les autres composants des verres A et B, suscite quelques remarques. En règle générale il y a beaucoup moins de variations dans la proportion de chacun des composants de la série B que dans celle des verres du type A. Sans tenir compte des verres B3 mal définis, nous remarquons de grandes différences dans la proportion de calcium qui est supérieure à 9% dans les verres A, et inférieure à 9% dans les verres B: différence normale, puisque les verres potassiques sont toujours plus riches en calcium que les autres. Le sodium, révélé par les analyses, provient très certainement de cendres de végétaux halophiles employés dans la composition du verre. De nombreux textes provençaux et languedociens attestent en effet dès le XIIIe siècle et jusqu'à la période moderne la culture en Camargue et autour des étangs languedociens de plusieurs espèces de plantes dont la combustion fournit la soude. Cette soude fut utilisée par les verriers et les savonneries médiévaux et post-médiévaux.[50]

47. N. Lambert, *op. cit.*, p. 84, fig. 10.

48. *Idem*, p. 83, fig. 9.

49. *Idem*, p. 81.

50. D. Foy, *Le verre médiéval . . . , op. cit.*, 1981, chapitre II, pp. 87–98. H. Amouric et D. Foy, "Notes sur la production et la commercialisation de la soude dans le midi méditerranéen du

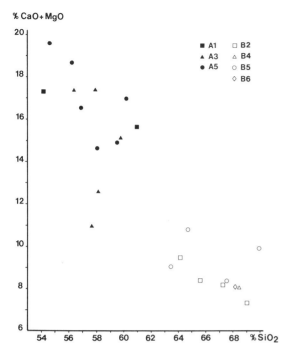

Fig. 21. *Pourcentage de la silice et des alcalins terreux dans les verres des XIIe et XIIIe siècles (formes A1, A3, A5, B2, B4, B5, B6).*

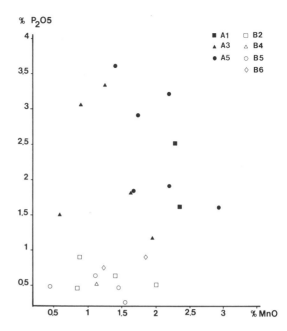

Fig. 22. *Pourcentage du manganèse et du phosphore dans les verres des XIIe et XIIIe siècles (formes A1, A3, A5, B2, B5, B6).*

Un graphique sur les teneurs en silice et alcalino-terreux (CaO+MgO) individualise nettement les verres des séries A et B (Fig. 21). Là, les verres A1 qui précédemment ne se distinguaient guère des types B, apparaîssent clairement dans le groupe des plus anciens. Des résultats identiques se manifestent dans un troisième graphique mettant en évidence les pourcentages de phosphore et de manganèse (Fig. 22). Ainsi les verres de la série A, du moins les formes A1, A3 et A5, qui n'ont pourtant pas un fondant potassique toujours supérieur au fondant sodique, doivent être rapprochés des verres dits potassiques à cause de leur richesse en alcalino-terreux et phosphore, éléments qui sembleraient être apportés dans les cendres des végétaux forestiers. A noter aussi leur pauvreté en silice.

La composition à fondant sodique des verres attribués à la fin du XIIIe siècle peut-elle être précisée par les séries d'analyses effectuées sur des déchets de verres provenant de Planier? Les

dix déchets de verres provenant de ce dernier atelier, montrent avant tout de grandes variations dans chacun des composants du verre (annexe 3). Si le fondant dominant est toujours le sodium, les rapports entre les fondants varient de 1,76 fois à plus de 9 fois. Les pourcentages de sodium restant toutefois semblables à ceux des verres B. Par contre les alcalino-terreux, surtout le magnésium, sont aussi importants que dans les verres A. Nous pouvons donc définir la composition des verres de Planier comme essentiellement sodique, mais encore très riche en MgO, comme l'étaient les verres, en partie potassiques, des XIIe–XIIIe siècles. Les variations observées dans les échantillons de Planier (CaO: $6 < 10,50$; Fe_2O_3: $0,63 < 1,60$; TiO_2: $0,10 < 0,17$; K_2O: $1,44 < 6,48$; SiO_2: $56 < 64,90$; Al_2O_3: $2,65 < 4,35$; MgO: $3,10 < 6,78$;

moyen âge au XVIIIe siècle," *Actes du colloque Techniques, technologie et histoire dans l'aire méditerranéenne*, octobre 1982, Cahiers du G.I.S., Aix-en-Provence, vol. VI (à paraître).

Na_2O: $10{,}60 < 16{,}00$; P_2O_5: $0{,}60 < 2{,}60$ et MnO: $0{,}94 < 2{,}30$) nous incitent à la prudence. La composition des verres de Planier ne doit être en aucune façon considérée comme celle des productions régionales de la fin du XIIIe siècle, mais seulement comme celle d'un seul atelier. Nous reviendrons sur les analyses de Planier pour les comparer aux verres des ateliers du XIVe siècle.

IX. Conclusion

La lecture des pages précédentes rend bien compte de notre méconnaissance de la verrerie antérieure au XIVe siècle dans le Midi de la France. Quelques formes des verres du haut moyen-âge (Ve–VIIe siècle) commencent à être reconnues à la faveur de fouilles stratigraphiques[51] et l'existence d'ateliers de verriers de cette époque est certaine.[52] En revanche nous ignorons tout des verres utilisés du VIIIe au XIe siècle: les fouilles de sites, et *a fortiori* la vaisselle de cette époque étant, jusqu'à présent, presque totalement absentes de nos régions.

Les objets de verre des siècles suivants restent encore peu nombreux et sont souvent incomplètement ou incertainement définis dans leur forme; leur datation est encore imprécise. Il est alors difficile dans ces conditions, d'établir des comparaisons avec les trouvailles—assez rares—des pays voisins. Notons cependant que le verre à tige, peu connu des pays méditerranéens, est en usage dans nos régions jusqu'au début du XIVe siècle. Il faut d'ailleurs chercher les parallèles de la forme B2, seule complètement restituée, dans le nord de la France et autres terres septentrionales; cette parenté (et non pas identité) n'implique pas une importation.

Le verre à tige n'est pourtant pas la forme prépondérante; différents types de gobelets ont été utilisés à la même période; ces gobelets sont certainement (B4) ou probablement (B5 et B6) des productions régionales. Nous ne connaissons pas l'origine du type B6, par contre les gobelets B4 et B5, connus dans d'autres pays méditerranéens, ont sans doute une origine orientale.

Sans doute existe-t-il, parmi les verres découverts, quelques pièces importées: il faut probablement être attribué aux rares fragments de verre émaillés trouvés dans les fouilles du Petit Palais d'Avignon et sur la fouille du prieuré de Notre-Dame de Pinel à Villariés (Haute-Garonne),[53] une provenance étrangère: orientale ou vénitienne?[54] On peut d'ailleurs s'étonner de la rareté de ces pièces émaillées qui pourraient correspondre à l'appellation "verres de Damas" qui apparaît dans les inventaires provençaux et languedociens.[55]

Remarquons enfin que les objets étudiés ici sont tous des verres à boire, ceci ne pouvant pourtant pas signifier l'absence totale de vases à liquide. A Planier des éléments de fioles, bien que rares, sont présents sous forme d'embouchure de petit goulot en verre incolore (Fig. 17,18) ou de paroi de flacon décorée de grosses côtes (Fig. 17,17). Il n'y a aucune raison de penser que les fioles connues par l'archéologie dans des régions proches, et par l'iconographie, soient totalement ignorées en Provence et Languedoc. Alors que les nécropoles de Cancabeau, de Sainte-Croix et de Digne[56] n'ont fourni que des verres, des tombes

51. D. Foy et M. Bonifay, "Eléments d'évolution des verreries de l'Antiquité tardive à Marseille d'après les fouilles de la Bourse (1980)," *Revue Archéologique de Narbonnaise* (à paraître).

52. Nous pouvons situer un atelier au IVe ou Ve siècle à Vienne: D. Foy et J. Tardieu, "Un atelier de verrier de la fin de l'Antiquité à Vienne," *Actes du 90e Congrès des Sociétés Savantes*, à paraître; à Marseille; et en Languedoc près de l'abbaye de Maguelonne à la fin du VIe ou au VIIe siècle: D. Foy et L. Vallauri, Témoins d'une verrerie du haut moyen-âge à Maguelonne, à paraître.

53. Dans ces dernières fouilles, M. Falco, responsable, a découvert un fragment de verre émaillé de blanc, vert et rouge portant dans un médaillon un lion; renseignement G. Villeval.

54. L. Zecchin, "Un decoratore di vetri a Murano alla fine del duecento," *Journal of Glass Studies*, XI, 1969, pp. 39–42; A. Gasparetto, 1979, *op. cit.*, pp. 93–94.

55. A titre d'exemple on peut citer en 1397 dans l'inventaire d'une juive d'Avignon une "*sculetta de vitro operate de opere de Damasco*" G. Arnaud d'Agnel, *Le meuble. Ameublement provençal et comtadin du moyen-âge à la fin du XVIIIe siècle*, Paris-Marseille, 1913, p. 122.

56. Des fouilles menées en 1936 dans la cathédrale de Digne ont mis à jour une série de tombes contenant des vases en

du XIIIe siècle dans l'église Saint-Georges à Vienne (Isère) ont livré plusieurs fioles à la panse et au col parfois décorés de filets en torsades ou de cordons rapportés en zigzag.[57] Des bouteilles à panse globulaire et long col sont connues par l'iconographie catalane des XIe et XIIe siècle. Des miniatures illustrant des repas montrent des bouteilles très grandes, sans doute même exagérément grandes, puisque certaines sont deux fois plus grosses que la tête des personnages buvant au goulot.[58] La schématisation de ces objets, simples boules munies d'un long col est frappante. Les fioles de Vienne et la bouteille trouvée en Italie à Castelmonardo,[59] n'ont pas de pied alors que la plupart des verres attribués aux XIIe et XIIIe siècles ont été formés en plusieurs opérations consistant à façonner la coupe puis le pied, et parfois même, la coupe, la tige puis le pied.

C.
LES PRODUCTIONS DU XIVe SIECLE EN VERRE INCOLORE ET FIN

La plupart des verreries datées du XIVe siècle, peuvent être attribuées à des productions locales d'après les trouvailles des ateliers de la Seube et de Rougiers du second quart du XIVe siècle, et de la verrerie de Cadrix de la seconde moitié du XIVe siècle. Les verres à boire, moins diversifiés qu'aux périodes précédentes, restent les verreries les mieux représentées.

I. Gobelets en Verre Très Fin, forme C1.

Le type C1 est, de très loin, l'objet de verre le plus répandu; il constitue, aussi bien à Rougiers qu'à Cadrix, la principale production de l'atelier. Ces gobelets dont la forme offre des variantes notables, se caractérisent essentiellement par leur matière mise en valeur par un décor approprié. Le verre épais des premiers gobelets de la fin du XIIIe siècle, est désormais réservé à quelques pièces particulières, tandis que les verres les plus nombreux sont d'une finesse remarquable souvent inférieure à 1 mm. La fragilité de ces pièces,

qui semblent pourtant d'un usage courant, est accentuée par la transparence presque parfaite d'un verre incolore ou à peine teinté de verdâtre ou de jaunâtre. Tous ces gobelets quelle que soit leur forme, ont un fond conique rentrant à l'intérieur de l'objet. Ce type de fond est celui de la plupart des verreries du XIVe siècle, aussi est-il très hasardeux d'attribuer les fonds trouvés isolés à un objet ou à un autre. Nous pensons pourtant que la plus grande partie des fonds recueillis sur de nombreux sites, appartiennent à des gobelets. Leur diamètre est compris entre 32 et 65 mm, et leur sommet conique est plus ou moins élevé, arrondi ou aigu. Tous ces gobelets ont aussi en commun des parois rectilignes, sans décrochement, et un rebord simple: la lèvre arrondie n'est jamais ourlée.

a. Les Formes

– Gobelets Cylindriques

Contrairement aux gobelets de la fin du XIIIe siècle, les gobelets du XIVe siècle sont généralement larges et trapus. Certains conservent la forme cylindrique caractéristique de ces premiers gobelets. Les pièces dites "cylindriques" n'ont entre le diamètre du rebord et celui du fond qu'une différence de l'ordre de 10 mm. On distingue ainsi les gobelets bas, beaucoup plus larges que hauts, les gobelets "cubiques" presque aussi hauts que larges et enfin les gobelets minces et hauts.

---

céramique grise (type pégau) et des verres. Cette fouille n'est pas publiée. Il reste aujourd'hui un seul verre, déposé au musée de Digne; c'est un verre tronconique au rebord à marli; trouvé en association avec un pégau, il peut être daté XIIe–XIIIe siècle. Ce verre et les verres (verres creux et vitraux) trouvés en 1983 et 1984 lors des fouilles du même site, par G. Demians d'Archimbaud, sont en cours d'étude.

57. M. Jannet et M. Soubeyran, *L'église Saint-Georges de Vienne (Isère): recherches archéologiques*, D.E.S. Lyon, dactylographié, 1978. *Des Burgondes à Bayard*, catalogue d'exposition, Grenoble, 1981, notices 563, 564.

58. Voir par exemple Paris, B.N., ms. lat. 6(3) f° 66, 97, 127 ou encore Bede Homilies, Gerone, Sant Feliu, f° 44.

59. D. Maestri et M. Maestri de Luca, *Castelmonardo, archeologia medievale e ricerca interdisciplinare*, Rome, 1978, pl. 59.

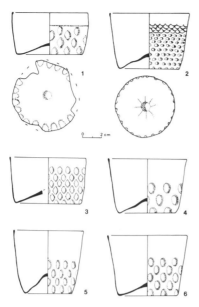

Fig. 23. *Gobelets, forme C1 (1 à 4: Petit Palais; 5 et 6: Cadrix).*

Les pièces les plus basses sont presque deux fois plus larges que hautes puisque leur hauteur est comprise seulement entre 40 et 45 mm, alors que la largeur maximale atteint 78 mm. Ces gobelets très trapus sont uniquement représentés par des trouvailles du Petit Palais d'Avignon (Fig. 23,1 & 3).

Le second sous-type cylindrique ne se différencie du premier que par sa hauteur plus importante variant entre 60 et 65 mm. S'ils restent plus larges que hauts comme les précédents, leurs proportions sont toutefois plus équilibrées, puisque leur largeur maximale est d'environ 70 mm. Ces gobelets presque "cubiques" proviennent uniquement de l'atelier de Cadrix (Fig. 24,2 & 4).

Le dernier gobelet dit cylindrique n'est en fait représenté que par une seule pièce issue de fouilles réalisées par G. Démians d'Archimbaud dans le jardin de l'hôtel de Brion en Avignon.[60] Cette pièce légèrement bleutée atteint 99 mm de haut et possède un diamètre à l'ouverture de 69 mm (Fig. 24,3).

– Gobelets Tronconiques

La différence entre le diamètre supérieur et le diamètre inférieur est pour les gobelets dits tronconiques de 20 à 30 mm. Leur hauteur varie entre 55 et 64 mm, et leur diamètre supérieur est compris entre 70 et 87 mm. Il est difficile de dire lesquels des gobelets cylindriques ou tronconiques sont les plus fréquents, car les formes complètes, trop peu nombreuses, ne peuvent représenter les nombreux exemplaires dont ne restent souvent que les fonds. Ces gobelets tronconiques sont cependant d'origine beaucoup plus diversifiée: le seul gobelet reconstitué de Rougiers est l'exemplaire le plus évasé (Fig. 24,1). D'autres pièces proviennent des fouilles du Petit Palais (Fig. 23,2 ou 25 et Fig. 23,4 ou 61) et de Cadrix (Fig. 23,5 & 6).

Les différents profils de ces gobelets ne peuvent être considérés comme significatifs d'une évolution. Les gobelets trouvés à la Seube sont hauts et cylindriques alors que le seul exemplaire reconstitué de Rougiers est très évasé: les deux ateliers semblent pourtant contemporains. A Cadrix nous trouvons des gobelets cylindriques et larges et des gobelets tronconiques. Entre les gobelets de la fin du XIIIe siècle et les nombreux gobelets produits au XIVe siècle, la seule transformation notable est l'abandon des gobelets hauts et cylindriques réalisés dans un verre assez épais, pour des gobelets tronconiques ou cylindriques mais presque toujours trapus et façonnés dans un verre très fin.

b. Les Décors

Les gobelets en verre très fin sont souvent décorés, certains par un décor rapporté de filets bleus, et d'autres par un décor moulé. Ce dernier décor est caractéristique du type C1. Quelques gobelets pourtant ne sont pas décorés. Il est impossible de définir parmi les trouvailles d'un site

60. D. Foy, Verres dans G. Demians d'Archimbaud, J. Thiriot, L. Vallauri, *Céramiques d'Avignon, les fouilles de l'Hôtel de Brion et leur matériel*, Mémoires de l'Académie de Vaucluse 1981, numéro hors série; les verres provenant de cette fouille et mentionnés dans ces pages, ont été publiés dans la revue citée ci-dessus, pp. 147–164.

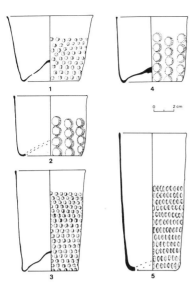

Fig. 25. *Gobelet, forme C1 (cf. Fig. 58,2; photo C. Hussy).*

Fig. 24. *Gobelets, forme C1 (1: Rougiers; 2 et 4: Cadrix; 3: coll. J. de Brion), forme C2 (5: Cadrix).*

la proportion des gobelets moulés et celle des non décorés. En effet le décor n'atteint jamais les rebords et apparaît souvent très estompé près des fonds; aussi les nombreux fragments de rebords et de fonds non décorés ne font pas forcément partie d'objets sans ornementation. L'existence de gobelets aux parois non décorées est pourtant certaine.

Le décor géométrique et répétitif obtenu par un moule fait d'une seule pièce, définit la série C1. Cette ornementation couvre la plupart du temps le fond de la pièce et ses parois sans atteindre le rebord sous lequel subsiste toujours un bandeau lisse.

Le motif décoratif le plus fréquent est celui de pastilles rondes en relief dont la taille et la disposition sont variables. Les plus grandes atteignent 8 à 10 mm de diamètre et sont disposées en rangs verticaux ou obliques. Différentes matrices donnaient ce décor de grandes pastilles tantôt espacées de quelques millimètres tantôt accolées (Fig. 24,2 & 4) ou bien encore se chevauchant jusqu'à former un réseau d'écailles (Fig. 25). Le décor semble uniforme sur toute la pièce, ce qui n'est pas toujours le cas des gobelets ornés de pastilles

rondes de très petite taille; celles-ci, disposées en rangs obliques, ont environ 3 mm de diamètre; ce décor couvre uniformément les parois (Fig. 24,3 & 4) ou bien se transforme dans la partie haute de la pièce, en emboîtements compacts (Fig. 23,2).

Les pastilles ovalisées ou losangées sont aussi très bien représentées. Ce décor de "grains de riz" ou de losanges est toujours en relief et chacune des pastilles est généralement bien espacée (Fig. 23,1 à 5 & 6).

Les fonds portent un décor, souvent très estompé et difficilement perceptible, qui ne rend pas forcément compte de celui que l'on trouve sur les parois. Le plus simple est celui de petits rayons partant du centre du fond où se trouve la marque du pontil.

II. Gobelets Cylindriques en Verre Epais, forme C2.

Ce type n'est malheureusement représenté que par une seule pièce; celle-ci, trouvée à Cadrix, fait probablement partie des productions de l'atelier. C'est un gobelet en verre relativement épais et verdâtre, qui atteint 135 mm de haut pour une largeur maximale de 67 mm. Les deux tiers des parois sont couvertes d'un décor de grains de riz imprimés en creux (Fig. 24,5 et Fig. 26).

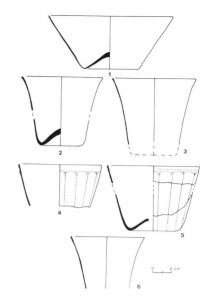

Fig. 26. *Gobelet, forme C2 (cf. Fig. 59,5; photo C. Hussy).*

Fig. 27. *Gobelets tronconiques, forme C3, Rougiers.*

III. Gobelets Tronconiques en Verre Epais, forme C3.

La tendance à l'élargissement des gobelets (en dehors de l'exception que constitue la forme C2) aboutit à l'apparition à l'extrême fin du XIVe ou au début du XVe siècle, de gobelets tronconiques en verre souvent épais et verdâtre et parfois décoré de côtes. Ces pièces très évasées ont le diamètre du rebord parfois presque égal ou supérieur au diamètre du fond (Fig. 27,1 & 5 et Fig. 28). Certains de ces gobelets moins larges et plus hauts, ont leur rebord déjeté vers l'extérieur (Fig. 27,2, 3, & 6). Ces pièces trouvées dans les derniers niveaux d'occupation du *castrum* de Rougiers sont probablement d'origine régionale. Les verres décorés de 16 ou 20 côtes verticales butant contre la fine moulturation qui délimite le bandeau lisse annonçant le rebord (Fig. 27,4 & 5), sont comparables à certains fonds côtelés trouvés à la verrerie

Fig. 28. *Verre tronconique (cf. Fig. 67,1: Rougiers, C. Hussy).*

du Monte Lecco datée du début du XVe siècle.[61]

Le gobelet apparu dès la fin du XIIIe siècle en France méditerranéenne et autres pays méridionaux a probablement ses origines en Orient. Parmi les trouvailles de la verrerie de Corinthe, datées du XIIe siècle, sont déjà représentés les

61. S. Fossati et N. Mannoni, "Lo scavo della vetreria di Monte Lecco," *Archeologia Medievale*, II, 1975, pp. 31–98, fig. 11, p. 58 et fig. 50, p. 59.

formes et les décors des gobelets connus en Provence au XIIIe et au XIVe siècle. Le décor de gouttes rapportées, de cordons, comme celui de pastilles moulées, technique décorative dite *optic blown*, ont probablement été reçus par l'Italie qui les a transmis à toute l'Europe. Cette diffusion ne s'est pas faite partout avec la même rapidité: en effet le gobelet, décoré ou non, n'est pas connu dans les pays septentrionaux avant le XVe siècle. Des gobelets cylindriques et tronconiques décorés de pastilles ou de côtes et découverts à Utrecht ne sont attribués qu'au début de ce siècle.[62] La même datation a été attribuée à un gobelet tronconique couvert de pastilles rondes moulées et trouvé à Southampton;[63] gobelet qui serait peut-être d'origine méridionale. De même les gobelets trouvés en Allemagne et Belgique, tels ceux conservés au musée de Namur, ne sont pas datés avant la fin du moyen-âge.[64]

En Italie, le type C1 est présent mais beaucoup moins répandu que sur les terres du Midi de la France. Ainsi parmi les découvertes de Tarquinia on note de nombreux gobelets à côtes verticales mais beaucoup moins d'éléments de verre au décor de pastilles moulées. La proportion de ce matériel dans l'ensemble des découvertes de cette ville est insignifiante. Quelle est l'origine de ces verres? En l'absence d'une documentation plus ample il serait vain de discuter sur ce problème. Cependant nous ne pensons pas que ces verres dont la matière fine et incolore se différencie des autres trouvailles, soient des productions régionales. Rien ne permet pourtant de considérer ces pièces comme des importations provençales. Sur l'atelier italien du Monte Lecco il n'existe pas de gobelets moulés en dehors de ceux qui possèdent des côtes. Mais on trouve sur ce même site daté du début du XVe siècle, le gobelet sans décor haut et cylindrique et le gobelet de forme basse et tronconique.[65] A la fin du XIVe et au XVe siècle, il semble donc que les ateliers italiens ne produisent pas—ou plus—des verres de type C1. Les découvertes provençales et languedociennes ne permettent pas de connaître précisément la longévité de ces gobelets: dans l'état actuel des recherches

nous situons l'apparition du type C1 dans le second quart du XIVe siècle et sa disparition au début du XVe siècle avec l'arrivée du gobelet C3 qui n'atteindra jamais l'importance du type précédent.

IV. Coupelles, forme C4.

Les coupelles, petits récipients bas et évasés, ne sont pas connues avant les productions régionales du second quart du XIVe siècle. Elles témoignent d'un enrichissement des formes à cette époque où les ateliers fabriquent des gobelets diversifiés. Comme les gobelets C1, les coupelles sont réalisées dans un verre extrêmement fin et presque incolore.

L'examen des rebords laisse penser à l'existence de deux types au moins. Les coupelles à marli plat sont malheureusement mal définies. Nous ne connaissons que le rebord de ces pièces probablement de petites dimensions, à en juger par le diamètre compris entre 90 et 120 mm. La lèvre arrondie, parfois épaissie, détermine à l'extérieur une petite mouluration (Fig. 31,1 à 4).

Les coupelles à marli concave sont parfaitement identifiées grâce à la découverte d'une pièce complète dont le profil confirme les restitutions des exemplaires incomplets. Les coupelles ou éléments de coupelles découverts à Rougiers, Psalmodi, Cadrix, et Avignon (collection J. de Brion et fouilles du Petit Palais) montrent des variantes dans les tailles et non dans les profils: le fond toujours concave a environ 55 mm de diamètre; les parois s'évasent ensuite jusqu'à un décrochement annonçant la courbure du rebord concave. La hauteur de l'objet est comprise entre

62. C. Isings et H. F. Wijman, *op. cit.*, fig. 2.

63. R. J. Charleston, "The Glass" dans C. Platt et R. Coleman-Smith, *Excavations in Medieval Southampton 1953–1969*, vol. 2, *The Finds*, Leicester, 1975, pp. 204–226, en part. fig. 222 n° 1508.

64. R. Chambon et F. Courtoy, "Verres de la fin du moyen-âge et de la Renaissance aux musées de Namur," *Annales de la Société Archéologique de Namur*, XLVI, 1951, pp. 100 à 120.

65. S. Fossati et L. Mannoni, *op. cit.*, p. 65, fig. n° 74 et 75.

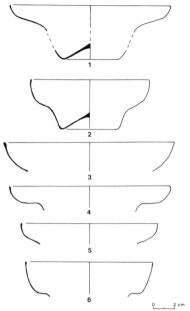

Fig. 29. *Coupelles, forme C4 (1: Rougiers; 2 et 4: Cadrix; 3 et 5: Psalmodi; 6: Avignon).*

Fig. 30. *Coupelle, forme C4 (cf. Fig. 69,2, Cadrix. Photo C. Hussy).*

45 et 60 mm; les variations du diamètre de l'ouverture, beaucoup plus importantes, se situent entre 110 et 160 mm (Fig. 29). La pièce complète découverte à Cadrix est l'un des plus petits exemplaires avec 45 mm de haut et 110 mm de large (Fig. 29,2 et Fig. 30).

Quelques coupelles sont dépourvues de tout décor (Fig. 29), en revanche d'autres ont un décor moulé de grains de riz (Fig. 31,5 & 6) ou de nervures (Fig. 31,8) comparable à celui des gobelets. Le décor rapporté est beaucoup plus rare sur les coupelles: nous n'en connaissons qu'un seul exemple découvert à Rougiers (Fig. 31,7).

La fonction de ces objets très fragiles, au rebord fin et concave et à la coupe large rendant difficile la préhension d'une seule main, reste énigmatique. Leur forme peu fonctionnelle pour être celle d'un verre à boire, était probablement destinée à contenir des liquides. L'évasement de ces pièces, et leur profil comparable à celui des lampes en verre, n'exclut pas une fonction de luminaire.

V. Verreries à Décor Bleu Rapporté, forme C5.

Le type C5 comprend plusieurs formes, mais doit son unité au décor rapporté de teinte bleu qui couvre totalement ou partiellement ces différentes formes: gobelets, coupelles, pots globulaires à embouchure étroite et fioles. Ce décor n'est pas l'unique caractère, commun de ces verreries, dont la matière parfois absolument incolore est très brillante. Peut-être faut-il identifier ce verre d'une qualité parfaite au *cristallin*, terme utilisé dans les textes tardifs du XVe siècle pour désigner un verre incolore. Le verre teinté dans la masse en bleu outremer et appliqué sous forme de filets ou de pastilles plates, met parfaitement en valeur la qualité exceptionnelle de la matière incolore et transparente. Cette ornementation et la qualité du verre font de ces pièces des objets précieux dont la plupart sont des coupelles à usage certainement décoratif. Les verreries à décor bleu produites dans les ateliers de la Seube et de Rougiers, sont encore fabriquées à Cadrix à la fin du XIVe siècle.

Les objets réunis dans cette rubrique ne sont peut-être pas tous du XIVe siècle, certains provenant de Psalmodi ou du Petit Palais peuvent être antérieurs puisque le décor bleu, nous l'avons vu, apparaît dans les productions de la fin du XIIIe siècle associé à un décor de gouttes ou de cordon dentelé rapportés. Le décor appliqué bleu, apparu à la fin du XIIIe siècle sur les verres

46

à tige A5 et B2 et sur les gobelets B4, s'est développé au début du XIVe siècle pour enrichir diverses formes de verreries.

a. Gobelets, forme C5a

Les gobelets en raison de leur fond comparable à celui des coupelles, sont difficiles à identifier; pourtant, bien que rares, des éléments attestent l'existence de gobelets décorés d'applications de verre bleu. Le cordon dentelé et incolore, entourant la base des objets et employé dans les premiers gobelets de la fin du XIIIe siècle, est maintes fois repris sur les gobelets et les coupelles décorés aussi de filets bleus.

Comme les gobelets à décor moulé, les gobelets C5a ont un profil cylindrique ou tronconique. Une seule pièce appartenant à la collection J. de Brion a pu être entièrement reconstituée. Presque parfaitement cylindrique (diamètre inférieur 61 mm et diamètre supérieur 65 mm), ce verre d'une matière très belle est mis en valeur par un décor couvrant sa moitié inférieure. Au-dessus du cordon pincé, le verre bleu forme une trame de losanges surmontée par trois filets grossièrement parallèles (Fig. 32,1).

Les verres tronconiques étaient tout aussi riches, comme en témoignent les trouvailles faites à Psalmodi. Un filet bleu, déposé sur le rebord, est peut-être la seule décoration de l'un d'entre eux (Fig. 32,2). Cependant, le rebord bleu peut parfois être associé à un décor moulé tel celui de côtes, fréquentes sur des gobelets cylindriques. Sur les parois d'autres gobelets évasés, les filets bleus décrivent des spirales (Fig. 32,3) et des croix pattées (Fig. 32,4). Ces derniers décors, uniquement connus à Psalmodi, sont aussi appliqués sur les panses des coupelles (Fig. 32,6).

b. Coupelles, forme C5b

Une certaine diversité existe dans le décor des coupelles. Déjà le type C4 offrait des variantes dans les pièces nues ou portant un décor fait au moule. Contrairement aux gobelets, décor moulé et applications bleues ne sont pratiquement jamais associés. Un seul rebord, souligné de bleu,

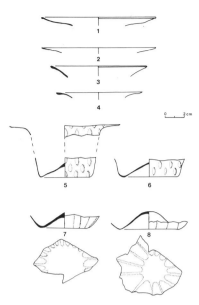

Fig. 31. *Coupelles, forme C4 (1 à 3, 5 à 7: Rougiers; 4 et 8: Cadrix).*

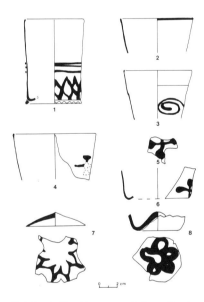

Fig. 32. *Gobelets à décor bleu rapporté, forme C5a (1: coll. J. de Brion; 2 à 7: Psalmodi; 8: Cadrix).*

47

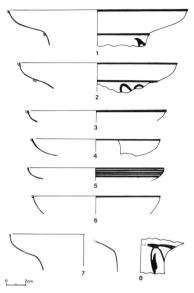

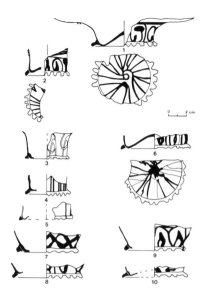

Fig. 33. *Coupelles à décor bleu rapporté, forme C5b (1 à 5, 7: Psalmodi; 6: Rougiers).*

Fig. 34. *Coupelles à décor bleu rapporté, forme C5b (1: La Bastide-des-Jourdans; 2 à 3, 7 à 9: Rougiers; 4: Psalmodi; 5 et 10: Cadrix; 6: Petit Palais).*

laisse deviner une côte moulée (Fig. 33,4). La variété de l'ornementation bleue sur les coupelles permet de distinguer trois types: d'abord les coupelles sans cordon pincé à la base (Fig. 32,6), celles qui en possèdent un (Fig. 34) et enfin les pièces munies de pieds (Fig. 35,1). L'attribution de quelques fonds, en particulier les plus simples, à des coupelles reste encore hypothètique; certains pourraient appartenir à des récipients à l'ouverture retrécie. En dehors de ces petites adjonctions, les coupelles ont toutes le même profil évasé. Quelques variantes sont à noter dans la largeur des fonds: les plus simples, relativement larges, ont un diamètre compris entre 58 et 75 mm. Si certaines bases munies d'un cordon atteignent 80 mm, d'autres se réduisent à 50 mm à peine. Les rebords à marli concave, toujours constitué d'un filet bleu, atteignent un diamètre de 130 à 180 mm. Parfois un faisceau de filets bleus est déposé parallèlement au rebord (Fig. 33,5) mais le plus souvent un seul fil coloré matérialise la séparation entre le corps et le rebord concave de l'objet; fil qui surmonte ainsi le décor organisé sur la panse (Fig. 33,1 & 2; Fig. 34,1).

Dans presque tous les cas cette ornementation consiste en la répétition d'un même motif. Le plus commun, et pourtant le plus savant, est celui d'arabesques, sorte de motifs floraux et abstraits faits de taches et d'arceaux; schéma essentiellement réservé aux coupelles munies d'un cordon pincé (Fig. 34,1 à 3, 6, & 8 à 10). Le décor d'une coupelle complète découverte à Montauban est plus original: il se présente sur deux registres.[66] Exceptionnellement la base d'une pièce possédé une ornementation rapportée de teinte incolore comme le reste de l'objet (Fig. 34,3). D'autres décors déposés sous forme de frises s'entrecroisent en délimitant des losanges (Fig. 34,7), ou bien forment des arceaux (Fig. 33,2). Un quatrième procédé ornemental, plus simple, couvre les parois des fonds avec ou sans cordon à la base: il s'agit de filets verticaux parfois associés deux à deux (Fig. 34,2).

66. Catalogue de l'exposition de Montauban n° 75, cf. note 27.

48

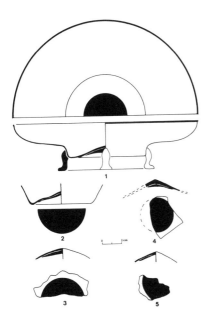

Fig. 35. *Coupelles à lentille bleue rapportée, forme C5b (1: La Seube, d'après N. Lambert; 2: La Bastide-des-Jourdans; 3: Rougiers; 4: Collioure; 5: Cadrix).*

Il est curieux de constater que la plupart des fonds simples ont leurs parois décorées de motifs isolés ne formant pas de frise; en dehors des croix pattées déjà signalées, nous trouvons des spirales aux lignes souples ou brisées ou des étoiles à six branches. D'autres schémas décoratifs existaient; ils restent imparfaitement définis à cause de la fragmentation excessive des pièces.

Le décor bleu n'ignore pas le fond des coupelles; sous le fond, à partir de la marque laissée par le pontil, s'organise l'ornementation; elle réside parfois dans quelques filets bleus désordonnés mais, plus souvent, forme un rayonnement de fils comme l'on peut le voir dans la coupelle trouvée à la Bastide-des-Jourdans (Fig. 34,1) ou dans les fouilles du Petit Palais (Fig. 34,6). Parfois ce décor est semblable aux arabesques qui couvrent le corps des gobelets et des coupelles.[67] Les motifs de rosace sous les fonds sont assez rares; nous en connaissons trois, l'un sur la coupelle complète découverte à Montauban, le second comparable mais au tracé plus irrégulier, apparaît sur un fragment de fond trouvé à Psalmodi (Fig. 32,7);

enfin la dernière rosace aux pétales plus souples décore un fond différent par sa teinte verdâtre et son épaisseur plus importante; bien que découvert sur la fabrique de Cadrix nous hésitons à considérer cette pièce (Fig. 32,8) comme une production locale.

La dernière catégorie de coupelles est caractérisée par un décor bleu qui couvre le fond de la pièce uniformément, et le rebord par un simple filet. Présentes sur les sites avignonnais, ainsi qu'à la Bastide-des-Jourdans, à Rougiers, à Cadrix et au château de Collioure, ces coupelles restaient incomplètes. La découverte d'une pièce au profil complet sur l'atelier de la Seube, permet une connaissance totale de l'objet.[68] Cette belle pièce incolore, très large (l'ouverture atteint 190 mm), serait dans sa forme comparable à toutes les autres coupelles si n'existaient pas trois petits pieds en forme de S surhaussant cet objet (Fig. 35,1). Nulle part ailleurs ne furent retrouvés les supports ou même leur arrachement. Pourtant la présence de fonds doublés, sur leur paroi externe d'une lentille de verre bleu, caractéristique de ces pièces, prouve bien que ces coupelles n'étaient pas plus exceptionnelles que les autres (Fig. 35,2 à 5). En revanche les coupelles simplement tronconiques, au rebord droit dans le prolongement des parois sont plus rares. Un exemplaire découvert dans les fouilles de la cathédrale d'Aix-en-Provence porte un décor de filets bleus parallèles.[69]

c. Récipients à Embouchure Etroite, forme C5c

Le pot globulaire est une des plus rares formes des verreries médiévales. Elle existait pourtant dans un verre fin et incolore décoré d'applications bleues. Seuls deux fragments trouvés à Rougiers attestent de cette existence.

---

67. *Idem.*

68. N. Lambert, *op. cit.*, p. 88, fig. 12 et 13.

69. D. Foy et L. Vallauri, "Céramique et verre" dans R. Guild, J. Guyon et L. Rivet, "Les origines du baptistère de la cathédrale Saint-Sauveur, Etude de topographie aixoise," *Revue archéologique de Narbonnaise*, 1983.

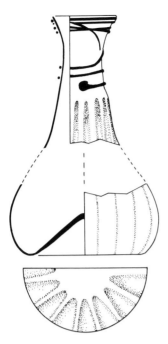

Fig. 36. *Fiole à décor bleu rapporté, forme C5c: Rougiers.*

Mieux représentées sont les fioles en verre fin plus ou moins incolores, enrichies d'un schéma décoratif de fils bleus. L'état fragmentaire du matériel ne permet pas d'observer ce décor sur d'autres parties que le goulot. La seule fiole restituée, livrant sa forme complète et provenant de Rougiers, montre que les filets bleus ne couvraient que le goulot.

La fiole de Rougiers, en verre brillant de belle qualité, très légèrement verdâtre, a une hauteur restituée de 165 mm; la panse piriforme est relativement courte par rapport au col terminé par une embouchure évasée. Le fond, comme dans les formes précédentes, est conique. L'ornementation est un filet bleu rapporté autour du goulot. Ce cordon se termine par une goutte de verre écrasée contre la paroi de l'objet. Ce motif décoratif bleu complète un décor moulé de seize côtes qui partent en rayonnant du centre du fond jusqu'au premier tiers du goulot (Fig. 36). Le double décor de cette belle pièce aux proportions harmonieuses se retrouve sur deux fragments de goulot

de taille plus réduite. Les applications bleues, plus modestes, consistent en un simple cordon qui bague la base du goulot. Au niveau de l'épaulement, apparaît l'extrémité du décor moulé et côtelé qui devait couvrir toute la panse de ces fioles (Fig. 37,8 & 12).

Les fils bleus couvrent des goulots de différentes tailles, les deux plus grands—de 135 et 150 mm—portent soit un faisceau de fils bleus parallèles et rapprochés (Fig. 37,1), soit trois cordons indépendants dont l'un est double (Fig. 37,2).

Un col plus fragmenté, mais probablement de même importance, a un simple cordon festonné à sa base (Fig. 37,7). Parfois le cordon bleu est surmonté d'un fil bleu très fin enroulé en spirale (Fig. 37,4). Un seul goulot a son embouchure évasée décorée de filets parallèles (Fig. 37,3). Notons enfin deux fragments éffilés appartenant à une forme inconnue, peut-être une sorte de rhyton décoré de filets bleus en zigzag (Fig. 37,5 & 9).

Bien que les fioles restent dans leur forme générale inconnues, les divers goulots laissent supposer des pièces différentes dans leur taille au moins. L'on voit aussi que les applications bleues ne sont pas réservées à un seul type de fiole.

Tous les fragments au décor rapporté de teinte bleue foncé, ne peuvent être identifiés à des formes précises; il semble cependant que la coupelle au rebord à marli concave soit la forme privilégiée de ce décor. Des pièces comparables aux types C5 se retrouvent en Yougoslavie et Italie,[70] mais sans doute pas dans des proportions aussi importantes. Dans la série des verres de l'extrême fin du XIVe siècle trouvés à Tarquinia seuls quelques fragments sont semblables à notre type C5. En revanche on trouve des filets bleus sur des verreries différentes, en particulier sur le goulot de bouteilles en verre plus épais, jaunâtre ou verdâtre.

Les trouvailles italiennes au décor rapporté bleu se situent dans une fourchette large comprise entre le XIIe et le début du XVIe siècle.[71] Nous

70. D. Whitehouse, 1979, *op. cit.*, pp. 168–169.
71. *Idem.*

proposons pour les pièces provençales et languedociennes, fabriquées par des ateliers régionaux
une datation plus serrée: nous les voyons apparaître au tout début du XIVe siècle et elles ne
semblent plus en usage au siècle suivant; le décor
de filet bleu rapporté est pourtant connu dans nos
régions dès le XIIIe siècle sur des verres à tige
(A5, B1, B2) et des gobelets (B4 et B5): cette
ornementation se limite alors à un filet bleu soulignant le rebord ou la base de la pièce. Nous
trouvons aussi sur des gobelets incolores parfois
côtelés, de la fin du moyen-âge, un fil bleu en
guise de rebord: ceci est très éloigné de la décoration exubérante des verreries C5.

Le type C5 est caractéristique des productions
du Midi de la France. D'autres ateliers ont pu
fabriquer des produits comparables mais actuel-
lement nous n'avons aucune preuve de cet artisanat en dehors des fragments découverts sur
l'atelier du Monte Lecco.[72] L'un des plus beaux
exemplaires italiens du type C5, une coupelle décorée d'une frise de losanges, découverte lors des
fouilles de Farfa[73] a probablement été fabriquée
par un centre italien. Les productions du type C5
en Italie se sont peut-être prolongées pendant le
XVe siècle?

Ce sont probablement les ateliers sis en Médi-
terranée occidentale (sud de la France ou Italie)
qui ont exporté ces produits luxueux découverts
dans le nord de l'Europe: quelques fragments ont
été mis au jour dans les fouille urbaines d'Orléans;[74] des rebords de coupelle et des fonds ont
été trouvés en Grande-Bretagne à Southampton
et Boston.[75]

VI. Autres Fioles en Verre Fin, forme C6.

Des fioles en verre fin, autres que les pièces à
décor bleu, témoignent de la variété des productions régionales. Toutes, bien que fragmentées, semblent de forme simple, soufflée dans
une seule paraison; le fond est conique (Fig. 39,5).
Rares sont les anses en forme d'oreillette et les
becs verseurs dont seuls quelques exemplaires
furent retrouvés à Rougiers. Sur cet atelier comme
à Cadrix, aucune bouteille sur pied ne fut fa-

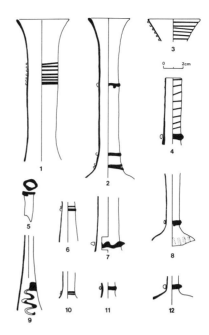

Fig. 37. *Fioles à décor bleu rapporté, forme C5c (1 à 4 et 7: Petit Palais; 5, 9 à 12: Psalmodi; 6 à 8: coll. J. de Brion).*

briquée. De grands pieds tronconiques découverts sur des sites avignonnais appartiennent
peut-être à des récipients plus tardifs.

La partie supérieure d'une fiole trouvée à
Rougiers est d'une grande richesse ornementale
avec ses nervures fines et moulées couvrant la
panse et se resserrant à la base du goulot souligné
par un cordon incolore rapporté en onde (Fig.
38,1). Cet exemplaire, ainsi que la fiole décorée de
fil bleu et décrite précédemment, prouvent bien
que ces récipients luxueux ne sont pas exceptionnels. Ces deux procédés ornementaux: côtes
moulées et cordon rapporté, se retrouvent sur

72. S. Fossati et T. Mannoni, *op. cit.*, p. 64.

73. D. Whitehouse, 1983, *op. cit.*

74. J. Barrera, *Ensembles de verres creux (XIVe–XVIe siècles) provenant des fouilles d'Orléans (1977–1981)*, Mémoire de l'Ecole des Hautes Etudes en Sciences Sociales, mai 1984, dactylographié, p. 146.

75. R. J. Charleston, 1975, *op. cit.*, p. 204 et fig. 221 et R. J. Charleston, "Some English Finds of Medieval Glass with Balkan Analogues," *Verre médiéval aux Balkans (V^e-XVe)*, Belgrade, 1975, pp. 101–107.

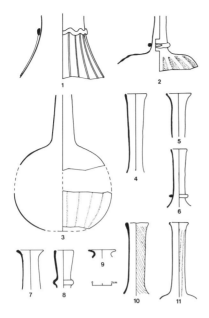

Fig. 38. *Fioles, forme C6 (1 et 4: Rougiers; 2: Cadrix; 3: coll. J. de Brion; 5 à 11: Petit Palais).*

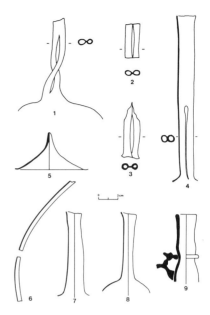

Fig. 39. *Fioles, forme C6 (1: Avignon; 2, 4 et 8: Cadrix; 3: Rougiers; 9: Psalmodi).*

d'autres objets (Fig. 38,2). Le décor moulé très léger s'estompe dans la partie supérieure d'une pièce à panse globulaire et en verre extrêmement fin (Fig. 38,3). A Rougiers comme à Cadrix les productions d'ampoule à col cylindrique, d'une exécution parfois fruste est certaine (Fig. 38,4 et Fig. 39,7 & 8). On remarquera que les cols sont toujours nus; ceci pourrait s'expliquer par l'utilisation d'un moule ouvert, d'une seule pièce, ne pouvant imprimer le décor que sur la panse. Deux goulots pourtant, découverts au Petit Palais, portent une ornementation moulée de nervures droites ou obliques (Fig. 38,10 & 11); décor peut-être plus tardif obtenu par une matrice en deux parties?

Des fioles très fragiles, au goulot particulier, méritent une attention. Ces goulots retrouvés en grand nombre à Avignon[76] et sur les ateliers de Rougiers et Cadrix, ont la particularité d'être à la base double et parfois torsadé sur une hauteur de 60 à 75 mm (Fig. 39,1 & 4); ensuite le goulot forme un canal unique. Sans doute faut-il imaginer la forme générale semblable à celle d'une ampoule découverte dans la région de Bordeaux;

la datation proposée de cet objet, XIIe–XIIIe siècles, étant probablement trop haute.[77]

D.
LES PRODUCTIONS EN VERRE VERT-BLEUTE ET EPAIS, XIVe SIECLE

Une partie des verreries produites régionalement au cours du XIVe siècle, ont été réalisées dans une matière lourde et translucide de teinte vert-bleuté. Ce verre épais est exclusivement réservé à des récipients de taille importante dont les bouteilles à long col forment la série la plus nombreuse.

76. Des goulots de ce type furent découverts au cours de travaux urbains en Avignon et dans les fouilles de la rue Racine. S. Gagnière et J. Granier, "Nouvelles découvertes archéologiques à Avignon, les fouilles de la rue Racine," *Revue annuelle d'information*, Mairie d'Avignon, 1976.

77. J. Barrelet, *op. cit.*, p. 29 et pl. XVI.

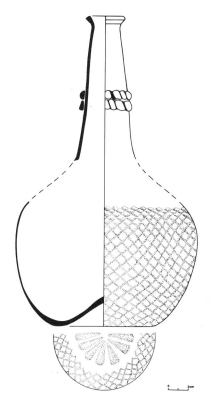

Fig. 40. *Bouteille, forme D1: Lérins.*

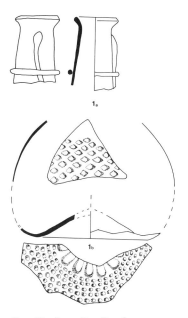

Fig. 41. *Bouteille, forme D1: Rougiers.*

I. Bouteilles à Long Col, forme D1.

Rares sont les récipients à embouchure étroite, munis d'une anse; un seul fragment découvert à Psalmodi ne permet pas de retrouver la forme complète de cet objet dont l'origine n'est pas assurée (Fig. 39,9). Contrairement à de nombreux exemplaires trouvés surtout en Italie,[78] les goulots, décorés dans leur partie médiane d'un renflement obtenu au moule et donnant l'aspect d'un cordon, sont peu nombreux (Fig. 38,8); aucun ne provient d'un site de production.

Les bouteilles à long col, rassemblées ici sous le type D1, ont en commun leur matière décrite précédemment, leur forme et leur décor. Le verre d'assez bonne qualité est à peine criblé de petits bouillons et légèrement irisé. Quelquefois une fine pellicule brunâtre couvre les surfaces. La teinte est vert-bleuté, plus franchement verte sur certaines pièces en particulier celles venant du Languedoc.

a. Les Formes

Si aucun objet ne fut retrouvé intact, la multitude des fragments recueillis sur divers sites de la Catalogne à la Ligurie, et la reconstitution possible d'une bouteille provenant de l'île Saint-Honorat de Lérins au large de Cannes,[79] permet une connaissance certaine de la forme D1. La diversité dans les dimensions des fonds et des goulots laisse supposer un échelonnement des formes compris au moins entre 195 mm et plus de 300 mm de haut (Fig. 40). Ces vases reposent sur un fond conique plus ou moins saillant et variant dans leur largeur du simple au double: les diamètres sont compris entre 58 et 115 mm. Les panses piriformes (Fig. 41) ou globulaires atteignent

78. Parmi les goulots portant ce décor, signalons les découvertes du Monte Lecco, Fossati et Mannoni, *op. cit.*, p. 58, fig. 2 et p. 65, fig. 76; les fragments siciliens: F. D'Angelo, *op. cit.*, 1976, pp. 379–389, en part. fig. 8; et des objets déposés au musée de cividale; A. Gasparetto, *Journal of Glass Studies*, XXI, 1979, *op. cit.*, pp. 76–95, en part. fig. 6.

79. Cette bouteille a été anciennement découverte dans la chapelle Saint-Pierre sur l'île Saint-Honorat.

dans leur plus grande largeur 150 à 185 mm. Elles sont emmanchées d'un long goulot parfois presque aussi haut que le corps de l'objet: trois cols complets atteignent respectivement 155 mm (Fig. 44,1), 145 mm (Fig. 40) et 130 mm (Fig. 42,3). Souvent légèrement renflé à leur base, ces goulots se rétrécissent vers le haut donnant naissance à une lèvre de section triangulaire ou arrondie. Quelquefois une petite gorge interne signifie le repliement de la lèvre vers l'intérieur. Un seul goulot a la particularité de posséder une embouchure en entonnoir (Fig. 44,6). Le rétrécissement du col du bas vers le haut, est plus ou moins marqué: l'écart entre la largeur du goulot à la base et le diamètre juste au-dessous du rebord est de 7 à 28 mm (42 > 35: Fig. 42,3; 44 > 32: Fig. 44,2; 50 > 35: Fig. 42,7; 57 > 29: Fig. 40).

La forme D1, archéologiquement reconstituée, est confirmée par la représentation d'une bouteille sur un retable catalan du XIVe siècle.[80] Le décor de ce vase, bien figuré dans l'iconographie, ne laisse aucun doute sur la similitude de l'objet peint et des pièces archéologiques.

b. Les Décors

Deux procédés ornementaux, toujours associés, se répètent inlassablement sur chacune de ces bouteilles: le premier est un cordon rapporté qui bague le goulot en son milieu ou légèrement plus haut. Ce cordon peut être simple ou double et lisse ou travaillé à l'outil.

–Décor Rapporté

Les bagues non façonnées, de section circulaire, sont les moins fréquentes. Larges de 3 à 6 mm, ces cordons d'une horizontalité plus ou moins parfaite, sont parfois doubles. Dans ce cas l'anneau supérieur très fin se réduit à un simple filet juxtaposé à un cordon inférieur plus large (Fig. 44,4 & 5). L'on peut souvent observer la jonction des deux extrémités du cordon qui se chevauchent (Fig. 44,1 & 2). Un seul goulot a la particularité de porter deux cordons lisses perpendiculaires (Fig. 41): le cordon vertical a été rapporté le premier; après avoir aplati une grosse goutte de verre contre la paroi de l'objet, le verrier

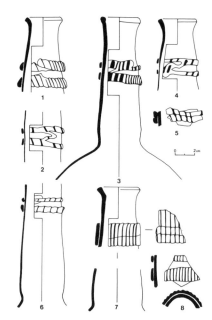

Fig. 42. *Goulots de bouteille à cordon incisé, forme D1 (1, 7 et 8: Rougiers; 2 et 6: Petit Palais; 3 et 4: coll. J. de Brion; 5: Cadrix).*

a étiré la pâte malléable en un filet. La bague de verre située à 47 mm de l'embouchure et parallèlement à celle-ci, a été déposée sur le premier cordon.

Plus nombreux sont les cordons de verre rapportés et façonnés après leur pose. Un unique exemplaire rassemble les deux types de décor rapporté: un fil déposé autour du col est parallèle à un cordon plus large travaillé à l'outil (Fig. 43,9).

Les bagues façonnées en godrons se présentent sur un (Fig. 43) ou plusieurs rangs (Fig. 42). Les creux et les reliefs verticaux et réguliers (Fig. 42,7 & 8) ou obliques et désordonnés (Fig. 42,3), ont été obtenus à l'aide d'un outil pointu qui incise rapidement à intervalles plus ou moins réguliers la coulée de verre chaud encore malléable que le verrier a appliqué autour du col. Cette décoration

80. Des vases à long col bagué d'un cordon façonné apparaissent dans la cène du retable exécuté par Jaume Serra et déposé au musée d'art catalan de Montjuich.

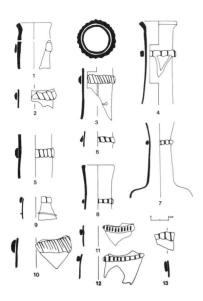

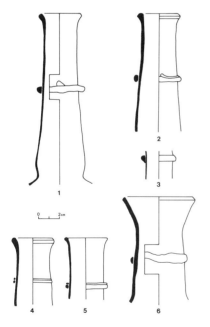

Fig. 43. *Goulots de bouteille à cordon incisé, forme D1 (1 et 2: Planier; 3 à 5: Psalmodi; 6: Collioure; 7, 8, 11 et 12: coll. J. de Brion; 9 et 10: Rougiers; 13: Cadrix).*

Fig. 44. *Goulots de bouteille à cordon lisse, forme D1 (1 et 3: Petit Palais; 2, 4 à 6: coll. J. de Brion).*

à chaud exige une grande rapidité et exclut tout repentir: ceci explique l'irrégularité des formes et des dimensions notamment dans la largeur des rangs (Fig. 43,10) et dans l'intervalle des doubles cordons: ceux-ci peuvent être distants de quelques millimètres (Fig. 42,1 à 4 & 6) ou étroitement juxtaposés (Fig. 42,5). Les cordons doubles ont été réalisés dans une même coulée de verre et dans un geste continu: un filet de verre reliant les deux bagues est parfois visible (Fig. 42,2 à 4).

Si la maladresse des artisans est souvent notable, la perfection de certains cordons à décors verticaux atteste d'une grande maîtrise d'exécution: sur un large cordon, constitué en fait de trois bandes de verres bien ajustées, les creux et les pleins sont d'une régularité parfaite (Fig. 42,7). A l'aide d'une spatule de bois mouillé, ou de métal, le verrier a incisé le triple cordon en rabattant après chaque incision l'outil sur le côté, ce qui donne au relief une arête légèrement aplatie; les vides sont ici légèrement plus importants que les pleins.

– Décor Moulé

Obtenu par un moule ouvert, le décor n'atteint jamais les parties de la bouteille situées au-dessus de l'épaulement (Fig. 45). Le schéma déjà observé sur les gobelets, se répète sous les fonds: à partir du centre, bien marqué par la trace du pontil, rayonnent de petits pétales formant une rosace incluse dans une série de cercles concentriques formés de petites dépressions, le plus souvent arrondies ou rectangulaires, dont la taille croît dans les cercles extérieurs (Fig. 46). Les motifs alvéolés se poursuivent sur toute la panse affectant la forme de losanges ou d'hexagones; les plus grands se trouvent toujours dans les parties inférieures du corps de l'objet. Dans la partie haute les alvéoles se rétrécissent et se transforment au niveau de l'épaulement en petits pointillés creux. Le décor s'estompe totalement sur l'épaulement.

Cette ornementation se répète sur tous les objets avec de légères variantes dues à la multiplicité des moules. Parfois estompé, le décor sous le fond n'est perceptible qu'au toucher. Il semble cependant qu'aucun pétale n'ait jamais été imprimé sur

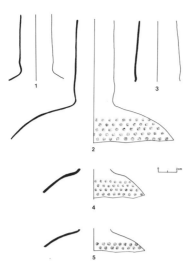

Fig. 45. *Bouteilles, forme D1 (1 et 2: Petit Palais; 3: Rou-giers; 4: Cadrix; 5: Psalmodi).*

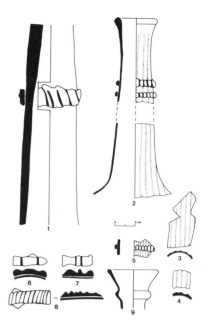

Fig. 47. *Bouteilles, forme D1 (1: Petit Palais; 2: La Môle; 3, 6 à 8: Rougiers; 4: Cadrix; 5: Psalmodi; 9: Beaucaire).*

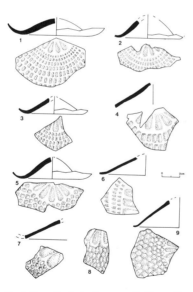

Fig. 46. *Bouteilles, fonds à décor moulé, forme D1 (1 à 5: Rougiers; 6 et 9: coll. J. de Brion; 7: Petit-Palais; 8: Collioure).*

un des exemplaires (Fig. 47). Tous les autres fonds ne portent pas le même nombre de pétales, nombre qui n'est pas proportionnel au diamètre de la pièce. Sur le seul site de Rougiers, le nombre des pétales varie de 7 à 19; ils sont de dimension variable et plus ou moins espacés; leur extrémité est généralement circulaire mais parfois les lignes sont plus anguleuses. La qualité de ce décor n'est pas partout la même; aussi on remarque, parmi toutes les nombreuses pièces recueillies en divers lieux, la netteté de l'impression du décor des fonds de Rougiers: chaque pétale et alvéole sont beaucoup mieux marqués; autour des pétales les alvéoles sont aussi plus ou moins rapprochées: tantôt quelques millimètres les séparent tantôt elles sont si resserrées qu'elles forment un gau-frage régulier.

Quelques fragments de goulots découverts sur le *castrum* de la Môle (Var), à Rougiers, Cadrix, et Psalmodi (Fig. 47,2 à 5) sont exceptionnels par leur décor de cannelures verticales peut-être ob-tenu par un moule en deux parties; les cordons façonnés en godron complètent ce décor (Fig. 47,2 & 5).

De véritables dames-jeannes étaient décorées de la même façon que les bouteilles; un goulot découvert dans les fouilles du Petit Palais et bagué d'un cordon à godrons, atteint une épaisseur moyenne de 55 mm (Fig. 47,1).

c. Datation

Les bouteilles D1 semblent avoir été plus longuement utilisées que les gobelets moulés et les verreries à décor bleu.

Les premières apparaissent probablement dès la fin du XIIIe siècle. Des fragments de goulots, portant le décor caractéristique et découverts à Planier, témoignent de cette précocité (Fig. 43,1 & 2) qui est confirmée par les rares trouvailles de fragments de godrons dans les niveaux anciens de Rougiers ainsi que par le matériel provenant de Montségur[81] et des fouilles de Montauban. Fabriqués, entre autres, par les verreries de la Seube, Rougiers et Cadrix, ces objets ont perduré après l'extinction de ces ateliers. En effet la répartition stratigraphique des bouteilles D1 à Rougiers, montre leur utilisation encore importante dans les niveaux les plus tardifs, postérieurs à la fixation de l'atelier c'est à dire au début du XVe siècle. La longévité de cette forme est vérifiée par les fouilles de l'atelier du Monte Lecco où furent exhumés goulots et fonds[82] et les fouilles du cloître San Silvestro à Gênes où un goulot avec son cordon caractéristique fut trouvé dans un niveau de la deuxième moitié du XVe siècle.[83] Il reste cependant dangereux d'identifier la forme D1 uniquement par la présence d'un cordon incisé car cette ornementation est toujours en usage dans les verreries modernes, en particulier sur les dames-jeannes.

La répartition du type D1 est beaucoup plus limitée que celles des verres C1 et C5; en effet en dehors de la Ligurie on ne connait pas ces produits en Italie. En revanche dans tout le midi de la France: dans le sud ouest (l'Escaladieu et Montauban) comme sur le pourtour méditerranéen ces bouteilles sont largement répandues. Le motif de la rosace entouré d'alvéoles connu dès le IXe siècle dans le Proche Orient et en Afrique du

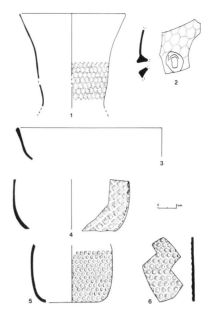

Fig. 48. *Récipients en verre épais, forme D1 (1 et 4: Cadrix; 2: Psalmodi; 3, 5 et 6: Rougiers).*

Nord a probablement été transmis par l'Espagne musulmane.

II. Autres Récipients en Verre Vert-Bleuté, Épais.

a. Bouteilles Diverses, forme D2

D'autres objets que les bouteilles D1 furent soufflés dans la même matière: certains même portaient sur leurs panses les cordons façonnés en godron, caractéristiques des bouteilles. Ces fragments de paroi, décorés de godrons (Fig. 47,6 à 8) appartiennent vraisemblablement à des pots comparables à une pièce déposée au Musée des Arts Décoratifs et d'origine supposée languedocienne.[84]

81. J. Tricoire et J. Mathieu, *op. cit.*, 1974, pp. 17–30, en part. p. 25.

82. S. Fossati et M. Mannoni, *op. cit.*, p. 61, fig. 69, 70 et 73.

83. D. Andrews, "Vetri, metalli e reperti minori dell'area sud del convento di S. Silvestro a Genova," *Archeologia Medievale*, 1977, pp. 162–188, en part. fig. XXXI, 20.

84. J. Barrelet, *op. cit.*, pl. XXVIII.

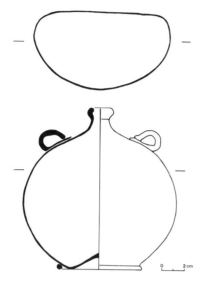

Fig. 49. *Gourde, forme D3, Lérins.*

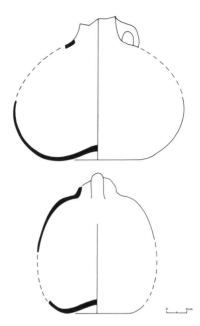

Fig. 51. *Gourde, forme D3, Rougiers.*

Fig. 50. *Gourde précédente (photo C. Hussy).*

Des fonds de 65 et 90 mm, aux parois rectilignes et couvertes d'un décor moulé d'hexagones (Fig. 48,5) ou de losanges (Fig. 48,4) ne peuvent qu'appartenir à des fioles fabriquées à la fin du XIVᵉ siècle, l'un de ces objets provenant de Cadrix. Un fragment de verre plat, toujours

décoré d'alvéoles hexagonales, provient sans doute aussi d'une pièce similaire (Fig. 48,6).

Certains vases étaient beaucoup plus importants, comme en témoigne un col tronconique large de 110 mm à l'ouverture et d'une hauteur évaluée à 110 mm. Le décor moulé, qui devait couvrir la panse, s'arrête à mi-hauteur du goulot (Fig. 48,1).

Aussi rare est le fragment de récipient globulaire trouvé à Psalmodi, muni d'une toute petite ouverture circulaire; le décor désormais traditionnel sur le verre épais, d'alvéoles hexagonales, est toujours présent (Fig. 48,2). L'état fragmentaire de cette pièce ne permet pas d'imaginer sa forme générale.

b. Les Gourdes, D3

Trois gourdes en verre vert, comparable à celui des bouteilles D1, ont été découvertes en Provence et en Ardèche.

Une pièce intacte provient d'un caveau situé dans l'abside de la chapelle Saint-Pierre sur l'île Saint-Honorat au large de Cannes.[85] Ce vase est

85. F. Benoit, *Histoire de Lerins*, Toulon, 1965, p. 78.

Fig. 52. *Gourde, forme D3, Viviers (Photo C. Hussy).*

aussi large que haut: il atteint 137 mm de hauteur pour une largeur à mi-panse équivalente. Le col très court possède un rebord épaissi et replié l'intérieur. L'un de ses côtés est aplati. Sur cette pièce ont été rapportés un cordon lisse formant un pied annulaire supportant le fond conique, et deux anses symétriques dans le dernier tiers de la hauteur (Fig. 49 et Fig. 50).

Divers fragments, provenant de Rougiers, permettent de reconstituer une gourde dont la forme générale reste encore incertaine. Contrairement à l'objet précédent, ce vase est beaucoup plus large que haut; il ne possède aucun pied annulaire. Sa panse ovoïde dissymétrique, avait un ou deux flancs aplatis; une anse ou deux, de part et d'autre du goulot, permettait son transport (Fig. 51).

Une gourde semblable, mais richement décorée de cordons qui enveloppent la panse, et munie de quatre anses symétriques, a été mise au jour dans les dernières fouilles de Viviers (Ardèche). Associée à un pégau en pâte vernissée, cette gourde découverte dans une sépulture mal-

heureusement violée peut être datée du XIVe siècle (Fig. 52, fouille Y. Esquieu).

La fonction, ou les fonctions exactes de cette forme restent inconnues; fragiles ces objets ne pouvaient être transportés, accrochés à la ceinture, aussi aisément que les gourdes de terre ou de métal. Ces vases en verre étaient peut-être protégés par une enveloppe de cuir ou d'osier comme certaines des verreries possédées par le roi René au XVe siècle. La présence de ces objets dans des sépultures témoigne de la fonction funéraire des verreries encore au XIVe siècle; mais pas plus que les pégaus, les gourdes n'ont certainement pas été réservées à une fonction exclusivement funéraire.

c. Les Bocaux, D4

Un seul objet a été suffisamment reconstitué pour permettre l'étude d'une nouvelle forme. Ce pot, à panse globulaire, possède un fond conique. L'ouverture large a un rebord déversé formant un bandeau extérieur. Le fond et la panse sont moulés de motifs géométriques formant une trame de quadrilatères qui se transforment dans la partie haute en petits losanges. Le décor n'atteint pas le rebord. Le fond incomplet ne permet pas de connaître le motif central qui était peut-être une rosace (Fig. 53).

Ce vase dont la forme générale rappelle celle du bocal, provient de Rougiers et se situe dans les niveaux correspondants au fonctionnement de la verrerie. L'iconographie médiévale n'offre pas de forme semblable au type D3; pourtant des bocaux de verre, parfois munis d'un couvercle et destinés à contenir des denrées, étaient utilisés au XVe siècle, comme le montre une iconographie du *Theatrum Sanitatis de Ubuchasym de Baldach.*[86]

d. Les Plats, D5

Fort rares aussi sont les formes ouvertes en verre. Seul un fragment identifié comme la paroi d'un plat a été découvert à Rougiers (Fig. 48,3). Son ouverture atteint 300 mm de diamètre; la lèvre est arrondie.

E.
LA COMPOSITION DES PRODUCTIONS DU XIVe SIECLE

Des analyses physico-chimiques permettent de connaître la composition des productions ver-

rières régionales au XIVe siècle. A partir des échantillons recueillis à Rougiers et Cadrix nous étudierons les variations de chaque constituant des verres provenant d'un même atelier.

Vingt-deux analyses ont été effectuées sur quatorze fragments d'objets présumés avoir été fabriqués à Rougiers et sur huit déchets de verre ou prélèvements de pâte vitreuse effectués sur des creusets trouvés à Rougiers (annexe 4). Quatorze autres analyses ont été effectuées sur les déchets trouvés à Cadrix (annexe 5).

Aucun élément ne permet de distinguer ces deux productions; le tableau suivant montre combien la composition du verre est variable à l'intérieur d'un même atelier. Dans ce tableau nous n'avons pas tenu compte des trois prélèvements effectués dans des creusets de Rougiers; ces trois échantillons riches en fer et aluminium ont peut-être été "contaminés" par la nature du réfractaire qui les contenait. De même les fragments violets n'ont pas été utilisés pour étudier la teneur du MnO, et le pourcentage en fer du déchet bleu de Cadrix n'a pas été relevé: le manganèse et le fer ayant été utilisés ici à titre de colorant.

---

86. Bibl. Casanatense, Rome codice 4182: édité par E. M. Parme 1970.

	CaO	Fe_2O_3	TiO_2	K_2O	SiO_2
Rougiers	4,3 < 11,5	0,35 < 0,96	0,05 < 0,34	3,10 < 10,2	59,1 < 68,2
Cadrix	4 < 9	0,62 < 1,10	0,15 < 0,44	3,26 < 8,26	58,8 < 66

	Al_2O_3	MgO	Na_2O	P_2O_5	MnO
Rougiers	1,55 < 4,3	1,35 < 2,80	10,8 < 18	0,55 < 1,60	0,05 < 1,65
Cadrix	3,25 < 4,5	1,38 < 2,20	12 < 17,8	0,60 < 1,3	0,72 < 0,96

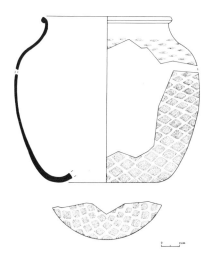

Fig. 53. *Bocal, forme D4, Rougiers.*

Ces chiffres extrêmes, significatifs des variations parfois du simple au double sur un même élément (le calcium ou le potassium par exemple) ne rendent pas compte de la composition la plus courante. Généralement, celle-ci a une teneur en silicium comprise entre 62 et 66%; le calcium est rarement supérieur à 9%; le potassium n'excède qu'exceptionnellement 6,5% et la teneur moyenne du sodium se situe entre 13 et 17%. Entre la composition des verres de Rougiers et celle des productions de Cadrix, la seule différence notable apparaît dans la teneur en aluminium habituellement plus élevée à Cadrix. Différence qui pourrait s'expliquer par la nature même des échantillons: ce sont tous des déchets de verre naturellement plus riches en oxydes que les fragments d'objets.

Deux autres séries de verres, supposés appartenir au XIVe siècle, ont été analysés. Il s'agit de trois verres trouvés à Psalmodi (annexe 6) et six déchets de verres recueillis près des ruines de l'abbaye de Pré-Bayon à Gigondas, (Vaucluse) sur l'emplacement d'une verrerie (annexe 7). Les résultats de ces analyses sont semblables aux deux premières séries; notons cependant la teneur relativement faible en sodium des déchets de Pré-Bayon, et le taux de manganèse des verres de Psalmodi atteignant 1,20 et 1,40%.

La principale différence entre les ateliers du XIVe siècle et la fabrique de Planier réside dans la proportion en magnésium, très élevée dans la verrerie la plus précoce. En effet, cet élément varie de 3,10 à 6.70% à Planier, contre 1,35 à 2,80% à Rougiers et 1,38 à 2,20% à Cadrix. Un graphique illustrant les teneurs en MnO et MgO des verres des trois ateliers varois, individualise les productions de Planier (Fig. 65). La teneur élevée du magnésium (plus de 3,10%) n'est pas caractéristique de l'atelier de Planier car d'autres verres attribués aux XIIe et XIIIe siècles atteignent le même pourcentage.

Les analyses réalisées sur les verreries à décor bleu, caractérisées par une matière de très belle qualité, ne permettent pas de les différencier des autres productions simultanées.

F.
LES VERRES DE L'EXTREME FIN DU MOYEN-AGE

Les verres de la fin du moyen-âge sont paradoxalement les moins connus. Ceci est du à la pauvreté des trouvailles et parfois à l'absence de tout contexte permettant de préciser la datation de ces rares objets. Nous ignorons le lieu de fabrication de ces pièces; sans doute certaines d'entre-elles proviennent-elles d'un des nombreux ateliers alors actifs en Provence et Languedoc. Le matériel présenté ici provient essentiellement d'Avignon (fouilles de l'hôtel J. de Brion), et de Martigues. Il s'agit presque uniquement de verres à boire parmi lesquels on peut distinguer des gobelets, des verres à pied et des verres à tige.

I. Les Gobelets, forme E1.

Les gobelets en verre fin, légèrement jaunâtre, sont hauts et tronconiques (Fig. 54,1) ou bien bas et larges (58 mm de haut pour 76 mm de diamètre maximum); leur rebord est rentrant (Fig. 54,2 et Fig. 55). Tous portent un décor moulé de côtes verticales qui s'épaississent à leur extrémité, ou bien une ornementation faite d'arceaux juxtaposés et superposés. Il s'agit ainsi d'un décor "*nipt diamond-waies*," les côtes d'abord imprimées par

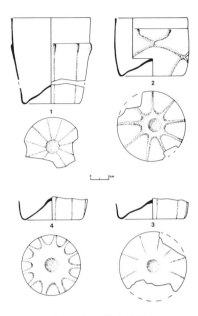

Fig. 54. *Gobelets, forme E1, coll. J. de Brion.*

Fig. 55. *Gobelet à décor moulé, forme E1 (cf. Fig. 54,2, photo C. Hussy).*

un moule ont été ensuite réunies à la pince ce qui explique le fort relief de cette ornementation. Sous le fond apparaît un motif rayonnant de nervures partant soit du centre, matérialisé par la marque du pontil (Fig. 54,1 & 2), soit du pourtour du fond (Fig. 54,3). Ces objets découverts dans les fouilles de l'hôtel de Brion sont malheureusement hors stratigraphie tout comme les verres à pied annulaire auxquels ils s'apparentent par leur décor. Sans doute faut-il les situer vers la fin du XVe siècle ou dans la première moitié du XVIe siècle comme des trouvailles comparables faites à Tours[87] et Orléans.[88]

II. Verres à Pied, formes E2 et E3.

Le décor de nervures verticales en fort relief se retrouve sur les verres à pied annulaire lisse ou le plus souvent dentelé (Fig. 56,2 à 5). Les formes hautes (105 mm) s'évasent régulièrement pour atteindre 92 mm au rebord (Fig. 56,1 et Fig. 57). L'élégance de ce profil et la finesse du décor rapporté et moulé sont bien mis en valeur par la matière fine et absolument incolore. Nous proposons de dater ces verres retrouvés dans les fouilles de l'hôtel de Brion et dans celles de

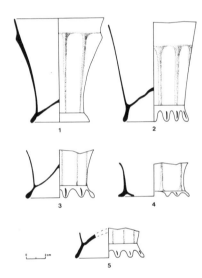

Fig. 56. *Verres à pied annulaire, forme E2 (1 à 3: coll. J. de Brion; 4 et 5: Psalmodi).*

Psalmodi (Fig. 56,4 & 5), dans le courant du XVe siècle. Nous pouvons comparer ces formes à un verre peint par Hugo Van der Goes, verre qui se différencie pourtant par son cordon pincé ne fai-

---

87. J. Motteau, "Gobelets et verre à boire XVe–XVIIe siècle," *Recherches sur Tours*, I, 1981, pp. 85–101, en part. fig. 4.
88. J. Barrera, *op. cit.*, pl. 11.

62

Fig. 57. *Verre à pied, forme E2 (cf. Fig. 56,1, photo C. Hussy).*

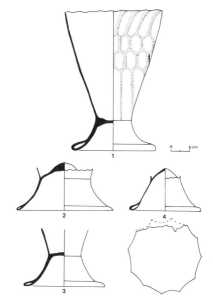

Fig. 59. *Verres à pied tronconique, forme E3, Martigues.*

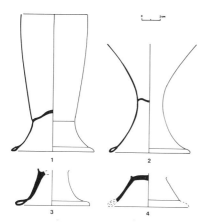

Fig. 58. *Verres à pied tronconique, forme E3 (1 et 2: coll. J. de Brion; 3 et 4: Psalmodi).*

sant pas office de pied mais entourant simplement la base d'un gobelet.

Un second type de verre à pied (forme E3) se caractérise par son pied tronconique nettement individualisé de la coupe; cette base soufflée indépendamment du restant de la pièce puis rapportée sous la coupe, varie dans ses proportions et correspond à des coupes très différentes: certaines sont très évasées (Fig. 58,2), d'autres au contraire presque cylindriques (Fig. 58,1); l'iconographie italienne et catalane de la fin du XIVe et du XVe siècle montrent de grands verres évasés sur des pieds hauts comparables aux découvertes avignonnaises. C'est probablement à l'extrême fin du XVe siècle qu'il convient de placer ces pièces ainsi que les verreries issues d'une fosse parfaitement datée à Martigues. Si la plupart des pieds provenant de Martigues sont semblables par leur matière incolore et fine aux verres d'Avignon, un objet reconstitué sur toute sa hauteur s'individualise par sa matière et son décor: Plus épais, ce verre aujourd'hui opaque et irisé porte sur sa coupe un décor complexe obtenu au moule: des nervures verticales couvrent la moitié de la coupe et se transforment ensuite en deux rangs d'alvéoles

63

Fig. 60. *Verre à pied tronconique (cf. Fig. 59,1), photo C. Hussy.*

hexagonales pour se terminer par des côtes inclinées sur la droite qui atteignent le rebord légèrement festonné (Fig. 59,1 et Fig. 60). Un verre de même forme, au décor comparable, a été mis au jour à Orléans.[89]

III. Verres à Tige, forme E4.

A Martigues, dans le même contexte que celui du verre à pied décrit précédemment, étaient d'autres verres dont des verres à tige fort bien représentés. Tous ont en commun une tige creuse et une matière légèrement verdâtre, toujours richement décorée. Deux procédés d'ornementation, pas toujours associés apparaissent: toutes les tiges sont baguées par un cordon ondé rapporté. Sur certaines pièces, ce décor recouvre en partie des spirales moulées qui partent du pied, s'enroulent autour de la tige et se développent sur la panse basse et évasée (Fig. 61,1 & 2). En revanche

---

89. *Idem*, pl. 13 n° 181.

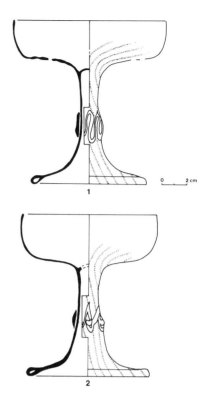

Fig. 61. *Verres à tige, forme E4, Martigues.*

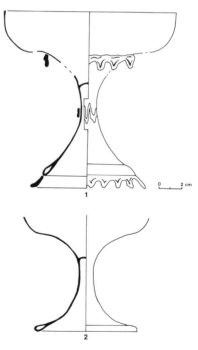

Fig. 62. *Verres à tige, forme E4, Martigues.*

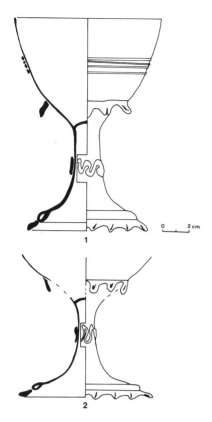

Fig. 63. *Verres à tige, forme E4, Martigues.*

Fig. 64. *Verre à tige, (cf. Fig. 113,1, photo C. Hussy).*

sur les autres verres le décor moulé est absent et le décor rapporté est beaucoup plus riche: il se répéte trois fois; le cordon pincé supérieur entoure la base de la coupe; un second cordon sur le pourtour du diamètre du pied surélève l'ensemble de la pièce; entre les deux cordon se trouve le filet ondé de la tige (Fig. 62,1). Exceptionnellement un faisceau de filets parallèles apparaît à mihauteur de la coupe. La pièce qui porte ce dernier décor se différencie aussi par sa coupe haute et beaucoup moins évasée que celle des autres verres à tige (Fig. 63,1 et Fig. 64). Enfin des verres de forme comparable, plus sobres, n'ont aucun décor (Fig. 62,2).

IV. Bouteilles.

Les récipients à liquide de la fin du moyen-âge sont presque inconnus. Les bouteilles D1 sont sans doute encore en usage. D'autres fioles de-

vaient être aussi employées comme en témoignent quelques goulots de petits récipients. La base d'une fiole aux flancs applatis et décorée d'un cercle en son milieu est connue à Martigues.

Tous ces vestiges d'un art verrier de la fin du moyen-dage découverts dans des villes importantes et commerçantes soulèvent le problème de leur origine. Artisanat local ou importation? Quelques céramiques en relation avec les verres de Martigues et d'origine italienne pourraient suggérer une origine semblable pour les verres. Ces pièces luxueuses rappellent déjà par leur élégance la "façon Venise." Cependant la présence de nombreux verriers italiens en Provence, à la fin du XVe siècle, n'exclue pas une provenance régionale.[90]

---

90. Les premiers verriers italiens sont connus en Provence en 1425. Entre 1425 et 1552, nous avons recensé en Provence et Comtat-Venaissin 127 verriers, tous semblent être des "altaristes."

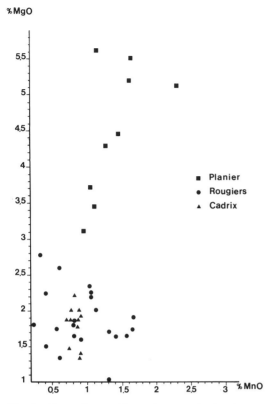

%MgO

%MnO

Fig. 65. *Teneur du magnésium et du manganèse dans les verres de Planier, de Rougiers et de Cadrix.*

CONCLUSION

La trentaine de formes de verres étudiés ici ne rend qu'imparfaitement compte de l'importance des productions verrières et de la multiplicité de la vaisselle de verre en usage dans le midi méditerranéen en particulier pour les XIIᵉ–XIIIᵉ siècle et pour l'extrême fin du moyen-âge. Sans doute faudra-t-il encore beaucoup de travail et de chance pour pouvoir compléter ce premier tableau évolutif de la verrerie médiévale, en France méditerranéenne (Fig. 66). Cependant, même si nous ne pouvons pas connaître tous les verres du XIVᵉ siècle, nous pouvons affirmer que l'essentiel des pièces utilisées quotidiennement sont des produits régionaux qui se limitent à trois types: le gobelet incolore portant un décor moulé de pastilles (C1); diverses formes (essentiellement

coupelles, et gobelets) ayant en commun une riche ornementation en verre bleu rapporté (C5) et des bouteilles en verre épais (D1).

L'originalité des verreries médiévales du Midi de la France s'affirme déjà face aux productions des pays méditerranéens tels l'Italie et la Yougoslavie et face aux trouvailles des terres septentrionales. Le seul point commun avec ses dernières régions est le décor côtelé des verres à tiges B2, et encore ce verre, produit vraisemblablement localement s'individualise par sa tige massive et le profil en tulipe de sa coupe. Les analogies avec les verres italiens, bien que plus évidentes doivent être nuancées. Ainsi les verres à gouttes rapportées si fréquents en Italie du XIIIᵉ au XVᵉ siècle, n'ont pas connus la même vogue dans les ateliers provençaux et languedociens qui n'ont adopté ce décor qu'à la fin du XIIIᵉ siècle uniquement. Par contre les gobelets à décor moulé et les verreries à filets bleus rapportés bien connus en Yougoslavie et Italie ont peut-être eu une plus grande faveur dans nos régions, mais seulement au XIVᵉ siècle; pourtant c'est vraisemblablement par l'intermédiaire de l'Italie que ces techniques se sont propagées en Provence et Languedoc. Quant aux bouteilles D1, si fréquentes dans le Sud de la France, elles semblent absentes en Italie sauf en Ligurie. Cette forme, comme les précédentes d'origine orientale, pourrait cette fois ci avoir été transmise, non pas par l'Italie, mais par l'Espagne du sud.

Les analyses physico-chimiques et les fouilles d'atelier permettent de penser que la plupart des verres trouvés dans nos régions sont d'une fabrication locale: seuls les verres bicontroniques (forme A3) à fondant potassique pourraient témoigner d'une origine nordique. D'autres verres étaient certainement importés comme le prouvent au XVᵉ siècle, les achats de "*voirres cristallins*" par le roi René sur des "*galliasses venitiennes*" à Marseille, ou encore l'achat du même personnage à un mercier venu de "*Gallé de France.*"[91]

---

91. Arnaud d'Agnel, *Les comptes du roi René*, T.1, 1908–1910.

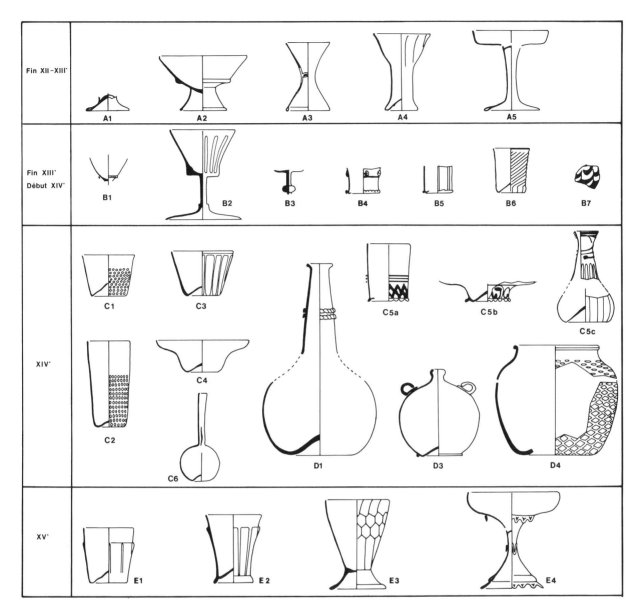

Fig. 66. *Typologie périodisée des verreries XIIᵉ–XVᵉ siècles.*

Notons aussi à la fin du XIVᵉ siècle la mention d'entrée de "veyre de Berri" dans Avignon.[92]

Les productions verrières du Midi semblent pourtant dès la fin du XIIIᵉ siècle, suffisantes pour la consommation locale; certains de ces produits ont pu être exportés. La verrerie provençale était sans doute estimée puisqu'on la trouve mentionnée dans les biens du Comte d'Artois,

mort en 1302.[93] A la fin du XVᵉ siècle les verriers provençaux, pour la plupart des "altaristes," étaient en mesure d'offrir des pièces très belles, qui pouvaient peut-être égaler les productions

92. P. Pansier, "Les gabelles d'Avignon de 1310 à 1397," *Annales d'Avignon et du Comtat Venaissin*, 1926, p. 53.

93. Gerspach, *L'art de la verrerie*, Paris, 1885.

vénitiennes: de 1473 à 1480, nous trouvons à Marseille Jean Fournier qui vend des aiguières de verre à des vénitiens au prix de 3 florins le cent.[94]

Les textes permettent-ils de connaître l'importance et le coût de l'objet de verre? La proportion de verres trouvés dans les fouilles est toujours insignifiante par rapport à la céramique, mais le verre a pu être récupéré, et dans la plupart des fouilles l'absence des pièces en bois et en étain ne permet pas de juger de l'importance du verre dans la vaisselle quotidienne. Dans les inventaires et les comptes de péage, le verre est peu cité, mais les céramiques que l'on sait abondantes, grâce aux fouilles archéologiques, sont presque toujours ignorées; aussi l'interprétation de ces textes reste difficile.

D'un usage sans doute limité (au moins jusqu'au XIVe siècle) le verre ne semble pourtant pas un produit bien cher. Le droit perçu sur les verreries aux péages est minime: En 1252 pour une *saumata* de verres il est exigé un seul denier à Mezel, et deux à Valensole;[95] au XIVe siècle la redevance est la même.[96] Les taxes parfois en nature, restent toujours modestes: seules une ou deux pièces sont prélevées sur un chargement de cent unités.[97] En fait la taxe prélevée en fonction de la quantité transportée, ne semble pas tenir compte de la qualité du produit: aussi la modicité de la redevance ne reflète peut-être pas le coût réel de l'objet de verre.

---

94. E. Baratier et F. Raynaud, *Histoire du commerce de Marseille*, T. II, de 1281 à 1480, Marseille, 1951, p. 830.

95. E. Baratier, *Enquêtes sur les droits et revenus de Charles Ier d'Anjou en Provence* (1252 et 1278), Paris, 1969.

96. Comptes de péage 1308–1309, Arch. Dep. Bouches-du-Rhône, B 1981.

97. Une *"cupa"* ou deux sont exigées en 1252 par saumée de verre aux péages de Tarascon, Saint-Gabriel et Trinquetaille; Deux pièces sont prélevées en 1308 à Meyrargues.

Les dessins ont été réalisés par D. Foy et L. Vallauri

English Summary

The Typology of Medieval Glass Vessels from Excavations in Provence and Languedoc

This article examines different types of medieval glass (twelfth–late fifteenth century) discovered in excavations of rural and urban sites in southern France. The material, presented in chronological order, is studied by form, decoration, and fabric. Physical and chemical analyses reveal the composition of the glass.

The rare examples dating from the twelfth and thirteenth centuries are for the most part incomplete. However, excavations of cemeteries have brought to light ribbed chalices and footed cups. The glasses of the late thirteenth and fourteenth centuries, on the other hand, are well known. There are regional variants, as shown by the excavations of workshops at Planier, La Seube, Rougiers, and Cadrix.

There is no doubt that drinking vessels were very widespread in the late thirteenth century. Important changes took place at this time: the appearance of the goblet and the use of a soda flux in the composition of the glass. Three types of glass predominate. The first type comprises cylindrical or flaring goblets of colorless glass with molded decoration of oval or rounded indentations. Next there are glasses decorated with bright blue trails; this decoration occurs on many forms (cylindrical goblets, shallow bowls, and bottles) and is sometimes associated with a pinched cordon around the base of the vessel. Finally, the container for liquids most often used in the fourteenth century is a bottle of bluish-green glass. The globular body has a mold-blown lattice decoration which terminates under the base in a rosette. The mouth is surrounded by a smooth cordon or is incised.

Prunted vessels, frequent in Italy and Yugo-slavia, are not common in southern France, and they do not appear before the end of the thirteenth century.

The list of late medieval forms is more limited. The goblets continue but new types appear: glasses on a conical or circular foot and with richly decorated stems.

Annexe N° 1
Analyses des verres attribués à la fin du XIIe et au XIIIe siècle.

Analyse	Type	Provenance	CaO	Fe$_2$O$_3$	TiO$_2$	K$_2$O	SiO$_2$	Al$_2$O$_3$	MgO	Na$_2$O	P$_2$O$_5$	MnO
VEM 40	A1	Rougiers	10,9	0,90	0,13	4,05	61,0	2,40	4,90	9,9	1,60	2,35
VEM 41	A1	Rougiers	11,4	1,00	0,08	5,70	54,1	3,05	5,85	13,6	2,40	2,30
VEM 8	A3	Rougiers	12,0	0,80	0,11	12,20	56,3	2,75	5,50	5,2	3,05	0,90
VEM 9	A3	Rougiers	13,8	1,95	0,36	0,35	58,9	6,80	1,85	0,00	7,40	2,20
VEM 34	A3	Rougiers	9,0	0,70	0,26	9,65	57,7	3,65	1,90	11,2	1,50	0,60
VEM 35	A3	Rougiers	10,8	0,90	0,31	8,90	58,2	3,90	1,60	9,9	1,15	1,95
VEM 105	A3	Psalmodi	12,30	0,00	0,13	10,15	57,70	2,46	4,97	7,45	3,32	1,26
VEM 142	A3	Beaucaire	10,50	0,61	0,13	7,82	59,75	2,11	4,55	9,10	1,80	1,62
VEM 37	A5	Rougiers	11,9	0,80	0,11	7,50	56,9	2,25	4,70	9,3	2,90	1,75
VEM 37'	A5	Rougiers	11,8	2,90	0,44	0,05	48,0	7,10	0,50	0,00	3,80	5,55
VEM 137	A5	St-Roman	10,80	0,81	0,13	5,28	60,30	1,46	6,02	9,80	1,80	1,65
VEM 138	A5	Psalmodi	9,70	1,14	0,17	4,66	58,00	2,95	4,90	11,90	1,60	2,94
VEM 139	A5	Psalmodi	10,80	0,95	0,15	6,38	59,50	2,75	4,18	10,30	3,20	2,20
VEM 140	A5	Psalmodi	12,80	1,26	0,20	4,99	55,20	4,63	5,92	10,00	1,90	2,20
VEM 141	A5	Psalmodi	13,80	0,71	0,13	8,69	54,60	2,10	5,64	8,00	3,60	1,50

Annexe N° 2
Analyses des verres de la fin du XIIIe siècle—début XIVe siècle.

Analyse	Type	Provenance	CaO	Fe$_2$O$_3$	TiO$_2$	K$_2$O	SiO$_2$	Al$_2$O$_3$	MgO	Na$_2$O	P$_2$O$_5$	MnO
VEM 131	B2	Petit Palais	6,40	0,69	0,10	4,61	67,40	1,95	1,76	13,10	0,62	1,40
VEM 132	B2	Petit Palais	7,10	0,63	0,10	4,32	65,60	2,20	1,48	13,80	0,50	2,02
VEM 133	B2	Petit Palais	8,20	0,55	0,09	5,18	64,15	2,18	1,48	15,60	0,90	0,88
VEM 134	B2	Petit Palais	5,85	0,49	0,10	5,86	69,00	1,75	1,46	15,60	0,45	0,84
VEM 18	B3	Rougiers	8,00	1,15	0,14	4,75	62,00	3,35	4,50	11,7	1,85	1,10
VEM 19	B3	Rougiers	11,7	0,70	0,11	9,75	57,3	2,10	4,90	5,0	3,05	1,35
VEM 39	B3 anneau	Rougiers	5,2	0,85	0,29	3,75	64,2	3,10	1,85	16,5	0,75	2,00
VEM 135	B4	Petit Palais	6,60	0,50	0,08	3,50	68,50	1,55	1,48	14,80	0,50	1,12
VEM 21	B5	Rougiers	8,9	0,58	0,12	3,55	64,75	1,80	1,88	16,2	0,49	0,45
VEM 22	B5	Rougiers	7,8	0,65	0,05	2,90	63,50	2,38	1,28	16,00	0,62	1,10
VEM 23	B5	Rougiers	5,6	0,48	0,12	2,95	69,95	1,11	4,20	15,80	0,45	1,45
VEM 24	B5	Rougiers	7,3	0,42	0,02	3,40	67,60	0,98	1,08	16,40	0,25	1,55
VEM 13	B6	Rougiers	6,6	0,67	0,12	3,15	68,20	1,32	1,50	16,40	0,90	1,86
VEM 20	B6	Rougiers	4,5	0,80	0,11	3,65	59,30	2,10	1,80	16,00	0,79	1,25

69

Annexe N° 3
Analyses des verres de l'atelier de Planier.

Analyse	CaO	Fe_2O_3	TiO_2	K_2O	SiO_2	Al_2O_3	MgO	Na_2O	P_2O_5	MnO
VEM 164	10,30	0,92	0,13	6,48	58,30	3,12	5,20	11,50	2,40	1,62
VEM 165	6,10	0,63	0,11	2,40	64,90	3,10	3,46	17,10	0,60	1,10
VEM 166	7,00	0,85	0,10	2,54	63,25	3,40	4,30	16,30	1,00	1,28
VEM 167	10,50	1,18	0,17	5,35	57,20	4,28	5,50	12,00	2,20	1,64
VEM 168	10,40	0,90	0,13	5,28	58,80	2,65	5,12	10,60	2,00	2,30
VEM 169	9,00	1,00	0,14	4,94	56,00	3,61	6,78	12,50	2,60	1,08
VEM 170	7,70	0,90	0,11	1,44	63,70	3,50	5,60	14,20	0,80	1,14
VEM 171	7,50	0,66	0,11	3,07	63,50	3,40	3,70	14,80	0,60	1,04
VEM 172	7,80	0,81	0,12	2,50	63,05	3,24	4,44	14,30	0,90	1,42
VEM 173	6,00	1,60	0,10	2,98	62,20	4,34	3,10	16,00	0,60	0,94

Annexe N° 4
Analyses des productions de Rougiers.

Analyse		CaO	Fe_2O_3	TiO_2	K_2O	SiO_2	Al_2O_3	MgO	Na_2O	P_2O_5	MnO
5	rebord gobelet C1	4,3	0,80	0,33	3,65	66,5	3,10	1,50	18,0	0,75	0,40
11	Fgt gobelet C1	6,2	0,55	0,22	5,80	65,5	2,30	1,35	16,7	1,25	0,60
12	Fgt gobelet C1	8,0	0,50	0,05	5,15	65,9	2,20	1,80	14,9	1,00	0,80
27	fond gobelet C1	7,7	0,40	0,09	3,65	65,0	1,55	1,85	16,0	0,60	0,80
29	fond gobelet C1	11,5	0,36	0,25	10,2	65,5	3,20	2,25	10,8	1,30	0,40
33	fond gobelet C1	7,8	0,50	0,23	5,15	61,5	2,80	2,00	14,8	1,40	1,10
38	fond gobelet C1	9,5	0,35	0,22	4,65	61,6	2,25	1,60	16,5	0,55	0,90
6	Fgt coupelle C4	10,2	0,80	0,36	8,40	59,1	4,30	1,75	13,0	1,60	0,55
32	rebord coupelle C4	8,0	0,60	0,21	6,65	63,0	2,50	2,25	11,8	1,30	1,05
28	coupelle C5b	6,7	0,90	0,10	3,60	62,1	2,90	2,60	17,5	0,50	0,60
1	fiole C5c	7,2	0,65	0,32	6,50	67,1	3,10	2,35	11,0	1,10	1,05
2	bouteille D1	8,0	0,80	0,14	4,10	63,5	2,25	1,90	15,5	0,90	1,70
3	bocal D4	6,6	0,85	0,13	4,00	64,3	3,50	1,65	17,5	0,75	0,80
4	gourde D3	8,2	0,80	0,21	5,15	64,7	2,75	2,20	13,9	1,10	1,05
174	déchet verdâtre	7,1	1,12	0,20	4,13	63,7	3,40	1,70	14,8	1,10	1,33
175	déchet verdâtre	7,7	0,94	0,17	4,05	62,6	2,70	1,64	15,4	0,75	1,40
176	déchet verdâtre	7,6	0,84	0,15	4,05	62,2	2,50	1,64	13,9	0,80	1,58
177	déchet verdâtre	6,5	0,64	0,30	3,74	64,7	3,60	2,80	17,8	1,10	0,32
178	déchet violacé	9,4	0,96	0,22	3,84	61,6	3,40	1,64	13,6	0,95	2,20
52	prélèvement ds un creuset	6,0	1,65	0,28	3,40	62,1	5,40	1,75	16,5	0,70	1,65
55	prélèvement ds un creuset	5,4	1,55	0,33	3,15	64,0	5,85	0,75	14,2	0,70	1,30
58	prélèvement ds un creuset	4,1	0,90	0,34	3,90	68,2	4,20	1,80	15,1	0,70	0,05

Analyses des productions de Cadrix.

Analyse		CaO	Fe_2O_3	TiO_2	K_2O	SiO_2	Al_2O_3	MgO	Na_2O	P_2O_5	MnO
152	Fgt forme D1	7,80	0,80	0,21	5,28	63,7	3,40	1,92	15,0	1,10	0,90
153	déchet incolore	6,0	0,65	0,29	8,26	64,90	3,50	1,40	12,8	1,65	0,92
154	déchet verdâtre	8,1	1,10	0,32	3,94	62,50	5,30	1,84	14,2	0,95	0,86
155	déchet jaunâtre	5,1	0,71	0,31	3,84	66,0	4,50	2,20	16,3	0,75	0,82
156	déchet verdâtre	7,3	0,96	0,22	5,57	63,3	4,25	1,78	13,4	1,30	0,94
157	déchet verdâtre	7,75	0,80	0,20	4,80	63,05	3,65	2,00	15,6	1,10	0,88
160	déchet verdâtre	7,30	0,94	0,20	4,22	65,30	3,75	1,38	13,2	0,70	0,90
161	déchet incolore	8,8	0,68	0,17	4,61	63,85	4,00	1,46	14,7	1,10	0,72
162	déchet bleuté	7,7	0,78	0,20	4,70	63,5	3,66	2,00	14,8	1,10	0,86
107	déchet verdâtre	7,8	0,80	0,19	5,15	64,0	3,66	1,84	14,7	1,02	0,96
106	déchet violacé	7,6	1,90	0,44	5,07	58,8	4,40	1,90	13,3	0,94	3,25
158	déchet violacé	4,0	0,62	0,32	3,26	65,7	3,46	1,94	17,8	0,60	1,36
163	déchet violacé	8,60	0,73	0,15	4,61	62,3	3,25	1,92	14,7	1,15	1,90
159	déchet bleu	9,0	2,02	0,19	4,08	63,85	4,25	1,84	12,0	0,95	0,70

Analyses des Verres de Psalmodi

Analyse		CaO	Fe_2O_3	TiO_2	K_2O	SiO_2	Al_2O_3	MgO	Na_2O	P_2O_5	MnO
104	Gobelet C1	5,50	0,30	0,04	4,30	68,4	1,68	0,98	16,8	0,82	1,2
102	Coupelle C5b	7,40	0,50	0,08	5,50	64,4	1,44	1,81	14,8	1,0	1,4
103	Bouteille D1	8,60	0,55	0,11	4,82	64,4	2,18	2,00	15,9	1,02	0,96

Productions de l'atelier de Pré-bayon (Gigondas)

Analyse		CaO	Fe_2O_3	TiO_2	K_2O	SiO_2	Al_2O_3	MgO	Na_2O	P_2O_5	MnO
143	déchet incolore	7,6	0,76	0,17	7,63	67,00	1,95	1,46	11,1	0,64	0,46
144	déchet incolore	8,0	0,38	0,12	6,77	66,70	1,80	1,56	11,15	0,90	0,84
145	déchet incolore	9,3	0,48	0,13	6,24	64,40	1,00	1,88	13,0	1,05	0,85
146	déchet incolore	9,0	0,50	0,12	6,86	64,35	1,80	1,76	11,9	0,90	1,18
147	déchet incolore	8,6	0,40	0,08	10,66	65,95	1,00	1,80	8,40	1,20	1,04
148	déchet violacé	8,1	0,60	0,11	5,86	65,00	2,09	1,64	12,8	0,50	1,54

GOTHIC GLAZIERS: MONKS, JEWS, TAXPAYERS, BRETONS, WOMEN

MEREDITH PARSONS LILLICH

MEDIEVAL stained glass windows have many admirers, but our information about the largely anonymous craftsmen who designed and made them is slim. The craft itself is not so mysterious; the process described by the twelfth-century monk Theophilus[1] is remarkably similar to the method employed up to the present day. The artists themselves are somewhat more elusive in history,[2] particularly in the Gothic period, traditionally and with reason regarded as the apogee of this beautiful, expensive, and highly complicated art.

Stained glass which dates before the thirteenth century is itself rare, and it is hardly surprising that information about those early glaziers is scant. In addition to Theophilus—who speaks eloquently but anonymously since we do not know his monastery, his work, or indeed anything about him but his name-in-religion—the glazier Gerlachus left his name and his "portrait" in glass he made for the Premonstratensians of Arnstein about 1160.[3] Only three glaziers are named in the early texts on architectural arts collected by Mortet. One is a monk, Valerius, remembered because he fell from his scaffold while installing his glass in the abbey of Saint-Mélaine in Rennes and bounced up unharmed. The second is a serf, Fulco, who was freed and provided for life with a house and land in return for his artistic services at the Abbey of Saint-Aubin in Angers. And the third is a "professional," the glazier Rogerus who was "brought from the city of Reims" to make the stained glass of the Abbey

of Saint-Hubert-d'Ardenne in Luxembourg.[4] All are late eleventh century, before we have anything but the most vestigial remains of any windows themselves.

It is even possible to suggest that some of these early craftsmen were Jewish. One of the miracles of the Virgin, introduced to western Europe by Gregory of Tours, describes her intercession to save a Jewish child who had taken communion

---

1. *On Divers Arts, the Treatise of Theophilus*, ed. John G. Hawthorne and Cyril Stanley Smith (Chicago: 1963), Book II: "The Art of the Worker in Glass." This edition of Theophilus places greater emphasis on the techniques he describes and their practical application, and is thus of greater use to art historians. The treatise has most recently been ascribed to the diocese of Cologne, about 1125: John Van Engen, "Theophilus Presbyter and Rupert of Deutz: the Manual Arts and Benedictine Theology in the Early Twelfth Century," *Viator* XI, 1980, pp. 147–163.

2. Studies on medieval glaziers are few; see Hans Wentzel, "Glasmaler und Maler im Mittelalter," *Zeitschrift für Kunstwissenschaft* III, 1949, pp. 53–62. The subject is mentioned in passing in: Françoise Perrot, "L'Art de la signature, VIII: La signature des peintres-verriers," *Revue de l'art* XXVI, 1974, pp. 40–41; Catherine Brisac and Jean-Jacques Gruber, "Le Métier de maître verrier," *Métiers d'art* no. 20, November 1982, pp. 23, 27–29.

3. Grodecki, *Le Vitrail roman*, Fribourg, 1977, pp. 151–161, 268. The inscription "Rex regum clare Gerlacho propiciare" encircles the image of Gerlachus, depicted with brush and paintpot in hand, the artist "in harness."

4. Victor Mortet, *Recueil de textes relatifs à l'histoire de l'architecture . . . XIe–XIIe siècles*, Paris, 1911, pp. 154–157 (Valerius), pp. 264–265 (Fulco), pp. 191–193 (Rogerus). For discussions of pre-twelfth century debris see Grodecki, *Vitrail roman*, pp. 45–50; Eva Frodl-Kraft, *Die Glasmalerei: Entwicklung, Technik, Eigenart*, Vienna, 1970, pp. 13–28.

F I G . 1 . *Miracle of the Jewish Child of Bourges: his father, a glazier, throws him into the furnace. Le Mans Cathedral, north choir, upper ambulatory Bay 105. (Photo: ARCH. PHOT. / SPADEM / VAGA, New York 1985)*

along with his Christian friends and had later been thrown into a fiery furnace by his angry father—a glazier.[5] The tale survives in this guise to the Gothic period (Fig. 1), when Cantiga IV of Alfonso el Sabio's *Cantigas de Santa María* and Gautier de Coincy's *Miracles de la Vierge* both describe the father as a glazier of Bourges—or in one mid thirteenth-century manuscript of the latter, of Chartres.[6] But if Jews did blow some of the glass in those majestic High Gothic cathedrals, no documentation attests to their precise contribution or to their names. And in the anti-Semitic thirteenth century, European Jews were forced out of the crafts into usury and were eventually expelled altogether. Blumenkranz[7] points out that the same miracle as related around 1225–1227 by Cesarius of Heisterbach, a Cistercian from the Rhineland, omits the father's profession, and the furnace becomes the water heater for the Jewish ritual bath which was a familiar part of every ghetto community.

At the other end of the Middle Ages, written documents, as would be expected, increasingly provide glaziers' names in contracts and some glimpse of their working relationships. Scholars have published this documentation since the late fourteenth century for Chartres Cathedral,[8] for

the cathedral of Rennes,[9] and for the great art patron Jean, duc de Berri.[10] Among the glaziers working for the Duke was Maistre Miles le Cavelier, rewarded upon one occasion with a diamond ring!

The Appendix to this study provides a selection of contracts for glaziers from Paris and Arras during the first third of the fourteenth century, which will be discussed below. But for the Gothic era of the late Capetians (thirteenth and beginning of the fourteenth centuries), however, there is nearly a void. Two glass painters signed their work: "Clemens vitrearius carnotensis" signed a window

5. Bernhard Blumenkranz, *Le Juif médiéval au miroir de l'art chrétien*, Paris, 1966, pp. 22–25; *idem, Les Auteurs chrétiens latins au moyen âge, sur les juifs et le judaisme*, Etudes juives III, The Hague, 1963, p. 68; *idem, Juifs et chrétiens dans le monde occidental (430–1069)*, Paris, 1960, p. 31. The father is a glazier in the Greek sixth-century source: see Theodor Nissen, "Zu den ältesten Fassungen der Legende vom Judenknaben," *Zeitschrift für Französische Sprache und Literatur* LXII, 1939, p. 393.

6. *Cantiga* IV: "En Beorges un judeu/ ouve, que fazer sabía/ vidro, et un fillo seu . . ." (Manuel Cardenal de Iracheta, ed., *Alfonso el Sabio*, Madrid, 1946, p. 229, lines 5–7). *Miracles de la Vierge*: "A Boorges, ce truis lisant,/ d'un Juïf verrier mesdisant/ fist nostre dame tex mervelles; . . ." (Theodor Pelizaeus, *Beiträge zur Geschichte der Legende vom Judenknaben*, Halle, 1914, p. 63, lines 1–3). Pelizaeus' edition is based on Brussels, Bibl. roy. Ms. 3357 (inv. 10747), fol. 34v (13th c.). The variant title "c'est dou juif verrier de Chartres" occurs in London, Brit. Lib. Harley Ms. 4401, fol. 32v (mid-13th c.); see Pelizaeus pp. 59, 63.

7. Blumenkranz, *Juif médiéval*, p. 22; *idem, Juifs et chrétiens*, pp. 31–32.

8. Maurice Jusselin, "La Maîtrise de l'oeuvre à Notre-Dame de Chartres; la fabrique, les ouvriers et les travaux du XIV siècle," *Mémoires de la Société archéologique d'Eure-et-Loir* XV (1915–1922) pp. 233–347 (on glaziers pp. 299–302); Yves Delaporte, *Les Vitraux de la cathédrale de Chartres*, Chartres, 1926, text vol., pp. 20–25.

9. M. Delavigne-Villeneuve, in *Bulletin archéologique et agricole de l'Association bretonne* IV, 1852, pp. 161–163, published accounts from 1375 at the cathedral of Rennes with the Beart family, glaziers.

10. Alfred de Champeaux and P. Gauchery, *Les Travaux d'art exécutés pour Jean de France, duc de Berry . . .*, Paris, 1894, pp. 115–116; Millard Meiss, *French Painting in the Time of Jean de Berry: the Late Fourteenth Century and the Patronage of the Duke*, London, 1967, v. 1, pp. 44–45. Studies of glaziers in the fifteenth and succeeding centuries are less uncommon and I have not collected them here.

FIG. 2. *Haina, west window, signed "Lupuldus frater."* (*Photo: Landesamt für Denkmalpflege Hessen, Aussenstelle Marburg*)

made for Rouen Cathedral about 1235–1240,[11] and "Lupuldus frater" signed a grisaille in the west window of the Cistercian Abbey of Haina about 1300 (Fig. 2).[12] To put it another way: a professional worked in Rouen Cathedral, and a Cistercian monk produced windows in his own abbey church. Such a working hypothesis may prove useful in attempting to track glazing ateliers on stylistic criteria alone.[13]

Names in published documents have been no more common than those in windows. In 1976 Grodecki published the accounts of the Abbey of Saint-Denis which—beginning in 1286—mention the glaziers, their payment and their work, chiefly restoration and upkeep.[14] The significance of this data has hardly been tapped, for these documents establish useful information about "professionals" who were paid an annual salary, robes, and lodging. The terminology varies, but Grodecki states: "Il ne semble pas qu'il y ait une différence réelle entre 'pensio,' 'salarium,' et 'dietae,' puisqu'il s'agit chaque fois d'un payement annuel, et non de la rétribution d'un travail spécifié et déterminé." Glaziers were also paid by the job, however, for example in the accounts of Saint-Lazare of Autun for 1294–1295: "Item, magistro Stephano pro vererriis beatorum Nazarii et Lazari reficiendis, XI lb. XVIs. VIII d. . . ."[15] In fact, the Appendix provides numerous examples of payment by the job, in situations

which might seem more adaptable to an annual stipend. The Count and later the Countess of Artois regularly paid the few glaziers whom they employed over many years by the job for new work and for repairs in their many properties and their equally numerous charities.

Clearly more documents will emerge for the thirteenth century, though probably not for the first half. The hypotheses of Delaporte for that era are nonetheless sound and bear examination, since we will see that they establish a basis for the interpretation of new documentation here presented. Delaporte suggests first that it is not necessary to suppose that there ever were very many glaziers. The very omission of the craft from

11. The "Clement of Chartres" panel is frequently illustrated; it appears in color in Jean Rollet, *Les Maîtres de la lumière*, Paris, 1980, p. 146. I have omitted from my argument three examples listed below, where the name inscriptions are problematical:

(1) Saint-Martin, Westhoffen, "Renbuldus me fecit" in the traceries (late 13th c.). Saint-Martin was a parish, but owned and staffed by the Alsatian abbey of Marmoutier; thus Renbuldus could have been a monk or a secular craftsman. See: Christiane Wild-Block, "Les Vitraux de Westhoffen," *Bulletin de la Société d'histoire et d'archéologie de Saverne et environs* no. 60, 1967, p. 5, fig. 8; the same journal nos. 79–80, 1972, is an entire volume devoted to Westhoffen.

(2) Auxerre Cathedral, choir clerestory, "Bartheolomevs." See: Perrot, pp. 40–41; Virginia Raguin, *Stained Glass in Thirteenth Century Burgundy*, Princeton, 1982, pl. 82.

(3) Dionysiuskirche, Esslingen, "Lampertus" at the feet of St. Denis, illustrated in Hans Wentzel, *Meisterwerke der Glasmalerei*, Berlin, 1954, pp. 35–36, fig. 23.

12. Brigitte Lymant, "Die Glasmalerei bei den Zisterziensern," in the catalog *Die Zisterzienser, Ordensleben zwischen Ideal und Wirklichkeit*, exhibition at Aachen, Cologne, 1980, p. 350, illustration p. 353; Perrot, p. 41.

13. See my study of a glazier, probably a Benedictine monk from Evron, whose thirty-year career can be traced in his own and two other Benedictine abbeys in western France: "Bishops from Evron: Three Saints in the Pitcairn Collection and a Fourth in the Philadelphia Museum," *Stained Glass of the Middle Ages*, ed. Caviness and Husband, New York, 1985.

14. Grodecki, *Les Vitraux de Saint-Denis I* (Corpus Vitrearum Medii Aevi France, Etudes I), Paris, 1976, pp. 32–33.

15. Victor Mortet and Paul Deschamps, *Recueil de textes relatifs à l'histoire de l'architecture . . . XIIe–XIIIe siècles*, Paris, 1929, p. 324.

Etienne Boileau's *Livre des métiers* of 1263 probably is a good indication that they were not numerous.[16] Delaporte further states: "Payés sans doute à la journée, les verriers du XIIIe siècle ne perdaient pas leur temps à la rédaction de devis et de mémoires." Probably many couldn't read, their illiteracy being suggested—as with other medieval artisans' works—by their mistakes in copying inscriptions.[17] The latest example in French stained glass where evidence of the glazier's illiteracy is probable is at the rural priory of Gassicourt near Mantes, about 1270.

Delaporte's third assumption is somewhat more problematical: that it is not likely in the Gothic period that the stained glass artists were themselves occupied in the actual fabrication of glass. This is a very significant point. It implies a division of labor which is difficult to document, since the words *vitrearius* and *verrier* were applied without distinction to both individuals, the glaziers who made glass (glassblowers), and the glaziers who designed, made, and repaired stained glass windows. It is, however, a distinction which is clear in the document of 1375 of Chartres Cathedral, in which Jehan Hannequin le verrier (living at Senonches near the forest of Dreux) agrees to sell to Guillemin le verrier (employed by the cathedral) various quantities of sapphire, green, and purple.[18] While Delaporte may not be correct in transferring this work division as far back as the High Gothic of about 1200–1235, Grodecki's documents from the Abbey of Saint-Denis establish this division of labor clearly as early as 1284 when the accounts list sums paid "pro vitro albo et colorato." These theories about the Gothic glazing craft can be tested by the Paris tax rolls of the late Capetian era, which will be discussed below.

Taxpayers

Four Parisian tax rolls have been published: 1292, 1296, 1297, and 1313.[19] These four as well as the three which remain unpublished (1298, 1299, 1300) have been studied by Françoise Baron for their references to manuscript illuminators, painters, and sculptors.[20] She lists 229 artists (alphabetically) with indices by first name, by parishes, and by crafts.[21]

It is a much simpler matter to list the glaziers, since there were far fewer. These will be listed

16. Delaporte, p. 16. For the *Livre des métiers* see: G. B. Depping, ed., *Réglemens sur les arts et métiers de Paris rédigés au XIIIe siècle et connus sous le nom du livre des métiers d'Etienne Boileau*, Paris, 1837; René de Lespinasse and François Bonnardot, *Le Livre des métiers d'Etienne Boileau*, Paris, 1879.

17. A perfect example is discussed by M. L. Campbell, "'Scribe faber lima': a Crozier in Florence Reconsidered," *Burlington Magazine*, CXXI No. 915, June 1979, pp. 364–369, a study of an English crozier of 1185–1200 on which the craftsman carefully copied, in niello-work lettering, the instructions to him "Inscribe, workman, with your file. . . ." For walrus-ivory carving of about 1200 in which the inscriptions include letters upside-down, reversed or running backward, see Meredith Lillich, *The Stained Glass of Saint-Père de Chartres*, Middletown, CT, 1978, p. 126 n. 24. The illiterate glazier of Gassicourt was trained in the chantier of Le Mans Cathedral: see ch. III of my forthcoming book *The Armor of Light* (Berkeley, in press).

18. Jusselin p. 300; Delaporte pp. 22–23; Arch. dépt. d'Eure-et-Loir G 159 fol. 100.

19. The roll of 1292 (Paris, Bibl. nat. fr. 6220) was published by Hercule Géraud, *Paris sous Philippe le Bel d'après des documents originaux*, Paris, 1837. The Swedish linguist Karl Michaëlsson published three of the seven existing rolls before he died: "Le Livre de la taille de Paris l'an 1296," *Göteborgs universitets årsskrift* LXIV, 1958, no. 4, pp. 1–308; "Le Livre de la taille de Paris l'an 1297," *Göteborgs universitets årsskrift* LXVII, 1961, no. 3 pp. 1-480; "Le Livre de la taille de Paris, l'an de grace 1313," *Göteborgs högskolas årsskrift* LVII, 1951, no. 3, pp. 1–349. For the rolls of 1296 and 1297 see n. 20 infra; the tax of 1313 (Bibl. nat. fr. 6736) was a special levy for the knighting ceremony of the king's sons. A very useful demographic analysis of the tax rolls appears in Raymond Cazelles, *Nouvelle histoire de Paris de la fin du règne de Philippe August à la mort de Charles V, 1223–1380*, Paris, 1972, pp. 29–30, 113–115, 131–136.

20. The five rolls of 1296–1300 are Archives nationales KK 283. See Françoise Baron, "Enlumineurs, peintres et sculpteurs parisiens des XIIIe et XIVe siècles d'après les rôles de la taille," *Bulletin archéologique du comité des travaux historiques et scientifiques*, n.s. IV, 1968, pp. 37–121.

21. There are 229 artists in her Répertoire A (Enlumineurs, peintres et ymagiers). Since the *Livre des métiers* of Etienne Boileau grouped painters and saddlers in the same corporation, and since sculptors were sometimes called *tailleurs de pierre*, Baron includes saddlers and stonecutters as Répertoire B for the convenience of future researchers. The grand total of artisans in both lists is 479.

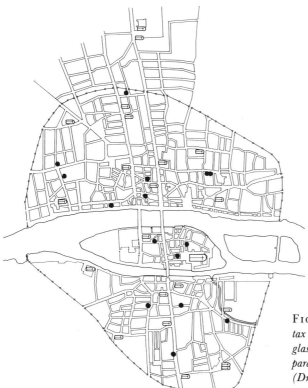

FIG. 3. *Plan of Paris with locations of glaziers listed in the tax roll of 1292. Two live in la rue de la Verrerie, location of the glassworks, in the northeast quadrant of the map (Right Bank, parallel to the river and just north of the Place de Grève). (Drawing: Jerry Bowes)*

below, in order as they occur in the rolls (thus by parish location), with those living at the glassworks (*la verrerie*) bracketed; if the glazier also appears on other rolls, the years are given. It can be seen by looking at the parishes (the right column) that the glaziers, in addition to being few in number, were spread all over town (see Figs. 3–6).[22] Only at the glassworks, rue de la Voirrerie, was there even a small cluster of glaziers, who can be assumed to be producers of glass—glassblowers—by virtue of their convenient location. La Voirrerie was near la Poterie (both requiring furnaces), in the parish Saint-Jehan just east of Saint-Merri and north of the Place de Grève. La rue de la Verrerie[23] is still there (4th arrondissement, metro Hôtel-de-Ville). The glassworks had been installed there about 1185.

All individuals identified as *verrier* have been listed, though it will be seen that a handful made supplemental income, usually but not always as tavern keepers. That situation is true for the other artists listed by Baron as well. It can be remarked in these rolls that glaziers tended to take on such supplemental "moonlighting" only as the financial situation of the reign of Philippe le Bel worsened, during France's economic crisis of 1295–1304. Another problem recognized by Baron is

22. On the location of the book-producing crafts in Paris see Robert Branner, "Manuscript-Makers in Mid-Thirteenth Century Paris," *Art Bulletin* XLVIII, 1966, pp. 65–67; Branner, *Manuscript Painting in Paris During the Reign of Saint Louis*, Berkeley, 1977, pp. 14–15, Appendix II.

23. Jacques Hillairet, *Dictionnaire historique des rues de Paris*, Paris, 1963, vol. II, pp. 621–622; Adrien Friedmann, *Paris, ses rues, ses paroisses du moyen âge à la Révolution*, Paris, 1959, pp. 361–363. It seems a fitting coincidence that the Abbot Suger's townhouse had been located at No. 76 on this same street.

Symon le verrier (1297)	12 den.	Saint-Huitace I
Guillaume le voirrier	3 sous	Saint-Germain-l'Auccerais III
Thomas Chace-Pie, voirrier (1297? as Maci)	36 sous	Saint-Germain-l'Auccerais IV
Gautier le voirrier	12 den.	Saint-Leu-et-Saint-Gile
Robert de Saint-Cloout, verrier	3 sous	Saint-Jaque-de-la-Boucherie III
Jehanne la verriere	2 sous	Saint-Jaque IV
LA VERRERIE		
Mestre Raoul, le verrier le roy (1297)	2 sous	Saint-Jehan-en-Greve II
Jehan de Tunes, verrier	12 den.	Saint-Jehan-en-Greve II
Robert le verrier	3 sous	Saint-Pere-des-Arsis
Jehanne la verriere	2 sous	Saint-Pere-aus-Bues
Nicolas le verrier (1296)	12 sous	Saint-Christofle
Ysabelot la verriere	2 sous	Saint-Sevrin-de-Petit-Pont
Lorenz le verrier (1296) (1297)	30 sous	Saint-Sevrin II
Alain le verrier	8 sous	Saint-Benoiet-le-Bestourne
Adam, verrier (1296) (1297)	18 sous	Sainte-Genevieve-la-Grant I

The following are listed for comparison:

Aalis l'ymaginiere (sculptress)	12 den.
Honoré l'enlumineur	10 sous
Mestre Jehan de Ceranz, maçon le Roi	6 livres
Jehanne la coiffiere le Roy	36 sous
Perronnele la maçonne	36 sous
Oudinnet son fuiz	
Maalot sa pucelle	12 den.

the possibility that *verrier* could already be merely a surname, since the beginning of that onomastic development, in both France and England, can be traced to this generation of the population.[24] On the basis of Karl Michaëlsson's general conclusions about that question in these tax rolls, I think it unlikely, though, as Baron admits, it is a possibility.

The problem of the ambiguous term *verrier* is

24. The further problem raised by Wentzel (see n. 2 supra), that glass painters may have gone under the general title "pictores," is probably only relevant for a much later period. But on the development of surnames in the period under discussion in this article, see: Karl Michaëlsson, *Etudes sur les noms de personne français d'après les rôles de taille parisiens (rôles de 1292, 1296–1300, 1313)* (Uppsala Universitets Årsskrift, I), Uppsala, 1927, esp. p. 87: Jean Favier, *Philippe le Bel*, Paris, 1978, pp. 107–108; Gustav Fransson, *Middle English Surnames of Occupation 1100–1350* (Lund Studies in English III), Lund, 1935, rpt. 1967, pp. 29–41, 185 (Verrer).

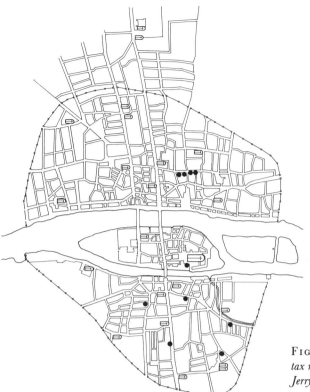

FIG. 4. *Plan of Paris with locations of glaziers listed in the tax roll of 1296. Four live on la rue de la Verrerie. (Drawing: Jerry Bowes)*

not as difficult as it might appear. Did these individuals blow glass, or did they produce glazed windows? The heavy energy consumption of a glass furnace and the constant danger of fire make it likely that, in urban Paris, only those taxpayers living at the Verrerie would have been glass-blowers—making not only flat glass for windows but also glass vessels. One of them, and only one on all the rolls, is so specified: "Jehanne la verriere, marcheande de teiles," whose flourishing shop can be traced in 1296, 1297, and 1313. Since *teile* (teille, telle, tele) means "pan, crucible, vase with a wide mouth,"[25] her wares were probably apothecary utensils, for glass was not in common use for either everyday or luxury household containers in the thirteenth century. Examples of post-antique European drinking glasses and bottles which date before the fifteenth century are rare.[26]

What conclusions may be drawn beyond those already mentioned, i.e., the scarcity of these crafts-

men and the spread of their locations throughout the city's parishes? Taxes range from 12 deniers (which is also the lowest tax paid by artists stud-

25. A glass *teille* is not mentioned in Old French dictionaries, and can be presumed rare; the normal materials were pottery, tin or wood. See: Tobler-Lommatzsch, *Altfranzösisches Wörterbuch*, Wiesbaden, 1974, vol. X, p. 150 ("teille, telle"); Frederic Godefroy, *Dictionnaire de l'ancienne langue française*, Paris, 1892, vol. VII, pp. 662c ("telle, tele").

26. See illustrations in *The Secular Spirit: Life and Art at the End of the Middle Ages*, New York, 1975, "The Household; *Medieval Art in Upstate New York*, ed. Lillich, Syracuse, 1974, pp. 13–17. On the scarcity of medieval glass and the four types of vessels which have survived see: A. Gasparetto and A. von Saldern, "Glass," *Encyclopedia of World Art* vol. VI, New York, 1962, cols. 378–379. The large find of fragments of footed and stemmed glass goblets excavated at the château of Caen is the earliest known, dated to the end of the thirteenth or beginning of the fourteenth centuries: Michel de Bouard, "Verres à boire du XIIIe siècle trouvés à Caen." *Annales de Normandie* XIV, 1964, pp. 231–240. Only one pre-fourteenth century example is cited (unillustrated) in the remarkable group of medieval glassware in: *Aujourd'hui le moyen âge*, Marseille, 1981, pp. 51–55 and color plate.

LA VERRERIE

Jehan de Chartres, verrier (1297)	10 sous	Saint-Jehan II
Jehanne la verriere, marcheande de teiles (1297)	24 sous	Saint-Jehan II
Huet l'englais, son vallet (1297) (1313)	8 sous	Saint-Jehan II
Jehan le prestre, verrier	8 sous	Saint-Jehan II
Nicholas le verrier (1292)	20 sous	Saint-Christofle
Phelippe le verrier	6 sous	Saint-Sevrin I
Lorenz le voirrier (1292) (1297)	30 sous	Saint-Sevrin II
Pierre de mont-le-heri, verrier (3 other rolls)	12 sous	Saint-Benoist I
Adam le chandelier, verrier (1292) (1297)	36 sous	Sainte-Genevieve-la-Grant I
Pierre le verrier, corratier (see A, below)	8 sous	Sainte-Genevieve-la-Grant II

A: *Corratier* (courratier, courretier, courtier) probably signifies a broker, dealer, wholesaler, since the term also occurs in the rolls as "corratier de vin," "corratier de chevaux," etc.

ied by Baron) to the high-scorer Hue who paid 4 livres 10 sous. Hue's tax is comparable to only two sculptors in the rolls[27] though ten saddlers made at least that much money in the same years.[28] Hue lived at the glassworks and inherited his thriving business from Dame Jehanne, merchant of glass vessels; hence he was probably a businessman in charge of a furnace and not an artist. It was a very rare glazier indeed who made enough income to be taxed a livre or more. Only two can be listed who have no evidence of supplementary trade or income, such as tavern keeping: Maci and Thomas Chace-Pie (probably the same individual since Maci is a diminutive of Thomas) and Nicholas. Only the smallest handful of these artisans can be traced through several rolls, unlike the artists studied by Baron, who often were clustered in dynasties. It therefore seems likely that glaziers in Paris at the end of the thirteenth century were still largely a peripatetic lot, going where the work was. Those employed more or less permanently by the bishop or the court would have escaped the tax in any case.[29]

In this regard the Paris tax rolls of the 1290s offer negative evidence; it can be stated more or less conclusively that in the capital city there were not—as yet—the established dynastic families of glaziers who would appear from the fourteenth

27. On the term *imagier* for sculptor see Baron pp. 40–41. In 1313 Huistace l'ymagier paid 6 livres and Jehan l'imagier, le mestre, paid the same as Hue (4 liv. 10 s.). Baron's list of highly taxed artists (p. 42 n. 26) must be used with caution since two of her high-scorers combined several occupations: Nicolas le peintre was a tavernier and Jehan de Taverni had his hand in several trades.

28. Although saddlers and painters were in the same guild (Baron p. 41), clearly saddlers made more money. Beautiful medieval saddles can be highly decorated: see for example *The Secular Spirit*, color pl. 14, p. 271.

29. Baron p. 40 n. 15.

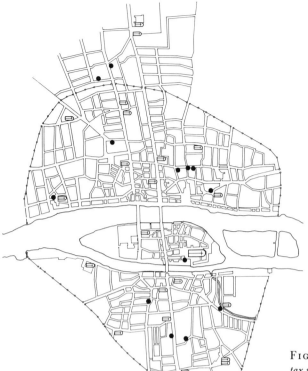

FIG. 5. *Plan of Paris with locations of glaziers listed in the tax roll of 1297. Three (one with an apprentice, also taxed) live on la rue de la Verrerie. (Drawing: Jerry Bowes)*

century on, whom some have suggested for the Gothic period. Stained glass was not—as Branner has established that books already were—designed and made in Paris and therefore ordered there, by customers arriving in the capital for that express purpose, and shipped to the provinces. This does not imply that some form of regular employment was not available, if one were lucky enough to receive an annual salary as "caretaker of the glass" from a great abbey like Saint-Denis or from the Victorines or the cathedral chapter. But the accounts published by Grodecki indicate that artisans who made their livings in that way were very few. Master Raoul, listed as the king's glazier (1292, 1297), did not make much money either year; and even the favorite glaziers of the Artois could not count on a steady income every year from that great family (see Appendix).

80

Women

One other conclusion can be reached from an examination of these taxpayers: in addition to Dame Jehanne who sold glass vessels, four others are women. Since many women worked in manuscript painting and as *imagières*[30] this should not

30. The best introduction to the subject of women artists in the Middle Ages is the article by Professor Annemarie Weyl Carr, "Women Artists in the Middle Ages," *The Feminist Art Journal* V no. 1, 1976, pp. 5–9, 26, an excellent and balanced introduction, the footnotes of which collect the important documentation thus far available. Women worked in the book arts and in tapestry and needlework, chiefly. The best study of the former is Dorothy Miner, *Anastaise and Her Sisters*, Baltimore, 1974. For illustrations see the less critical studies by Karen Petersen and J. J. Wilson, *Women Artists*, New York, 1976, ch. 2; and Hugo Munsterberg, *A History of Women Artists*, New York, 1975, ch. 2.

Maci le voirrier (1292?)	48 sous	Saint-Germain II
Symonnet le voirrier (1292)	6 sous	Saint-Huitace IV
Jehan le voirrier, tavernier (see B, below)	8 sous	Saint-Sauveeur
Colart l'escuëlier, verrier	10 sous	Saint-Gerves III
LA VERRERIE		
Mestre Jehan de Chartres, voirrier (1296)	10 sous	Saint-Jehan II
Dame Jehanne la voirriere (1296) Rogerin, son fuiz	24 sous	Saint-Jehan II
Huet, son vallet (1296) (1313)	8 sous	
Raoul le voirrier (1292)	6 sous	Saint-Jehan II
Lorens le voirrier, tavernier (1292) (1296) (see B, below)	20 sous	Saint-Sevrin II
Pierre le voirrier (1296)	12 sous	Saint-Benoiet I
Adam le voirrier (1292) (1296)	36 sous	Sainte-Genevieve-la-Grant I
Robert le voirrier	2 sous	Saint-Leu-et-Saint-Gile
Guillaume le voirrier	2 sous	Saint-Pol I
Vincent le voirrier	2 sous	Saint-Christofle

B: Compare: Thomasse l'enluminerresse, taverniere (1313); Nicolas le paintre, tavernier (1296); Eude le barbier, tavernier (1296).

---

be so surprising. Michaëlsson and Baron have interpreted differently the women taxpayers on the rolls, Baron (pp. 42–43) suggesting that they were not practicing craftswomen but merely widows directing a shop in order to hold it together for minor sons. The evidence in the book trades has been given a different reading by Branner, where it is becoming increasingly evident that women found a ready employ. Karl Michaëlsson's observations (1313, pp. xviii–xix) about women in the tax rolls underline the latter view. He notes that while there were professions reserved for women and others where a widow might continue the trade of her husband, it was by no means unusual for a woman to have a different occupation from her husband, and that some women were taxed as "head of household" while working wives paid half the family impost.

The percentage of the four taxed women glaziers to the total is exactly the percentage of women to men discovered by Douglas Farquhar[31] for the painters' guild in Bruges in 1454: 12%. There is no reason to assume that they were not practicing artisans, a long-maintained tradition in French stained glass production. To mention

---

31. Miner, p. 24.

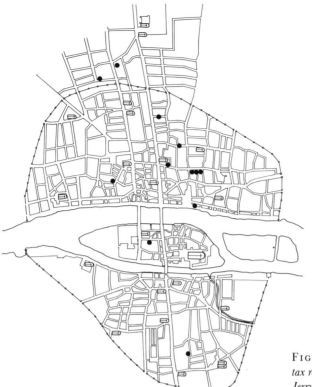

FIG. 6. *Plan of Paris with locations of glaziers listed in the tax roll of 1313. Three live on la rue de la Verrerie. (Drawing: Jerry Bowes)*

only three documented restoration accounts of the eighteenth century: (a) the stained glass of Poitiers Cathedral was restored in 1775–1778 by "la veuve Reverad et son gendre Descantes, peintres verriers . . .";[32] (b) the *fabrique* at the Cathedral of Dol in 1731–1734 made payment for restorations "a dernault vitrier et a sa souer";[33] (c) a large repair and releading job was undertaken at Dol in 1768 by the widow "duvergee vitrier."[34] Glassblowing is hard physical work and was probably done by men. But since the late thirteenth-century documentation establishes that glass was regularly purchased for stained glass projects, there is no reason to assume that the four Parisian women *verrières* were not practicing artisans, glass painters.

The form of payment for the caretaker-glazier was an annual salary, as we have seen at Saint-Denis from the 1280s and at Chartres by at least 1317.[35] Delaporte was no doubt correct that High

Gothic apprentices and journeymen were compensated by the day or perhaps piecemeal, since the early fourteenth-century glaziers in the Appendix paid their workmen that way. But how was a great commission for a new monument paid? For this we know of no evidence from the churches of the capital or indeed any of the great cathedrals glazed in the thirteenth century. There is some evidence in, of all places, Brittany.

---

32. Louis Grodecki, "Les Vitraux de la cathédrale de Poitiers," *Congrès archéologique* CIXe session, 1951, p. 141.

33. Arch. dépt. Ille-et-Vilaine G 377c.

34. Arch. dépt. Ille-et-Vilaine G 281. Women appear infrequently in the illustrations of glaziers in the *Diderot Encyclopedia, The Complete Illustrations 1762–1777*, New York, 1978, Vol. IV pp. 2571, 2580, 2612.

35. Jusselin published the contract of March 5, 1317, between the chapter at Chartres and Gaufridus vitrarius (pp. 299–300); see also Delaporte, p. 20.

Pierre verrier, esmailleur (see C, below)	12 sous	Saint-Germain V
Remont le verrier	3 sous	Saint-Sauveur
Robert le verrier, talemelier (1297) (see C, below)	60 sous	Saint-Leu-et-Saint-Gile
Edeline la verriere	18 sous	Saint-Nicolas-des-Champs
Robert de gaillo, verrier	6 sous	Saint-Merri II
Thomas l'anglois, verrier	3 sous	Saint-Merri IV
Bernart le verrier	3 sous 6 den.	Saint-Jehan I

LA VERRERIE

Guiart le verrier (added: lorrein)	18 den.	Saint-Jehan II
Jehan de ses, verrier (see Appendix for his contracts with Countess of Artois)	18 sous	Saint-Jehan II
Hue le verrier (1296) (1297)	4 livres 10 sous	Saint-Jehan II
Richardin le voirrier, orfevre (see C, below)	18 den.	Saint-Maciel
Bertran le voirier	12 sous	Saint-Benoit II

C: Michaëlsson (*Etudes sur les noms de personne*) noted the frequency of several occupations listed for the same taxpayer. A talemelier was a baker.

Bretons

One says "of all places, Brittany" because it is commonly believed that Breton glazing flourished only from the fifteenth century on, when indeed great dynasties of glaziers produced much beautiful work marked by a noteworthy regional expressionism.[36] There is, however, Gothic stained glass still existing in Brittany: at the Cathedral of Dol (Ille-et-Vilaine);[37] in the former Benedictine priory of Saint-Magloire, Léhon (Côtes-du-Nord);[38] in the former Benedictine Abbey of

36. For an introduction see Jean Lafond's paragraphs on Brittany in *Le Vitrail français*, Paris, 1958, pp. 194, 235–236. See most recently, with bibliography: *Le Vitrail breton, Arts de l'Ouest* no. 3 (November 1977) (Centre de recherches sur les arts anciens et modernes de l'ouest de la France, U.E.R. des arts, Université de Haute-Bretagne, Rennes); reviewed by Catherine Brisac in *Bulletin monumental* v. 136, 1978, pp. 370–371. In the Arch. dépt. Ille-et-Vilaine, Fonds Couffon (28 F 41): manuscript of René Couffon listing the Breton glaziers from the late fourteenth through eighteenth centuries, with concentration on those of the fifteenth and sixteenth centuries.

37. René Couffon, "La Cathédrale de Dol," *Congrès archéologique* v. 126, 1968, pp. 55–56 and bibliography.

38. René Couffon, "Contribution à l'étude des verrières

Saint-Méen (Ille-et-Vilaine);[39] and in the parish church of Saint-Alban (Côtes-du-Nord).[40] The windows of Dol include the arms of Bishop Thibaud de Pouancé, an agent of King Philippe-le-hardi as well as of his son; the glass of Léhon was a benefaction of the Beaumanoir family and in 1636 still contained their arms; and the fragments at Saint-Méen and the borders of the east window of Saint-Alban still include the arms of the dukes of Brittany.

For a contract made by a duke of Brittany with a named glazier, however, it is necessary to investigate the destroyed Carmelite church at Ploërmel (Morbihan), *château-fort* often used as residence by the dukes. The future Jean II, as Count of Richmond, brought two Carmelites to Ploërmel in 1273, and upon becoming Duke of Brittany in 1286 he began construction of a monastery for the growing community.[41] Title passed in 1304 though the complex was not yet complete, and following Jean II's accidental death in Lyons the following year, he was buried at Ploërmel in a white marble tomb of which the gisant still remains.[42] In his will, Duke Jean left the following provisions for the project:[43]

"As Freres du Charme de Ploermel M. lib. turon. a asouir [achever] les edifices par la main des esecuteurs. . . .
"Au Vitrier de Redon XXVII lib. XII s."

Who the glazier of Redon was and what the contract included can be established by a document of 1307, now in the Archives départementales de la Loire-Atlantique:[44]

Sachent touz que ge Loranz le vitrier de Redon ay eu et receu por totes les vitres du Carme que ge ay mis en liglese du Carme et en lenfermerie trente et set lbr. dez souz par la men Jean Le Rey borgois de Plermel [,] conte fet ou jour de vendredi en la feste de la Mad. O Monsour Bertran de la Hasaye chapeleen mon segnour le duc et o metre Andre de Joe [,] as dites trente et set lbr. dez souz por totes chouses. De laquelle some dargent davant dite ge me tien a bien

paye. En tesmoyg de laquelle chouse ge done ces letres seelees du seaul Pierres Baltoh . . [Baden?] a mes preeres [,] porquoi ge n'avoye propre seaul. Done ou jor davant D . . . [=dit?] lan de graece mil treis cenz et set.

Item je receuy pour celle besoigne neuf livres diz et oict solz. Donne comme dessus.

This document establishes that the "glazier of Redon" was named Laurent and that he was paid by men who can be identified from the will as the Duke's agents: Pierre de Baden, Mons. Bertrant de la Hasaye, Jean le Roy. Laurent was paid, for the windows of the church and the infirmary of the Carmelite monastery, the sum of 37 liv. 10 sous. By deducting from that total the amount of the Duke's bequest we arrive at what had been paid him by the Duke as an advance, or 9 liv. 18 sous—the amount that he acknowledges having received at the end of the document. The total sum is roughly comparable to that which the

anciennes du département des Côtes-du-Nord," *Bulletin et mémoires de la Société d'émulation des Côtes-du-Nord* LXVII, 1935, pp. 84–86. Illustrated in color in Louis-Michel Gohel, *Les Vitraux de Bretagne*, Rennes, 1981, p. 2.

39. A. André, "De la verrerie et des vitraux peints dans l'ancienne province de Bretagne," *Bulletin et mémoires de la Société archéologique du département d'Ille-et-Vilaine* XII, 1878, pp. 196–197.

40. Couffon, "Contribution," pp. 87–93 and fig. 4. Illustrated in color in Gohel, *Bretagne*, p. 4.

41. Arthur de la Borderie, *Histoire de Bretagne*, Rennes, 1899, v. III, p. 365; M. R. Michel-Dansac, "Ploërmel," *Congrès archéologique* 81st session, 1914, p. 293.

42. The tombs of Jean II and of Jean III (d. 1341) now share a common slab in the more recent church of Saint-Armel in Ploërmel; the Carmelite church was demolished in 1596. Michel-Dansac p. 301.

43. The testament of Duke Jean II of Brittany is published by: Dom Hyacinthe Morice, *Mémoires pour servir de preuves à l'histoire ecclesiastique et civile de Bretagne*, Paris, 1742, vol. I, cols. 1193–1200. For the vitrier, col. 1198; receipted, col. 1200. I would like to thank Rosaline Landy of Cambridge for help with the language of this will.

44. This document was found in the Château de Nantes by A. de la Borderie and was published, as far as I am aware, only by Arthur Ramé in the *Journal de Rennes* of March 29, 1855 (12e année, no. 38). It is now Arch. dépt. Loire-Atlantique E 22 no. 79. I am grateful to the director of the archives, X. du Boisrouvray, for help in identifying this document.

Chapter of Chartres in 1317 contracted to pay their glazier Geoffroy for a complete repair of all the windows of Chartres Cathedral (30 livres chartr.), work expected to take him at least a year.[45] That is, Laurent was commissioned for this work and paid an advance of nearly three-quarters of the sum by the Duke, the final 25% coming to him upon completion.

The glass which Laurent put into the infirmary was probably grisaille; one can compare, for example, the thirteenth-century grisailles of the chapter house and refectory of the Abbey of Saint-Germain-des-Prés, which still remained in the eighteenth century.[46] But the church itself no doubt received some colored and historiated windows. The Carmelite Convent of Ploërmel was destroyed in 1596, but the Benedictine abbey church of Saint-Sauveur still remains in Redon, Laurent's home base, with a handsome Gothic chevet bearing a family resemblance to the Cathedral of Tours and other rayonnant Capetian structures.[47] Of its glazing (removed just before the Revolution) we have two partial accounts: one provides a stylistic dating to the late thirteenth century, and the other suggests the noble patrons. The date can be established by the fragment of border which still existed in the early nineteenth century,[48] with the fleurs-de-lys and castles which are common coin in French stained glass of the second half of the thirteenth century[49] and which still exist in Brittany in the stained glass of Dol and Léhon. The donors can be established by the 1780 description of the windows by Jean Ogee:[50]

> Sur les anciennes vitres de l'Eglise de cette Maison, on remarque les portraits de plusieurs Ducs & Duchesses de Bretagne, & de quelques Seigneurs des maisons de Rohan, de Rieux, de Rochefort, de Châteaubriand, & de Malestroit.

All of these families were represented in the forces of the Duke of Brittany whose coats of arms are preserved in the Wijnberghen Roll of about 1280.[51]

Thus the Benedictine church of Redon was without reasonable doubt glazed with Gothic windows in the same generation as Saint-Méen (where the Duke's arms still appear) and the Carmelite convent of Ploërmel. One glazier could probably have been established at Redon and supported himself by commissions in the region very comfortably.

Redon is near the south Breton coast, above the mouth of the Loire. The bishop-counts of Dol on the north Breton coast, not far from Mont-Saint-Michel, were powerful temporal lords in constant conflict with the dukes of Brittany in the thir-

45. After the total restoration he was to be paid 6 liv. as an annual salary for their continued upkeep. Jusselin pp. 299–300.

46. Henri Sauval, *Histoire et recherches des antiquitez de la ville de Paris*, Paris, 1742, pp. 340–341. The Cathedral of Dol still has remnants of many handsome grisailles in the choir, dating about 1280–1285.

47. *Dictionnaire des églises de France*, ed. Laffont (Paris: 1968) IV A 122–124, dates the beginning of Gothic building to 1256 and its completion to Abbot Jehan de Guipry (d. 1307). See also Pierre Héliot, "Le Chevet de Saint-Sauveur à Redon," *Bulletin et mémoires de la Société archéologique du département d'Ille-et-Vilaine* LXXIX, 1976, pp. 31–51.

48. Arthur Ramé found this border at Redon (*Journal de Rennes* 1855). Couffon (1968) p. 56 states that Ramé found the border and some grisaille; Ramé only states he found the border.

49. It has long been recognized that the border France/Castille does not indicate a royal commission but was a ubiquitous design employed by glaziers in this generation: Louis Grodecki, *Vitraux des églises de France*, Paris, 1947, pp. 23–25.

50. Jean Ogee, *Dictionnaire historique et géographique de la province de Bretagne*, Nantes, 1780, vol. IV, p. 7. The glass was not destroyed in the Revolution, but removed intentionally by the monks between Ogee's visit and that event: (Anonymous), *Histoire abrégée de la ville et de l'abbaye de Redon*, Redon, 1864, p. 339 n. 1.

51. Paul Adam-Even and L. Jéquier, "Un Armorial français de XIIIe siècle: l'armorial Wijnbergen," *Archives héraldiques suisses*, v. 65–68 (1951–1954): the *marche* of Brittany is #921–1020. This *marche* cannot be dated precisely, though it must predate 1308: Adam-Even suggests about 1280. In the roll the families named in the Redon glass are: Rohan (#927), Rieux (#990), Rochefort (#940), Châteaubriand (#937), and Malestroit (#970). Since families normally die out or branch in less than six generations it is unlikely that this same confluence would occur very much after the Gothic era.

teenth century[52] and one would expect their fiefs to support a separate economy. It is, in fact, possible to establish the existence of a family of glaziers at Dol. Their names occur in the obituary of the cathedral chapter known as the *Livre rouge*, which can be dated on internal evidence to the period between 1312 and 1323.[53] Arranged by the logic of what they tell us, the undated entries are:[54]

Septembri F. Kal	. . . Item cum *heredibus Guillelmi le Vitrier* V sol. . . .
Januarius A. XVI. Kal.	Objit Johannes Hastivel clericus qui dedit ad anniversarium suum faciendum XXti. sol. annui redditus super quod platea sita in parrochia Beate Marie inter domum Gregorii de Hirel presbiteri ex una parte et *domum heredum Guillelmi le Vitrier* ex altera.
Aprilis. E. VIII. Idus.	. . . Item IX sol. & I caponem cum *heredibus Guillelmi Bordin videlicet cum Onessia la Vitrere*. . . .
Septembri E. II Kal.	. . . Item cum *Juliano Bordin* in domibus suis. Item XL. sol. super domos suas . . .
Januarius D. II Idus.	Objit *Julianus Bordin* qui dedit ad anniversarium suum faciendum XLII. sol. videlicet XX. sol. super domum Roberti Maunorri presbiteri. Item XX sol. super domum (Rad(ulf)i Herpin. Item II sol. super domum magistri Hernandi Seguim.

FIG. 7. *Dol Cathedral, east window, Washing of the Feet (Passion cycle), glazier Guillaume Bordin? (Photo: ARCH. PHOT. / SPADEM / VAGA, New York 1985)*

What relationship Julian had to the defunct Guillaume is undeterminable and Julian may have turned his obvious business acumen to a trade other than glazing—his gifts are huge by the standards of this cartulary—but it is possible to

52. Pierre Mauclerc's violences against Dol were investigated by the King's agents at the inquest of 1235. Relations with Mauclerc's son Jean I le Roux were calm, but definitely not with Jean II, who came to power in 1286. An old tradition I have been unable to verify maintains that the Bishop of Dol attempted to get Jean II excommunicated by the Pope in the early 1290s; it seems clear that the episcopal châteaux were fortified at the start of the fourteenth century for fear of the Duke's retaliation. F. Duine, "Histoire civile et politique de Dol jusqu'en 1789," *L'Hermine, Revue litteraire et artistique de Bretagne* v. 37, 1907, pp. 84, 86.

53. The *Livre rouge* is now in Arch. dépt. Ille-et-Vilaine G 281; a nineteenth-century copy is in the same archives, Fonds Delabigne-Villeneuve (1 F 204). The original scribal hand includes obits of 1312 (Bishop Thomas de Moreac of Dol and Bishop Guillaume Bouvet of Bayeux); it has no entries for the next bishops of Dol (d. 1324, 1328, etc.) and has notes in an added hand datable 1349, 1357, etc.

54. I would like to thank Professor Philip Gallagher for verification of my transcriptions and for cautionary suggestions.

FIG. 8. *Dol Cathedral, east window, St. Samson with the dragon on a leash, glazier Onessia Bordin? (Photo: ARCH. PHOT. / SPADEM / VAGA, New York 1985)*

FIG. 9. *Dol Cathedral, east window, the Wheel of St. Catherine, glazier Julian Bordin? (Photo: ARCH. PHOT. / SPADEM / VAGA, New York 1985)*

assume that Guillaume Bordin the glazier left, at his death, Onessia la vitrere his widow (possibly daughter) and established financial assets.

I have been tempted to see in this family group the three hands of the great east window-wall of Dol Cathedral,[55] where the artist in charge (Guillaume Bordin?), as well as the second in seniority (Onessia?), both train and produce cartoons for a third (Figs. 7, 8, 9). The final few panels in the mature style of the third artist are among the most spectacular explosions of expressionism in western France. One can easily imagine him as the young Julian Bordin, later to achieve success and the riches which appear in the Dol cartulary entries. To add credence to this hypothesis: it would be reasonable that Julian had been named for his grandfather—the normal Gothic practice; and the first glazier at Dol, whose style precedes those of the great east window where his patternbook remains in use, was probably trained at Le Mans Cathedral. Le Mans is the cathedral of St. Julian.

At any rate the great east window of Dol, and the precious scraps still in nearby abbeys which enjoyed ducal and aristocratic patronage, all provide evidence of established regional craftsmen—whom the Dol cartulary possibly names by name.

The Stained Glass Craft After 1280

Without the evidence, faulty and skimpy as it is, from the Paris tax rolls, any interpretation at all of the fragmentary documentation of these Gothic glaziers of Brittany would be unthinkable. With the Paris rolls, it is possible to hypothesize that a few provincial glaziers were, by the late Capetian era, not peripatetic in work habits but established and stable and earning a good living from the work their regions provided. While we have assumed that this "Late Gothic" development took place during the troubled fourteenth century—when so many social patterns changed—the evidence in Brittany shows otherwise.

---

55. My theories about the several generations of glaziers working at Dol will appear in *The Armor of Light* ch. V.

87

There must have been a similar situation in Arras; the Appendix records that the first glazier working for the Count of Artois, probably by 1294, was Master Othon of Arras, who made his panels in Arras and was paid to transport and install them; Othon was still working for the House of Artois in 1311, and in 1312 his son, Master Jacques, was in charge of the shop.

In the last decades of the thirteenth century glass was clearly not being ordered in Paris and shipped out, and just as clearly large mobile cathedral *chantiers* were no longer required, whether or not any still operated in that old pattern. In 1279, at Tours, for example, Richardus the glazier rented a house in the cathedral's cloister next door to the house of Etienne de Mortagne, master mason of the cathedral.[56] Such a cluster of craftsmen at work on a campaign of reconstruction would suggest that they were peripatetic still, and had come *to* Tours *for* this job.

But that was 1279. A definite change in the practice of the stained glass craft was under way, beginning in the 1280s. Previously, in the twelfth and early thirteenth centuries, it is reasonable to presume glaziers had moved from job to job and had probably set up their own furnaces to produce much of their material themselves. The treatise of Theophilus gives instructions in close succession for making glass in a furnace and for making stained glass windows and painting them. He also tells us how to make the furnace. Whether or not the great chantiers (such as Chartres and Bourges) made their own glass cannot be proven, but there is no documentary evidence whatsoever for the purchase of such large amounts of glass by the Chapter, which did keep records. On the basis of style, art historians have assumed, probably correctly, that the personnel of the great chantiers fluctuated as glaziers came and went. It seems likely that they were trained in all aspects of their craft, as Theophilus demonstrates, and that, probably, the toilsome or boring tasks around the furnace would be assigned to apprentices, while only those men more advanced in their careers might —at least in a large chantier—be able to "specialize" in glassblowing or in designing and painting.

By the last decades of the thirteenth century this picture changed. The distinction between glaziers who make glass and sell it, and glaziers who buy it and paint it and make decorative windows from it, indicated this change. Both art historians[57] and archeologists[58] have recognized the appearance of a new glass technology at about this same moment. Glass by 1300 was thinner and clearer, and it came in larger pieces. Is this technological improvement an indication of specialization, either its cause or its effect? Perhaps, after about 1280, not everyone *could* blow glass of sufficient quality to satisfy the rising expectations of craftsmen or of the public.

Research in another area may verify this hypothesis. The technique of silver stain, by which yellow spots are produced on glass by touching it with a silver compound and then firing, was probably transferred from Arabic sources to Paris between 1280 and 1285, via the *Lapidario* of Alfonso el Sabio.[59] In addition to "ecce" (the stone

56. A. Salmon, "Documents sur quelques architectes et artistes de l'église cathédrale de Tours," *Mémoires de la Société archéologique de Touraine* IV, 1847–1853, pp. 130–138; Linda Papanicolaou, "Stained Glass Windows of the Choir of the Cathedral of Tours," Ph.D. dissertation, New York University, 1979, pp. 27–28.

57. The pioneer study is Jean-Jacques Gruber, "Quelques aspects de l'art et de la technique du vitrail en France (Dernier tiers du XIIIe siècle, premier tiers du XIVe), published in Université de Paris, Faculté des lettres, *Travaux des étudiants du Groupe d'histoire de l'art*, Paris, 1927–1928, pp. 71–94. See also exhibition catalogs: *Art and the Courts: France and England from 1259–1328*, National Gallery of Canada, Ottawa, 1972, v. I, pp. 108–112; *Transformations of the Court Style: Gothic Art in Europe 1270 to 1330*, Rhode Island School of Design, Providence, 1977, pp. 100–109.

58. See "Artisanat du verre" in *Aujourd'hui le moyen âge* (cited in n. 26 supra), pp. 51–53. The thesis of D. Foy, "Le Verre médiéval et son artisanat en France méditerranéenne: état de la question," Université d'Aix (3e cycle), 1981, should be mentioned; I have not had the opportunity to read it.

59. On silver stain (with bibliography) see: Lillich, "European Stained Glass around 1300: The Introduction of Silver Stain," *Papers of the XXVth International Congress of the History of Art, 1983*, Vienna to appear.

which produces yellow on glass), the *Lapidario* also describes "caoz":[60]

> Its properties are such that if its powder is mixed with glass when it is being made (melted), it will not shatter when it is later removed from the fire, as is often the case, and (the glass) can be stretched by hammering it (!), and it stands the hammer blows, and can be shaped as you wish, in the same way as gold or silver, without losing its clarity.

This remarkable stone, which smells of vinegar, will also stick to the tongue and is helpful for intestinal ulcers and for menstruating women. While hammering would seem to be an extreme test of success, it does appear that a stronger glass was being developed in northern Europe at about the same time that silver stain was introduced.

The careful search for evidence of this development must take place, at least in part, in the scientific laboratory. But equally careful historical research can also play a role. Grodecki estimated that, despite centuries of destruction, some 15,000 to 20,000 stained glass panels of the thirteenth century alone still remain in France, most of them unstudied.[61] The meticulous archival documentation of this fragile but vast treasure can certainly continue to produce much new data not only for art history but for the social, economic, and technological history of the Middle Ages as well.

---

60. Alfonso el Sabio, *Lapidario & Libro de las formas & ymagenes*, ed. Roderic C. Diman and Lynn W. Winget, Madison, Wisconsin, 1980, p. 106. I would like to thank Joanne Foxford and Professor Reinaldo Ayerbe for much assistance with this translation.

61. *Vitrail français*, Paris, 1958, p. 115.

APPENDIX

Glaziers' contracts with the House of Artois. The texts are selected from Jules-Marie Richard, *Une Petit-nièce de Saint Louis, Mahaut, comtesse d'Artois et de Bourgogne (1303–1329)* (Paris: 1887).

I. Jean de Sées, Parisian glazier
   He was the only glazier employed by the Countess for work in her properties in Paris and Conflans. I have hypothesized about Jean de Sées' career in "European Stained Glass around 1300: The Introduction of Silver Stain," *Papers of the XXVth International Congress of the History of Art* (Vienna: to appear), at notes 71 ff.

   A. 1312–13, Hôtel d'Artois, Paris: Jean de Sées worked under the direction of Evrart d'Orleans (for whose career see *Thieme-Becker* vol. 11:115)
   En celle année fist Jehan de Seez, verrier, les verrieres des chasis qui furent en la sale et les verrieres de la chapele de la chambre madame et de la garde robe, et seur ces verrieres bailla Everart à mestre Jehan de Sez, XLVI lb. par.
   (Richard p. 303: Arch. nat. KK 393, fol. 35)

   B. 1316–19, hôtel de Conflans
   Je Jehan de Ses, voirrier, fais savoir à touz que j'ai eu et receu de maistre Estiene, tresorier madame la contesse d'Artois et de Bourgongne, pour XXVII paniaus de voirre ouvrés et une chapelle d'ymagerie à tabernacles, qui montoient VIIxx piés, mis as fenestres de la tour del hostel madite dame à Conflans, IIII s. VI d. le pié, trente et une livres dis soulz parisis. Item, pour clous pour les dis voirres, dis soulz. Et m'en tien à bien paié. En tesmoing de ce j'ai mis mon seel à ces lettres faites le IIIIe jour d'aoust à Conflans l'an mil CCC et XVIII.
   (Richard pp. 294, 303 n. 4: A 366)
   140 feet of glass, at 4 sous 6 deniers the foot.

Since this is the price for colored designs, the "chapelle d'ymagerie à tabernacles" can be presumed to describe the glazing design. Jean de Sées sealed with his own seal.

C. 1319

A Jehan de Ses, voirrier de Paris, pour IIII petis paniaus de voirre vigneté, tenanz V pies et demie, II s. VI d. le pié, mis es chasseis des II clotés coste la chapele, III paniaus de voirre blanc mis au drecheur, et I O de voirre blanc mis en la garde robe haute coste le celier, et IIII paniaus de voirre blanc mis en chasseis de la chambre coste le viex chapelle tenanz XXX pies, II s. le pié. Pour V piés de voirre d'ymagerie mis en la fourme du grant clotel coste la chapele, III s. VI d.

(Richard pp. 303–4: A 372)

"Verre vigneté" costs 2 sous 6 deniers the foot; white glass, 2 sous; "verre imagé," 4 sous 6 deniers. "Verre vigneté" is now known as grisaille.

D. 1318–23, Hôtel d'Artois, repairs following the fire of 1317

A Jehan de Ses, verrier pour le viex voirre de la fourme du pignon ou le feu se prist, apparellier, dessendre et rasseoir par marchié fait par monsgr le prevost d'Ayre, C s.

Item, audit Jehan pour LXII piés de voirre es hoetaus du pignon, vigneté et armoié à listres de couleurs de ladite fourme, III s. le pié, valent IX lb. VI s.

Item, audit Jehan pour III paniaus de voirre blanc tenans IX piés, qui sunt haut delez l'huis de la paneterie, II s. VI d. du pié, valent XXII s. VI d.

Item, audit Jehan pour les verrieres de la consirgerie apparellier pour plon, voirre et estain, X s.

Item, audit Jehan que on lui devoit de viel pour l'aparellement des verreries de la

chambre madame pour plon, verre et estain, pour journées d'ouvriers et les escucheons changer, XIIII s.

Item, audit Jehan pour apparellier les verrieres de la chapelle et pour I crucefiement dedans, XII s.

Item, audit Jehan pour IIII piés de voirre assis en la fruiterie de Paris pour le vent, VIII s.

Item, audit Jehan pour la grant voirriere du bout de la salle devers le praiel et les fenestres de la petite salle delez la chambre madame dessus et dessous, pour plon, voirre et estain et journées, XX s. VI d.

(Richard pp. 304–5: A 359, dated Chandeleur 1318)

This account includes grisailles "armoié" in colored bands, new coats of arms, and a crucifixion scene. The glazier is paid for lead, tin (solder), and glass for repairs, and for his workmen's wages, as well as for an old bill for previous work.

His receipt follows:

(18 l. 13 s. par.) pour le viex voirre du pignon de la salle reparellier, LXII piés de voirre mis es hocteaus dudit pignon vignetez et armoiés, III paneaus de voirre delez la paneterie et en la verriere du bout de la salle devers les praiaus.

(Richard p. 305 n. 1: A 365)

E. 1321, Hôpital Saint-Jacques
Jean de Sées was paid 10 lb., probably for colored designs.

(Richard p. 305: A 400)

F. 1323

A Jehan de Ses, verrier, pour II panniaus de verres tenant X piez mis en la chambre neue, pour II panniaus mis aus aloes de coste la neue chambre, tenant V piez, pour IIII panniaus mis ou palleur de coste la neue chambre tenant XXI piez, III s. pour pié, valent CVIII s. Et pour I pannea mis en I chassis en la chapelle neue, tenant V piez et demi, IIII s. VI d. pour pié, pour XVIII panniaus mis en la viese chambre madame, tenant LXVI piez IIII s. VI d. pour pié, valent XVI lb. XXI d. Sont en somme XXI lb. IX s. IX d.

(Richard p. 305: A 412)

Included is glass at 3 sous/foot (grisailles with coats of arms) and colored designs at 4 sous 6 deniers/foot.

G. 1329: The new husband of Jean de Sées' widow Marguerite, a glazier named Guillaume Doucet, finishes the work at the hôtel d'Artois. He gives as his address "demeurant à la verriere à Paris," that is, la rue de la Verrerie, where Jean de Sées lived according to the tax roll of 1313. See that roll, supra.

(Richard p. 305)

II. The Artois accounts mention glaziers from Arras and the vicinity for work not at Paris or Conflans. These accounts continue into the second half of the fourteenth century. Included here are those accounts for the period during the lifetime of Jean de Sées, for comparison.

A. Payments to Master Othon, glazier of Arras, for work at the château d'Hesdin

1. 1294 (Othon's name is not mentioned)
    pour le grant fourme de le sale VIIIxx piés de voirre parmi couleurs parmi blanc XII d. le pié VIII lb. Por voire amené d'Arras, por mettre à le grant sale deseure la boutellerie, V s.

    (Richard p. 298: Arch. nat. KK 393)

2. 1299
    A maistre Oste le verrier pour le voirre de gloriette, cest assavoir VIIc et LXXIII piés de voirre blanc XII d. le pié, XXXVIII l. XIII s.
    Pour CV piés de voirre peint d'imagerie II s. le pié, X l. X s. Pour tout ce voirre amener d'Arras à Hesdin XII s. Item XX s. pour toile dont on fist verrieres as fenestres du mares quant li Rois i fu.

    (Richard p. 298: A147)

White glass costs 12 deniers (= 1 sou) the foot, and designs cost 2 sous/foot. The glazier is paid to transport the glass from Arras to Hesdin and install it. Canvas is installed as a temporary measure for the king's visit.

3. 1304—Othon and his son Jacques
    A maistre Hoste, le voirrier d'Arras, por refaire raparlier les voirrieres, des noeves chambres du chastel, Jakemon fix maistre Othe et ses vallés, chascun VI jors, II s. par jor, XII s. Item, III lb. de blanc voirre, VI s. Item, II lb. de voirre de couleur, VI s. Item, pour ce faire, II lb. d'estain, II s. VI d.

    (Richard p. 299 n. 2: Arch. nat. KK 393)

    The atelier (master, son, and two workmen) paid 2 sous per day; glass sold by weight, and a charge for solder, for a repair job. White glass is 2 sous per pound, colored glass is 3 sous/pound. In 1312 the price had fallen: white glass was sold for 1 sou and colored glass for two sous the pound.

    (Richard p. 299: A 297)

B. Payments to Master Jean Le Sauvage, glazier of Arras

1. 1322, Monastery of Sainte-Claire
    (28 l. II s. parisis) pour la demeure de CIX lb. et II s. qui me furent deu pour voirres mis à Sainte-Claire d'ales Saint-Omer tant de couleur comme blanc.

    (Richard pp. 299–300)

2. 1322, chapel of the hospital at Hesdin
    A maistre Jehan le verrier pour le grant fourme de le capele, XLVI piés de blanc voirre, II s. pur chascun pié, sont IIII lb. XII s.

    Item, pour ledite fourme, LIII piés de voirre de couleurs, III s. pour chascun pié, sont VIII lb.

    Item, les II fourmettes des II costés de le capele, XXI piés de blanc voirre, II s. le pié, sont XLII s.

Item, pour desdites fourmettes, XI piés de couleurs, III s. le pie, sont XXXIII s.

Item, pour IX fenestres qui sont ès pans dudit ospital emplies de voirre, si tient chascune fenestre XIIII piés de blanc voirre qui sont en somme VIxv et VI piés, II s, pour chascun pié, XII lb. XII s.

Item, pour chascune de ches IX fenestres V piés de voirre de couleurs qui sont en somme XLV piés, VI lb. XV s.

Item, pour les II fourmes du pignon qui est devers le mer, pour chascune XIIII piés et demi de blanc voirre, XXIV piés, II s. le pié, LVIII s.

Item, pour lesdites fourmes, XXII piés de couleur, III s. le pié, XLVI s.

Somme pour tout cest voirre aporté d'Arras, assis et mis en oevre tout au court del ouvrer, acaté par signeur Andriu de Courcheles et mesuré par maistre Jake de Bouloigne au pié d'Arras, XLI lb. XVIII s. VI d.
(Richard p. 300 n. 1: A 404)

The price of white glass is 2 sous/foot; colored glass, 3 sous/foot. The glazier is paid to transport the work from Arras and install it. Because it is billed by the foot, it was measured to verify the bill.

3. 1323, Hospital of Gosnay
Annexed to the glazier's receipt is a letter verifying the work by the man instructed to measure it, the mason Thomas Harouet.

Très chiers et redoutez sires, j'ai recheu vos lettres esqueles il est contenu que je vous fache savoir la mesure du voirre que li voirriers d'Arras à fait Gosnay. Je signefie pour chertain à votre grant benignité que veschi la mesure des piés des verrieres du moustier des chartrous. Premièrement, pour le grande fourme derriere l'autel, XXVI piés et I quart de blanc voirre. Item, XLIII piés et demi de couleurs en chele fourme meisme. Item, pour I autre fourme, dont il en y a VII qui sont toutes accomplies, et contient en cheli fourme XXIII piés et demi de blanc voirre et XXV piés et demi de couleurs. Item, pour V verrieres petites qui sont devers le cloistre, pour chascune XIII piés et III quars de blanc voirre et V piés et I quart de couleurs. Somme pour tout le blanc voirre XIIxx XIX piés et demi et XIIxx et VII piés et I quart de couleurs, mesuré du pié d'Arras par Jehan Clabaut et par mi qui fu presens au mesurer.
De par Thumas Harouet vostre vallet.
(Richard pp. 300–1: A 421)

4. 1324, château de Beuvry, repair
A Jehan le verrier d'Arras, pour les verrieres du chastel de Beuvri refaire, primes pour I penel de couleurs u quel me sires d'Artois est, qui contient larghement V piés, IIII s. pour chascun piet, XX s.
(Richard p. 301 n. 2: A 423)

The window contains the figure of the Count d'Artois; the charge (for colored design) 4 sous/foot.

Jean Le Sauvage continued to work for the House of Artois until his death around 1333, when he was replaced by his brother Jacques.
(Richard p. 301)

92

A "WEEPING" GLASS BOWL AT THE ASHMOLEAN MUSEUM

Roy Newton and Robert H. Brill

In mid-1979, Dr. Donald B. Harden called Roy Newton's attention to the existence of a strange glass bowl which had been in the Ashmolean Museum for nearly 100 years.[1] It was known to be "weeping" and then was generally believed to be late Hellenistic or early Roman in date. It seemed inconceivable that such a deteriorating object could have existed intact for nearly two millennia.

The surface was permanently sticky to the touch, and any original labels had long been lost, but David Brown, an Assistant Keeper at the museum, succeeded in identifying it as Glass No. 73 of the Fortnum gift. Described in Fortnum's list as having been "cracked by fire," it was bought in Rome in 1882, lent to the Ashmolean in 1886, and given in 1888. It is said to have been on exhibition in the museum for some years before there was much evidence of the slow, spontaneous cracking which Donald Harden subsequently observed. In the 1880s it appears to have been "whole but cracked," whereas in 1929 it was in several pieces. Harden arranged for its repair, but the glue did not hold, and it was not long before the bowl fell to pieces again. In 1980 it was in many pieces, and there seems to be little doubt that much deterioration had occurred since 1929.

Two chemical analyses have been carried out. The first, by Dr. A. M. Pollard of the Research Laboratory for Archaeology and the History of Art at the University of Oxford,[2] revived questions about the bowl's origin. The second analysis was arranged by Dr. Robert H. Brill of The Corning Museum of Glass and carried out by Dr. Brant Rising of Lucius Pitkin, Inc., New York City. The results of the latter, a quantitative analysis, are given in the accompanying table (Fig. 1).

In 1981, David Brown, Mark Pollard, and Robert Brill examined the bowl at Oxford. A light amber color, it is heavily crizzled and was apparently blown. The base has a shallow kick and seems once to have had a pontil mark; the form seems peculiar for an ancient piece.

The chemical analyses show that the bowl is a modern object which could not have been made in antiquity. The following comments support this conclusion:

Comparison with Compositions of Ancient Glasses[3]

1. The analyzed composition of this bowl does not resemble the composition of any category of ancient glass familiar to the authors. Neither does the analysis match those of any of the several hundred individual glasses analyzed by The Corning Museum of Glass.

2. The alkali content is one unusual feature. The glass contains considerably more potash

---

1. Letter to R. G. Newton from D. B. Harden, June 7, 1979.

2. Letters from A. M. Pollard to R. G. Newton, October 7, 17, 1980.

3. Robert H. Brill, Report on the Chemical Analysis of a "Late Hellenic" Bowl in the Ashmolean Museum, May 27, 1981 (unpublished).

TABLE 1. Chemical Analysis of the "Weeping" Bowl

CMG sample *no. 4068*

SiO_2	Δ	~ 77.3%
Na_2O	a	7.99
CaO	a	0.33
K_2O	a	13.4
MgO	a	0.01
Al_2O_3	a	0.14
Fe_2O_3	a	0.29
TiO_2		nf
Sb_2O_5	a	nf
MnO	a	<0.005
CuO		0.032
CoO		nf
SnO_2		nf
Ag_2O		nf
PbO		0.40
BaO		<0.01
SrO		nf
Li_2O		0.02
Rb_2O		0.10
B_2O_3		0.01
V_2O_5		nf
Cr_2O_3		nf
NiO		nf
ZnO		0.011
ZrO_2		nf
Bi_2O_3		nf
P_2O_5		–
As_2O_5		nf

Analysis by Dr. Brant Rising and co-workers, Lucius Pitkin, Inc., New York City. (LP918358)

a= by atomic absorption; all other values by emission spectrography.

Δ = SiO_2 estimated by difference from 100%.

(K_2O) than soda (Na_2O), whereas the majority of ancient glasses contain much more soda than potash.[4] (Only rarely has a predominance of potash over soda been found. One instance is a group of glasses from northern Italy dating about 1000–800 B.C. They have a similar K_2O/Na_2O ratio, but the percentages of the other oxides do not at all match the analysis of this bowl.)

3. Similarly, the analysis of the bowl does not resemble the composition of any of the approximately 400 medieval glasses analyzed at

4. This is in marked contrast to Turner's conclusion that ancient glasses are always complex in character. W. E. S. Turner, "Studies in Ancient Glasses and Glassmaking Processes. Part IV. The Chemical Composition of Ancient Glasses," *Journal of the Society of Glass Technology*, 40, 1956, pp. 162T–186T, see p. 171T.

Corning. Although similar K_2O/Na_2O ratios can be found among medieval glasses, the percentages of the other oxides differ greatly from those in the bowl.

4. Rubidium oxide (Rb_2O), probably introduced with the alkali, is decidedly higher than in most ancient glasses, although occasionally rubidium is found in medieval glasses. The lithium oxide (Li_2O) is higher than in most ancient glasses except for some we have analyzed which are known to have been made in Turkey. They, however, are soda glasses with only minor levels of potash.

5. The lime (CaO) content (0.33%) is very much lower than that of any ancient or medieval glass analyzed from any source. Only rarely does the lime content of any ancient or medieval glass fall below about 4%. (There are probably no reliable values at all reported as less than 2.5%—unless the glass is a high-lead glass.)

6. The magnesia (MgO) content (0.01%) is also much lower than those of any ancient or medieval glasses we have analyzed. Only occasionally are magnesia values less than 0.5% found, and the lowest found in any early glass is about 0.3%.

7. It is unusual to find an ancient glass which is virtually free of barium (BaO) and strontium (SrO) oxides, as this one is. However, because these elements are generally thought to be introduced along with calcium, it is not surprising that these two elements are very low in this particular glass.

8. The alumina (Al_2O_3) content (0.14%) is markedly lower than in the large majority of ancient and medieval glasses. The lowest are in the range of 0.4–0.5%.[5]

9. The iron (Fe_2O_3) content (0.29%) is lower than in most ancient glasses. However, there are precedents for iron values of about 0.3–0.4%. Interestingly, some of these low-iron glasses are also amber-colored, but the rest of their compositions are entirely different from that of the bowl.

10. The manganese (MnO) content (0.005%) is lower than in most ancient glasses. Normally, one finds a background level of at least 0.05% MnO, although a few groups are consistently as low as about 0.02%.

11. The amber color of the glass is probably due to the presence of the ferri-sulfide colorant frequently found in ancient glasses. There is nothing else in the composition which would produce an amber color. This coloring species is so intense that even as little iron as is present in this glass would be sufficient to produce some amber color, providing that sulfur was also present and that the glass was chemically reduced. The analytical method would not have detected sulfur but the analysis done by Dr. Pollard could have shown some because he used x-ray fluorescence.

The chemical durability of this glass, as judged from its analysis, is expected to be very poor because of the lack of lime which is needed as a stabilizer. In fact, this is not a soda-lime or potash-lime glass at all, but really has just an alkali-silicate composition, one which is notoriously susceptible to attack by atmospheric moisture. Such a glass would have shown signs of surface attack within a few weeks (or possibly a few days) of manufacture, if exposed to ordinary room humidities. The attack would initially have taken the form of cloudiness, dullness, or slipperiness to the touch. After a few years the deterioration would have become severe and, unless stored in an extremely dry environment, the glass would have shown some variant of crizzling, spalling, or internal cracking. Consequently, if this bowl is known to be at least a century old, then it should

---

5. Data quoted by Caley show that the alumina content of Egyptian and Roman glasses is rarely less than 1%. E. R. Caley, *Analyses of Ancient Glasses, 1790–1957*. Corning, New York: The Corning Museum of Glass, 1962, pp. 58, 111.

be expected to show some form of extensive deterioration. If the glass were actually ancient and had been buried in the earth, in any but the most arid climate, the likelihood is that it would now be so heavily weathered that little glass at all would remain, only weathering products.

Conclusions

Based on the chemical analysis, the authors conclude that the glass bowl definitely was not manufactured in ancient or medieval times. Moreover, because of the "purity" of the glass, that is, the lack of oxides invariably introduced unintentionally in early glasses, it seems likely that this glass was melted from relatively "pure" laboratory chemicals, rather than from common batch materials. It was probably made only shortly before it was originally acquired, a conclusion entirely in keeping with its overall form and character. Furthermore, we suspect that it was melted in a platinum crucible by someone who was not an experienced glassmaker, as an experiment or possibly as an attempt to deceive a potential purchaser. The chemical composition of the glass indicates that it would be very susceptible to attack by moisture, so it is not at all surprising that the bowl is in such poor condition even though it is not very old. The absence of stabilizing oxides explains why the glass is unstable.[6] Its (R) value has been calculated as -1573, similar to a badly crizzled glass reported earlier,[7] which is also consistent with its seriously corroded state.[8]

6. R. G. Newton and A. Paul, "A New Approach to Predicting the Durability of Glasses from Their Chemical Compositions," *Glass Technology*, 21, 1980, pp. 307–309.

7. R. H. Brill, "Crizzling—A Problem in Glass Conservation," *Proc. IIC Congress on Conservation in Archaeology and in the Applied Arts*, Stockholm, 1975, pp. 121–134, see p. 122, glass no. 4011.

8. R. G. Newton, D. G. Holloway, and L. L. Hench, "A Note on the Spontaneous Cracking of Ancient Glass Samples," *Ann. 8ᵉ Cong. Assoc. Int. du Verre*, London and Liverpool, Sept. 18–25, 1979. Liège, 1981, pp. 355–367, 385.

Recent Important Acquisitions

MADE BY PUBLIC AND PRIVATE COLLECTIONS
IN THE UNITED STATES AND ABROAD

1

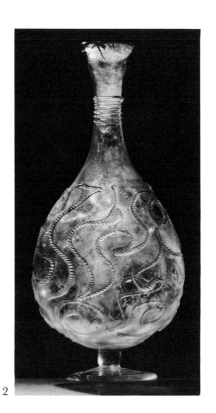

2

3

1. Kohl tube with stopper, core-formed, black with turquoise and yellow thread decoration. Achaemenid, Northern Iran, 5th–4th century B.C. H. (tube) 8.1 cm; L. (stopper) 2.5 cm. *The Newark Museum* (84.39).

2. Flask, colorless, blown, with snake-thread trailed decoration. Roman, found in Neusserstrasse, Cologne, about A.D. 150–220. H. 19.4 cm. *The British Museum,* Department of Greek and Roman Antiquities (1984.7-16.1).

3. Beaker, blown, with white, yellow, green, black, and red enamel. Venice, late 13th-early 14th century, found in Nuremberg with the prunted beakers (no. 4). H. 11 cm. *Germanisches Nationalmuseum Nürnberg* (G1 644).

4

5

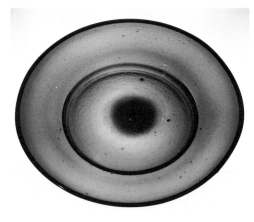

7

4. Two beakers, prunted, light green. Southern Germany, 14th century, found in Nuremberg with the enameled beaker (no. 3). H. (tallest) 9.8 cm. *Germanisches Nationalmuseum Nürnberg* (G1 617, G1 630).

5. The Behaim Beaker, colorless, enameled and gilt, arms of Behaim, depictions of St. Michael and St. Catherine. Venice, about 1495. H. 10.7 cm. *The Corning Museum of Glass* (84.3.24; Houghton Endowment Fund).

6

8

9

6. Ewer, blue, blown, enameled and gilt. Italy, Venice, about 1500. H. 25.4 cm. *Los Angeles County Museum of Art* (84.2.1; purchased with funds provided by William Randolph Hearst, Decorative Arts Council Acquisition Fund, and others).

7. Plate, transparent dark green. Probably Venice, 16th century. D. 43.3 cm. *The Corning Museum of Glass* (84.3.224; gift of Rainer Zietz).

8. Tazza, colorless with white and colored filigree and millefiori. Venice, about 1500–1600. H. 10.3 cm. *The Corning Museum of Glass* (84.3.235; gift of Jerome Strauss, insurance funds).

9. Tazza with Strozzi Arms, colorless, mold-blown, enameled and gilt. Italy, Venice, about 1525–1550. D. 28.2 cm. *Los Angeles County Museum of Art* (84.2.10; purchased with funds provided by William Randolph Hearst, Decorative Arts Council Acquisition Fund, and others).

10. Rondel, *St. Michael*, colorless, enameled, silver (yellow) stained. Europe, lower Rhine, about 1530. D. 23.6 cm. *The Corning Museum of Glass* (84.3.236).

10

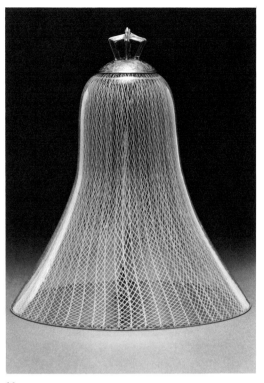

11

12

13

14

15 16

17

11. Bell, blown, with white canes, *vetro a retorti*, silver mount and clapper. Italy, Venice, or the Netherlands, about 1600. H. 12.8 cm. *Los Angeles County Museum of Art* (84.2.6; purchased with funds provided by William Randolph Hearst, Decorative Arts Council Acquisition Fund, and others).

12. Plate with Arms of the Von Czettritz family, blue, blown, diamond-point engraved, signed "W.N.". Silesia, dated 1649. *Los Angeles County Museum of Art* (84.2.9; purchased with funds provided by William Randolph Hearst, Decorative Arts Council Acquisition Fund, and others).

13. Handled decanter, colorless, mold-blown, with pincered decoration. Northern Netherlands, about 1650. H. 24.1 cm. *Westfries Museum*, Hoorn, Netherlands (0111).

14. Beaker, colorless, blown, with *Schwarzlot* enameling, Nuremberg, probably Johann Schaper (1621–1670), dated 1667. H. 10.5 cm. *Badisches Landesmuseum Karlsruhe* (84/171).

15. Goblet, colorless, blown, cut and engraved with arms of the Wimpfen and Thurn families. Bohemia, about 1720. H. 14 cm. *Moravská Galerie v Brně*, Czechoslovakia (28.097).

16. Goblet, colorless, blown, engraved. Nuremberg, Anton Wilhelm Mäuerl (1672–1737), signed, dated 1723. H. 19 cm. *Badisches Landesmuseum Karlsruhe* (84/170).

17. Goblet, colorless, blown, wheel-engraved. Crest and letters F.A.R.P.E.S. honoring Frederick Augustus, King of Poland and Elector of Saxony. Germany, late 18th century. H. 72 cm. *Royal Ontario Museum* (982.92.1).

101

18

20

19

21

102

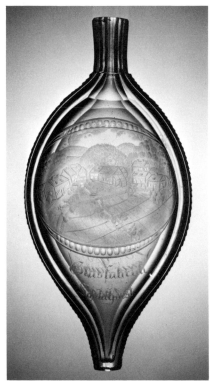

22

23

24

18. Casket, gilt metal and blue and white enamel plaques. England, probably Birmingham or London, possibly James Cox, about 1760–1770. OH. 19.6 cm. *The Corning Museum of Glass* (84.2.54; gift of Lucy Smith Battson by exchange).

19. Plaque, colorless, engraved, reverse-painted depiction of Napoleon I, engraved and signed by St. Quirin. France, about 1810–1820. OH. 49 cm. *The Corning Museum of Glass* (84.3.34; gift of Mr. and Mrs. Peter O. Brown).

20. Pocket bottle, mold-blown, attributed to H. W. Stiegel. United States, Lancaster County, PA, 1763–1774. H. 14 cm. *Los Angeles County Museum of Art* (84.95; purchased with funds provided by the Antiquarian Society in Honor of Mrs. Gregor Norman-Wilcox).

21. Flask, blown-molded, used in presidential campaign of William Henry Harrison. Western Pennsylvania, about 1839–1840. H. 16.8 cm. *Old Sturbridge Village* (13.14.120). Photo by Henry E. Peach.

22. Flask, colorless, blown, cut, engraved view of *Glasfabrik Schildhorst*, engraved by Louis Vaupel. Bohemia, dated 1850. L. 21.2 cm. *The Corning Museum of Glass* (84.3.6).

23. Goblet, blown, colorless, frosted, overlaid with blue, engraved by Franz Paul Zach (signed F. Zach); color twist stem with faceted collar. Bohemia, about 1860. H. 25.5 cm. *Dr. and Mrs. Leonard S. Rakow, New York City.*

24. Salad set, colorless, blown, cut. Corning, New York, probably Hawkes or Hoare, about 1893. OH. (bowl and stand) 20.1 cm. *The Corning Museum of Glass* (84.4.58; gift of Mr. and Mrs. John C. Huntington, Jr.).

25

26

25. Panel, *Flora*, stained, leaded, designed by Sir Edward Burne-Jones. England, William Morris and Company, 1896. H. 117 cm. From the collection of *The Morse Gallery of Art*, Winter Park, Florida, through the courtesy of The Charles Hosmer Morse Foundation (GL-25-84).

26. Pair of stained glass windows, Dante and Beatrice. William Willet, Philadelphia, about 1910–1920. OH. 119.5 cm. *The Corning Museum of Glass* (84.4.3; gift of Dr. Thomas H. English).

27. Vase, blown, cameo-carved and intaglio-engraved, brown over yellow over pink over green over colorless. France, Paris, Daum Brothers blank carved and signed by Louis Damon, about 1900. H. 34.35 cm. From the collection of *The Morse Gallery of Art*, Winter Park, Florida, through the courtesy of The Charles Hosmer Morse Foundation (GL-26-84).

28. Vase, *Crown of Thorns*, blown, transparent deep pink shading to amber with applied decoration. France, Nancy, Cristalleries Daum, 1911. H. 57.2 cm. *The Corning Museum of Glass* (84.3.46).

29. Vase, blown, with enameled decoration. Bohemia, Loetz Witwe, Klostermühle, designed by Dagobert Peche, about 1914. H. 19.8 cm. *Kunstsammlungen der Veste Coburg* (107/84).

30. Covered box, blown, with applied feet and finial. Bohemia, Loetz Witwe, Klostermühle, designed by Dagobert Peche or Michael Powolny, about 1914. H. 11.3 cm, D. 11 cm. *Kunstsammlungen der Veste Coburg* (104/84).

27

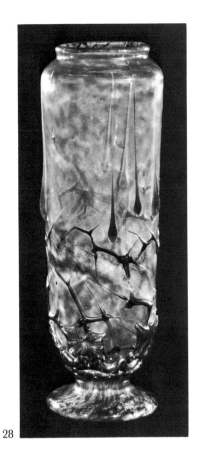

28

29

30

31

32

33

31. Chalice, colorless, blown, with black enamel decoration. Vienna, Wiener Werkstëtte, signed "WW", designed by Dagobert Peche, 1916. H. 18.3 cm. *Edgar Kindler, Basel, Switzerland* (no. 845).

32. Vase, blown, with canes. Designed by Vittorio Zecchin, made by Artisti Barovier. Italy, Murano, about 1914–1920. H. 25.7 cm. *The Toledo Museum of Art* (84.72; Decorative Arts Purchase Fund).

33. Vase, blown with bubble inclusions. France, Cristallerie Schneider, Charles Schneider, about 1930. H. 28.8 cm. *Los Angeles County Museum of Art* (M 83.152; gift of Oktabec Gallery, Los Angeles, California).

34. Covered rose jar. Engraved, green overlay on colorless, designed by H. P. Sinclaire, Jr. H. P. Sinclaire & Co., Corning, NY, 1926. OH. 20.4 cm. *The Corning Museum of Glass* (84.4.165; gift of Mrs. Douglas Sinclaire).

35. Salad bowl, colorless, blown, with white enamel, designed and made by Maurice Heaton. Valley Cottage, NY, about 1930. D. 35.7 cm. *Yale University Art Gallery* (1984.41.2; Henry P. Wheeler, B.A. 1942, and Leslie Wheeler, B.A. 1940, Fund).

34

36

37

36. Set of modular containers, colorless, pressed, designed by Wilhelm Wagenfeld. Lausitzer Glasverein, Weiswasser, Germany, 1938. OH. 21.5 cm. *The Corning Museum of Glass* (84.3.263; gift of Barry Friedman and Patricia Pastor).

37. Vase, blown, flashed and cut, emerald green on colorless. Acid stamp on base. Belgium, Val St. Lambert, 1938–1939. H. 30.5 cm. *The Newark Museum* (84.137; gift of Mrs. Leonilda Tedford).

38

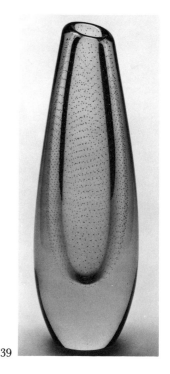

39

40

38. Three vases, blown, colorless with colored inclusions, by André Thuret. France, about 1945–1955. H. (tallest) 28 cm. *The Corning Museum of Glass* (84.3.222, 220,219; gift of Mme. André Thuret).

39. Vase, blown, with inclusions, by Gunnel Nyman. Finland, Nuutajarvi, 1948. H. 26 cm. *Musée des Arts Décoratifs*, Paris (54790).

40. Sculpture, aqua and polychrome glass, blown elements embedded in a cast block. Italy, Fulvio Bianconi, about 1950–1960. H. 28.1 cm. *The Corning Museum of Glass* (84.3.2).

41. Vase, blown. Italy, Luciano Ferro, about 1950–1954. H. 33 cm. *The Toledo Museum of Art* (84.73; Decorative Arts Purchase Fund).

42. Sculpture, *Spaceman*, colorless, painted, assembled, by Gino Colucci. Italy, about 1950–1960. H. 27.4 cm. *The Corning Museum of Glass* (84.3.3).

43. Cocktail glass and shaker, blown, by Kaj Frank. Finland, Nuutajarvi, about 1950–1955. H. (shaker) 25 cm. *Musée des Arts Décoratifs*, Paris (54807/808; gift of B. Kulvik and A. Siltavuori).

44. Sculpture, formed, painted, assembled, by Gino Colucci. France, about 1960. H. 15.4 cm. *Musée des Arts Décoratifs*, Paris (Dépôt F.N.A.C.).

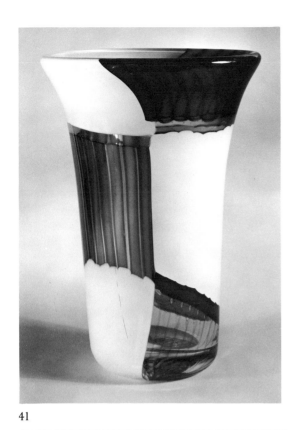

41

43

42

44

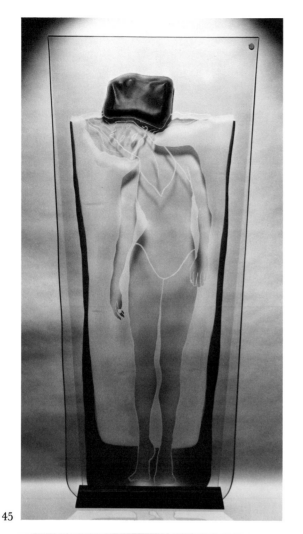

45

46

45. Sculpture, *Blocks*, colorless, layered sheet glass, sandblasted, by Bonnie Biggs. Elkins Park, PA, 1983. H. 182.5 cm. *The Corning Museum of Glass* (84.4.40; gift of Anne and Ronald Abramson).

46. Sculpture, *Space Cup*, colorless, blown, cut, fabricated. United States, Michael Cohn, 1983. H. 18 cm, w. 28 cm. *High Museum of Art*, Atlanta (1984.41).

47. Six-part sculpture, *Acid Rain #2*, translucent dark blue and green, cast, by Alan Klein. Cambridge, MA, 1983. ow. 31.4 cm. *The Corning Museum of Glass* (84.4.8).

47

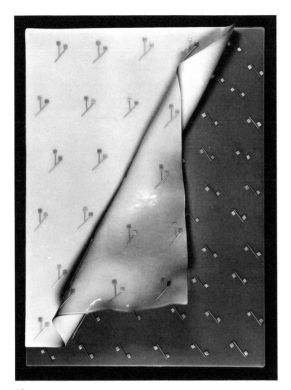

48

49

48. Wall sculpture, *Wall Paper Panel*, blown, slumped, by Molly Stone. Emeryville, CA, 1983. OH. 76 cm. *The Corning Museum of Glass* (84.4.11).

49. Leaded glass panel, *Homage to the Abstraction Creation Group*, green, red, and amethyst, by Dick Weiss. Seattle, WA, 1983. OH. 191.8 cm. *The Corning Museum of Glass* (84.4.45).

50. Sculpture, *Spring Head*, colorless, multicolored, blown, with enameled metal attachments, by Hank Murta Adams. Austria, Baden, 1984. H. 39.2 cm. *The Corning Museum of Glass* (84.3.228).

50

Notes

Netherlands, her work raised the area of glass studies, particularly Roman glass, to a status of its own within archeology when she was appointed Professor of Archeology by the University of Utrecht in 1972. All those who know her personally are familiar with Clasina Isings' enthusiasm and her interest in glass of all periods including contemporary studio glass.

Many of her friends have wished to express their recognition of Clasina Isings' achievements in a tangible manner. Therefore they are grateful to the editor of the *Journal of Glass Studies* for his offer to print articles written in her honor. The first one appeared in volume 26, and this volume contains another. In fact, the editor received so many contributions written for the occasion that they are likely to become a regular feature of the following *Journal*s as well. It is on this page, however, that her friends gather to raise glasses to Clasina Isings and to wish her health, happiness, and many more years of work in the field of glass: PROSIT!

E. Marianne Stern

* * *

August 1984
The Editor
Journal of Glass Studies
Corning, New York 14831

So Who *Was* Ennion?

In Honor of Clasina Isings

Clasina Isings was sixty-five years old on February 15, 1984—an appropriate occasion to recognize and honor her as a remarkable glass scholar. Ever since the publication of her book *Roman Glass from Dated Finds* in 1957, all those working on Roman glass have profited from her guiding hand. Her classification of the datable material known at that time was based on sound archeological methods; it not only had a great impact when it appeared but set the international standard for modern research in this field. In the

I was interested to read Dr. Yael Israeli's interpretation of the working methods of the Sidonian glassmaker, Ennion.[1] Dr. Israeli appears to think

---

1. Yael Israeli, "Ennion in Jerusalem," *Journal of Glass Studies* 25, 1983, pp. 66–68.

112

that the glassmakers made the clay molds which they used to give the shape and decoration to their vessels. The molds were, in fact, made by a separate group of craftsmen, specialized potters, and, in some cases at least, creative artists.

Dr. Israeli further concludes, after a study of unsigned vessels whose decoration shows close affinities to the signed Ennion vessels, that at least one of these pieces, no. 65.1.2 in The Corning Museum of Glass, cannot be an Ennion product, or even from his workshop. The two seams on the mold "run vertically between the palmettes, and in contrast to Ennion's usual manner, are not integrated into the design. This technical difference seems to me to offer sufficient evidence that the unsigned vessels were not made by Ennion and perhaps not even in his workshop, as has been suggested by some scholars."[2]

But if Ennion was so particular about his seams, how is it that this publicity-conscious old maestro permitted the handles on two of his famous group of four jugs to be placed, not on the opposite side of the rectangle containing his signature, as on the Museum Haaretz jug, where it shows his name to maximum advantage, but directly over the signature, which is dwarfed by the sweep of the handle above it? In certain circumstances, such as pouring, the name would be entirely concealed.

This brings us again to the rather disturbing question: what, in fact, was it that Ennion claims to have made? Was he not, after all, a master glassmaker, or instead the master potter who made the molds? The names Aeennean, Eannion, Aniane, and variants also appear among the names of fabricants stamped on the bases of clay lamps of this period.[3] We have already shown the relationship between the glassmakers and the lamp makers.[4]

The name appears again among the names of potters stamped on the widely dispersed *terra sigillata* ware of the last centuries B.C. and the first centuries A.D. An Annius was making and exporting *sigillata* ware in the Augustan period. The ware of Anio was found in Olbia, of C. Anni in Corfu, of Enni in Alexandria and Eubastis. An Ennius-signed object was believed to have been made in Arezzo. Sextius Annius was an Arretine potter of the Augustan period. His ware, as well as that containing other significant names, is found in Athens, Puteoli, Antioch, Alexandria, and Samaria.

We could extend this list indefinitely by including potters who signed their work with the same names as the glassmakers associated with Ennion. Among these are Jason, Aristeas, and variants of Neikais, such as Neikh, Niko, and the double signature of Nikia-Nicia, who operated, possibly, in Italy and employed bilingual stamps, the Greek forms being used for the Eastern markets.[5]

The field of signed pottery is well researched and documented. It offers a fascinating new approach, and a firm springboard into the still unexplored world of the ancient glassmakers. There is really no place any more for unbased speculation and uninformed assumptions.

Anita Engle, Editor
Readings in Glass History

*   *   *

Chinese Glass Display
The City of Bristol Art Gallery

The City of Bristol Museum & Art Gallery's Oriental Section, containing over 320 items, is one of the two largest holdings of Chinese glass vessels outside China. Its collection is based on that of H. F. Burrows Abbey and was bequeathed to the National Art-Collections Fund in 1950, presented by the Fund to Bristol. In 1982 the redesign of the area allocated to it was undertaken with support from the South-West Area Museums Council, and on February 17, 1983, the Asian Art Society for the South-West celebrated the opening of this new display.

---

2. *Ibid.*, p. 68, f.n. 10.

3. E. Joly, *Lucerne del Museo di Sabratha*, (Monographie di Archeologia Libica, XI), Rome, Bretschneider, 1974.

4. Anita Engle, *Readings in Glass History* 17, chap. 7.

5. Iliffe, "Sigillata Wares in the Near East", *Quarterly of the Dept. of Antiquities of Palestine* 6, 1938, pp. 4–53.

At present ninety-six pieces are displayed in five humidity-controlled units back-lit through translucent plexiglass. The five units form a sequence telling the story of glass in China: the earliest pieces imitating jades; the seventeenth-century free-blown wares; the development of facet cutting and carving in the early and middle eighteenth century; the simultaneous development of surface decoration in color or incised line; and

finally the carved polychrome multi-layer wares of the late eighteenth and nineteenth centuries. Explanatory labels describe these developments. Access to the material now in storage may be granted by prior appointment; the collection is fully cataloged on index cards (in process of trans-

fer to computer) while a catalog is being prepared.

The display is adjacent to the Schiller Room which houses a comprehensive collection of Chinese ceramics and other arts.

> Peter Hardie, Curator
> Oriental Art
> City of Bristol Museum & Art Gallery

*   *   *

Charleen Edwards, the Managing Editor for the *Journal of Glass Studies* and all publications of The Corning Museum of Glass, retired as of April 30, 1985. Mrs. Edwards and her husband have moved to Ashland, Oregon. Richard Price is the new Managing Editor for publications of The Corning Museum of Glass.

*   *   *

Gabriella Gros-Galliner
1923–1984

After a long illness, Mrs. Gabriella Gros-Galliner has died in London. An active member of the English Glass Circle, Mrs. Gros was particularly interested in glass of the Art Nouveau period.

Her book *Glass—A Guide for Collectors* (1970) and numerous articles emphasized that period. The life and works of Emile Gallé were also the focus of her research. She was Joint Editor of *Glass Circle News*, the Glass Circle journal.

*   *   *

Philip Hofer
1898–1984

Philip Hofer, a former member of the Board of Trustees of The Corning Museum of Glass, has died at the age of eighty-six. The secretary of the Fogg Museum at Harvard for twelve years, Mr. Hofer founded the university's department of printing and graphic arts in 1938, the first university department of its kind in the country.

Previously he had been curator of the Spencer Collection of the New York Public Library and first assistant director of the Morgan Library. As a book collector, he emphasized eighteenth-century German, Iberian, and Italian publications, and his Italian book collection was known as the finest outside Italy.

Mr. Hofer was also a trustee of the American School for Classical Studies in Athens and chairman of the Bernard Berenson Villa I Tatti Committee in Florence. He gave wise counsel to the Board of The Corning Museum of Glass from 1952 to 1974.

*　　*　　*

Hugh Wakefield
1916–1984

Glass studies have been greatly impoverished by the untimely death on February 8, 1984, of Hugh Wakefield, formerly Keeper of the Circulation Department in the Victoria and Albert Museum.

Hugh Wakefield was born in 1916 and educated at King Edward's School, Birmingham, and at Trinity College, Cambridge. In 1938 he joined the Royal Commission on Historic Monuments, to which he returned at the end of his war-time army service. In 1948, however, he left the Commission to become Assistant Keeper in the Department of Circulation at the Victoria and Albert Museum. Here he laid the foundation of his knowledge of the arts of the Victorian and Edwardian periods, a particular spur to work in this field being his experiences in the organization of the pioneer exhibition of Victorian and Edwardian Decorative Arts which was mounted to commemorate the Museum's centenary in 1952. In the preparation of this Exhibition he assumed responsibility for the ceramics and glass, and his research in both these areas had issue in published form—*Victorian Pottery* in 1962 and *Nineteenth Century British Glass* in 1961 (with a second edition in 1982). The former work appeared in the Victorian Collector series which he also edited for the publishers Herbert Jenkins.

On the death of his predecessor in 1960 Hugh Wakefield became Keeper of the Circulation Department, thereby assuming responsibility for the preparation and distribution of small and medium-sized exhibitions for display in the regional museums of England. This was a very extensive task, and the Circulation Department became the largest in the Museum, assuming also a general responsibility for the study of the Victorian and later periods, and for the building of the Museum's collections of nineteenth and twentieth century decorative arts. His Departmental experience admirably fitted him for membership on the Crafts Advisory Council between 1971 and 1975, and he was chairman of the Committee for Museums of Applied Art of the International Council of Museums in 1974 and 1975.

On his retirement from the Museum in 1976, Hugh Wakefield became for a while secretary of a sub-committee of the Standing Commission on Museums, and he was also an executive committee member and judge of the National Heritage Museum of the Year Award, an assignment to which he brought special qualifications derived from his previous experience with the country's museum services: these qualities he combined with great enthusiasm for the job, which had for him the added attraction of allowing him to travel about the country, travel being one of the abiding passions of his life.

The relative leisure and detachment which retirement brought to Hugh Wakefield was partially spent in preparing a second edition of his *Nineteenth Century British Glass*, a book which had played a pioneering role when it first appeared, but which by the 1970s had been rendered in a degree out-of-date by subsequent publications in the field. This revision he undertook with characteristic care and thoroughness, insisting on a meticulous standard of scholarship which also showed in his fastidious use of the English language.

Apart from his book, Hugh Wakefield wrote a number of authoritative articles on various aspects of nineteenth-century glass—whether on individual makers such as Apsley Pellatt or the Richardsons, or on subjects such as the development of flower-stand centerpieces or the influence of Venetian glass on nineteenth-century British glass. Just before his death he had finished preparing for the press his paper on "Early Pressed

115

Glass in England" delivered to the 1983 conference of the International Association for the History of Glass at Nancy.

Those who knew Hugh will mourn the passing not only of an influential scholar who made important contributions to his chosen subjects, but also of a warm and kindly personality. He was always appreciative of the efforts of others and in his turn ready to help wherever he could.

Robert J. Charleston

*   *   *

Luigi Zecchin
1905–1984

Chi ha conosciuto personalmente Luigi Zecchin ne ricorda la figura asciutta e sempre agile ed il volto illuminato da occhi azzurri idagatori e benevoli ma ancor più la cortese disponibilità verso chiunque lo consultasse sulla vetraria veneziana, la materia da lui prediletta, e la vasta cultura ed il rigore scientifico che caratterizzavano le sue pubblicazioni. L'importante contributo dato da Luigi Zecchin alla storia della vetraria veneziana è stato dovuto, oltre che alla passione ed alla serietà con le quali conduceva le sue ricerche, anche al fatto che la sua formazione culturale gli permetteva di considerare i fatti vetrari sia sotto l'aspetto storico-artistico che sotto quello tecnologico.

Nato a Murano, dove sempre visse, nel 1905, fu a stretto contatto con l'ambiente vetrario dell'isola ed in particolare con lo zio Vittorio Zecchin, pittore e designer a cui si dovette tra il secondo ed il terzo decennio del nostro secolo il rinnovamento della vetraria veneziana. Luigi Zecchin da ragazzo collaborò con lo zio e sotto la sua guida si interessò al design ed alla grafica.

Parallelamente i suoi studi lo portarono nel 1928 alla laurea in Ingegneria Civile Edile presso l'Università degli Studi di Padova ed alla collaborazione con la facoltà di Economia e Commercio dell'Università di Venezia, dove tenne dall'anno accademico 1949–50 la cattedra di Matematica Finanziaria ed Attuariale. Sfruttò la sua preparazione tecnico-scientifica anche in campo vetrario, come direttore ed insegnante presso la Scuola Tecnica a specializzazione vetraria in Murano, dalla quale uscirono molti tecnici ancora operanti nelle fornaci dell'isola, dal 1937 al 1946. Si fece promotore nel dopoguerra, quale Assessore del Comune di Venezia, della fondazione della Stazione Sperimentale del Vetro, centro di ricerche vetrarie, sempre in Murano. Della Stazione Sperimentale fu membro del Consiglio di Amministrazione e poi membro del Comitato di Redazione della "Rivista".

Già dal 1930 circa Luigi Zecchin iniziò i suoi studi di storia vetraria ma dal dopoguerra essi ebbero un salto di qualità quando egli cominciò a frequentare l'Archivio di Stato di Venezia, uno dei più importanti del mondo per l'antichità e la ricchezza delle sue carte, data la millenaria durata della Repubblica Veneta. Luigi Zecchin infatti iniziò pazientemente ad esaminare le carte dei Podestà di Murano, delle quali le prime risalgono al 1279, ed altre carte dell'Archivio, a studiare le "Mariegole" o statuti dell'Arte vetraria ed antichi ricettari manoscritti. Egli potè interpretare il tutto grazie alle sue conoscenze della tecnologia vetraria e, nell'ultimo decennio, potè procedere ad uno studio comparativo grazie alla collaborazione dei tecnici della Stazione Sperimentale del Vetro, che sotto la sua guida analizzavano i vetri frammentari recuperati nella laguna di Venezia.

Certamente si devono a Luigi Zecchin i più importanti contributi degli ultimi decenni sulla storia della vetraria veneziana. Gli studiosi più aggiornati conoscono le sue pubblicazioni ma noi ci rammarichiamo che i loro contenuti siano arrivati solo indirettamente al grande pubblico perché Luigi Zecchin scrisse circa duecento densissimi e brevi articoli per il "Giornale Economico" della Camera di Commercio di Venezia, per "Tecnica Vetraria", per "Vetro e Silicati", per il "Journal of Glass Studies", per il "Bollettino della Stazione Sperimentale del Vetro", per "La Voce di Murano" e per la "Rivista della Stazione Sperimentale del Vetro" ma non volle purtroppo mai condensare in un'opera organica i risultati delle sue ricerche.

E' impossibile sintetizzare in poco spazio i temi da lui trattati, spaziando dal XIII al XIX secolo. I risultati più validi riguardano il medioevo vetrario veneziano di cui fece conoscere i prodotti, i produttori, le materie prime, le tecniche. La sua scoperta più importante, anche a suo parere, fu quella relativa alla presenza a Murano tra l'ultimo ventennio del XIII secolo e la prima metà del XIV di decoratori a smalti fusibili su vetro. Ciò ha permesso di attribuire definitivamente a Vene-

zia un gruppo di vetri smaltati, datati a quella stessa epoca.

Altro argomento di importanza fondamentale è stato la definizione del ruolo svolto da Angelo Barovier nella rivoluzione tecnologica verificatasi nel vetro veneziano attorno al 1450 e delle fasi di preparazione del cristallo, elaborate dall'antico vetraio. Altri campi di indagine furono i ricettari manoscritti veneziani o di origine veneziana e toscani, il libro di Antonio Neri, l'organizzazione della corporazione dei vetrai nei secoli, le loro emigrazioni all'estero, le dinastie vetrarie di Murano, gli inventari di vetrerie medievali e rinascimentali.

Le ricerche di Luigi Zecchin hanno chiarito molti problemi ed hanno dato nuove prospettive alle indagini ma soprattutto hanno fatto capire quanto sia errato accettare acriticamente i numerosi dati infondati e leggendari di cui è infarcita la storiografia vetraria veneziana. Da lui ci viene un monito ad affrontare con pazienza le carte, di cui fortunatamente i nostri archivi sono assai ricchi, nella convinzione che esse soltanto possono fornire quella griglia di dati nella quale inquadrare i monumenti conservati nei musei e recuperati con gli scavi. Luigi Zecchin ha inoltre richiamato gli studiosi della vetraria veneziana all'aspetto strettamente tecnologico, che è stato per secoli la ragione del suo primato e che è stato troppo a lungo trascurato.

Rosa Barovier Mentasti

Note to Authors and Readers

The *Journal of Glass Studies* was created by The Corning Museum of Glass in 1959 to serve as a vehicle for international scholarship in the history, art, and early technology of glass. Previously unpublished articles of original research on topics of glass history from its beginnings to the mid-twentieth century should be sent to the Editor, who will submit them to *Journal* Advisors or Museum staff Readers for decision on acceptance for publication. The *Journal* does not accept articles concerned with living artists or glassmakers.

The *Journal* publishes articles in English, French, Spanish, Italian, and German; articles written in other languages must be submitted in an English translation. Information of less than article length which may be of interest to the scholarly world of glass, as well as "Letters to the Editor," will be considered for publication in the "Notes" section. Authors are requested to submit clean, typed, double-spaced manuscripts. Illustrations for articles and for "Recent Acquisitions" should be approximately 8 x 10 inch (131 cm x 164 cm), glossy black and white photographs suitable for publication. Such materials will be returned to the sender, if this is requested at the time of publication acceptance, once the *Journal* has been issued. Manuscripts and illustrations not accepted for publication shall be returned at once to the author or institution. In general, articles should be of reasonable length (10 or so pages); unduly long articles or articles with too copious a bibliography or footnotes may have to be turned down since they preclude the publication of other scholarship. For similar reasons, the *Journal* will no longer devote space to *Festschrifts*. Footnote and bibliographic style should follow the pattern used in recent *Journals*.

Manuscript materials should be addressed to:

> The Editor
> *Journal of Glass Studies*
> The Corning Museum of Glass
> Corning, New York 14831

As a non-profit publication, the *Journal* does not offer payment for work published. However, as a courtesy, a complimentary copy of the *Journal* in which the article appears and twenty-five offprints of the article are sent to the author. Additional copies of the offprints can be made available to the author at cost if these are ordered at the time the article is accepted for publication.

The *Journal* staff normally restricts its editing to matters of clarity and correct usage once the article has been approved by the Readers or Advisors. An edited typescript and first galleys are sent to authors for confirmation as to the faithful reproduction of the approved text.

CHECK LIST

of Recently Published Articles and Books on Glass

This list includes publications added to The Corning Museum of Glass Library since the Check List for *Journal* 26. In some cases, older material new to the library collection has been added, excluding any article or book prior to 1940 listed in *Bibliography of Glass* by George S. Duncan, Sheffield: Society of Glass Technology, 1960. *Journal of Glass Studies* readers are reminded that Check List sections on Contemporary Glass, i.e., blown and other, flat glass (architectural, mosaic, painted, stained), and technology are now found in *New Glass Review*.

INDEX

I. General Publications (not limited to a specific period or form)

II. Technological Publications, including Conservation (application of scientific knowledge and methods of research to glass art and history)

III. Historical Publications

    Ancient
    Islamic, to fourteenth century
    Medieval, fifth to thirteenth century
    Renaissance to Present
        General
        Australia, New Zealand, South Pacific
        British Isles: England, Ireland, Scotland, Wales
        French
        Germanic, including Austria, Bohemia, Czechoslovakia, Germany,
            Lichtenstein, Moravia, Poland, Silesia, Switzerland
        Italian, including *façon de Venise*
        Netherlandish, including Belgium, Luxembourg, Holland
        North American
            Canada
            United States, including Colonial period, Alaska, Hawaii
            Bottles, Flasks, Insulators, Jars
        Oriental, including China, Japan, Korea
        Russian
        Scandinavian, including Denmark, Finland, Iceland, Norway, Sweden
        Art Nouveau and Art Deco
        For Contemporary (post 1945), see the annual *New Glass Review*
        Stained Glass (pre-1945)
        Beads

Fewer than four citations from any area are included under Renaissance to Present, General.

Only substantive book reviews are listed and may be found under the author of the work reviewed.

Collectibles are included under country of origin.

Articles on restoration and conservation of Stained Glass are listed under Technological Publications.

GENERAL

ANONYMOUS

"Acquisitions: Glass"
The Toledo Museum of Art 1983 Annual Report, Toledo, Ohio: the museum, 1983, pp. 8–9, ill.
50 objects.

"Cleaning Glass"
Early American Life, v. 15, no. 4, Aug. 1984, pp. 13–14, ill.

"Fachausschuss V: Glasgestaltung und Glasveredelung. Sitzung vom 2. und 3. Juli 1983 in Hamburg"
Glastechnische Berichte, v. 56, no. 11, 1983, pp. R225–R226.
Summarizes conference papers on historical subjects by E. M. Stern, P. C. Ritsema van Eck, G. Haase, S. Beeh-Lustenberger.

"Glassets Museum"
Glas & Mennesker, v. 5, no. 9, April 1984, p. 16, ill.
Holmegaard glass museum.

"Juliette & Leonard Rakow Honored at Corning Museum"
Antiques & The Arts Weekly, v. 12, no. 47, Nov. 23, 1984, p. 5.

"Museum Acquires Ancient Glass"
The Toledo Museum of Art Calendar, April 1984, p. 3, ill.
Islamic flask; Mughal gilded bowl and an amethyst cut hookah base; 19th c. yellow Chinese bowl.

"Recent Important Acquisitions Made by Public and Private Collections in the United States and Abroad"
Journal of Glass Studies, v. 26, 1984, pp. 136–151, ill.

"Thüringer Glas 1597 entstand die erste Glashütte—Produkte auf DDR-Briefmarken"
Glas + Rahmen, no. 22, Nov. 1983, p. 1178, ill.
Postage stamps commemorating Thuringer glass industry since 1597.

"Le verre était une des grandes vedettes du SAD 83"
Verre Actualités, no. 54, Dec. 1983, pp. 44–45.
Opening of Centre National du Verre in Paris and formation of Centre International du Verre in Aix-en-Provence.

"Vive émotion parmi les professionnels et les amateurs de l'art du verre"
Le Courrier des Métiers d'Art, no. 31, March 1984, p. 17.
Earthquake in Liège, Nov. 1983, damages 50 pieces of glass in the museum.

"Winners of Rakow Awards Announced"
Antiques & The Arts Weekly, v. 12, no. 47, Nov. 23, 1984, p. 49.

American Institute of the History of Pharmacy: Calendar, 1985 (Ed. by Dr. D. A. Wittop Koning, Amsterdam)
Madison, Wis.: the institute, [1984], 7 pp., ill.
Includes glass beakers; prints and paintings showing pharmaceutical containers.

Art at Auction: The Year at Sotheby's 1982–83
London: Sotheby Publications, 1983, 416 pp., ill.

BASEL. HALLE 24, GEBÄUDE D DER SCHWEIZER MUSTERMESSE
Schweizerische Kunst- und Antiquitätenmesse Basel
Basel: Schweizerische Kunst- und Antiquitätenmesse, 1984, 147 pp., ill.
Antique show and sale; includes glass of various periods.

BENJAMIN, SUSAN
Enamels. Cooper-Hewitt Museum (Ed. by Nancy Akre)
[Washington, D.C.]: The Cooper-Hewitt Museum, the Smithsonian Institution's National Museum of Design, 1983, 128 pp., ill.
From ancient times to the present.

BYRNE, J.
"UK Handmade Glass Sector Review"
Glass (U.K.), v. 61, no. 8, Aug. 1984, p. 284.
Quality handmade glass survives despite high labor costs and competition.

CARPENTIER, DIDIER and BACHELET, JOËL
Painting on Glass
New York, N.Y.: Arco Publishing, Inc., 1984, 64 pp., ill.
Hobby craft book.

Catalogue of Egyptian, Mediaeval & Continental Glass in the Cecil Higgins Museum
[Bristol: the museum, n.d.], 21 typescript pp.
Also includes English and American glass.

Christie's Review of the Season 1983
Oxford: Phaidon-Christie's Ltd., 1983, 504 pp., ill.

CODY, DAN
"A Story in Glass"
Sky (Delta Air Lines Inflight Magazine), v. 13, no. 2, Feb. 1984, pp. 80–84+, ill.
The Corning Museum of Glass, Lalique and Tiffany, Harvey Littleton and other contemporary glassmakers, etc.

DEAN, PATRICIA
The Official Identification Guide to Glassware
Orlando, Fla.: The House of Collectibles, Inc., 1984, 340 pp., ill.

Décoration sur verre
Paris: Dessain et Tolra, 1981, 48 pp., ill.
Hobby book: cold painting containers, mirrors; imitation stained glass.

DEXEL, THOMAS
"Formen und ihre Geschichte"
Kunst & Antiquitäten, no. 2, March/April 1984, pp. 54–60, ill.
Household items, including glass flasks, jugs, etc.

Gebrauchsglas: Gläser des Alltags vom Spätmittelalter bis zum beginnenden 20. Jahrhundert
Munich: Klinkhardt & Biermann, 1983, 304 pp., ill.
Tableware, flasks, bottles, and other utilitarian glassware through the ages.

DOWNING, JEANNETTE D.
"Where Lalique Meets the Egyptians: A Survey of Glass Art Techniques"
Arts Quarterly (New Orleans Museum of Art), v. 3, no. 2, April/May/June 1981, p. 12, ill.
Exhibit that describes the molding process.

DRAHOTOVÁ, OLGA
L'Art du verre en Europe
Paris: Gründ and Prague: Polygrafia, 1983, 232 pp., ill.
General survey using examples from the decorative arts museum, Prague.
European Glass
New York, N.Y.: Excalibur Books, 1983, 232 pp., ill.
The development of hollow glass through the ages.

Durobor: Verrerie, Glaswerk, Glassware, Glaswerk, Vetraia, Vidrieia [trade catalog]
Soignies, Belgium: Durobor, 1984, u.p. folder, ill.
Drinking glasses.

European Tableware Buyers Guide 1984
[Produced by *Tableware International*]
Redhill, Surrey: International Trade Publications, Ltd., 1984, 111 pp., ill.

FAUSTER, CARL U.
"What You Should Know About 'Fluting' Techniques"
The Hobstar, v. 7, no. 2, Oct. 1984, pp. 2–3, ill.
In cut glass.

FOURASTIÉ, FRANÇOISE and JEAN
"En marge de l'histoire du verre et de la vitre"
Mélanges de Préhistoire, d'archéocivilisation et d'ethnologie (offerts à André Vera- gnac., Paris) 1971, pp. 279–291, ill.
Window glass.

FRASER, B. KAY
Découper bouteilles et verres perdus
Paris: Dessain et Tolra, 1981, 63 pp., ill.
Translation of original book, *Creative Bottle Cutting*.

General Foods Catalog
[Rye Brook, N.Y.: General Foods, 1984, 24 pp.].
Exhibition of food utensils, including glass tableware, teapots, reamers, bottles, funnels, etc.

GICKLHORN, BRIGITTE
Peintures sur verre
Annecy: Gardet Editeur, 1975, 32 pp., ill.
Hobby book.

Glasgow Museums & Art Galleries: The Burrell Collection (Text by Richard Marks and others)
London and Glasgow: William Collins Sons & Co., in association with the museums, 1984, 160 pp., ill.
Stained glass; European glass 16th–19th c.

HALDANE, SUZANNE
The See-Through Zoo: How Glass Animals Are Made
New York, N.Y.: Pantheon Books, 1984, 37 pp., ill.
Children's book on lampworking.

HOLL, FRIEDRICH
Die Poesie des Glases: des Glases Lob, der Arbeit Lied, Symbol und Gleichnis
[Zwiesel/Bayern]: Friedrich Holl, 1983, 128 pp., ill.
Glass and glassmaking in poetry.

HUGGER, PAUL
Spiegel und Spiegelmacher
Basel: G. Krebs, in commission by Rudolf Habelt Verlag, 1973. (Schweizerische Gesellschaft für Volkskunde, Abteilung Film, Reihe: Altes Handwerk, Heft 35), 39 pp., ill.
Mirrors and mirror making, past and present.

ISENBERG, SI
"Crafting with Bottles"
GlassCraft News, v. 1, no. 6, 1984, p. 11+, ill.
Making bowls and other items.

JEBSEN-MARWEDEL, H.
"Handschmeichler aus Glas"
Glaswelt, v. 36, no. 8, Aug. 1983, p. 626, ill.
Millefiori "hand-coolers" or amulets of unknown origin from a Danish collection.

KEEFE, JOHN
"Masterworks of Glass"
Arts Quarterly (New Orleans Museum of Art), v. 6, no. 2 and 3, May–Sept. 1984, p. 23, ill.
Exhibition of 50 pieces from the museum's collection.

KLEIN, DAN and LLOYD, WARD
The History of Glass (Foreword by Robert Charleston)
London: Orbis, 1984, 288 pp., ill.

Kunst, Kultur, Köln 2. Neuerwerbungen der Kölner Museen aus dreissig Jahren (Ed. by Gerd Biegel)
Cologne: Horst Keller and Greven & Bechtold, 1979, 493 pp., ill.
Acquisitions in Cologne's nine museums in last 30 years.

LeMAY, NANCY A.
"Glassychord Is Back"
Americana, v. 12, no. 5, Nov./Dec. 1984, p. 10, ill.
Glass harmonicas made by Gerhard Finkenbeiner of Waltham, Mass.

LYON, KENNETH W.
"Engraved or Etched?"
The Glass Club Bulletin, no. 144, Fall 1984, pp. 6–9, ill.
Differences between wheel engraving and acid etching.

MATTHEWS, GLENICE LESLEY
Enamels, Enameling, Enamelists
Radnor, Pa.: Chilton Book Co., 1984, 177 pp., ill.

McCORQUODALE, CHARLES
History of the Interior

New York, N.Y.: The Vendome Press, 1983, 224 pp., ill.
Includes Roman mosaics, chandeliers, mirrors, decorative window glass, etc.

Miniatures. Compiled for the Cooper-Hewitt Museum, the Smithsonian Institution's National Museum of Design
[Washington, D.C.]: the Smithsonian Institution, 1983, 123 pp., ill.
Includes glass items, pp. 91–97, from various countries and periods.

MOODY, B. E.
"Effects of Legislation on the Competitiveness of Glass"
Glass Technology, v. 25, no. 1, Feb. 1984, pp. 31–37, ill.
Traces the history of legal measures affecting glass manufacture.

O'CONNELL, ANNETTE
"Glass Rolling Pins"
Old Bottle Magazine, v. 17, no. 11, Nov. 1984, pp. 3–7, ill.

PAULSON, HOMER
"Cleaning Cruets"
Heisey News, v. 8, no. 5, May 1984, p. 8.

PAZAUREK, GUSTAV E.
Guter und Schlechter Geschmack im Kunstgewerbe
Stuttgart: Deutsche Verlags-Anstalt, 1912, 365 pp., ill.
Considers taste and design in art objects; glass examples from various periods and countries.

PHILIPPE, JOSEPH
"Propos sur l'histoire de la fenêtre"
Beauté Magazine, no. 65, 1er trimestre, 1983, pp. 3–4+, ill.

POLITZER, CATHERINE and MICHEL
Jeux de verre
Paris: Dessain et Tolra, 1983, 64 pp., ill.
Hobby book: making vitrines, scenes inside bottles, terrariums, etc.

PRAT, VÉRONIQUE
"La Collection de verres anciens du roi du Vermouth"
L'Actualité, July 21, 1984, pp. 70–74, ill.
Cinzano collection.

QUEEN, CHRISTINE J.
"Island Beaches Hold Treasures Released by the Sea"
Collectors News, v. 24, no. 9, Jan. 1984,

p. 11, ill.
Glass fishing balls found in Okinawa.

ROMERO, JULIA MAE
"Extant Enamel Artifacts and Language"
Glass on Metal, v. 3, no. 6, Dec. 1984, pp. 81–83.

SASSER, ELIZABETH SKIDMORE
"A Short History of Glass and Glassmaking in Western Civilization"
The Museum Journal (West Texas Museum Association, Lubbock), no. 22, 1983, pp. 71–122.

SHERIFF, NANCY and BILL
"The Portland Museum of Art"
The National Early American Glass Club Gatherings, v. 8, no. 3, Oct. 1984, pp. 6–7.
The glass displays in the new wing.

SMIT, F. G. A. M.
"Engraved and Cut Glass on Postage Stamps"
The Glass Engraver, no. 34, Winter 1983/84, pp. 16–19+, ill.
Various countries, 1950s–1983.

SPILLMAN, JANE SHADEL
"The Connoisseurship of Glass"
The Minneapolis Institute of Arts Antiques Show, Presented by the Decorative Arts Council, [Minneapolis, Minn.: the institute], 1984, pp. 70–77, ill.

ST. JOHNSTON, ALFRED
"A Lost Art Revived"
Magazine of Art (London), v. 10, 1887, pp. 187–193, ill.
Cameo glass, both ancient and some Stourbridge pieces of 1880s.

STÖBER, OTTO
Glas. 1. Glas-Zeit-Tafel, mit einer Kurzgefassten Literaturübersicht der verschiedenen Wissensgebiete vom Glase
Linz: Länderverlag, 1947, 112 pp., ill.
A glass time line covering both artistic and technical developments; includes a register and bibliography.

STRUCK, BIRGIT
"Die Entwicklung des Glas-Designs, Teil 1"
Sprechsaal, v. 116, no. [5], 1983, pp. 343–4, 346.
Development of glass design. Part 1: the move from handwork to industrial designing; Jugendstil designers.

SWOYER, DAVID
"Glass Casting"
Arts Quarterly (New Orleans Museum of Art), v. 3, no. 2, April/May/June 1981, p. 13, ill.
Exhibit that displays glass casting and molding processes.

THIEL BAUER, ANA MARIA
Diseño de un sistema de objetos de cristal para la mesa
Mexico City: [thesis for] Universidad Iberoamericana, 1984, 178 pp., ill.
In Spanish and English. A system and criteria for designing tableware.

WATTS, DAVID C.
"The Glass Carafe, by Mrs. Jennifer Frost"
Glass Circle News, no. 29, July 1984, p. 3.
Summary of a paper given for the Glass Circle.
"Old Glassmaking Techniques by Ray Flavell"
Glass Circle News, no. 29, July 1984, pp. 3–4.
Summary of a lecture given for the Glass Circle.

WELANDER, ELSEBETH
"Hur gammalt är glaset?"
Nya Antik et Auktion, no. 1, Jan. 1984, pp. 22–26, ill.
Distinguishing between old glass and new copies.

WRIGHT, ADELA
"Windows and Frames"
The Antique Collector, v. 55, no. 8, Aug. 1984, pp. 50–53, ill.
History, styles, repair methods.

YOSHIMIZU, TSUNEO
Garasu nyūmon
Tokyo: Heibon Kabushiki Kaisha, 1983, 161 pp., ill.
[In Japanese only] General history and introduction to glass; glass forming and decorating techniques.

ZURICH. KUNSTGEWERBE-MUSEUM DER STADT.
MUSEUM FÜR GESTALTUNG
Die Vase (Text by Werner Oechslin and Oskar Bätschmann)
Zurich: the museum, 1982, 215 pp., ill.
Exhibition of the vessel form in drawings, paintings, prints, catalogs, etc.

TECHNOLOGY

ANONYMOUS
"Festival Window on the World: A Guide to the International Garden Festival"
Pilkington News, April 18, 1984, pp. 7–9, ill.
Greenhouse pavilion and theme park using Pilkington glass for Liverpool festival.
"Flachglaserzeugung seit der Jahrhundertwende"
Glas + Rahmen, no. 11, June 1983, pp. 640–641.
100 years of flat glass.
"Il genio di Leonardo nelle macchine del vetro"
Il Vetro, v. 17, no. 8, Aug. 1939, pp. 283–287, ill.
Exhibit of machines designed by Leonardo for grinding optical glass.
"Glass—The Answer to Nuclear Waste"
Glass (U.K.), v. 61, no. 8, Aug. 1984, p. 280, ill.
Vitrification process whereby nuclear waste is solidified into a block of borosilicate glass for safe storage.
"Making Glass by Hand"
Heisey News, v. 13, no. 5, May 1984, pp. 14–17. Part 2: v. 13, no. 6, June 1984, pp. 8–10.
[reprint, source unknown].
"Modern Expression of 19th Century Hothouse in Garden Festival's International Pavilion"
Glass (U.K.), v. 61, no. 7, July 1984, p. 254, ill.
Liverpool conservatory follows architectural principles developed in 1817.
"Das Rätsel der römischen Diatretgläser ist gelöst"
Porzellan + Glas, no. 3, 1984, pp. 90–91, ill.
Josef Welzel and Christinenhütte factory recreate Roman diatreta glasses.
"A U.S. Company Celebrates Its First Century by Recalling Its Philosophy of Meeting Change and Challenge"
American Glass Review, v. 104, no. 5, Nov. 1983, pp. 6–8, ill.
History of U.S. flat glass industry.

ADAMS, P. BRUCE, and OTHERS
All About Glass
Corning, N.Y.: Corning Glass Works, 1984, 35 pp., ill.
General book about structure, properties, and manufacturing of glass.

BASTOW, HARRY
"Decorative Color Effects in Glass"
Glass and Pottery World, v. 16, no. 4,
April 1908, pp. 32–33.

BERDUCOU, MARIE
and RELIER, CAROLINE
"La Conservation sur les chantiers du
Proche et Moyen-Orient des céra-
miques et verres archéologiques"
*Lettre d'Information Archéologie Orien-
tale*, no. 7, April 1984, pp. 53–67.
On-site conservation of glass.

BETTEMBOURG, JEAN-MARIE
"Dégradation et conservation des
vitraux anciens"
Dossiers de l'Archéologie, no. 26, Jan./
Feb. 1978, pp. 102–111, ill.

BIRKHILL, FREDERICK
A Concise History of Lampworking
[Pinckney, Mich.: unpublished manuscript from Frederick Birkhill Studios,
1984?], 12 pp., ill.

BISER, BENJAMIN F.
Elements of Glass and Glass Making
Pittsburgh, Pa.: Glass and Pottery
Publishing Co., 1899; reprint: [s.l.]:
Roy C. Horner, 1974, 174 pp.

BLUME, MARY
"Have the French Been 'Shockingly
Negligent of Their Greatest Artistic
Glory'?"
Art News, v. 77, no. 2, Feb. 1978, pp.
36–40, ill.
Restoring Chartres windows.

BRADLEY, S. M.; BOFF, R. M.;
and SHORER, P. H. T.
"A Modified Technique for the Light-
weight Backing of Mosaics"
Studies in Conservation, v. 28, no. 4,
1983, pp. 161–170, ill.

BRETZ, SIMONE
"Die Restaurierung eines Glases aus
dem Mittelalter"
MALTECHNIK Restauro, v. 90, no. 1,
Jan. 1984, pp. 51–56, ill. English
summary.
Restoration of a *krautstrunk*.

BRILL, ROBERT H.
"Ben tornato a Napoli"
The Corning Museum of Glass Newsletter,
Summer 1984, pp. 1–2, ill.
Corning restores damaged Venetian
and *façon de Venise* glasses from two
Naples museums.

BURGOYNE, IAN and
SCOBLE, RACHEL
*Two Thousand Years of Flat Glass Mak-
ing*

St. Helens, Merseyside: Pilkington
Brothers P.L.C., Printing and Stationery Department, 1983, 14 pp., ill.

BUTTS, SHELDON
"Photographing Glass"
The Hobstar, v. 9, no. 8, May 1984, pp.
4–5, ill.

*Carl Zeiss, Optische Werkstätte, Jena. Mi-
croscopes and Microscopical Accessories*
[Catalog no. 29]
Jena: Carl Zeiss, Optische Werkstätte, 1891, 125 pp., ill.

*Conservation and Preservation of Stained
Glass with Special Reference to Post-Medieval Glasses in The Netherlands* [Interna-
tional conference, Lunteren 1981]
Amsterdam: Centraal Laboratorium/
Central Research Laboratory for Objects of Art and Science, [1984?], 120
pp., ill.

CROMPTON, WALTER H.
"The Corning Ribbon Machine"
Glass (U.K.), v. 61, no. 2, Feb. 1984,
p. 64+, ill.
History, process, products.

DALY, JAMES C.
Fiber Optics
Boca Raton, Fla.: CRC Press, Inc.,
1984, 246 pp., ill.

DAVISON, SANDRA
"The Problems of Restoring Glass
Vessels"
The Conservator, v. 2, 1978, pp. 3–8, ill.

DIETZEL, ADOLF
"Das 100 Jahre alte Thermometer
problem und der 'Mischalkalieffekt' "
Glastechnische Berichte, v. 56, no. 11,
1983, pp. 291–293. English summary.
The 100 year old thermometer problem and the "mixed alkali effect."

DOWN, JANE L.
"The Yellowing of Epoxy Resin Ad-
hesives: Report on Natural Dark
Aging"
Studies in Conservation, v. 29, no. 2,
May 1984, pp. 63–76, ill.
Resins used in glass conservation.

EMSLEY, JOHN
"Glass: Past Elegant, Future Thin"
New Scientist, no. 8, Dec. 1983, pp.
728–732, ill.
Changes in the glass industry to
higher technology.

FAHRENKROG, HANS-HERMANN
Glas am Bau, Produktion und Einsatz
Grafenau/Württ.: Expert Verlag
[Kontakt und Studium, Bd. 85],
1983, 198 pp., ill.

FITZ, STEPHAN
"A New Method of Cleaning Browned
Medieval Glass"
*ICOM Committee for Conservation, 6th
Triennial Meeting Preprints*,
(Ottawa, 21–25 Sept. 1981), Paris:
International Council of Museums,
1981, 4th vol., article no. 81/20/5.

FRAUDENIENST, HEINZ
"Fully Automatic Acid Polishing"
Glass (U.K.), v. 51, no. 4, 1974, pp.
146–148, ill.

FREESTONE, I. C.; LaNIECE,
S. C.; and MEEKS, N. D.
"A Bronze Statuette of Minerva: A
Study in Mineralogical Provenanc-
ing"
MASCA Journal, v. 3, no. 1, June
1984, pp. 10–12, ill.
Natural (volcanic) glass in corrosion
products of bronze statuette point to
its origin as Pompeii.

*The Future of Glass and Ceramic Decorat-
ing: Society of Glass Decorators Twentieth
Annual Seminar, Pittsburgh, Pa.*
Port Jefferson, N.Y.: the society,
1984, 105 pp., ill.

GENEVA. MUSÉE RATH
Sauver l'art? Conserver, analyser, restaurer
Geneva: Musée d'art et d'histoire;
Editions du Tricorne, 1982, 332 pp.,
ill.
Exhibition that included restoration
of glass and stained glass.

GIRARD, SYLVIE
"Jalons historiques"
La Revue de la Céramique et du Verre, no.
17, July/Aug. 1984, pp. 22–23, ill.
Glass and architectural landmarks:
Crystal Palace, Paxton's "Great
Stove" at Chatsworth, Institute of
Technology at Leicester.

GRODECKI, LOUIS
"Sauvons les vitraux anciens"
Dossiers de l'Archéologie, no. 26, Jan./
Feb. 1978, pp. 12–25, ill.

HACKER, MICHAEL
"Glass Technology in Secondary
Schools—an Experimental Pro-
gram"
American Ceramic Society Bulletin, v. 62,
no. 12, Dec. 1983, pp. 1341–1342, ill.

HAEVERNICK, THEA ELISABETH
"'Moldawite'"
Beiträge zur Glasforschung. Die wichtigsten Aufsätze von 1938 bis 1981, Mainz am Rhein: Philipp von Zabern, 1981, pp. 12–13.
[Originally published in *Germania*, v. 30, no. 1, 1952]. Tektites from Moravia.

HENAU, P. DE and FONTAINE-HODIAMONT, C.
"Selectie uit de werkzaamheden van 1980 en 1981/Sélection des activités des années 1980 et 1981"
Bulletin de l'Institut royal du Patrimoine artistique/Koninklijk Instituut voor het Kunstpatrimonium, (Brussels), no. 19, 1982/83, pp. 205–206, ill.
Restoration of a floral vase by F. Zitzmann, Wiesbaden, 1899.

HLAVÁČ, JAN
The Technology of Glass and Ceramics: an Introduction
Amsterdam: Elsevier Scientific Publishing Co., 1983, 431 pp., ill.

ILEY, G. N.
"Float Glass and Its Impact on the Flat Glass Industry"
Glass International, March 1984, pp. 51–56, ill.
History, development, future trends.

JACKSON, PATRICIA R.
"Resins Used in Glass Conservation"
Proceedings of the Symposium, Edinburgh 1982, (Ed. by J. O. Tate, N. H. Tennent, and J. H. Townsend), Scottish Society for Conservation & Restoration, 1983, pp. 10–1 to 10–7.

KACZMARCZYK, ALEXANDER and HEDGES, ROBERT E. M.
Ancient Egyptian Faience: An Analytical Survey of Egyptian Faience from Predynastic to Roman Times
Warminster, U.K.: Aris & Phillips Ltd., 1983, 587 pp., ill.

KERLIN, EWALD
"Erhaltung wertvoller Glasmalereien"
Glas + Rahmen, no. 24, Dec. 1983, p. 1242, ill.
Stained glass conservation efforts.

LÁJOS, HORVÁTH
"The Use of Sial Glass Piping in the Hungarian Wine Industry"
Czechoslovak Glass Review, no. 1, 1962, pp. 22–24, ill.

LEARNER, RICHARD
Astronomy Through the Telescope
New York, N.Y.: Van Nostrand Reinhold Co., 1981, 224 pp., ill.
500 years of mirrors, lenses, optical instruments.

LINDBERG, DAVID C.
Studies in the History of Medieval Optics
London: Variorum Reprints, 1983, 302 pp., ill.

LONGWORTH, G.; TENNENT, N. H.; TRICKER, M. J.; and VAISHNAVA, P. P.
"Iron-57 Mössbauer Spectral Studies of Medieval Stained Glass"
Journal of Archaeological Science, v. 9, no. 3, Sept. 1982, pp. 261–273, ill.

LUTZ, EGON
"Glasrestaurierung im Rheinischen Landesmuseum Trier"
Trierer Zeitschrift, v. 46, 1983, pp. 281–283, ill.
Restoring Roman glass pieces.

MALIES, HAROLD
"Introduction to Microscopes"
The Antique Collector, v. 55, no. 8, Aug. 1984, pp. 56–61, ill.
19th c. types.

MARCHESE, B. and GARZILLO, V.
"An Investigation of the Mosaics in the Cathedral of Salerno. Part II: Characterization of Some Mosaic Tesserae"
Studies in Conservation, v. 29, no. 1, Feb. 1984, pp. 10–16, ill.

McLELLAN, GEORGE and SHAND, ERROLL B.
Glass Engineering Handbook. Third Edition
New York, N.Y.: McGraw-Hill Book Co., 1984, 512 pp., ill.

MILLS, JOHN FITZMAURICE
Encyclopedia of Antique Scientific Instruments
New York, N.Y.: Facts on File Publications, 1983, 255 pp., ill.

MORETTI, C. and HREGLICH, S.
"Opacizzazione e colorazione del vetro mediante le 'anime.' 1-a parte: indagine nei ricettari del '700 ed '800"
Rivista della Stazione Sperimentale del Vetro, v. 14, no. 1, Jan./Feb. 1984, pp. 17–22, ill. English summary.
18th and 19th c. recipe books on use of opacifiers and coloring agents.

MORETTI, EMILIO
"Lavorazione del vetro a mano: le cannette per zanfirico/Hand-made Glass: Rods for zanfirico"
Vetro Informazione, v. 3, no. 18, Nov./Dec. 1983, pp. 35–36, ill. English summary.
Canes.

"La lavorazione del vetro a mano: il lampadario classico muranese/Hand-made Glass: the Classical Chandelier of Murano"
Vetro Informazione, v. 3, no. 16, July/Aug. 1983, pp. 23–25, ill.

"La lavorazione del vetro a mano: il vetro doublé con lavorazione ad asporto/Hand-made Glass: Double Glass with Cutting Decorations"
Vetro Informazione, v. 4, no. 20, March/April 1984, pp. 42–43, ill.

Mosaics No. 2: Safeguard. Carthage 1979; Périgueux 1980
[Rome]: ICCROM/International Committee for the Conservation of Mosaics, 1983, 63 pp., ill.
English edition.

NEWTON, ROY and NORMANDALE, OLIVER
"Correspondence on alcohol and lead glass"
The Glass Engraver, no. 36, Summer 1984, pp. 7–11.
Question regarding safety of drinking alcoholic beverages from lead glasses.

NRIAGU, JEROME O.
Lead and Lead Poisoning in Antiquity
New York, N.Y.: John Wiley & Sons, 1983, 437 pp.
Glass and glassmaking, pp. 223–232.

OBERMAN, LADISLAV
"Glass Fibres in the Electrical Engineering Industry"
Glass Review, v. 39, no. 4, 1984, p. 9, ill.

PARTRIDGE, J. H.
Glass-To-Metal Seals
Sheffield: Society of Glass Technology, 1949, 238 pp., ill.

PAUL, AMAL
Chemistry of Glasses
New York, N.Y.: Chapman and Hall; Methuen, 1982, 293 pp., ill.

PERRY, ROBERT C.
"The Float Glass Process: A New Method or an Extension of Previous Ones?"
Glass Industry, v. 65, no. 2, Feb. 10, 1984, pp. 17–19+, ill.
Historical survey.

PFAENDER, HEINZ G.
Schott Guide to Glass
New York, N.Y.: Van Nostrand
Reinhold Co., 1983, revised edition,
179 pp., ill.

PINCUS, ALEXIS G.
Forming in the Glass Industry, Part 1:
Forming Machines and Methods
New York, N.Y.: Ashlee Publishing
Co., Books for the Glass Industry Di-
vision, 1983, 248 pp., ill.
Forming in the Glass Industry, Part 2:
Accessories to Glass Forming
New York, N.Y.: Ashlee Publishing
Co., Books for the Glass Industry Di-
vision, 1983, pp. 250–508, ill.

POPE, FRANKLIN LEONARD
The Evolution of the Electric Incandescent
Lamp
New York, N.Y.: Boschen & Wefer,
1894, 91 pp., ill.

Proceedings of the 28th Symposium and Exhi-
bition on the Art of Glassblowing [Cherry
Hill, N.J.]
Toledo, O.: The American Scientific
Glassblowers Society, 1983, 59 pp.,
ill.

RAMBUSCH, VIGGO BECH
"The Lead Cames of Stained Glass
Windows: Purpose, Problems, &
Preservation"
Technology & Conservation, v. 8, no. 3,
Fall 1983, pp. 46–49, ill.

RANDALL, J. E.
A Practical Treatise on the Incandescent
Lamp
Lynn, Mass.: Bubier Publishing Co.,
1891, 82 pp., ill.

Restaurieren kunstgerecht. Eine Dokumenta-
tion der Werkstätten des Museums für Kunst
und Gewerbe
Hamburg: Museum für Kunst und
Gewerbe, 1983, 252 pp., ill.
Includes restoration of several glass
pieces by Margarete Meyer, pp. 17–
25.

SALDAÑA DE GOUST, C.
"Avance d'une bibliographie de conservation et restauration de matéri-
aux siliceux"
ICOM Committee for Conservation, 6th
Triennial Meeting (Ottawa, 21–25 Sept.
1981) Preprints, Paris: International
Council of Museums, 1981, 4th vol.,
no. 81/21/1.
Toward a bibliography of glass and
ceramic conservation.

SANDERSON, D. C. W.
and HUNTER, J. R.
"The Neutron Activation Analysis of
Archaeological Glasses from Scandi-
navia and Britain"
Pact, no. 7, Part 2, 1982, pp. 401–411,
ill.

SANDERSON, D. C. W.;
HUNTER, J. R.;
and WARREN, S. E.
"Energy Dispersive X-ray Fluores-
cence Analysis of 1st Millenium AD
Glass from Britain"
Journal of Archaeological Science, v. 11,
no. 1, Jan. 1984, pp. 53–69, ill.

ŠČAPOVA [SCHAPOVA], JULIA L.
"Rezul'taty spektral'nogo analiza
stekla iz Tanaisa"
Drevnosti Nizhnego Dona (Materialy i
Issledovaniä po Arkheologii SSSR), no.
127, 1965, pp. 249–255.
Results of spectral analysis of glass
from Tanais.

SCHILLINGER, KLAUS
"Herstellung von Brennspiegeln und
Brenngläsern im 17. und 18. Jh. und
ihre Anwendung zur Erzeugung
hoher Temperaturen"
NTM-Schriftenreihe für Geschichte der
Naturwissenschaften, Technik, und Medi-
zin, (Leipzig), v. 20, no. 2, 1983, pp.
67–85, ill.
History of making concave mirrors
and lenses, used to produce high
temperatures.

SCHREURS, J. W. H.
and BRILL, R. H.
"Iron and Sulfur Related Colors in
Ancient Glasses"
Archaeometry, v. 26, no. 2, 1984, pp.
199–209, ill.

SHOEMAKER, ARTHUR F.
"Glass in the Space Age"
Glass (U.K.), v. 61, no. 9, Sept. 1984,
pp. 301–303, ill.
Use of glasses in space shuttles.

SUTTON-JONES, KEN
and BURGOYNE, IAN
"A New Light for a Redundant Optic"
Museums Journal, v. 82, no. 4, March
1983, pp. 237–238, ill.
Display of lighthouse lens units by
Chance Brothers at Pilkington Glass
Museum.

TALIAFERRO, T. L.
Standardization of Glass Finishes
Chicago, Ill.: [s.n.], 1934, 40 pp., ill.
In container industry.

TEAGUE, WALTER DORWIN
"Structural and Decorative Trends in
Glass"
American Architect, no. 141, May 1932,
pp. 40–43+, ill.

TENNANT, N. H. et al.
"Major, Minor, and Trace Element
Analysis of Medieval Stained Glass
by Flame Atomic Absorption Spec-
trometry"
Archaeological Chemistry III. Based on a
Symposium Sponsored by the Division of
the History of Chemistry . . . , Washington, D.C.: American Chemical Society, 1984, pp. 133–150, ill.

TERWEN, P. A.
"The Mending of Stained Glass; A
Technical Instruction"
Proceedings of the Symposium, Edinburgh
1982, (Ed. by J. O. Tate, N. H. Ten-
nant, and J. H. Townsend), Scottish
Society for Conservation & Restora-
tion, 1983, pp. 11-1 to 11-5.

TURNER, GERARD L. 'E.
Nineteenth-Century Scientific Instruments
Berkeley and Los Angeles, Cal.: Uni-
versity of California Press for Soth-
eby Publications, 1983, 320 pp., ill.
"Three Late-Seventeenth Century
Italian Telescopes, Two Signed by
Paolo Belletti of Bologna"
Annali dell'Istituto e Museo di Storia della
Scienza di Firenze, v. 9, no. 1, 1984, pp.
41–64, ill.

USSELMAN, MELVYN CHARLES
"Michael Faraday's Use of Platinum
in His Researches on Optical Glass"
Platinum Metals Review, v. 27, 1983,
pp. 175–181, ill.

VINCENT, KEITH
"Developments in Household and
Fluorescent Lamp Making Ma-
chinery"
Glass (U.K.), v. 61, no. 2, Feb. 1984,
pp. 68–71+, ill.

VRBKA, IVAN
"Possibilities of the Use of Glass Balls
and Balotina"
Glass Review, v. 38, no. 11, 1983, p. 17,
ill.
Industrial glass balls made at Ja-
blonecké Sklárny Glassworks.

WHITBY, GARRY
Glassware Manufacture for Developing
Countries
London: Intermediate Technology
Development Group, 1983, 45 pp.,
ill.

WILLIAMS-THOMAS, D.
"Domestic Glassware Production:
Complementary—Not Competitive"
Glass (U.K.), v. 61, no. 1, Jan. 1984,
p. 29, ill.
Handmade glassware business.

ZARUBA, BARBARA
"Der Spiegel—Vergangenheit und
Gegenwart"
Glaswelt, v. 36, no. 11, Nov. 1983, p.
886+, ill.
Mirror production, past and present.

ZECCHIN, LUIGI
"Il ricettario di Giovanni Darduin"
*Rivista della Stazione Sperimentale del
Vetro*, v. 1, no. 3, May/June 1971, pp.
21–24, ill. English summary.
Late 16th c. Muranese opaque
enamel formulas.

HISTORICAL
PUBLICATIONS

ANCIENT

ANONYMOUS
"Ancient Glasswares Excavated at
Begram, Afghanistan. Interview with
Mrs. Haruko Motamedi"
Glass (Tokyo), no. 16, March 1984,
pp. 9–14, ill. In Japanese, English
summary.
1st–3rd c. Roman glasses in Kabul
Museum.

AVIGAD, NAHMAN
Discovering Jerusalem
Nashville, Tenn.: Thomas Nelson
Publishers, 1980, 270 pp., ill.
Molded and freeblown glass fragments and the remains of a factory,
pp. 186–192.
"Jerusalem Flourishing: A Craft Center for Stone, Pottery, and Glass"
Biblical Archaeology Review, v. 9, no. 6,
Nov./Dec. 1983, pp. 48–65, ill.
1st c. glass factory site with evidence
of earliest phase of glassblowing; also
quantity of molded fragments, "kohl
sticks."

BARAG, DAN
"Glass Inlays and the Classification
and Dating of Ivories from the Ninth-
Eighth Centuries B.C."
Anatolian Studies (Ankara), v. 33,
1983, pp. 163–167, ill.
"Glass Vessels"
'Atiqot, v. 16, 1983, pp. 37–38, ill.

Bottle and other vessel fragments
from an excavation at Kursi, Israel.
"Two Masterpieces of Late Antique
Glass"
The Israel Museum Journal, v. 2, Spring
1983, pp. 35–38, ill.
4th c. A.D. jugs in the museum collection.

BATTAGLIA, GABRIELLA
BORDENACHE
*Corredi funerari di età imperiale e barba-
rica nel Museo Nazionale Romano*
Rome: Edizioni Quasar di Severino
Tognon, 1983, 165 pp., ill.
Glass (glass paste cameos, molded
boat, etc.): pp. 27–29, 70–74, 90.

BORGARD, PHILIPPE
"Le Village de la Colline du Château à
Fontaine de Vaucluse (Vaucluse):
un site de l'antiquité tardive (V-VIe
siècle)"
Bulletin Archéologique de Provence, v. 13,
no. 4, 1984, pp. 1-14, ill.
Fragments from site in southern
France.

BUCOVALĂ, MIHAI
"Roman Glass Vessels Discovered in
Dobrudja"
Journal of Glass Studies, v. 26, 1984, pp.
59–63, ill.

BUJNA, JOZEF and
ROMSAUER, PETER
"Späthallstatt- und frühlatènezeit-
liches Gräberfeld in Bučany"
Slovenská Archeológia, v. 31, no. 2,
1983, pp. 277–322, ill.
Beads.

BÜRGES, JOST
"Pfyn—Ad Fines"
Archäologie der Schweiz, v. 6, no. 4,
1983, pp. 146–160, ill. French, Ital-
ian summaries.
Late Roman finds at Swiss site.

CURTIS, JOHN
Nush-i Jan III: The Small Finds
London: The British Institute of Persian Studies, 1984, 71 pp., ill.
Beads, spindle whorls, vessel fragment from Median and Parthian
levels.

DAUPHIN, CLAUDINE
"Une mosaïque romaine"
Archéologia, no. 186, Jan. 1984, pp.
44–53, ill.
3rd c. mosaic, Naplouse, Israel.

DAYTON, J. E.
"The Mycenaeans and the Discovery
of Glass"

*International Congress of Mediterranean
Pre- and Protohistory* (Amsterdam:
Gruener), 1980, pp. 169–177, ill.

DEKOULAKOU, IPHIGENEIA
"Archaiotētes kai mnēmeia: Achaïas"
Archaiologikon Deltion, v. 30 (1975),
1983, pp. 99–120, ill.
Unguentaria, bottles, flasks.
"Archaiotētes kai mnēmeia achaïas:
Pátra"
Archaiologikon Deltion, v. 31 (1976),
1984, p. 103, ill.
Roman glass from excavations at
Photila St. and Trikoupe St., Patras.

DOTHAN, MOSHE
*Hammath Tiberias, Early Synagogues and
the Hellenistic and Roman Remains*
Jerusalem: Israel Exploration Society; University of Haifa, Department of Antiquities and Museums,
1983, 88 pp., ill.
Includes molded glass kantharos
with metallic coating.

DUNAND, FRANÇOISE
"Les 'têtes dorées' de la nécropole de
Douch"
*Bulletin de la Société Française d'Egypto-
logie* (Paris), no. 93, 1982, pp. 26–43,
ill.
Includes glass finds, 2nd–4th c.
A.D.: simple bowl and square bottle,
and more elaborate Alexandrian-
type decorated fragments.

ENGLE, ANITA
*The Proto-Sidonians: Glassmakers and
Potters* (Readings in Glass History no.
17)
Jerusalem: Phoenix Publications,
1983, 103 pp., ill.

ERDÉLYI, I. and SALAMON, Á.
"Bericht über die Ausgrabungen in
Pilismarót, Öregek-dülö (1973–
1974)"
*Mitteilungen des Archäologischen Instituts
der Ungarischen Akademie der Wissenschaften*, v. 10/11, 1980/81, pp. 147–
162, ill.
Vessels from Roman and Avar cemetery at Hungarian site.

FARIOLI CAMPANATI,
RAFFAELLA, ed.
*III colloquio internazionale sul mosaico
antico, Ravenna, 6–10 settembre 1980* (2
vols.)
Ravenna: Edizioni del Girasole/
Mario Lapucci, 1983, 591 pp., ill.
Conference papers on ancient mo-
saics.

FISCHER, CHRISTIAN
"En romersk glasskål med jagtmotiv fra en yngre romersk jernaldergrav"
Kuml, 1981, pp. 165–182, ill. English summary.
Bowl engraved with hunting scene from a late Roman Iron Age grave, Denmark.

FISCHER, THOMAS; RIECKHOFF-PAULI, SABINE; and SPINDLER, KONRAD
"Grabungen in der spätkeltischen Siedlung im Sulztal bei Berching-Pollanten, Landkreis Neumarkt, Oberpfalz"
Germania, v. 62, no. 2, 1984, pp. 311–372, ill.
Glass bangles and beads from Iron Age settlement at Berching-Pollanten.

FREMERSDORF, FRITZ and POLÓNYI-FREMERSDORF, EDELTRAUD
Die farblosen Gläser der Frühzeit in Köln. 2. und 3. Jahrhundert
Cologne: Archäologische Gesellschaft; Bonn: Dr. Rudolf Habelt, 1984, 144 pp., ill.
Large quantity of vessels, many forms and types of decoration.

GABRIČEVIĆ, BRANIMIR
"Antička nekropola u Sinju. Prilog proučavanju prapovijesnih vjerovanja"
Vjesnik, v. 76, 1983, pp. 5–101, ill. French summary.
Includes vessels from the Roman cemetery at Sinj in Dalmatia.

GAITZSCH, W.
"Ausgrabungen und Funde 1981, Römische Zeit: Niederzier, Kr. Düren"
Bonner Jahrbücher, v. 183, 1983, pp. 647–654, ill.
Bracelet; balsamarium and other vessel fragments.

GENING, V. F. and KORYAKOVA, L. N.
"Likhachovo i Chernoozerye kurgany rannego železnogo veka zapadnoǐ sibiri"
Sovetskaiā Arkheologiiā, no. 2, 1984, pp. 165–187, ill. English summary.
Iron Age burials in W. Siberia; includes beads.

GROSE, DAVID F.
"Glass Forming Methods in Classical Antiquity: Some Considerations"
Journal of Glass Studies, v. 26, 1984, pp. 25–34, ill.

HAEVERNICK, THEA ELISABETH
"Antike Glasarmringe und ihre Herstellung"
Beiträge zur Glasforschung. Die wichtigsten Aufsätze von 1938 bis 1981, Mainz am Rhein: Philipp von Zabern, 1981, pp. 8–11, ill. [Originally published in *Glastechnische Berichte*, no. 25, 1952, pp. 212–215].
Bracelets from Manching.

"Einige Glasperlen aus Gräbern der Lausitzer Kultur in Sachsen"
Beiträge zur Glasforschung. Die wichtigsten Aufsätze von 1938 bis 1981, Mainz am Rhein: Philipp von Zabern, 1981, pp. 14–17, ill. [Originally published in *Arbeits- und Forschungsberichte zur sächsischen Bodendenkmalpflege*, 1951, 2. Teil 1953, pp. 52–56].

Glasperlen der vorrömischen Eisenzeit I (Nach Unterlagen von Thea Elisabeth Haevernick, Herausgegeben von O.-H. Frey)
Mainz am Rhein: Philipp von Zabern, 1983, 178 pp., ill. (Marburger Studien zur Vor- und Frühgeschichte, Band 5).
Pre-Roman zig-zag beads and their locations; also Hallstatt beads and Roman window glass.

"Der Hortfund von Allendorf. Hals- und Haarschmuck"
Beiträge zur Glasforschung. Die wichtigsten Aufsätze von 1938 bis 1981, Mainz am Rhein: Philipp von Zabern, 1981, pp. 18–23, ill. [Originally published in *Prähistorische Zeitschrift*, no. 34/35, 1953, pp. 213–217].
Includes glass beads.

"Ein keltischer Glasarmring im Memminger Museum"
Beiträge zur Glasforschung. Die wichtigsten Aufsätze von 1938 bis 1981, Mainz am Rhein; Philipp von Zabern, 1981, pp. 39–40, ill. [Originally published in *Der Spiegelschwab*, no. 3, *Memminger Zeitung*, 1956].

"Römische Fensterscheiben"
Beiträge zur Glasforschung. Die wichtigsten Aufsätze von 1938 bis 1981, Mainz am Rhein: Philipp von Zabern, 1981, pp. 24–27, ill. [Originally published in *Glastechnische Berichte*, no. 27, 1954, pp. 464–466].

"Spätlatènezeitliche Gräber aus Brücken an der Helme"
Beiträge zur Glasforschung. Die wichtigsten Aufsätze von 1938 bis 1981, Mainz am Rhein: Philipp von Zabern, 1981, pp. 1–6, ill. [Originally published in *Marburger Studien* 1938, pp. 77–82].
Bracelet; blue and clear glass fragments.

HAEVERNICK, THEA ELISABETH and HAHN-WEINHEIMER, PAULA
"Untersuchungen römischer Fenstergläser"
Beiträge zur Glasforschung. Die wichtigsten Aufsätze von 1938 bis 1981, Mainz am Rhein: Philipp von Zabern, 1981, pp. 33–38, ill. [Originally published in *Saalburg-Jahrbuch*, no. 14, 1955, pp. 65–73].

HAGENOW, GERD
Aus dem Weingarten der Antike: der Wein in Dichtung, Brauchtum und Alltag
Mainz am Rhein: Philipp von Zabern, 1982, 248 pp., ill.
Includes glass vessels, pp. 128–135.

HARDEN, DONALD B.
Catalogue of Greek and Roman Glass in the British Museum. Vol. 1: Core- and Rod-formed Vessels and Pendants and Mycenaean Cast Objects
London: British Museum Publications, 1981, 187 pp., ill. Reviewed by Dan P. Barag in *The Antiquaries Journal*, v. 64, Part 1, 1984, pp. 149–151. Reviewed by David F. Grose in *Archaeological News*, v. 13, nos. 1/2, Spring/Summer 1984, pp. 43–45. Reviewed by Axel von Saldern in *Glastechnische Berichte*, v. 57, no. 1, 1984, pp. 18–19.

"Study and Research on Ancient Glass: Past and Future"
Journal of Glass Studies, v. 26, 1984, pp. 9–24.

Highlights of Archaeology: The Israel Museum, Jerusalem
Jerusalem: the museum, 1984, 159 pp., ill.
Mosaics, molded bowls, snake-thread bottle.

HIRAI, NAOSHI
"A Newly Discovered Glass Cup Found in South Russia"
Kōkogaku Zasshi (Journal of the Archaeological Society of Nippon), v. 41, no. 2, Jan. 1956, pp. 66–70, ill. In Japanese only.
Facet-cut vessel, possibly Sasanian.

The Israel Museum Guide (Text by Rafi Grafman)
Jerusalem: the museum, 1983, 174 pp., ill.
Ancient glass, pp. 102–105; also mosaics.

KOUKOULĒ-CHRUSANTHAKĒ, CH.
"Makedonia: Phílippoi"
Archaiologikon Deltion, v. 30, (1975)
1983, p. 285, ill.
2nd c. A.D. phial from funerary deposit at Philippi.

KRÄMER, WERNER
"Manching II. Zu den Ausgrabungen in den Jahren 1957 bis 1961"
Germania, v. 40, no. 2, 1962, pp. 293–317, ill.
Colored bracelets, La Tène period.

KUNOW, JÜRGEN
Der römische Import in der Germania libera bis zu den Markomannenkriegen: Studien zu Bronze- und Glasgefässen
Neumünster: Karl Wachholtz, 1983, 208 pp., ill.
Roman *Rippenschalen* and footed cups imported into northern Europe: their transport, origins, etc.

KÜNZL, ERNST
"Zwei silberne Tetrarchenporträts im RGZM und die römischen Kaiserbildnisse aus Gold und Silber"
Jahrbuch des Römisch-Germanischen Zentralmuseums Mainz, v. 30, 1983, pp. 381–402, ill.
Roman silver presentation plate with a portrait bust in blue glass.

KURASHIKI. OHARA BIJUTSUKAN IV [Ohara Art Museum IV]
Kōdai Egiputo to Chūkintō no Bijutsu
Kurashiki, Okayama: the museum, n.d., 134 pp., ill. [In Japanese only].
Egyptian and Near Eastern art; includes glass.

LANDES, CHRISTIAN
Verres gallo-romains
Paris: Musée Carnavalet, 1983, 117 pp., ill. (Bulletin du Musée Carnavalet, 36ᵉ année, 1983, no. 1–2).

LEES-CAUSEY, CATHERINE
"Some Roman Glass in the J. Paul Getty Museum"
The J. Paul Getty Museum Journal, v. 11, 1983, pp. 153–156, ill.

LIEBOWITZ, HAROLD
"News and Notes: Tel Yin'am, 1981"
Israel Exploration Journal, v. 33, no. 1-2, 1983, pp. 115–116.
Beads and an 'Egyptian blue' bowl.

LITH, SOPHIA M. E. VAN
"Glas aus Asciburgium"
Rheinische Ausgrabungen 23. Beiträge zur Archäologie des römischen Rheinlands IV, 1983, pp. 211–281, ill.

Large groups of beads and vessels show a variety of forms and decorative techniques.

MACCABRUNI, CLAUDIA
I vetri romani dei musei civici di Pavia. Lettura di una collezione
Pavia: Ticinum Edizioni in collaboration with the Comune di Pavia, 1983, 195 pp., ill.
Guide to the collection.

MACKENSEN, MICHAEL
Resafa I
Mainz am Rhein: Philipp von Zabern, 1984, 97 pp., ill.
Beaker, flask, and footed glass fragments; bracelets; beads from Northern Syrian fortified site.

MATTUSCH, CAROL, ed.
"Field Notes: California"
Archaeological News, v. 13, nos. 1/2, Spring/Summer 1984, p. 34.
Punic and Etruscan pendants acquired by the Getty Museum.

MENTASTI, ROSA BAROVIER
"La coppa incisa con 'Daniele nella fossa dei leoni' al Museo Nazionale Concordiese"
Aquileia Nostra, v. 54, 1983, pp. 158–171, ill.
Late Roman wheel-cut glass with Christian scene.

Mosaïque: recueil d'hommages à Henri Stern
Paris: Editions Recherche sur les Civilisations, 1983, 374 pp., ill.

MULHERN, ALICE
"L'Orante, vie et mort d'une image"
Dossiers de l'Archéologie, no. 18, Sept./Oct. 1976, pp. 34–47, ill.
Includes Early Christian gold glasses.

NÄSMAN, ULF
Glas och handel i senromersk tid och folkvandringstid/Glass and Trade in the Late Roman and Migration Periods
Uppsala: Uppsala Universitet höstterminen/Uppsala University Institute of North-European Archaeology, 1984, 166 pp., ill. English summary.
4th–6th c. glass found in Eketorp fort, Oland, Sweden, and a study of sources for these imports.

NELLIST, MICHAEL
"Roman Glass: A Transparent Deception"
Antique Collecting, v. 19, no. 7, Dec. 1984, pp. 66–67, ill.
Distinguishing fakes.

NOELKE, PETER
"Reiche Gräber von einem römischen Gutshof in Köln"
Germania, v. 62, no. 2, 1984, pp. 373–423, ill.
Grave groups with many glass flasks, bottles, bowls.

Notice sur le Musée Dodwell et catalogue raisonné des objets qu'il contient
Rome: L'Institut de Correspondance Archéologique, 1837, 71 pp.
Includes list of 134 glass items, pp. 43–49, formerly in a private collection in Rome.

OKAYAMA. OKAYAMA SHIRITSU ORIENTO BIJUTSUKAN [Municipal Oriental Art Museum]
Kodai garasuten. Oriento kaikan i shūnen kinen
Okayama: the museum, 1980, 63 pp., ill. [In Japanese only].
Exhibition of ancient glass, commemorating the first anniversary of the museum's opening.

OLIVER, ANDREW, JR.
"Early Roman Faceted Glass"
Journal of Glass Studies, v. 26, 1984, pp. 35–58, ill.
"Tomb 12 at Episkopi"
Report of the Department of Antiquities. Cyprus 1983, pp. 245–256, ill.
Cast and blown vessels from a collective tomb used 200 B.C.–100 A.D.

ONAĬKO, N. A.
"Pogrebenie voina u poselka Myskhako"
Kratkie Soobshcheniĩa, no. 174, 1983, pp. 82–86, ill.
Unguentarium, 1st c. A.D.

PARFITT, KEITH
"An Iron Age Bead from the Lydden Valley, Worth"
Kent Archaeological Review, v. 76, 1984, pp. 135–136, ill.

PILLINGER, RENATE
Studien zu römischen Zwischengoldgläsern 1: Geschichte der Technik und das Problem der Authentizität
Vienna: Verlag der Österreichischen Akademie der Wissenschaften, 1984, 121 pp., ill.

POTTER, T. W.
Roman Britain
Cambridge, Mass.: Harvard University Press, 1983, 72 pp., ill.
Urn, cut beaker, and other vessels from the British Museum.

ROTHENBERG, BENO
"The Timna Mining Sanctuary"
Israel—People and Land, Haaretz Museum Yearbook (Tel Aviv, ed. by R. Zeevy), v. 1 (19)-5743 (1983-4), New Series, pp. 85–120, ill.
Group of 19th–20th Dynasty Egyptian glass and beads.

RÜTTI, BEAT
"Das Schlangenfadenglas von Cham-Hagendorn"
Helvetia Archaeologia, v. 14, no. 55/56, 1983, pp. 217–224, ill.
Snake-threaded bottle found in Switzerland, probably made in Cologne.

SČAPOVA [SCHAPOVA], JULIA L.
Ocherki Istorii Drevnego Steklodelija (po materialam doliny Nila, Bliznego Vostoka i Evropy)
Moscow: Izdatelstvo Moskovskogo Universiteta, 1983, 199 pp., ill.
Essay on "the history of ancient glass, with material from the Valley of the Nile, Near East, and Europe."

SCHWAB, HANNI
"Die Sondiergrabungen 1978 auf dem Mont Vully mit einem Anhang über die Untersuchungen der Jahre 1979–1982"
Jahrbuch des Römisch-Germanischen Zentralmuseums Mainz, v. 30, 1983, pp. 233–264, ill.
Beads, bracelet.

SEAR, FRANK B.
Roman Wall and Vault Mosaics
Heidelberg: F. H. Kerle Verlag, 1977, 202 pp., ill.

SINGH, RAVINDRA N.
"Antiquity of Gold-Glasses in India"
Purātattva. Bulletin of the Indian Archaeological Society (New Delhi) no. 12, 1980–81, pp. 157–159.

SINGH, RAVINDRA N.
and KUMAR, SUNIL
"Glass from Megaliths: A Technological Appraisal"
Bhāratī (Bulletin of the Department of Ancient Indian History, Culture & Archaeology, Banaras Hindu University, Varanasi) New series, no. 1, 1983, pp. 164–168.
Beads, bracelets.

SINGH, RAVINDRA N.
and SARAN, SANTOSH
"Colours and Colouring of Ancient Glasses"
Prajna. Journal of The Banaras Hindu University (Varanasi) v. 29, no. 2,

1984, pp. 55–62.
Indian glasses, 2300 B.C.
"A Note on Glass Objects from Gupta Levels"
Brāratī (Bulletin of the Department of Ancient Indian History, Culture & Archaeology, Banaras Hindu University, Varanasi) New series, no. 1, 1983, pp. 155–158.
Vessels, beads, bangles from various Indian sites, 4th–8th c. A.D.

SIREIX, MICHEL
and CHRISTOPHE
"Une ville-marché gauloise"
Archéologia, no. 197, Dec. 1984, pp. 60–66, ill.
Late prehistoric bracelets and beads from Lacoste, Aquitaine.

SMART, J. D.
"Notes: The Portland Vase Again"
The Journal of Hellenic Studies, v. 104, 1984, p. 186, ill.
New suggestion concerning the identity of figures on the Portland vase.

SOREL, PHILIPPE
"Exposition à Paris: Lutèce, de César à Clovis"
Archéologia, no. 191, June 1984, pp. 26–35, ill.
Roman vessels at Musée Carnavalet exhibition.

STAWIARSKA, TERESA
Szkła z Okresu Wpływów Rzymskich z Północnej Polski: Studium Technologiczne
Wrocław: Zakład Narodowy Imienia Ossolińskich; Warsaw: Polska Akademia Nauk, Instytut Historii Kultury Materialnej, 1984, 156 pp., ill. English summary.
Study of Roman glasses excavated in northern Poland.

STERN, EPHRAIM
Material Culture of the Land of the Bible in the Persian Period 538–332 B.C.
Warminster: Aris & Phillips Ltd., 1982, 287 pp., ill.
Phoenician-style head beads.

STERN, EVA MARIANNE
"Antikes Glas in der Südtürkei"
Glastechnische Berichte, v. 57, no. 5, 1984, pp. 132–139, ill. English summary.
Quantity of 2nd–3rd c. glass found in province of Cilicia, southern Turkey.

STOLPIAK, BARBARA
"Z badań nad wyrobami szklanymi w kulturze Przeworskiej na Kujawach Centralnych"

Archeologia Polski, v. 25, 1980, pp. 167–181, ill. French summary.
Analysis of late La Tène fragments indicates a possible local glass factory.

SÜSSENBACH, UWE
"Die 'Konstantinischen Prinzen' des Goldglases von Köln-Braunsfeld"
Wallraf-Richartz-Jahrbuch, v. 44, 1984, pp. 11–28, ill.
4th c. gold-glasses.

SZŐNYI, ESZTER T.
"Arrabona késő római temetői—I., Vasútállomás környéki temető"
Arrabona, no. 21, 1979, pp. 5–57, ill. German summary.
Late Roman cemetery with glass finds.

TABORELLI, LUIGI
"Vasi di vetro con rilievi di 'ludi circenses' e 'gladiatorii', nuovi contributi"
Archaeologia, no. 49, 1984, Studi di Antichità in onore di Guglielmo Maetzke, pp. 561–576, ill.
Gladiator and sports cups.

TANIICHI, TAKASHI
"Ancient Glass Excavated in China (1). Zhou and Han Dynasties, Focused on Recent Discoveries"
Museum (Tokyo), no. 397, April 1984, pp. 24–34, ill. [In Japanese only].
Beads; mosaic ribbed bowl fragments.

"Pre-Roman and Roman Glass Recently Excavated in China"
Bulletin of the Okayama Orient Museum, no. 3, 1983, pp. 83–105, ill. [pp. 83–85 only are in English].

"Roman Mosaic Glass Bowl Excavated in China"
Proceedings of the 31st International Congress of Human Sciences in Asia and North Africa, Tokyo-Kyoto, 31st August–7th September 1983 (Ed. by Yamamoto Tatsuro), Tokyo: The Tōhō Gakkai (The Institute of Eastern Culture), 1984, pp. 399–400.

"Western Designed 'Composite Eye' Glass Beads Recently Excavated in China"
Bulletin of the Ancient Orient Museum, v. 5, 1983, pp. 323–340, ill. English summary.
Core-formed kohl tube and beads from 5th c. B.C.

TEJRAL, JAROSLAV
"Mähren und die Markomannenkriege"

Slovenská Archeológia, v. 31, no. 1, 1983, pp. 85–117, ill.
Roman ribbed bowls, Markomannen, Moravia.

THÜRY, GÜNTHER E.
and STRAUCH, FRIEDRICH
"Zur Herkunft des römischen Austernimports in der Schweiz"
Archäologie der Schweiz/Archéologie suisse/Archeologia Svizzera, v. 7, no. 3, 1984, pp. 100–103, ill. French, Italian summary.
Oyster bed at Puteoli shown on bottle from Populonia.

TRIER. RHEINISCHES
LANDESMUSEUM
Trier—Augustusstadt der Treverer. Stadt und Land in vor- und frührömischer Zeit
Mainz am Rhein: Philipp von Zabern, 1984, 323 pp., ill.
Includes *Rippenschalen* and *Balsamarien*, mosaic ware, jewelry.
Trier—Kaiserresidenz und Bischofssitz. Die Stadt in spätantiker und frühchristlicher Zeit
Mainz am Rhein: Philipp von Zabern, 1984, 368 pp., ill.
Large finds of many vessel types, including diatreta, cut circus beakers, animal and head flasks, drinking horns.

TZIAPHALIAS, ATH.
"Perisulloges—paradoseis archaiōn"
Archaiologikon Deltion, v. 31 (1976), 1984, p. 183, ill.
Vessels from excavations at Karditsa.

URNER-ASTHOLZ, HILDEGARD
"Auserlesene Gläser aus dem spätrömischen Friedhof von Stein am Rhein-Vor der Brugg" [in]
Spiegelungen: Neue Studien zur Kunst- und Kulturgeschichte, Bern and Munich: Francke Verlag, 1984, pp. 159–177, ill.
3rd–4th c. vessels in Schaffhausen Museum, including hunting bowl and a jug-within-a-jug.

VADAY, A. H.
"Tiszaföldvár"
Mitteilungen des Archäologischen Instituts des Ungarischen Akademie der Wissenschaften, v. 10/11, 1980/81, pp. 274–276, ill.
Glass beads from Sarmatian cemetery at Hungarian site.

VANPEENE, NICOLE
"Les Verres gallo-romains"
Histoire et Archéologie, no. 76, Sept.

1983, pp. 46–55, ill.
Finds from Epiais-Rhus, Val-d'Oise.

WARTKE, RALF-B.
Glas im Altertum. Zur frühgeschichte und Technologie antiken Glases
Berlin: Staatliche Museen zu Berlin (DDR), 1982, 31 pp., ill.
Exhibited at Vorderasiatisches Museum.

WELLS, PETER
"Prehistoric Charms and Superstitions"
Archaeology, v. 37, no. 3, May/June 1984, pp. 38–43, ill.
La Tène beads from the Vinica cemetery, Slovenia.

WESTERMARK, ULLA
and AMBROSIANI, BJÖRN
"En romersk aureus från Tetricus funnen i Östergötland Västanstång"
Fornvännen, v. 78, 1983, pp. 81–87, ill. English summary.
Includes Roman glass from Gotland.

WHITE, K. D.
Greek and Roman Technology
Ithaca, N.Y.: Cornell University Press, 1984, 272 pp., ill.
Glass, pp. 41–42; mosaic, pp. 42–44.

WINTER, NANCY A.
"News Letter from Greece 1982"
American Journal of Archaeology, v. 88, no. 1, Jan. 1984, pp. 51–58.
Finds at Corinth and Idaean Cave, Crete.
"News Letter from Greece 1983"
American Journal of Archaeology, v. 88, no. 4, Oct. 1984, pp. 461–469, ill.
Includes reference to 3rd c. A.D. glass factory at Corinth.

YOSHIMIZU, TSUNEO
Kodai garasu
Tokyo: Heibonsha, 1980, 144 pp., ill. [In Japanese only]. Egyptian, Roman, Islamic glass.

ZAPHEIROPOULOU, PHŌTEINĒ
"Ephoreia klasikōn archaiotētōn Delphōn: nomos aitōloakarnanias"
Archaiologikon Deltion, v. 31 (1976), 1984, pp. 169–171, ill.
Head bead and other beads from excavation at Arsinóe.

ZHITNIKOV, V. G.
and MARCHENKO, K. K.
"Novye dannye o stroitel'nykh kompleksakh Elizavetovskogo gorodishcha na Donu"
Sovetskaĭa Arkheologiiā, no. 3, 1984,

pp. 162–170, ill. English summary.
Head bead pendant from Elizavetovskoe on the river Don.

ISLAMIC

ANONYMOUS
"INA's 1983 Season: The Glass Wreck"
Institute of Nautical Archaeology, v. 10, no. 4, Winter 1984, pp. 1–2, ill.
Serçe Liman.

ANN ARBOR, MICHIGAN.
THE UNIVERSITY OF MICHIGAN
MUSEUM OF ART
The Meeting of Two Worlds: The Crusades and the Mediterranean Context (Text by C. V. Bornstein and P. P. Soucek)
Ann Arbor, Mich.: the museum, 1981, 103 pp., ill.
12th–13th c. Syrian bottle in the shape of a horse.

BALOG, PAUL
"The Fātimid Glass Jeton"
Annali Instituto Italiano di Numismatica, v. 18/19, 1971/72, pp. 175–264, ill. Part 2: v. 20, 1973, pp. 121–212, ill.

BASS, GEORGE F.
"The Nature of the Serce Limani Glass"
Journal of Glass Studies, v. 26, 1984, pp. 64–69, ill.

BERLIN. MUSEUM FÜR VOR-
UND FRÜHGESCHICHTE
Land des Baal: Syrien—Forum der Völker und Kulturen (Text by Kay Kohlmeyer and Eva Strommenger)
Mainz am Rhein: Philipp von Zabern, 1982, 380 pp., ill.
Pressed tile and an engraved beaker, 9th c., Raqqa.

BRUSSELS. MUSÉE
ARCHÉOLOGIQUE DE
L'UNIVERSITÉ LIBRE DE
BRUXELLES
Otrante: archéologie d'une cité (Text by Francesco D'Andria and David Whitehouse)
Brussels: Université Libre du Bruxelles, Musée Archéologique, 1983, 23 pp., ill.
Bottle and a Near Eastern glass coinweight.

HELLENKEMPER, HANSGERD
"Die Beute des Dogen"
die Kunst, no. 11, Nov. 1984, pp. 828–

835, ill. English summary.
San Marco treasures: 10th c. gilded and painted glass bowl and two chalices incorporating glass, from Constantinople.

KRÖGER, JENS
Glas. Staatliche Museen Preussischer Kulturbesitz, Museum für Islamische Kunst, Berlin, Band 1
Mainz am Rhein: Philipp von Zabern, 1984, 242 pp., ill.
[Islamische Kunst: Loseblattkatalog unpublizierter Werke aus deutschen Museen].

MONOD, THÉODORE
"A propos des bracelets de verre sahariens"
Bulletin de l'Institut Fondamental d'Afrique Noire, v. 37, 1975, pp. 702–748, ill.
Bracelets found in sub-Saharan Africa have parallels in Ethiopian/Yemen coastal areas.

"Sur un site à bracelets de verre des environs d'Aden"
Raydan, no. 1, 1978, pp. 111–124, ill.
Colored bracelets found and locally made at Kawd am-Saila near Aden.

TOKYO. CHŪKINTŌ BUNKAI SENTA [Middle Eastern Culture Center]
Oriento no Bijutsu/Treasures of the Orient
Tokyo: the center, 1979, 270 pp., ill.
[In Japanese, English check list].
Glass from Persia, Egypt, Syria.

TOKYO. TENRI GALLERY
Sasan-chō no kōgei/Exhibition of Arts of [the] Sasanian Dynasty in the Collection of Tenri Sankōkan Museum
Tokyo: Tenri Kōkan, 1968, 24 pp., ill. English captions.
Includes glass vessels.

TOKYO. TOKYU NIHONBASHI
Perusha Bijutsuten: Perusha teikoku kenkoku nisen gohakyu nen Kinen (Text by Namio Egami)
[s.l.: s.n.], 1971, 104 pp., ill.
[In Japanese only]. Exhibition of Persian art commemorating 2500th anniversary of founding of Persian empire.

VALDÉS FERNÁNDEZ, FERNANDO
"Kalifale Lampen"
Madrider Mitteilungen, v. 25, 1984, pp. 208–215, ill.
Earthenware objects from Madīnat az-Zahrā' (Spain) identified as lamps on basis of parallels in glass.

WHITEHOUSE, DAVID B.
"Islamic Wheel-cut Vessels of the 9th–12th Centuries"
The Corning Museum of Glass Newsletter, Winter 1984, pp. 1–2, ill.

WILLIAMS, DAVID W.
"Islamic Glass Vessel Fragments from the Old Vicarage, Reigate, Surrey"
Medieval Archaeology, v. 27, 1983, pp. 143–146, ill.
Identified by R. J. Charleston as Syrian, 13th c.

MEDIEVAL

ARTHUR, PAUL
"Le terme romane di via Carminiello ai Mannesi, Napoli: relazione preliminare di scavo"
Archeologia Medievale, v. 10, 1983, pp. 387–391, ill.
Possible evidence for glassmaking in Naples, 6th–7th c.

BAYLEY, JUSTINE
"Non-ferrous Metal and Glass Working in Anglo-Scandinavian England: An Interim Statement"
Pact, no. 7, Part 2, 1982, pp. 487–496, ill.

CLARK, JOHN
"Medieval Enamelled Glasses from London"
Medieval Archaeology, v. 27, 1983, pp. 152–156, ill.
'Syro-Frankish' or 'Aldrevandin' type.

DEKOULAKOU, IPHIGENEIA
"Archaiotētes kai mnēmeia achaïas: Pátra"
Archaiologikon Deltion, v. 31 (1976), 1984, pp. 97–102, ill.
Medieval bottle excavated at Patras, Hermes St.

DONCHEVA-PETKOVA, L. and ZLATINOVA, ZH.
"St'klarska rabotilnitsa kraĭ zapadnata krepostna stena v Pliska"
Arkheologiya, v. 20, no. 4, 1978, pp. 37–48, ill. French summary.
Furnace and melt remains of a glass workshop near western fortress wall in Pliska, 9th–10th c.

EVRARD, MAURICE
"La Sépulture mérovingienne no. 19 de Wellin (Belgique)"
Archäologisches Korrespondenzblatt, v.

14, no. 2, 1984, pp. 203–208, ill.
Glass bottle and beads from Merovingian cemetery.

GALKIN, L. L.
"Steklodel'naĭa masterskaĭa na gorodishche Selitrennoe"
Sovetskaĭa Arkheologiĭa, no. 2, 1984, pp. 213–221, ill. English summary.
14th c. glassmaker's workshop at Sarai Batu, Selitrenoye; beads, bracelets.

GIESLER, JOCHEN
"Frühmittelalterliche Funde aus Niederkassel, Rhein-Sieg-Kreis"
Bonner Jahrbücher, v. 183, 1983, pp. 475–579, ill.
Beaker fragments, beads.

HAEVERNICK, THEA ELISABETH
"Die Reihengräber der Karolingisch-ottonischen Zeit in der Oberpfalz"
Beiträge zur Glasforschung. Die wichtigsten Aufsätze von 1938 bis 1981, Mainz am Rhein: Philipp von Zabern, 1981, pp. 28–32, ill.
[Originally published in *Matieralhefte zur Bayer*. Vorgeschicte, Heft 4, 1954, pp. 34–39].
Beads.

"Zu einem silbernen Körbchenohrring"
Beiträge zur Glasforschung. Die wichtigsten Aufsätze von 1938 bis 1981, Mainz am Rhein: Philipp von Zabern, 1981, p. 7, ill. [Originally published in *Germania*, v. 29, no. 3/4, 1951].
Earring with glass inlay.

HEJDOVÁ, DAGMAR; FRÝDA, FRANTIŠEK; ŠEBESTA, PAVEL; and ČERNÁ, EVA
"Středověké sklo v Čechách"
Archaeologia Historica, no. 8, 1983, pp. 243–266, ill. German summary.
Origins and styles of medieval Bohemian glass.

KESSLER, HERBERT L.
"Mosaics of San Marco"
Smithsonian, v. 15, no. 6, Sept. 1984, pp. 42–53, ill.

KITZINGER, ERNST
Byzantine Art in the Making: Main Lines of Stylistic Development in Mediterranean Art
Cambridge, Mass.: Harvard University Press, 1977, 175 pp., ill.
Mosaics.

MALYGIN, P. D.
"Raskopki na nizhnem gorodishche v Torzhke"

Kratkie Soobshcheniiā, no. 179, 1984, pp. 76–84, ill.
Vessel fragments and beads from Torzhok.

NÜRNBERG. GERMANISCHES NATIONALMUSEUM
Aus dem Wirtshaus zum Wilden Mann: Funde aus dem mittelalterlichen Nürnberg (catalog by Rainer Kahsnitz, Rainer Brandl and others)
Nuremberg: the museum, 1984, 216 pp., ill.
Eating and drinking practices; medieval glassmaking; extensive vessel finds (flasks, nuppenbechers, etc.) from tavern site.

OKKEN, LAMBERTUS
"Die Glasspiegel in der Deutschsprachigen Literatur um 1200"
Janus (Leiden), v. 70, no. 1–2, 1983, pp. 55–96, ill.
Numerous references to mirrors in German literature.

ŠČAPOVA [SCHAPOVA], JULIA L.
"Khimiko-tekhnologicheskoe izuchenie stekol iz masterskoǐ na gorodishche Selitrennoe"
Sovetskaiā Arkheologiiā, no. 2, 1984, pp. 222–224, ill.
Analytical report on finds from 14th c. glassmaker's workshop in Selitrenoye [see Galkin, L. L.].

SCHOFIELD, JOHN
"The Search for London's Medieval Past"
The Illustrated London News, v. 272, no. 7034, Sept. 1984, pp. 56–57, ill.
14th c. Venetian beaker fragment.

SCHÜTTE, SVEN
5 Jahre Stadtarchäologie: Das neue Bild des alten Göttingen
Göttingen: Stadt Göttingen; Städtisches Museum, 1984, 80 pp., ill.
Includes many types of glass vessels, 8th–17th c.

SEILLIER, CLAUDE
"Le Nord de la France de Théodose à Charles Martel"
Archéologia, no. 188, March 1984, pp. 20–27, ill.
Exhibition at Boulogne that includes glass vessels.

STOICOVICI, EUGEN and BLĂJAN, MIHAI
"Cercetări arheologice în cimitirul din secolul VIII e.n. de la Ghirbom —'Gruiul Măciuliilor' (jud. Alba)"
Apulum, v. 20, 1982, pp. 139–153, ill.

French summary.
Obsidian and colored beads from 8th c. A.D. cemetery, Romania.

VANNINI, GUIDO
"Un percorso pilota"
Archeologia Viva, v. 3, no. 4, April 1984, pp. 18–35, ill.
Hedwig beaker recently discovered in a bishop's palace, Pistoia.

WILSON, DAVID M.
Anglo-Saxon Art from the Seventh Century to the Norman Conquest
Woodstock, N.Y.: The Overlook Press, 1984, 224 pp., ill.
Sutton Hoo clasps, bowl mounts, and brooch incorporating glass inlays and millefiori.

RENAISSANCE TO PRESENT

GENERAL

ANONYMOUS
"Acquisitions"
Bergstrom-Mahler Museum Preview, no. 5, Sept./Oct. 1984, p. 7, ill.
19th c. French and contemporary American paperweights; Ysart "Monart" millefiori bowl.

"The Christmas Collector"
Early American Life, v. 15, no. 6, Dec. 1984, pp. 53–55, ill.
Ornaments.

"The Collection of Mr. and Mrs. Fritz Biemann"
Art at Auction: The Year at Sotheby's 1983–84, London: Sotheby Publications, 1984, pp. 302–305, ill.
Sale of Venetian and German pieces.

"L'Expo des Expos"
Revue des Industries d'Art Offrir, no. 198, Dec. 1983, pp. 17–29, ill.
Musée des Arts Décoratifs exhibition of 19th and 20th c. expositions, including glassware.

"Important Antique Paperweights"
Annual Bulletin of the Paperweight Collectors' Association, 1984, pp. 38–39, ill.

"Marvelous Marbles Mark Man's History"
Marble-Mania, v. 33, Jan. 1984, p. 1.

"Museum News: Bergstrom-Mahler Museum"
Hobbies, v. 89, no. 2, April 1984, pp. 64–65, ill.
Exhibit of Victorian art glass and fairy lamps.

"Notable Gifts"
The Corning Museum of Glass Newsletter,

Winter 1984, p. 3, ill.
American and European glass and archival material.

"Preview 1: Ruby and Rose-Colored Glass"
The Bergstrom-Mahler Museum Calendar, Dec./Jan. 1983–84, p. 1.

"Victorian Art Glass, Annual Display from Permanent Collection and Anonymous Loans"
Bergstrom-Mahler Museum Preview, no. 2, Feb./March 1984, p. 2, ill.

BENDER, GEORGE A. and PARASCANDOLA, JOHN, eds.
Historical Hobbies for the Pharmacist
Madison, Wis.: American Institute of the History of Pharmacy, 1980, 57 pp., ill.
Includes "Pharmacy Glass" by John Crellin, pp. 25–30, ill.

BLANCHETTE, JEAN-FRANÇOIS
The Role of Artifacts in the Study of Foodways in New France, 1720–60
Ottawa: National Historic Parks and Sites Branch, Parks Canada, 1981, 184 pp., ill.
French and English bottles and stemware.

BOHNE, MILDRED T.
"Reverse Paintings on Glass"
Ohio Antique Review, v. 10, no. 1, Jan. 1984, pp. 33–35, ill.

BOORE, J. P.
"Glossary of Terms Used by Glass Paperweight Collectors"
Bulletin of the Paperweight Collectors' Association, June 1961, u.p. [2 pp.].

BRENNER, ROBERT
"Collecting Christmas Tree Ornaments"
The Antique Trader Weekly, Annual of Articles on Antiques, v. 15, 1983, pp. 65–71, ill.

"Fruit & Vegetable Christmas Tree Ornaments"
The Antique Trader Weekly, Annual of Articles on Antiques, v. 15, 1983, pp. 34–38, ill.

CALLTORP, INGRID
"Billigt samla saltkar"
Nya Antik et Auktion, no. 3, March 1984, pp. 40–41, ill.
Salts, including glass ones.

CALLTORP, INGRID and WOLLIN, CHRISTIAN
"Fotogenlampor"
Nya Antik et Auktion, no. 7/8, July/Aug. 1984, pp. 26–31, ill.
19th c. petroleum (kerosene) lamps.

CASPER, GERRIE
"Old Glass Paperweights, September 16-November 25, 1984"
Bergstrom-Mahler Museum Preview, no. 5, Sept./Oct. 1984, p. 2, ill.
Exhibit of weights featured in Evangeline Bergstrom's book.

CLARK, RUTH
"Carnival Glass Buttons"
The Carnival Pump, v. 17, no. 2, Dec. 1983, p. 5, ill.

CLARKE, T. H.
"The Guggenheim Collection"
Bulletin of the Paperweight Collectors' Association, June 1961, pp. [1-10], ill.
French and American weights, sulphides.
"Notes on a Terminology for French Paperweights"
Bulletin of the Paperweight Collectors' Association, v. 1, no. 3, April 1955, pp. 9-17, ill.
Applicable to all paperweights.

COOK, JOHN R.
"Opalescent Glassware"
Antique Showcase (Ontario), v. 18, no. 4, Oct. 1982, p. 6, ill.

CRONIN, J. R.
Fake & Forged Trade Marks on Old & New Glass
Pueblo, Col.: Grafika, 1976, 39 pp., ill.

DAHLBERG, GRACE CAROLYN
"Knife Rests"
The Antique Trader Weekly, Annual of Articles on Antiques, v. 15, 1983, pp. 124-125, ill.

DIKE, CATHERINE
Cane Curiosa: From Gun to Gadget
Paris: Les Editions de l'Amateur and Geneva: the author, 1983, 374 pp., ill.
Canes containing flasks and drinking glasses, perfume vials, spectacles, optical devices, etc.

DOLEZ, ALBANE
"Le Verre et la flamme"
L'Oeil, no. 351, Oct. 1984, pp. 48-53, ill.
Candlesticks and candelabras.

DUNLOP, PAUL
"Paperweight Collections in the U.S., Part 3"
The Weight Paper (Phoenix, Ariz.) v. 2, no. 3, July 1984, p. 1.

ECKSTEIN, EVE
"Some Thoughts on Hairpins, Hatpins and Tiepins"
Antique Collecting, v. 18, no. 8, Jan. 1984, pp. 17-19, ill.
Includes glass examples.

ELDER, ROBERT A., JR.
"The Lillie and Aaron Straus Paperweight Collection"
Bulletin of the Paperweight Collectors' Association, June 1961, u.p. [5 pp.], ill.
Smithsonian collection.

ELZEA, BETTY
Glass (Guides to European Decorative Arts, no. 4)
Philadelphia, Pa.: Philadelphia Museum of Art, 1984, 48 pp., ill.

ENDRES, WERNER
Silberglas. Bauernsilber: Formen, Technik und Geschichte
Munich: Callwey Verlag, 1983, 283 pp., ill.
Technique and history of silvered glass, c. 1850–1918.
"Das Silberglas: Geschichte, Formen und Verwendung"
Weltkunst, v. 54, no. 4, Feb. 15, 1984, pp. 290–293, ill.

EVANS, LINDA and SELMAN, LAWRENCE
"1000 Flowers"
Skald (Royal Viking Line), v. 1, no. 1, Fall 1984, pp. 6–7, ill.
Paperweights.

GEESER, JOYCE LEE
"Scent Bottles, Treasured Reminders"
Hobbies, v. 89, no. 9, Nov. 1984, pp. 56–59, ill.

GONZALES-PALACIOS, ALVAR; RÖTTGEN, STEFFI; and PRZYBOROWSKI, CLAUDIA
The Art of Mosaics: Selections from the Gilbert Collection
Los Angeles, Cal.: Los Angeles County Museum of Art, revised edition 1982, 224 pp., ill.
Post-Renaissance mosaics, including those made of glass tesserae.

GRUBERT, HALINA
"Mr. Higgins' Fine Art Museum"
Antique Collector, v. 55, no. 1, Jan. 1984, pp. 24–29, ill.
Cecil Higgins Art Gallery, Bedford (U.K.), includes 300 pieces of glass.

GÜNTHER, RUDOLF
"Zierschiffe und Segelschiffsmodelle aus Glas"
Glastechnische Berichte, v. 57, no. 8, 1984, pp. 214–220, ill. English summary.

Ornamental ships and sailing ship models of glass, 16th–19th c.

HABERSCHILL, M. H.
"Les Marques de pontil dans les bouteilles anciennes"
Vieux Papier, Bulletin de Société Archéologique et Artistique, no. 251, Jan. 1974, pp. 161–165, ill.
Pontil marks on old bottles help determine the origin and date.

HALLAM, ANGELA
Carnival Club of Great Britain Newsletter, 4 issues: no. 6, Winter 1983/84—no. 9, Winter 1984/85.

HARTILL, COLIN
"Commemorative Souvenirs of the Great Exhibitions"
Antique Collecting, v. 18, no. 9, Feb. 1984, pp. 38–40, ill.

HEYERT, ELIZABETH
The Glass-House Years: Victorian Portrait Photography 1839–1870
Montclair and London: Allanheld & Schram/George Priour, 1979, 158 pp., ill.
Glass rooftop studios.

HOLLISTER, PAUL
"Paris in the Spring, 1878"
The Glass Club Bulletin, no. 143, Spring 1984, pp. 11-14, ill.
Paris Universal Exposition of 1878, and commentary on glass and glassmaking at this time.

HUBERT, MARIA
"To Decorate a Christmas Tree"
Antique Collecting, v. 19, no. 7, Dec. 1984, pp. 18–22, ill.

HUFFMAN, JUNE
"Childhood Christmas Ornaments Generate Collection"
Collectors News, v. 25, no. 8, Dec. 1984, p. 10, ill.

HYAMS, HARRIET
"Stippled Glass: One Dot at a Time"
Glass Studio, no. 40, Jan. 1983 [1984], pp. 42–43, ill.
Review of Steuben exhibit of 18th c. works.

The Illustrated Catalogue of the Paris International Exhibition, 1878
London: Virtue & Co., Ltd., [1879?], 212 pp., ill.
Stourbridge firms, Lobmeyr, Osler, and others.

JAENNICKE, FRIEDRICH
Führer für Sammler und Liebhaber von

*Gegenstände der Kleinkunst, von Anti-
quitäten sowie von Kuriositäten*
Leipzig: G. Schönfeld's Verlags-
buchhandlung, 1905, 246 pp., ill.
Directory of craftsmen, firm names,
and marks, 15th–19th c. Includes
glass, stained glass, and mosaics.

JOHNSON, PETER
"Glass"
Antique Collecting, v. 19, no. 3, July/
Aug. 1984, p. 86, ill.
The market for collecting drinking
glasses and other wares.

JONES, NORA OWENS and
FUOSS, EDITH MATTISON
Black Glass Buttons
Ypsilanti, Mich.: University Litho-
printers, 1945, 150 pp., ill.

KAMINSKY, DENA
"Sulphides: 'The Noble Simplicity
and Quiet Grandeur' "
*Annual Bulletin of the Paperweight Col-
lectors' Association*, 1984, pp. 30–37, ill.

KAPLAN, ARTHUR GUY
*The Official 1984 Price Guide to Antique
Jewelry*
Orlando, Fla.: The House of Collect-
ibles, Inc., 1984, 656 pp., ill.
Includes glass snuff boxes and scent
bottles.

KAPLANS, THE
"A Bed of Pansies"
*Annual Bulletin of the Paperweight Col-
lectors' Association*, 1984, pp. 24–29, ill.

KEEFE, JOHN W.
"The Arthur Rubloff Gallery of
Paperweights"
Bulletin of the Art Institute of Chicago, v.
72, no. 6, Nov./Dec. 1978, pp. 10–11,
ill.
"New Orleans Collects: Paperweights"
Arts Quarterly (New Orleans Museum
of Art), v. 6, no. 4, Oct./Dec. 1984, p.
30, ill.
Exhibition from Billups and other
collections at the museum.

KEENAN, ANNETTE
"Leeches, Nostrums and Sweet Al-
mond Oil: Antique Pharmacies for
the Collector"
The Australian Antique Collector, v. 28,
July/Dec. 1984, pp. 59–63, ill.
Specie jars, carboys, shop rounds.

KELSAY, STEVE
"Christmas in July"
Antiques Dealer, v. 36, no. 7, July 1984,

pp. 23–26, ill.
Glass figural tree ornaments.

KELSAY, STEVE, ed.
Spirit of Christmas (Santa Ana, Cal.:
Steve Kelsay), quarterly newsletters,
1981–1982.
Ornaments.
Spirit of Christmas (special edition)
Santa Ana, Cal.: Steve Kelsay, 1984,
28 pp., ill.
Includes ornaments and tree light
bulbs.

KING, CONSTANCE E.
"Christmas Miracles in Glass: Tree
Decorations"
The Doll & Toy Collector, v. 1, no. 2,
Nov./Dec. 1983, pp. 20–25, ill.

KNIGHT, HEATHER and SMITH,
SHIRLEY
"A Look at Carnival Glass"
Australian Antique Bottle Collector, v. 2,
no. 10, Dec. 1983/Jan. 1984, pp. 8–11,
ill.
General history of carnival glass with
special reference to Australian patterns.

KOVEL, RALPH and TERRY
*The Kovels' Antique & Collectibles Price
List, 16th Edition*
New York, N.Y.: Crown Publishers,
Inc., 1983, 801 pp., ill.

LANMON, DWIGHT P.
"The Clara S. Peck Collection"
*Annual Bulletin of the Paperweight Col-
lectors' Association*, 1984, pp. 2–13, ill.

LEVITT, AMOS
"The Romance of Lanterns"
Home Lighting & Accessories, v. 67, no.
12, Dec. 1984, p. 114+, ill.

MACKAY, JAMES
An Encyclopedia of Small Antiques
London: Bracken Books, 1984, 320
pp., ill.
Beads, marbles, paperweights, wine-
glasses, *verre églomisé*, bottles, etc.

MARTIN, HAZEL
*A Collection of Figural Perfume & Scent
Bottles, Vol. 1*
Lancaster, Cal.: Hazel Martin, 1982,
72 pp., ill.

MATHEWS, OLIVER
"Early Wine Bottles: Walter Sichel"
The Antique Collector, v. 55, no. 9, Sept.
1984, pp. 86–87, ill.
Collection of 17th–19th c. bottles.

McCAWLEY, PATRICIA K.
Glass Paperweights
London: Charles Letts Books Ltd.,
1982, 71 pp., ill.

MERCK, ROBERT
"The Light of Christmas: Collecting
Figural Christmas Light Bulbs"
Collectors' Showcase, v. 4, no. 2, Nov./
Dec. 1984, pp. 42–44, ill.
German, Japanese, and American.

MILLER, MARTIN and JUDITH
Miller's Antiques Price Guide 1984 (Vol.
5)
Cranbrook (U.K.): M.J.M. Publica-
tions Ltd., [1983], 763 pp., ill.
Glass, pp. 550–578.

MONREAL, LUIS and
BARRACHINA, JAUME
*El castell de Llinars del Vallès: un casal
noble a la Catalunya del segle XV*
Monserrat (Barcelona): Publicacions
de l'Abadia de Monserrat, 1983, 332
pp., ill.
Catalan castle with indigenous glass
remains, both luxury and utilitarian
types.

MOORE, DON
"The Case of the Purloined Pattern"
*Heart of America Carnival Glass Associa-
tion Bulletin*, Feb. 1984, pp. 20–22, ill.
Imperial Co. pattern used by Sow-
erby.

MORRIS, ROLAND
"More Finds from Scilly Islands
Wrecks"
*The International Journal of Nautical
Archaeology and Underwater Exploration*,
v. 13, no. 3, Aug. 1984, pp. 254–262,
ill.
17th c. telescope; wine bottles from
1650–1707 and 1798.

MULLER, HELEN
Jet Jewellery and Ornaments
Aylesbury, Bucks: Shire Publications
Ltd., 1980, 32 pp., ill.
Includes "French jet" and "Vaux-
hall," glass imitations of jet.

MUNICH. DEUTSCHES MUSEUM
*Flaschen und Behälter. Zur Geschichte des
industriellen Markenartikels im 19. Jahrhundert* (Text by Eugen Leitherer)
Munich: the museum, 1983, 36 pp.,
ill.
Exhibition of flasks and bottles.

NELSON, BONNIE
"Jenny Lind"
The National Button Bulletin, v. 43, no.

5, Dec. 1984, pp. 175–179, ill.
19th c. buttons.

NEW HAVEN, CONN. YALE
UNIVERSITY ART GALLERY
The Folding Image: Screens by Western Artists of the Nineteenth and Twentieth Centuries (Text by Michael Komanecky and Virginia Fabbri Butera)
New Haven: the gallery, 1984, 312 pp., ill.
Stained glass, etched, etc. screens by artists in styles from Art Nouveau to contemporary (Patsy Norvell).

NOËL HUME, AUDREY
Food. Colonial Williamsburg Archaeological Series no. 9
Williamsburg, Va.: The Colonial Williamsburg Foundation, 1978, 68 pp., ill.
Bottles, tableware.

NOTLEY, RAY
"Carnival Glass As an Export"
Heart of America Carnival Glass Association Bulletin, May 1984, pp. 13–15. Part 2: June 1984, pp. [18–19], ill.

"An Important Announcement"
Heart of America Carnival Glass Association Bulletin, Sept. 1984, pp. 8–10, ill.
Notley-Lerpiniere collection of carnival glass at Broadfield House Glass Museum.

OBERHEIDE, JENS
Logengläser. Die Gläsersammlung Bodo Nährer im Rahmen einer kulturhistorischen Betrachtung der Entstehung und Entwicklung von Trink- und Tafelsitten
Graz: Akademische Druck- u. Verlagsanstalt, 1983, 72 pp., ill.
Masonic glasses, mostly Germanic, 18th–20th c.

The Official Price Guide to Glassware (Ed. by Thomas E. Hudgeons III, text by Patricia Dean)
Orlando, Fla.: The House of Collectibles, Inc., 1984, 656 pp., ill.

The Official Price Guide to Toys (Ed. by Thomas E. Hudgeons III)
Orlando, Fla.: The House of Collectibles, Inc., 1983, 228 pp., ill.
Includes marbles.

PANCAKE, EVAN
"Other Antique Weights"
Paperweight Collectors Association Newsletter, no. 65, Sept. 1984, pp. 3–4.
From other countries: Venetian, Belgian, Bohemian.

PEARSON, AILSA
"A Look at the 23rd Seminar on Glass, The Corning Museum of Glass, Oct. 19th–22nd, 1983"
Glasfax Newsletter, v. 16, no. 1, Feb. 1984, pp. 24–25.
Summary of lectures on pressed glass.

QUINTIN-BAXENDALE, MARION
"From My Notebook"
Carnival Club of Great Britain Newsletter, continuing series: no. 6, Winter 1983/84—no. 9, Winter 1984/85.
English and Scandinavian Carnival glass.

ROBINSON, HARVEY [GALLERY]
Fine Glass Paperweights Newsletter (Waban, Mass.), 3 annual issues, 4 pp. each.
Includes background information on French, American, and contemporary weights.

ROCHE, SERGE
Mirrors (Trans. by Colin Duckworth)
London: Gerald Duckworth & Co. Ltd., 1957 (1st published by P. Hartmann, Paris, 1956), [321] pp., ill.

ROGERS, MAGGIE and HAWKINS, JUDITH
The Glass Christmas Ornament: Old and New. A Collector's Compendium and Price Guide
Portland, Ore.: Timber Press, 1983, 2nd edition, 126 pp., ill.

SCHIFFER, HERBERT F.
The Mirror Book: English, American, & European
Exton, Pa.: Schiffer Publishing Ltd., 1983, 256 pp., ill.
Also includes glass frames and églomisé decoration.

SCHIFFER, MARGARET
Christmas Ornaments: A Festive Study
Exton, Pa.: Schiffer Publishing Ltd., 1984, 168 pp., ill.

SINCLAIRE, ESTELLE
"Fine Glass at the Great World's Fairs, Part 2"
The Hobstar, v. 9, no. 8, May 1984, pp. 6–8+, ill.
[Reprinted from *Hobbies*, July 1979].

SLUSSER, ESTHER
"Swirl and Sulphide Marbles"
Bulletin of the Paperweight Collectors' Association, June 1961, u.p. [4 pp.], ill.

SMITH, CAROLINE and
FUOSS, EDITH
Return Engagement of Black Glass Buttons
Ypsilanti, Mich.: University Lithoprinters, 1952, 144 pp., ill.

SPEIGHTS, M. W.
"Enamel Buttons"
The National Button Bulletin, v. 43, no. 5, Dec. 1984, pp. 193–207, ill.

"A Photographic Glossary of French Terms on Buttons"
The National Button Bulletin, v. 43, no. 1, Feb. 1984, pp. 4–8, ill.
Includes glass.

"The Strangest Animal in the World—on Buttons"
The National Button Bulletin, v. 43, no. 1, Feb. 1984, pp. 16–23, ill.
Snakes on glass buttons.

STAIR, LYNNE
"The Franklin Schuell Collection of Miniature Paperweights"
Annual Bulletin of the Paperweight Collectors' Association, 1984, pp. 40–42, ill.

STRATTON, DEBORAH
Candlesticks
Radnor, Pa.: Chilton Book Co., 1976, 112 pp., ill.

THOMSON, MADELEINE
"Travelling Treasures"
Glasfax Newsletter, v. 16, no. 2, Spring 1984, pp. 21–22, ill.
Mustard pots with glass liners.

WALKER, ALEXANDRA
"Scent Bottles at Preston"
The Glass Cone, no. 3, Sept. 1984, pp. 3–5, ill.
18th–19th c. French and English bottles at Harris Museum.

Warman's Antiques and Their Prices, 18th Edition
Elkins Park, Pa.: Warman Publishing Co., Inc., 1984, 719 pp., ill.

WATSON, HENRY D.
"Antique Marbles"
Marble-Mania, v. 35, July 1984, p. 3.
Excerpted from a 1942 article in *American Collector*.

WEBSTER, D. B. and TERRELL, FRANCESCA
"Georgian Elegance in Canada"
Canadian Collector, v. 19, no. 3, May/June 1984, pp. 29–36, ill.
Exhibit at Royal Ontario Museum that includes English and American glass.

WENRICH, JEANNE P.
"Shedding Light . . . on Some Often Misidentified Lamps"
The New York-Pennsylvania Collector, v. 9, no. 3, May 1984, p. 1+, ill.
Distinguishing between Argand, Astral, Solar, and Sinumbra lamps.

WESSELS, ERNST
Die Hinterglasmalerei, Anleitungen zur Herstellung von Malereien hinter oder unter Glas, sowie Glasmalerei-Imitation, Glas-Vergoldung und dergl.
Esslingen: Paul Neff Verlag, 1913, 86 pp., ill.

WHALLEY, JOYCE IRENE
Writing Implements and Accessories
Detroit, Mich.: Gale Research Co., 1975, 144 pp., ill.

WITTENBORG, HERBERT and others
" 'Millefiori'—oder 'Tausendblumenglas' "
Porzellan + Glas, no. 12, 1983, pp. 68–72, ill.
Old and new paperweights.

WOODS, JAN
"Ornamental Boots, Shoes"
Australian Antique Bottle Collector, v. 2, no. 12, April/May 1984, pp. 19–22, ill.
China and glass.

WRAY, MARGARET
"Carnival Glass"
Heart of America Carnival Glass Association Bulletin, Feb. 1984, pp. 15–16, ill.

YOUNG, ANNE MORTIMER
"Bleeding Antiques"
Antique Collecting, Part 1: v. 18, no. 11, April 1984, pp. 27–30, ill. Part 2: v. 19, no. 1, May 1984, pp. 51–54, ill. Part 3: v. 19, no. 2, June 1984, pp. 27–30, ill.
Cups, leeching jars, etc.

AUSTRALIA, NEW ZEALAND, SOUTH PACIFIC

ANONYMOUS
"The Cascade Brewery Company Limited"
Australian Antique Bottle Collector, [v. 3, no. 4?, 1984], pp. 11–13, ill.
Includes list of Tasmanian bottlers and breweries.
"A Letter from Home"
Australian Antique Bottle Collector, [v. 3,

no. 4?, 1984], pp. 24–28, ill.
Australian ink bottles.
"SA Glass Bottle Co."
Australian Antique Bottle Collector, v. 3, no. 2, Aug./Sept. 1984, pp. 27–28, ill.
Adelaide bottle factory, 1874–1913.

ARNOLD, KEN
Australian Preserving & Storage Jars pre 1920
Bendigo, Vic.: D. G. Walker Pty. Ltd., 1983, 320 pp., ill.

DRAKE, DANNY and VALERIE
"Glass Companies in N.S.W. and Victoria from 1866 to the Present"
The Australiana Society Newsletter, no. 2, April 1979, pp. 22–27, ill.
Includes trademarks.

GRIFFITHS, COL.
"The Cowburns, Early Hobart Town Brewers"
Australian Antique Bottle Collector, v. 2, no. 12, April/May 1984, pp. 7–9, ill.
19th c. soda and beer bottles.

TOMSETT, D.
"Bits and Pieces"
The Australiana Society Newsletter, no. 2, April 1979, p. 28, ill.
Commemorative pressed plate.

BRITISH ISLES: ENGLAND, IRELAND, SCOTLAND, WALES

ANONYMOUS
"At the Allen Gallery, Alton, Hampshire: A Rare Piece of Davenport Glass"
The Northern Ceramic Society Newsletter, no. 53, March 1984, pp. 40–42, ill.
Early 19th c. stemmed goblet with hunting scene executed by Davenport's patented process.
"Brewery Bygones"
Collectors World, v. 1, no. 11, July 1984, p. 20, ill.
18th c. engraved decanter, tumblers, stems.
"Famous Museum Bottle Finds True Owner"
Collectors World, v. 1, no. 6, Jan./Feb. 1984, p. 15, ill.
1660 wine bottle with seal, Worthing Museum.
"The Growing Collections"
Rotunda, v. 17, no. 2, Summer 1984, pp. 42–43, ill.

Tassie collection, Royal Ontario Museum.
"Memory Lane"
Pilkington News, Sept. 19, 1984, Newslink p. 2, ill.
St. Helens Crown Glass Works School and other programs for workers' children, 1850–1920s.
"Mystery of Rare Antique Wine Bottle"
Collectors World, v. 1, no. 7, March 1984, p. 19, ill.
17th c. seal shaft and globe.
"Reflections"
The Glass Cone, no. 3, Sept. 1984, p. 7.
An account of the glassmakers and their wares shown at a glassmakers' picnic and procession, near Stourbridge, 1859.
"Reflections 100 Years Ago: Crystal Glass Billiard Table"
The Glass Cone, no. 1, March 1984, p. 7.
By Joseph Webb of Stourbridge for an East Indian merchant.
"Shearings, News & Views: Glassworks Closed"
The Glass Cone, no. 1, March 1984, p. 7.
Trent Valley Glassworks in Staffordshire (U.K.), formerly called Royal Castle Flint Glass Works.

ANGUS-BUTTERWORTH, L. M.
"Glassmaking at Warrington 1757–1933"
Glass Technology, v. 25, no. 4, Aug. 1984, pp. 192–202, ill.

ASHFORD, ROGER
"Collecting English Slagware"
Antiques Dealer, v. 36, no. 11, Nov. 1984, pp. 20–23, ill.

BARKER, T. C.
Lord Pilkington 1905–1983: the End of a Great Glassmaking Era
[Pilkington]: Group Public Relations [Pilkington Brothers], 1983, 8 pp., ill.

BICKERTON, L. M.
English Drinking Glasses 1675–1825
Aylesbury, Bucks: Shire Publications Ltd., 1984, 32 pp., ill.

BRAY, MAURICE I.
"The Yorkshire Lady & The Man of Glass"
Collectors World, v. 1, no. 8, April 1984, pp. 2–4, ill.
Stourbridge glass collection at Broadfield.

CAMPBELL, W. A.
"Joseph Priestly's Soda Water"
Endeavor, v. 7, no. 3, 1983, pp. 141–143.
Mention of Hamilton and Codd bottles developed for marketing soda water.

CHARLESTON, ROBERT J.
English Glass and the Glass Used in England, circa 400–1940
London: George Allen and Unwin, 1984, 288 pp., ill.

COTTLE, SIMON
"Showcase: Glass on Tyne & Wear"
The Glass Cone, no. 1, March 1984, pp. 3–5, ill.

DARBY, MICHAEL
British Art in the Victoria and Albert Museum
London: Philip Wilson, in association with the Victoria and Albert Museum, 1983, 128 pp., ill.
Includes stained glass and pieces by Verzelini, Ravenscroft, Beilby.

DAVIS, FRANK
"The Scream in Nature" (Talking About Salerooms series)
Country Life, v. 175, no. 4510, Jan. 26, 1984, pp. 208–209, ill.
George Woodall cameo plaque, "Cupid in Disgrace."

"Time and the Fisherman" (Talking About Salerooms series)
Country Life, v. 175, no. 4522, April 19, 1984, pp. 1054–1055, ill.
Jacobite wineglass, about 1750.

DAY, JOAN, ed.
"BIAS Views: Nailsea Glassworks"
BIAS Journal (Bristol Industrial Archeological Society), no. 16, 1984, p. 4.
Progress report on excavation of the site.

DEWEESE-WEHEN, JOY
"Cecil Higgins Museum: Fine Place to Study Glass"
Antique Monthly, v. 17, no. 6, May 1984, p. 8B, ill.

EDINBURGH. HUNTLY HOUSE MUSEUM
Glass, By George! An Exhibition of Edinburgh Glassware Donated to Huntly House Museum by George R. Gay
Edinburgh: City of Edinburgh Museums and Art Galleries, 1983, [4] pp., ill.
19th and 20th c. glassware from Holyrood, Leith, and other firms.

English Glass, Royal Scottish Museum
Edinburgh: Her Majesty's Stationery Office, 1964, [30] pp., ill.

Glassware Throughout the Home . . . "The Claymer Series"
London: Clayton Mayers & Co., Ltd., [1927?], [24] pp., ill.
Catalog of sets of tableware.

GRIFFITHS, RODNEY
"Bristol Drinking Glasses"
The Antique Dealer & Collectors Guide, May 1984, pp. 48–50, ill.

A Guide to Harveys Wine Museum
Bristol: John Harvey & Sons Ltd., n.d., [21] pp., ill.
Collection of 18th c. wineglasses and decanters.

HAJDAMACH, CHARLES R.
"The Bohemian-English Connection"
The Glass Club Bulletin, Winter 1984, pp. 4–8, ill.

HAMILTON, D. L. and WOODWARD, ROBYN
"A Sunken 17th-Century City: Port Royal, Jamaica"
Archaeology, v. 37, no. 1, Jan./Feb. 1984, pp. 38–45, ill.
Onion-shaped liquor bottles.

HANSELL, JEAN
"Eye Baths through the Ages. Part 1: B.C.—1800"
Antique Collecting, v. 18, no. 9, Feb. 1984, pp. 27–30, ill. Part 2: "1800–1950," v. 18, no. 11, April 1984, pp. 23–26, ill.
Some 17th–18th c. English glass examples.

Harveys Glass Gallery [checklist of glasses]
[Bristol: John Harvey & Sons, n.d.], 11 typescript pp.

HEALE, D. A.
"The Crystal Palace Remembered"
Industrial Archaeology, v. 17, no. 1, Spring 1984, pp. 69–70.

HENDER, V. C.
"The Worshipful Company of Glass Sellers"
Glass Technology, v. 25, no. 5, Oct. 1984, pp. 217–220.
History of the organization since 1635.

HOLLAND, MARGARET
"Bristol Blue"
Antiques Dealer, v. 36, no. 11, Nov. 1984, pp. 24–26, ill.

JACKSON, J. T.
"Long-Distance Migrant Workers in Nineteenth-Century Britain: A Case Study of St. Helens' Glassmakers"
Historic Society of Lancashire and Cheshire. Transactions, v. 131, 1982, pp. 113–137, ill.

JAMES, ELIZABETH
"Glassmaking in King's Lynn"
Glass Circle News, no. 29, July 1984, pp. 4–5.

KIHLSTEDT, FOLKE T.
"The Crystal Palace"
Scientific American, v. 251, no. 4, Oct. 1984, pp. 132–143, ill.
How its construction and materials anticipated modern methods and aesthetics.

KINGSTON, ONTARIO. AGNES ETHERINGTON ART CENTRE
The Age of Elegance: British Tablewares 1775–1825
Kingston, Ont.: the art center, 1983, 28 pp., ill.
Cut and engraved decanters, sweetmeat dishes, etc.

LEAMINGTON SPA, U.K. ROYAL LEAMINGTON SPA ART GALLERY AND MUSEUM
F. H. Jahn Collection of 18th Century Glass
Leamington Spa: the museum, n.d., [16] pp., ill.
English drinking glasses, coin jugs and tankards, Nailsea jugs, spirit bottles.

LESTER, ANTHONY J.
"Auction Report: Glass"
Antique Collecting, v. 18, no. 10, March 1984, pp. 66–68, ill.
Various 17th–19th c. wineglasses, decanters, bottles; Jacobite glasses.

"A Toast for Christmas"
Antique Collecting, v. 19, no. 7, Dec. 1984, pp. 50–51, ill.
18th c. English drinking glasses.

MATSUMURA, TAKAO
The Labour Aristocracy Revisited: The Victorian Flint Glass Makers 1850–80
Manchester: Manchester University Press, 1983, 196 pp., ill.

MORTIMER, MARTIN
"English Decanters"
The Antique Dealer & Collectors Guide, Dec. 1984, pp. 55–57, ill.

MURRAY, SHEILAGH
"Coloured Pressed Glass of the 19th

Century"
Antique Collecting, v. 18, no. 8, Jan. 1984, pp. 20–22, ill.

NOTLEY, RAY
"The Carnival Glass Society (UK)"
The Glass Cone, no. 1, March 1984, p. 2.

"Scroll Embossed Ashtray and Another"
Heart of America Carnival Glass Association Bulletin, March 1984, pp. 23–24, ill.
Sowerby pattern.

"Sowerby Carnival Glass"
Heart of America Carnival Glass Association Bulletin, irregular series: Jan. 1984–Nov. 1984.

PETTIFER, DON
"Joseph Locke: The Legacy of a Master Glass Artist"
The Journal, A Newsletter for Friends of Wheaton Village, v. 7, no. 4, Oct./Dec. 1984, p. 1, ill.

ROBERTSON, IAN G.
"The Finds: Ceramics and Glass" [in] "Excavations at Tilbury Fort, Essex" by Patricia M. Wilkinson,
Post-Medieval Archaeology, v. 17, 1983, pp. 111–162, ill.
Late 17th–18th c. bottle fragments.

ROOTES, NICK
"Eighteenth Century Drinking Habits"
The Antique Collector, v. 55, no. 12, Dec. 1984, pp. 72–76, ill.
Footed drinking glasses.

SILLIMAN, BENJAMIN
A Journal of Travels in England, Holland, and Scotland, and of Two Passages over the Atlantic in the Years 1805 and 1806
Boston, Mass.: T. B. Wait and Co. for Howe and Deforest, and Increase Cook and Co., New Haven, 1812, pp. 10–15, 38–40, 307–310.
Viewing Dr. Herschell's great telescope, bottle making at Bristol, crown window glass production at Leith.

SMITH, E. ANN
"Drinking Practices and Glassware of the British Military, ca. 1755–85"
Northeast Historical Archaeology, v. 12, 1983, pp. 31–39, ill.
Bottles and tableware used by officers in Canada and U.S., mostly imported.

STEDMAN, JEREMY THOMAS
"Make It Plain This Christmas"

Antique Collecting, v. 18, no. 7, Dec. 1983, p. 16, ill.
17th c. wineglasses, a 19th c. feeding bottle, a glass funnel.

SUNDERLAND, U.K. MUSEUM AND ART GALLERY
Pyrex: 60 Years of Design
[Newcastle upon Tyne]: Tyne and Wear County Council Museums, 1983, 95 pp., ill.
Exhibition of the kitchenware made by James A. Jobling/Corning Ltd.

TRESISE, CHARLES E.
Tavern Treasures, A Book of Pub Collectables
Poole, Dorset: Blandford Press, 1983, 176 pp., ill.
Spirit jars, bottles and glasses, seltzer and water fountains.

WARREN, PHELPS
"Apsley Pellatt's Table Glass 1840–1864"
Journal of Glass Studies, v. 26, 1984, pp. 120–135, ill.

WATTS, DAVID C.
"Victorian Dealers and Their Innovations, by Hugh Wakefield"
Glass Circle News, no. 28, March 1984, p. 5.
Review of a talk given to the Glass Circle some time ago.

WITT, CLEO
Introducing Bristol Glass
Bristol: Redcliffe Press Ltd. for the Bristol and West Building Society in conjunction with the City of Bristol Museum & Art Gallery, 1984, 30 pp., ill.

WITT, CLEO; WEEDEN, CYRIL; and SCHWIND, ARLENE PALMER
Bristol Glass
Bristol: Redcliffe Press Ltd. for the Bristol & West Building Society in conjunction with the City of Bristol Museum & Art Gallery, 1984, 94 pp., ill.
Includes section on Bristol glass and the American trade.

WOOD, ERIC S.
"A 16th Century Glasshouse at Knightons, Alfold, Surrey"
Surrey Archaeological Society, v. 73, 1982, pp. 1–47, ill.
Two furnaces, one for annealing crown sheets, and quantity of early type forest glass.

WOODWARD, H. W.
The Story of Edinburgh Crystal

[Chesterfield, Derbys.]: Dema Glass Ltd., 1984, 92 pp., ill.

FRENCH

ANONYMOUS
"Cup and Saucer Sulphide of Henri IV"
Annual Bulletin of the Paperweight Collectors' Association, 1984, pp. 22–23, ill.
Probably made in Paris about 1819–1825.

"Lalique"
Revue des Industries d'Art Offrir, no. 207, Sept. 1984, pp. 78–91, ill.
History of the company and overview of past and present products.

"Le Musée du Cristal"
Revue des Industries d'Art Offrir, no. 207, Oct. 1984, pp. 12–21, ill.
Baccarat.

"News and Views: The Cartier Lighter Collection"
Antique Collecting, v. 19, no. 6, Nov. 1984, p. 52, ill.
Late 19th c. hydrogen lighters on exhibition.

BLOCH-DERMANT, JANINE
Le Verre en France d'Emile Gallé à nos jours
[s.l.]: Les Editions de l'Amateur, 1983, 312 pp., ill.

Bronze et Appareillage Général Electrique, Paris/B.A.G. Catalogue No. 50
Paris: Ateliers-Bureaux-Magasins à Paris, 1939, 55 pp., ill.
Lights and lamps, neon signs, chandeliers.

C & L. Orfèvrerie d'art argentée: fantaisies artistiques, cristaux montés
[s.l.: s.n.] Imprimeries réunies de Nancy-Paris, [about 1900], 74 pp., ill.
Silver-mounted bowls, coupes, decanters, epergnes, etc.

CLARKE, T. H.
"The Applewhaite-Abbott Silkworm Letter-weight"
Art at Auction: The Year at Sotheby's 1983–84, London: Sotheby Publications, 1984, pp. 306–309, ill.

CORBIÈRE, CLAUDE DE
"Une industrie d'art à travers le temps: le cristal et la verrerie à la main"
Revue des Industries d'Art Offrir, no. 204, June 1984, pp. 33–41, ill.

Includes brief histories of major French firms.

DAVIET, JEAN-PIERRE
"Saint-Gobain et l'industrie des glaces: Entreprise et marché du produit (1921–1938)"
Cahiers d'Histoire (Lyon), v. 26, no. 4, 1981, pp. 313–336.

DUNLOP, PAUL
"Antique Baccarat Bouquets"
The Weight Paper (Phoenix, Ariz.) v. 2, no. 3, July 1984, p. 4, ill.

ELLIS, ANITA
"Limoges Enamels in the Cincinnati Art Museum"
Glass on Metal, v. 3, no. 6, Dec. 1984, pp. 70–72, ill.
Five items dating from late 12th to early 17th c.

ERBSLÖH, ROSWITHA
"Die Blumenwelt in der Glaskugel"
Kunst & Antiquitäten, no. 6, Nov./Dec. 1984, pp. 58–65, ill.
French paperweights.

HAMON, MAURICE
"De l'artisanat à la manufacture"
Monuments Historiques, no. 128, Aug./Sept. 1983, pp. 15–19, ill.
18th c. glass factory at Le Creusot.

JOKELSON, PAUL
"A Superb French Collection of Antique Sulphides"
Annual Bulletin of the Paperweight Collectors' Association, 1984, pp. 44–54, ill.

LEGOUPIL, DOMINIQUE
"Cent ans de verre et de cristal: Daum"
Revue des Industries d'Art Offrir, no. 204, June 1984, pp. 41–44, ill.

Livre de différente marchandises fabriquées aux Verreries Royales de Monthermé, Cahier I
Monthermé: Verreries Royales, [1777, 176] pp.
Designs for drinking glasses.

LORRAINE, XAVIER DE
"Saint-Louis, un patrimoine artistique . . ."
Revue des Industries d'Art Offrir, no. 195, Sept. 1983, pp. 239–244, ill.

MARTINON, J.-F. and RIOU, R.
"Conditions de travail et de santé au XIXe siècle: Les verriers de Rive-de-Gier"
Cahiers d'Histoire (Lyon), v. 26, no. 1, 1981, pp. 27–39.
Health and working conditions of 19th c. Loire glassworkers.

MÉNÉTRA, JACQUES-LOUIS
Journal de ma vie: Jacques-Louis Ménétra, compagnon vitrier au 18e siècle (présenté par Daniel Roche)
Paris: Montalba, 1982, 431 pp., ill.
The life and travels of a Parisian glazier, written in 1764.

Les Presse-papiers de Baccarat: une marveilleuse histoire
[Paris: Baccarat], 1983, (English translation by Gail Bardhan), folder of 14 leaves.

SELMAN, LAWRENCE H.
"Unraveling the Mystery of Pantin"
Paperweight News, v. 6, no. 1, March 1984, pp. 5–6, ill.

THOMSON, MADELEINE
"The Silkworm Story"
Glasfax Newsletter, v. 16, no. 1, Feb. 1984, pp. 12–13, ill.
Well-known silkworm paperweight, now in Rubloff collection.

VASSE, JEAN
"Considerations sur l'histoire de la verrerie pharmaceutique"
Revue d'Histoire de la Pharmacie, Dec. 1957, pp. 157–169.
History of pharmaceutical containers, especially French.

GERMANIC

ANONYMOUS
"Das alte Glas bekommt Zuwachs"
Antiquitäten-Zeitung, no. 24, Nov. 9–22, 1984, p. 514, ill.
16th–17th c. Spessart glass at auction.

"An der Wiege des gläsernen Christbaumschmucks"
Die Schaulade, v. 59, no. 6, June 1984, pp. 1030–1031, ill.
Thuringian Christmas tree decorations, past and present.

"Ausstellen"
Deutsches Museum Jahresbericht 1983, p. 18, ill.
Exhibit of 19th c. packaging articles included flasks and bottles.

"Collection Corner: The Mahler Collection of Germanic Glass"
The Bergstrom-Mahler Museum Calendar, Dec./Jan. 1983–84, p. 3, ill.

"Deutsche Glasauktion in London"
die Kunst [formerly *Die Kunst und das schöne Heim*], no. 8, Aug. 1984, p. 631, ill.
Nuremberg *Schwarzlot humpen*, Biemann collection.

"Entwicklung der Glashüttenproduktion: ein Rückblick"
Glaswelt, v. 36, no. 11, Nov. 1983, p. 882+, ill.
Overview of German glasshouse history and production.

"Ein Händler kauft fast die halbe Auktion auf"
Antiquitäten-Zeitung, no. 14, June 22–July 5, 1984, p. 289+, ill.
Auction results for the Biemann sale.

"Die Hoffnung ist eine Hauptperson im barocken Glasschnitt"
Antiquitäten-Zeitung, no. 21, Sept. 28–Oct. 11, 1984, pp. 428–429, ill.
Auction results of Christian Gottfried Schneider engraved pokals.

"Jubiläum: Hundert Jahre Schott Glaswerke"
Glaswelt, v. 37, no. 9, Sept. 1984, pp. 810+, ill.
Schott laboratories and glassworks, Jena.

"Das Porträt auf Glas und Porzellan"
die Kunst, no. 9, Sept. 1984, pp. 655–656, ill.
Exhibit of a collection that includes 18th c. glasses with portraits, Karlsruhe.

"Preissprünge beim alten Glas"
Antiquitäten-Zeitung, no. 23, Oct. 26–Nov. 8, 1984, p. 473+, ill.
Mohn pieces, milk glass, enameled, cut, and engraved items at auction.

"Rattenberg: la cité du cristal"
Revue des Industries d'Art Offrir, no. 207, Sept. 1984, pp. 283–285, ill.
Brief history of the Tyrolean city and its glass firm.

"Rund und im Oval"
Antiquitäten-Zeitung, no. 11, May 11–24, 1984, p. 247, ill.
Auction of an oval portrait of a lady engraved by Dominik Biemann.

"Sammlung Biemann wird versteigert"
Antiquitäten-Zeitung, no. 9, April 13–26, 1984, pp. 1–2, ill.
Auction of Fritz Biemann collection.

"Schmuck wird versteigert, aber nur für einen Baum"
Antiquitäten-Zeitung, no. 23, Oct. 28–Nov. 10, 1983, pp. 518–519, ill.
Lauscha ornaments.

"Snuff-Bottles aus dem Bayerischen Wald"
Antiquitäten-Zeitung, no. 8, March 30–April 1984, pp. 170–172, ill.

Auction of Bavarian snuff bottles, mostly 1890–1920.

ADLER, JIŘÍ
"Zaniklé sklárny na panství Lipnice nad Sázavou. 1. část"
Sklář a Keramik, v. 34, no. 3, 1984, pp. 78–80. Part 2: v. 34, no. 6, 1984, pp. 177–181.
18th c. glassworks on the estate of Lipnice nad Sázavou: Staré Hutě, Kejžlice, Loukov.

ADLEROVÁ, ALENA
České užité umění 1918–1938
Prague: Odeon, 1983, 263 pp., ill.
Includes Czech glass: engraved, enameled, pressed, overlay. Also lampworking and stained glass.

BABCOCK, HERB
"The Glass Paintings of Kandinsky"
Glass Art Society Journal 1983–1984, pp. 18–23, ill.
During artist's Munich years under influence of Bavarian *hinterglasmalerei*.

BAUMGÄRTNER, SABINE
"Zwei südböhmische Gläser: ein spanisches Geschäft"
Weltkunst, v. 54, no. 15, Aug. 1, 1984, pp. 2012–2017, ill.
10-sided beaker with engraved panels and 8-sided flask engraved with allegorical subject, both 1700–1710.

BERLIN (DDR).
KUNSTGEWERBEMUSEUM
Böhmisches Glas des 19. Jahrhunderts aus dem Kunstgewerbemuseum Prag (Text by Helena Brožkova)
Berlin: Staatliche Museen, 1983, 82 pp., ill.
Exhibit of Bohemian glass from Prague museum.

BLAŽKOVÁ, JARMILA
"Jak přišla číše k svému autoru"
Sborník Statí [Memorial volume of essays in honor of 60th birthday of Dagmar Hejdová], Prague: Uměleckoprůmyslové Muzeum v Praze, ACTA UPM XV, C. Commentationes 2, 1980, pp. 103–113, ill.
Enameled drinking glass with hunting scene, 1673.

BORNFLETH, ELISABETH
"Die historistischen Gläser der Rheinischen Glashütten AG, Köln-Ehrenfeld"
Weltkunst, v. 54, no. 18, Sept. 15, 1984, pp. 2429–2435, ill.
Nuremberg collections of 19th c. historismus glass from Cologne-Ehrenfeld glassworks.

BRAUNOVÁ, DAGMAR
Renesanční a barokní emailované sklo
Plzeň: Západočeská Muzeum, [1980], 144 pp., ill.
German summary. Catalog of the museum's collection of Renaissance and Baroque enameled glass.

BRESACK, GÜNTHER
"100. výročí sklářského závodu Jeně (1884–1984)"
Sklář a Keramik, v. 34, no. 7, 1984, pp. 193–194. English summary.
German glassworks at Jena: optical glass, technical glasses, tableware.

BROŽOVÁ, JARMILA
"Classical Period of Bohemian Cut Glass: 1800–1850"
Glass Review, v. 39, no. 8, 1984, pp. 16–21, ill.
"The Glassworks at Chřibská in the Early 19th Century"
Glass Review, v. 39, no. 4, 1984, pp. 5–8, ill.
"K původu Johanna Josefa Mildnera, brusiče a malíře skla v Dolnorakouském Gutenbrunnu"
Sborník Statí [Memorial volume of essays in honor of 60th birthday of Dagmar Hejdová], Prague: Uměleckoprůmyslové Muzeum v Praze, ACTA UPM XV, C. Commentationes 2, 1980, pp. 133–142, ill. German summary.
The origins of Johann Mildner, Austrian glass cutter and painter.

BUIJNSTERS-SMETS, L.
"Een verloren zoon achter glas"
Antiek, v. 18, no. 5, Dec. 1983, pp. 240–246, ill. English summary.
4 19th c. Bavarian reverse paintings on glass illustrating the Prodigal Son.

CHARON, MURAL K.
Ludwig (Ludvik) Moser, King of Glass
Hillsdale, Mich.: Charon/Ferguson Publishers, 1984, 111 pp., ill.

CUADRADO, JOHN A.
"Antiques: In Times of Greeting and Celebration. Festive Bohemian Enameled Glass"
Architectural Digest, v. 41, no. 11, Nov. 1984, pp. 172–177, ill.

DAVIS, FRANK
"Given in Friendship" (Talking About Salerooms series)
Country Life, v. 176, no. 4539, Aug. 16, 1984, pp. 438–439, ill.
Biemann collection pieces: covered goblet engraved by Friedrich Winter and a glass decorated by Johann

Schaper of Nuremberg.
"Heirs to Giotto and Botticelli" (Talking About Salerooms series)
Country Life, v. 176, no. 4536, July 26, 1984, p. 226, ill.
Biemann gilt-decorated roemer.

DO PAÇO, ANIBAL
and DECKER, KARL VIKTOR
"Mittelalterliche-neuzeitliche Funde"
Mainzer Zeitschrift, v. 79/80, 1984/85, p. 249, ill.
18th–19th c. bottles from Mainz.

DORSCH, KLAUS J.
"Glasschnittpokale von Georg Ernst Kunckel und aus seinem Umkreis im Germanischen Nationalmuseum"
Anzeiger des Germanischen Nationalmuseums, 1984, pp. 77–91, ill.
Engraved *pokals* by Kunckel and his circle.

DRAHOTOVÁ, OLGA
"Schürerové a Preusslerové jako výrobci kobaltorého skla"
Sborník Statí [Memorial volume of essays in honor of 60th birthday of Dagmar Hejdová], Prague: Uměleckoprůmyslové Muzeum v Praze, ACTA UPM XV, C. Commentationes 2, 1980, pp. 72–95, ill. German summary.
Cobalt glassmaking by Schürer and Preussler and correlation with Bohemian and Saxon enamel-painted glasses.

DREYER, HERBERT
"Der Porzellanmaler August O. E. von dem Busch 1704–1779"
Kunsthistorische Studien, (Provinzial Museum, Hanover) v. 3, 1931, pp. 7–38, ill.
Includes diamond-point engraved glassware.

FUCHS, LUDWIG F.
"Ein signierter Pokal von Elias Rosbach"
Belvedere, v. 8, no. 12, 1929, pp. 436–438, ill.
About 1740, bacchanalian scene.

Glaswaaren-Fabrik Eduard Dressler
Berlin: Eduard Dressler, 1901, 24 pp., ill.
[Includes *1901 Preis-Liste* insert, 11 pp.] Inkwells, cut glass paperweights, and other desk articles.

HEIN, JØRGEN
"De røde glas"
Skalk, no. 4, 1984, pp. 27–30, ill.
Ruby glass at Rosenborg Palace, Denmark.

HEJDOVÁ, DAGMAR
and REICHERTOVÁ, KVĚTA
"Nález sklářské pece v bývalém Anež-ském klášteře v Praze I, Na Fran-tišku"
Archaeologica Pragensia, no. 3, 1982, pp. 169–188, ill. German summary.
Late 16th–17th c. glass furnace remains and fragments in Prague monastery.

HOFMANN, JOSEF
Die ländliche Bauweise. Einrichtung und Volkskunst des 18. und 19. Jahrhunderts der Karlsbader Landschaft
Karlsbad: Arbeitsgemeinschaft für Heimatkunde des Bezirkes Karlsbad, 1928, 234 pp., ill.
Enameled flasks and drinking glasses, reverse paintings on glass.

HOLEŠOVSKÝ, KAREL
"Předobraz designu 1780–1830"
Umění a Řemesla, no. 1, 1984, pp. 44–50, ill. English summary.
Includes Bohemian glassware of about 1800.

HORAT, HEINZ
"Die Ausgrabung einer Glashütte des 18. Jahrhunderts im Entlebuch"
Zeitschrift für Schweizerische Archäologie und Kunstgeschichte, v. 41, no. 4, 1984, pp. 283–284, ill.
Note on excavation of a glasshouse of 1723–60 at Entlebuch, Switzerland.

HUCKE, KARL
"Zwei Keulengläser des 16. Jahrhunderts aus der Kieler Altstadt"
Offa, no. 38, 1981–82, pp. 387–390, ill.
Fragments of two 16th c. Bohemian *keulen*-glasses from Baltic coast.

H. Klein Crystallglas-Fabriken, Raffinerien Waldstein [catalog reprint, ca. 1890]
[Leipzig: C. G. Naumann?, 1983, 70 pp.], ill.
Large range of Bohemian glass.

KLIVAR, MIROSLAV
"Výstava čs. skla v Corning Museum"
Domov, (Československý Ustav Zahranicni), v. 35, no. 3, 1982, pp. 3–6, ill.
Czech glass exhibit, Corning, 1982.

KOMMER, BJÖRN R.
"Gläserne Kronen in Norddeutschland"
Weltkunst, v. 54, no. 19, Oct. 1, 1984, pp. 2624–2627, ill.
18th–19th c. chandeliers made at Lübeck and other northern firms.

KOSSOWSKA, KRYSTYNA
"Początki Huty Szkła w Zawierciu"
Szkło i Ceramika, v. 35, no. 4, 1984, pp. 158–160, ill.
History of glass production at Zawiercie, Poland.

KREISEL, HEINRICH
Deutsche Spiegelkabinette
Darmstadt: Franz Schneekluth Verlag, [1958], 32 pp., ill.
Mirrors and mirrored rooms in 18th c. palaces.

KRIMM, STEFAN
Die mittelalterlichen und frühneuzeitlichen Glashütten im Spessart
Aschaffenburg: Geschichts- und Kunstverein Aschaffenburg e.V., 1982, 264 pp., ill.
History of glasshouses in Spessart region.

KUBACH-REUTTER, URSULA
"Erwerbungen, Geschenke und Leihgaben 1983: Madonna"
Anzeiger des Germanischen Nationalmuseums, 1984, p. 122, ill.
Silver-cased Madonna figurine from Haida (Nový Bor), second half 19th c.

KUTAČ, VINCENC
"150 Years of Existence of the Glassworks at Lenora"
Glass Review, v. 39, no. 6, 1984, pp. 7–9, ill.
Late 19th c. pieces.

LANGHAMER, ANTONÍN
"Reminiscences of Jindřich Tock-stein"
Glass Review, v. 39, no. 11, 1984, pp. 14–18, ill.
Czech designer and engraver, 1940s.

LEPOVITZ, HELENA WADDY
"The Industrialization of Popular Art in Bavaria"
Past and Present (Oxford), v. 99, 1983, pp. 88–122, ill.
Late 18th and 19th c. glass paintings: history of the craft in Bavaria, centers of production, distribution patterns.

LERNER, FRANZ
Geschichte des deutschen Glaserhandwerks
Schorndorf: Hofmann-Verlag, 1981, 2nd edition, 284 pp., ill.
History of German window glassmaking.
"Glück und Glas"
Glas + Rahmen, no. 19, Oct. 1984, p. 1016+.
Exhibition of Spessart glass at Lohr and Dortmund.

LÖSKEN, MANFRED
"Schreiberhau—Haida—Hadamar: Der Glasgestalter Alexander Pfohl"
Glas + Rahmen, no. 18, 1984, pp. 943–944, ill.
Glass designer Alexander Pfohl (born 1894), based on information from upcoming book by Dr. Helmut Ricke.

MEJER, LESZEK
"Kryształowe żyrandole—specjal-ność czechosłowackich szklarzy"
Szkło i Ceramika, v. 35, no. 3, 1984, pp. 116–117, ill.
History of Czech chandelier production.

"Nieco historii szklarskiej naszych zachodnich sąsiadów"
Szkło i Ceramika, v. 34, no. 5–6, 1983, pp. 203–204.
Short history of glassmaking in Thuringia, especially Lauscha.

MUCHA, MARIA
"Badania archeologiczne na terenie nowożytnej Huty szkła w miejsco-wości Bukowe"
Rocznika Konińskiego, no. 7, 1979, pp. 181–199, ill.
17th–18th c. bottle and other vessel fragments from area of glass factories near Bukowe, Poland.

NAWROLSKI, TADEUSZ
"Archaeology in the Investigations of the Renaissance City and Fortress of Zamość"
Archaeologia Polona, v. 21/22, 1983, pp. 125–172, ill.
16th–19th c. glassware, mostly locally produced, from Polish city.

OCHOCKA, BOGUSŁAWA
"100 lat Huty Szkła Gospodarczego 'Zawiercie'"
Szkło i Ceramika, v. 35, no. 3, 1984, pp. 112–113.
History of Zawiercie glassworks, Poland.

OLCZAK, JERZY
"Szkło okienne (XVI wiek)"
Materiały Sprawozdawcze z Badań Zespołu Pobenedyktyńskiego w Mogilnie. Zeszyt 3/Proceedings of the Studies on the Post-Benedictine Complex at Mogilno. Volume 3 (Biblioteka Muzealnictwa i Ochrony Zabytów Seria 8, Tome LXII), 1983, pp. 113–127, ill.
16th c. window glass found at Polish site.

PARTSCH, CARL
"Der Preusslerhumpen"

Schlesiens Vorzeit in Bild und Schrift N.F., v. 9, 1928, pp. 121–130, ill.
The 1727 *humpen* associated with the Bohemian-Silesian family of glass-makers.

PAZAUREK, G. E.
"Einige Arbeiten von Friedrich Siebenhaar"
Schlesiens Vorzeit in Bild und Schrift N.F., v. 9, 1928, pp. 139+, ill.
19th c. gem and cameo glass cutter.

PITTROF, KURT
"Böhmische Meister der Glaskunst im Ausland"
Glastechnische Berichte, v. 57, no. 7, 1984, pp. 188–199. English summary.
The travels and influence of Bohemian glassmakers and engravers in the 18th and 19th c.

RÖSSLER, SUSANNE
Gablonzer Glas und Schmuck. Tradition und Gegenwart einer kunsthandwerklichen Industrie
Munich: Verlagshaus Sudetenland GmbH., 1979, 104 pp., ill.
History and present production of glass and glass jewelry, Gablonz.

SCHMIDT, ALBERT
"Ein Querschnitt durch die Zunftzeit der Glaser in Hamburg"
Glaswelt, v. 4, no. 1, Jan. 1960, pp. 27–28. Part 2: v. 4, no. 2, Feb. 1960, p. 56.
Study of the glass trade in Hamburg during guild times to 1865.

SCHNYDER, RUDOLF
"Der Tell der Helvetischen Gesellschaft, ein wiedergefundenes Werk von Alexander Trippel"
Zeitschrift für Schweizerische Archäologie und Kunstgeschichte, v. 41, no. 3, 1984, pp. 193–206, ill. English summary.
Engraved *pokal*, c. 1830, inserted in a carved sculpture of William Tell.

SPIEGL, WALTER
"Parfumflakons der Biedermeierzeit, 1.Teil"
Weltkunst, v. 54, no. 5, March 1, 1984, pp. 506–511, ill.
2.Teil: v. 54, no. 6, March 15, 1984, pp. 716–720, ill.

SWARZENSKI, GEORG
Die Kunstsammlung im Heylshof zu Worms. Beschreibender Katalog [reprint, 1927] (Translations by Jack Lowenstein)
Frankfurt am Main: Joseph Baer &

Co., 1927. Reprint: Kingston, N.J.: Stein Collectors International Publications, 1984, 55 pp., ill.
Includes 16th–17th c. enameled glass *humpens*.

WERTHEIM. GLASMUSEUM
Mainfränkische Weingläser
Wertheim: the museum, 1982, 41 pp., ill.
Exhibit of drinking vessels, 16th–19th c., from the Spessart area.

ZRŮBEK, RUDOLF
"Historie sklářství v Orlických horách, 1. část"
Sklář a Keramik, v. 33, no. 8, 1983, pp. 226–227, English summary. Part 2: v. 33, no. 10, 1983, pp. 275–278, ill. Part 3: v. 34, no. 2, 1984, pp. 44–47, ill.
History of glass manufacturing in Eagle Mountains region.

ITALIAN

ANONYMOUS
"Altare vetro ieri/oggi. 6–28 agosto 1983"
Vetro Informazione, v. 3, no. 17, Sept./Oct. 1983, p. 46, ill.
Exhibition review: old and new Altare glass.

"Italian Glass Exhibited"
MassBay Antiques, v. 5, no. 2, May 1984, p. 23, ill.
At a N.Y. gallery.

"Il vetro da tavola ieri ed oggi. Murano, Museo Vetrario"
Vetro Informazione, v. 3, no. 17, Sept./Oct. 1983, pp. 45–46, ill.
Exhibition of tablewares, 1500s to present.

COPENHAGEN. ROSENBORG [Castle]
Venetianske Glas
Copenhagen: Rosenborgsamlingen, 1984, 96 pp., ill.
Exhibition of the 18th c. Venetian glass collection at Rosenborg.

DOORNINK-HOOGENRAAD, M. M.
"Zutphens glas? Twee 'façon de Venise' bokalen in het Stedelijk Museum van Zutphen"
Antiek, v. 18, no. 10, 1984, pp. 516–523, ill.
Two covered vessels with *vetro a retorti* decoration.

FREEMAN, LAURA
"Collecting Venetian-Murano Glass"

The Antique Trader Weekly, Annual of Articles on Antiques, v. 15, 1983, pp. 130–132, ill.
1920s–1950s.

GABORIT-CHOPIN, DANIELLE
"Le Trésor de Saint-Marc de Venise"
Archéologia, no. 191, June 1984, pp. 36–47, ill.
Byzantine enamels, objects of rock crystal, and Venetian glass.

GAYNOR, SUZANNE
Wallace Collection Glass
London: The Trustees of the Wallace Collection, 1984, [15] pp., ill.
Mostly Venetian or *façon de Venise*, 16th and 17th c.

GUIDOTTI, GABRIELLA CANTINI
Tre inventari di bicchierai toscani fra cinque e seicento
Florence: Presso L'Accademia della Crusca, 1983, 185 pp., ill.
Inventories of three 16th and 17th c. Tuscan glassmakers, with additional historical material.

HEIN, JØRGEN
"Das Glaskabinett in Schloss Rosenborg"
Kunst & Antiquitäten, no. 4, July/Aug. 1984, pp. 18–27, ill.
Venetian glass collection of Frederick IV.

HELFAND, WILLIAM H.
"Early Hospital Pharmacy Featured in Italian Exhibit"
Pharmacy in History, v. 26, no. 1, 1984, p. 42, ill.
Rome, 1983; included jars, bottles.

The Jack and Belle Linsky Collection in The Metropolitan Museum of Art
New York: the museum, 1984, 361 pp., ill.
Enameled Venetian standing cup, c. 1530.

KEEFE, JOHN W.
"The Venetian Tradition"
Arts Quarterly (New Orleans Museum of Art), v. 6, no. 4, Oct./Dec. 1984, p. 30, ill.
Glass exhibit at the museum.

MALANDRA, GUIDO
I vetrai di Altare
Savona: Cassa di Risparmio di Savona, 1983, 323 pp., ill.
History and products of L'Altare glassmaking center.

MURANO. MUSEO VETRARIO
*Vincenzo Zanetti e la Murano dell'Otto-
cento*
Murano: the museum; Venice: Comune di Venezia Assessorato alla
Cultura, 1983, 135 pp., ill.
Abbot who founded Museo Vetrario
and helped to revive Muranese glassmaking, 1860s–1870s.

POTOČNIK, UTA
"Aktuelle Ausstellungen: Venezia-
nisches Glas"
die Kunst, no. 11, Nov. 1984, p. 818+.
Exhibit in Bad Honnef.

PULVER, ROSALIND
"The Art of Venetian Glass"
Antique Collecting, v. 18, no. 11, April
1984, pp. 12–16, ill.

RICOUR, MONIQUE
"Treasures from Venice"
Antiques, v. 125, no. 6, June 1984, p.
1318+, ill.
Loan exhibition of 40 objects from
treasury of St. Mark's Cathedral on
display in Paris.

*Rosenborg: De Danske Kongers Kronologiske
Samling/The Royal Danish Collections/Les
Collections des Rois de Danemark/Die
Sammlungen der Dänischen Könige*
Copenhagen: Rosenborg, 1982, 80
pp., ill.
Guide. Includes Venetian glass room
of Frederick IV.

THEUERKAUFF-LIEDERWALD,
ANNA-ELISABETH
"Gläserne Albarelli"
Kunst & Antiquitäten, no. 2, March/
April 1984, pp. 28–35, ill.
Venetian drug jars in Veste Coburg
collection.

WYMER, WENDY
"Glass and the Island of Murano"
The Museum Journal (West Texas Museum Association, Lubbock), no. 22,
1983, pp. 123–128.

ZECCHIN, LUIGI
"I Cappa, vetrai a Murano nel XIV e
nel XV secolo"
*Rivista della Stazione Sperimentale del
Vetro*, v. 14, no. 3, May/June 1984,
pp. 131–135. English summary.
The Cappas, a Muranese glassmak-
ing family in the 14th and 15th c.
"Una fornace muranese all'insegna
della Sirena"
*Rivista della Stazione Sperimentale del
Vetro*, v. 1, no. 2, March/April 1971,
pp. 19–23. English summary.

Serena family factory established
1520.
"Giorgio Ballarin, vetraio a Murano
tra il XV secolo ed il XVI"
*Rivista della Stazione Sperimentale del Ve-
tro*, v. 13, no. 5, Sept./Oct. 1983, pp.
213–218, ill. English summary.
Muranese glassmaker, late 15th c.
"Nicolò di Biagio, albanese, vetraio a
Murano dal 1459 al 1512"
*Rivista della Stazione Sperimentale del Ve-
tro*, v. 13, no. 6, Nov./Dec. 1983, pp.
273–278, ill. English summary.
Inventory of work by an Albanian
glassmaker working in Venice.
"Ricordi vetrari dei Seguso, a Mu-
rano, fino al 1679"
*Rivista della Stazione Sperimentale del Ve-
tro*, v. 14, no. 4, 1984, pp. 177–182, ill.
English summary.
Seguso family history.
"Vetrerie muranesi dal 1276 al 1300"
*Rivista della Stazione Sperimentale del Ve-
tro*, v. 1, no. 4, July/Aug. 1971, pp.
17–20, ill. English summary.
"Vetrerie muranesi dal 1301 al 1325"
*Rivista della Stazione Sperimentale del Ve-
tro*, v. 1, no. 5, Sept./Oct. 1971, pp.
17–20, ill. English summary.
"Vetrerie muranesi dal 1326 al 1350"
*Rivista della Stazione Sperimentale del Ve-
tro*, v. 1, no. 6, Nov./Dec. 1971, pp.
21–24, ill. English summary.
"Vetrerie muranesi dal 1351 al 1400"
*Rivista della Stazione Sperimentale del Ve-
tro*, v. 2, no. 1, Jan./Feb. 1972, pp.
19–22, ill. English summary.
"Vetrerie muranesi dal 1401 al 1415"
*Rivista della Stazione Sperimentale del Ve-
tro*, v. 2, no. 2, March/April 1972, pp.
73–76, ill. English summary.
"Vetrerie muranesi dal 1416 al 1425"
*Rivista della Stazione Sperimentale del Ve-
tro*, v. 2, no. 3, May/June 1972, pp.
109–112, ill. English summary.
"Vetrerie muranesi dal 1426 al 1440"
*Rivista della Stazione Sperimentale del Ve-
tro*, v. 2, no. 4, July/Aug. 1972, pp.
165–168, ill. English summary.

NETHERLANDISH

*L'Art verrier au pays de Liège d'antan et d'au-
jourd'hui* (Text by Joseph Philippe in
collaboration with André Wilmotte)
Villers-le-Temple: Rotary-Club
d'Amay, 1984, 144 pp., ill.
Liège glass and glassmaking, 19th c.
to present.

BOVESSE, J.
"A propos de Sébastien Zoude, maître
de verrerie namurois, et de son
épouse Marguerite Petiaux (1768–
1785)"
*Annales de la Société archéologique de Na-
mur*, v. 59, 1979, pp. 149–173.
First Belgian glassmaker of English
style crystal.

ECK, PIETER C. RITSEMA VAN
"Early Wheel Engraving in the Netherlands"
Journal of Glass Studies, v. 26, 1984, pp.
86–101, ill.

KLOEK, W. TH. and
KOK, J. P. FILEDT
"'De Opstanding van Christus,' gete-
kend door Lucas van Leyden"
Bulletin van het Rijksmuseum, v. 31, no.
1, 1983, pp. 4–20, ill. English sum-
mary.
Resurrection drawing by Lucas van
Leyden, probably a design for an ex-
tant glass panel.

LEERDAM. NATIONAAL
GLASMUSEUM
400 Jaar Gebruiksflessen
Leerdam: the museum, 1983, 19 pp.,
ill.
Exhibition of flasks and bottles.

MASSART, DANIEL
*Verreries et verriers du Centre (de 1764 à
nos jours)*
Haine-Saint-Pierre, Belgium: Cercle
d'Histoire et de Folklore Henri Guillemin, La Louvière, v. 19, 1983, 175
pp., ill.
History and production of Belgian
glass factories.

NORTH AMERICAN
CANADA

QUARTERMAIN, MANSELL
"Glass in Perspective as a Collectible"
The Atlantic Advocate, Nov. 1981, pp.
14–17, ill.
Collectible items, especially Cana-
dian-made.

THOMSON, MADELEINE
"Glass for the New National Gallery of
Canada"
Glasfax Newsletter, v. 16, no. 1, Feb.
1984, p. 9, ill.
Plans include a "Great Hall of
Glass," by 1988, Ottawa.

WARREN, JOYCE
"Cruets & Castors"
Glasfax Newsletter, v. 16, no. 2, Spring 1984, pp. 1–4, ill.
Bick collection of Canadian and U.S. silver-mounted Victorian pickle castors.

WATSON, JOHN and THOMSON, MADELEINE
"Excerpts Concerning Como"
Glasfax Newsletter, v. 16, no. 2, Spring 1984, pp. 8–9.
History of Ottawa Glass Works, Vaudreuil.

WEBSTER, DONALD BLAKE; CROSS, MICHAEL S.; and SZYLINGER, IRENE
Georgian Canada: Conflict and Culture, 1745–1820
Toronto, Ont.: Royal Ontario Museum, 1984, 225 pp., ill.
British and American-made wineglasses, decanters, case bottle, etc.

UNITED STATES

ANONYMOUS
"A. B. Knight"
Heisey News, v. 13, no. 7, July 1984, pp. 9–10.
Fairmount, W. Va. glass etching and decorating shop, 1918–1930s.
"American Heritage Paperweights"
Heartbeat, v. 3, no. 10, Jan./Feb. 1984, p. 3, ill.
Weights with Washington and Lincoln pictures made by Degenhart brothers, Cambridge Glass Co., 1930–1950.
"America's Steuben Celebrates 50 Years with Major Presentation"
American Glass Review, v. 105, no. 3, Sept. 1984, pp. 8–9, ill.
"Ask Hobie Hobstar"
The Hobstar, v. 6, no. 6, Feb. 1984, p. 9.
Questions on cut glass patterns.
"Auctions: Sandwich Lamps of the 1860s"
The Sandwich Collector, v. 1, no. 3, July 1984, pp. 16–17, ill.
"Brilliant Cut Glass Gifts"
The Corning Museum of Glass Newsletter, Winter 1984, pp. 2–3, ill.
Hawkes, Hoare, Giometti pieces.
"Carl U. Fauster Discusses Libbey Historical Cut Glass"
Antiques & The Arts Weekly, v. 12, no. 21, May 25, 1984, p. 80, ill.

"Centenary Celebrations at PPG"
Glass (U.K.), v. 60, no. 12, Dec. 1983, pp. 469–470, ill.
History of the company.
"Christensen Agate Company"
Heartbeat, v. 3, no. 10, Jan./Feb. 1984, p. 1+.
Cambridge, Ohio, marble factory, 1927–1934.
"Cruets on Exhibit"
Heartbeat, v. 4, no. 1, May/June 1984, p. 1, ill.
Late 19th–20th c. cruets at Degenhart Museum.
"Currents in Collecting"
Collector Editions, v. 12, no. 3, Fall 1984, pp. 12–14, ill.
Steuben Glass anniversary exhibition.
"Depression Glass Department"
Glass Review (Ohio), v. 14, no. 9, Nov. 1984, pp. 26–28, ill.
Pages from a 1930 Indiana Glass Co. catalog.
"Depression Glass Department"
Glass Review (Ohio), v. 14, no. 10, Dec. 1984, pp. 26–27, ill.
"Epergnes"
Cambridge Crystal Ball, no. 135, July 1984, pp. 7–10, ill.
Catalog pages.
" 'Fifty Years on Fifth' Opens at Steuben Glass October 5"
Antiques & The Arts Weekly, v. 12, no. 40, Oct. 5, 1984, pp. 130–131, ill.
"First National Milk Glass Convention Set for March 31"
Antiques & The Arts Weekly, v. 12, no. 10, March 9, 1984, p. 20.
"Fish Hatchery Jar"
Cambridge Crystal Ball, no. 135, July 1984, pp. 2–3, ill.
"Fry Society Seeks Information"
Ohio Antique Review, v. 10, no. 6, June 1984, p. 3.
Study group of H. C. Fry Glass Co. of Rochester, Pa.
"Glass Collector Rescues Relics Just in Time"
Glass Studio, no. 43, April 1984, pp. 37–38.
Fragments from site near Smith Brothers Glass House, New Bedford, Mass.
"Glass Happenings"
Glass Review (Ohio), irregular series: v. 14, no. 1, Jan./Feb. 1984—v. 14, no. 10, Dec. 1984.
"Glass Industry in 19th Century America"
The Sandwich Collector, v. 1, no. 4, Oct. 1984, p. 17.

Portland Museum of Art exhibition.
"Glass Show November 23–25, Massapequa, New York"
Antiques & The Arts Weekly, v. 12, no. 46, Nov. 16, 1984, p. 20.
Cambridge, Heisey, etc.
"The Great North American Kerosene Lamp Exhibition and Forum"
The Rushlight, v. 50, no. 2, June 1984, p. 2, ill.
Review.
"Guernsey Glass Co., Inc."
Heartbeat, v. 4, no. 1, May/June 1984, pp. 1–2.
Cambridge, Ohio, plant begun in 1967.
"Hoare Glass Gifts"
The Corning Museum of Glass Newsletter, Spring 1984, p. 1, ill.
Recent acquisitions.
"Holiday Parties"
The Hobstar, v. 7, no. 4, Dec. 1984, pp. 2–8, ill.
Variety of cut glass pieces.
"Importer to Stop Using Heisey Mark"
Hobbies, v. 88, no. 12, Feb. 1984, p. 53.
"Learning from Fakes and Reproductions"
The Rushlight, v. 50, no. 1, March 1984, pp. 12–13, ill.
Lamps and lighting devices.
"Lighting Devices: The Acorn Lantern"
The Sandwich Collector, v. 1, no. 2, April 1984, pp. 16–17, ill.
"Lighting the Old House"
Southern Antiques, v. 10, no. 8, Sept. 1984, pp. 2–3B+, ill.
[Reprinted from *The Old House Journal*, n.d.].
"Lion Head Lamps"
Maine Antique Digest, v. 12, no. 10, Oct. 1984, p. 4-A, ill.
"The Manufacture and Cutting of Flint Glass"
The Scientific American, v. 8, no. 5, Jan. 31, 1863, u.p.
Description of a visit to Gilliland's Brooklyn Flint Glass Works.
"Master Glass Engraver at The Jones Gallery"
Antiques & The Arts Weekly, v. 12, no. 34, Aug. 24, 1984, p. 21, ill.
Louis Vaupel pieces.
"Milk Glass Enthusiasts Hold First Convention"
Collectors News, v. 24, no. 12, April 1984, p. 3.
"Mosser Glass, Inc."
Heartbeat, v. 4, no. 2, July/Aug. 1984,

pp. 1–3.
Cambridge, Ohio, plant begun in 1971.

"Museum's New Acquisition"
The Journal, A Newsletter for Friends of Wheaton Village, v. 7, no. 1, 1984, p. 1, ill.
Pairpoint lamp.

"News Corner: The Toledo Club"
Hobbies, v. 89, no. 5, June 1984, p. 77, ill.
Libbey punch bowl, twin of one made for President McKinley, 1898.

"The Old Inspires the New"
The Thistle, v. 5, no. 3, Summer 1984, p. 3, ill.
Reproductions of old cup plates.

"One Hundred Ten Years Ago: Geo. Duncan & Sons"
Duncan Glass Journal, v. 9, no. 4, Oct./ Dec. 1984, p. 5.
1874 quote from Pittsburgh city directory.

"Patents: Christmas Salts"
The Sandwich Collector, v. 1, no. 2, April 1984, pp. 15–16, ill.

"Pattern Glass: Sandwich Pressed Glass Patterns"
The Sandwich Collector, v. 1, no. 2, April 1984, pp. 17–18.
List of known patterns, derived from fragments recovered, company records, pattern models.

"Recent Museum Acquisition: Findlay Onyx Glass"
The Journal, A Newsletter for Friends of Wheaton Village, v. 7, no. 2, 1984, p. 1, ill.
Creamer and spooner made in Findlay, Ohio.

"Reinstallation of Glass Collection at Bennington Museum"
Antiques & The Arts Weekly, v. 12, no. 22, June 1, 1984, p. 1+, ill.

"Reproductions & Adaptations: The Acorn Boat Salts"
The Sandwich Collector, v. 1, no. 2, April 1984, p. 17, ill.

"Russel Wright: American Designer on View at the Renwick Gallery"
Antiques & The Arts Weekly, v. 12, no. 7, Feb. 17, 1984, p. 51, ill.

"Salem Glass Works, Established 1862"
The Heritage Newsletter, v. 15, no. 5, May 1984, p. 1, ill.

"Sandwich Glass Honored the Candidates"
Southern Antiques, v. 10, no. 7, Aug. 1984, p. 1+, ill.
Cup plates and other items with political campaign themes.

"Steuben Glass Celebration"
Glass International, Sept. 1984, p. 58, ill.

"Steuben Glass Exhibition on St. Petersburg Agenda"
Southern Antiques, v. 10, no. 9, Oct. 1984, p. 24A, ill.
Carder glass from a private collection.

"Super Glassware"
The Hobstar, v. 7, no. 4, Dec. 1984, p. 11.
1878 article describes a large cut and engraved punch bowl set by Wilhelm & Graef.

"Techniques & Terminology: Overlay"
The Sandwich Collector, v. 1, no. 3, July 1984, p. 18, ill.

"Variety Glass, Inc."
Heartbeat, v. 3, no. 11, March/April 1984, pp. 1–2.
Cambridge, O., pharmaceutical-scientific glassware plant begun in 1960; uses some old Cambridge Glass Co. machinery, molds.

"Walter Dorwin Teague Designs Glass"
Design (Columbus, O.), no. 37, March 1936, p. 40.
Teague hired by Pittsburgh Plate Glass Co. to develop new uses and designs.

ADAMS, JACK
"How Carnival Glass Is Made"
The Carnival Pump, v. 18, no. 1, Sept. 1984, pp. 23–26, ill.
Making a souvenir bowl at Fenton.

"Marigold"
The Carnival Pump, v. 17, no. 4, June 1984, pp. 4–5, ill.

ALLISON, GRACE C.
"Kemple Glass: Whimsies, Miniatures, Bottles and/or Vases"
Glass Review (Ohio), v. 14, no. 8, Oct. 1984, pp. 22–31, ill.

ANDERSON, SCOTT
" 'Visible' Gas Pump Collectibles of Yesteryear"
The Antique Trader Weekly, Annual of Articles on Antiques, v. 15, 1983, pp. 166–168, ill.
Gas pump globes.

BAKER, GARY E.
"The People's Choice: Images of American Presidents in The Chrysler Museum Collection"
The Chrysler Museum Bulletin, v. 14, no. 11, Nov. 1984, p. [3].

Flasks and pressed glass items on display.

BALLENTINE, PAUL and MARY
"April May-Day at Garth's"
Ohio Antique Review, v. 10, no. 6, June 1984, pp. 33–34, ill.
Courtney collection of early midwestern glass.

BARNETT, JERRY
"Boyd's Crystal Art Glass"
The Antique Trader Weekly, Annual of Articles on Antiques, v. 15, 1983, pp. 312–314, ill.

"Fostoria Glass Company Lamps"
The Antique Trader Weekly, Annual of Articles on Antiques, v. 15, 1983, pp. 238–239, ill.

BERG, ED
"Identifying the Late Puritan Salt Dish"
Heisey News, v. 13, no. 12, Dec. 1984, p. 8.

BERG, ED and KAY
"Salty Comments: Observations and Opinions on Open Salt Collecting"
Heisey News, v. 13, no. 11, Nov. 1984, pp. 5–6.

BERKE, IAN
" 'Queens' by T. G. Hawkes & Co."
The Hobstar, v. 7, no. 1, Aug./Sept. 1984, p. 12.
Pattern made c. 1903–1930s.

BISHOP, BARBARA and
HASSELL, MARTHA
Your Obdt. Servt., Deming Jarves: Correspondence of the Boston & Sandwich Glass Company's Founder, 1825–1829
Sandwich, Mass.: The Sandwich Historical Society, 1984, 116 pp., ill.

BLACK, LINDA L.
"Collecting Kerosene Lanterns"
The Rushlight, v. 50, no. 4, Dec. 1984, pp. 2–8, ill.

Kerosene Lantern Lecture, Clinton, N.J.
[s.l.: the author], 1983, 10 pp. Presented by the Rushlight Club at Clinton Historical Museum Village.

Lantern Enlightenment: A Kerosene Lantern Reference Guide
[Wharton, N.J.: the author] and East Hanover, N.J.: Craftsmen Photo Lithographers, 1982, 81 pp., ill.

BLAKE, JOYCE E.
Glasshouse Whimsies
Buffalo, N.Y.: Keller Bros. and Miller, 1984, 83 pp., ill.

Also includes old postal views of some U.S. glasshouses and two interviews with glassmakers.

BLIZZARD, AVALON
"Fenton Hats"
Butterfly Net, v. 7, no. 5, May 1984, pp. 3–5.

BOGGESS, BILL and LOUISE
Identifying American Brilliant Cut Glass
New York, N.Y.: Crown Publishers, Inc., 1984, 273 pp., ill.

BOGGESS, LOUISE
"Nappies and Similar Pieces"
The Hobstar, v. 6, no. 6, Feb. 1984, pp. 6–7, ill.
"The Versatile Bonbon"
The Hobstar, v. 6, no. 11, July 1984, pp. 1–3, ill.

BOND, CONSTANCE
"Nostalgia for Neon Signs"
Smithsonian, v. 15, no. 4, July 1984, p. 128, ill.
SITES traveling exhibition of neon, 1930s–1950s.

BOONE, GRAY
"Pressed Glass Still Captures the Imagination"
Renninger's Antique Guide, v. 9, no. 20, Oct. 8–21, 1984, p. 1, ill.

BOYKIN, ELIZABETH M.
"The Grace of Modern Glass Design"
Arts and Decoration, v. 37, Sept. 1932, p. 15+, ill.
Steuben glass and designer Walter Dorwin Teague.

BREDEHOFT, NEILA
"The Close Relationship of Navy and New Era"
Heisey News, v. 13, no. 2, Feb. 1984, pp. 4–5, ill.
1930s Heisey patterns.
"Heisey Decorations"
Heisey News, irregular series: v. 13, no. 1, Jan. 1984—v. 13, no. 12, Dec. 1984.
"Heisey Salts"
Heisey News, irregular series: v. 13, no. 1, Jan. 1984—v. 13, no. 12, Dec. 1984.

BRENNAN, T. PATRICK
The Wheeling Glass Houses
Wheeling, W. Va.: Oglebay Institute, [1981], 16 pp., ill.

BRITT, JOHN and LUCILE
"Educational Mug Series"
The Carnival Pump, continuing series:

v. 17, no. 2, Dec. 1983—v. 18, no. 2, Dec. 1984.
"Educational Series"
The Keystoner, continuing series: v. 1, no. 1, Aug. 1984—v. 1, no. 3, Dec. 1984.
Carnival glass.
"Educational Tumbler Series"
American Carnival Glass News, continuing series: v. 19, no. 1, Jan. 1984—v. 19, no. 4, Sept. 1984.
"Educational Tumbler Series"
Heart of America Carnival Glass Association Bulletin, continuing series: Jan.—Nov. 1984.
"Pictorial Pattern Parade"
Heart of America Carnival Glass Association Bulletin, continuing series: Jan.—Nov. 1984.

CAREY, DON
"The Charm of Velvex"
The Mystic Light of the Aladdin Knights, v. 12, no. 6, Nov. 1984, pp. 1–2, ill.
Aladdin lamp of 1935–1938.

CASPER, GERRIE
"History Commemorated in Glass"
Bergstrom-Mahler Museum Preview, no. 3, April/May 1984, pp. 3–4, ill. Part 2: no. 4, June/Aug. 1984, pp. 2–3, ill.
Exhibit of American historical glass from the museum's collection.

CHAMBERLAIN, CAROL
"Degenhart Museum to Exhibit 145 Cruets from Collection"
Glass Review (Ohio), v. 14, no. 6, July/Aug. 1984, p. 3, ill.

CHAMBERLAIN, GEORGIA S.
"Early American Portrait Medallions on Glass Paperweights"
Bulletin of the Paperweight Collectors' Association, v. 1, no. 3, April 1955, pp. 18–22, ill.

The Charles Shipman Payson Building
Portland, Me.: Portland Museum of Art, 1983, [41] pp., ill.
Includes 1840 pressed glass bowl and a Portland Glass Co. pressed sugar and creamer.

CLARK, GORDON
"Stem of the Month"
Pony Express, continuing series: v. 11, no. 1, Jan. 1984—v. 11, no. 12, Dec. 1984.

Colors in Cambridge Glass by National Cambridge Collectors, Inc.
Paducah, Ky.: Collector Books, 1984, 128 pp., ill.

COOKE, LAWRENCE S., ed.
Lighting in America, from Colonial Rushlights to Victorian Chandeliers (New and expanded edition)
Pittstown, N.J.: The Main Street Press, 1984, 176 pp., ill.
Articles were originally published in *Antiques*, 1924–1983.

Corning Glass Works. Tumblers and Tableware [sales catalog]
Charleroi, Pa.: Corning Glass Works, [1942?], 40 pp., ill.

COURTER, J. W.
"Aladdin: the Last Holdout in an Era of Electric Power"
The Rushlight, v. 50, no. 2, June 1984, pp. 16–18, ill.

The D. C. Jenkins Glass Company, Kokomo, Indiana—Arcadia, Indiana. Manufacturers of Pressed and Blown Glassware (catalog reprint, undated)
Berkley, Mich.: National Greentown Glass Association, 1984, [32] pp., ill.
Lamp globes, jars, hotel and home tableware, kitchen items, etc., produced between 1901 and 1930.

DAVIS, BOB
"Agata with Silver Holder"
Toothpick Bulletin, v. 10, no. 7, July 1984, p. 8, ill.
N.E. Glassworks toothpick holder.
"Beaded Match"
Toothpick Bulletin, v. 10, no. 4, April 1984, p. 6, ill.
"Bow Knot"
Toothpick Bulletin, v. 10, no. 6, June 1984, p. 7, ill. and v. 10, no. 8, Aug. 1984, p. 9.
Old pattern being reproduced today.
"Co-Op's Rex"
Toothpick Bulletin, v. 10, no. 1, Jan. 1984, p. 6, ill.
Toothpick holder with pattern made by Cooperative Flint Glass Co. of Pa., 1907.
"Diamond Mirror"
Toothpick Bulletin, v. 10, no. 4, April 1984, p. 4, ill.
Fostoria pattern.
"Duncan"
Toothpick Bulletin, v. 10, no. 10, Oct. 1984, p. 6, ill.
"Fostoria Carmen"
Toothpick Bulletin, v. 10, no. 12, Dec. 1984, p. 1, ill.
"Iowa—on a Base"
Toothpick Bulletin, v. 10, no. 5, May 1984, p. 7, ill.
U.S. Glass Co. states series pattern.

"Long Diamond"
Toothpick Bulletin, v. 10, no. 7, July 1984, p. 10, ill.
U.S. Glass Co. pattern, 1891.

"McKee Colonial No. 75"
Toothpick Bulletin, v. 10, no. 3, March 1984, p. 6, ill.

"Stars & Stripes"
Toothpick Bulletin, v. 10, no. 2, Feb. 1984, p. 8, ill.
McKee pattern, 1898.

DIPBOYE, MARILYN
"A Glass (Cat) Menagerie"
Ohio Antique Review, v. 10, no. 5, May 1984, p. 55, ill.
Collecting glass cats: covered dishes, pressed plates, novelties.

DONEGAN, FRANK
"In the Marketplace: Catching Up"
Americana, v. 12, no. 5, Nov./Dec. 1984, p. 20+, ill.
Recent developments in the American blown glass market.

The Eclipse Electric Lamp. Eclipse Electric Lamp Co., Buffalo, N.Y. [catalog reprint, n.d., c. 1895]
[s.l.]: The Rushlight Club, 1984, 12 pp., ill.
Portable lamps for use with bicycles, carriages, etc.

EDWARDS, BILL
"Millersburg Rarity News"
Heart of America Carnival Glass Association Bulletin, Nov. 1984, p. 15, ill.

EHRENBERG, RAYMOND W.
"Mystery Paperweight: The Telephone Blue Bell"
Bulletin of the Paperweight Collectors' Association, v. 1, no. 3, April 1955, pp. 28–31, ill.
Souvenirs made by U.S. Glass Co. and/or Fenton, 1907–1930s.

FAUSTER, CARL U.
"Famous Cut Glass Table"
The Hobstar, v. 6, no. 10, June 1984, pp. 1–2, ill.
By Libbey, for St. Louis World's Fair, 1904.

"Glass Chess Sets—For Show, Not Play"
Spinning Wheel, v. 39, no. 3, May/June 1983, p. 21+, ill.
Set by Libbey's Ernst Widlund, and other sets.

"The Importance of Monogrammed Glass"
The Hobstar, v. 7, no. 3, Nov. 1984, pp. 4–5, ill.

"Learning from Libbey Ads—Cut Glass 1892–1920"
The Antique Trader Weekly, Annual of Articles on Antiques, v. 15, 1983. Part 2: pp. 88–91, ill. Part 3: pp. 249–251, ill.

"Libbey Cut Glass Baskets, Reviewed 1905–1920"
The Hobstar, v. 6, no. 7, April 1984, pp. 1–2, ill.

"More about Brilliant Cut Punch Bowls"
The Hobstar, v. 6, no. 7, March 1984, p. 1+, ill.
In museum collections.

FELT, TOM and O'GRADY, BOB
Heisey Candlesticks, Candelabra, and Lamps
Newark, O.: Heisey Collectors of America, Inc., 1984, 436 pp., ill.

FENTON, FRANK
"SGS 1981 Convention Presentation"
Stretch Glass Society Newsletter, Part 3: v. 9, no. 4, 1983, pp. 4–8, ill.
Continuation of talk on early days at Fenton.

FINCH, RALPH
"The Courtney Glass Collection"
Maine Antique Digest, v. 12, no. 7, July 1984, pp. 1C–6C, ill.

"Glass Auction Earns Raves"
Antique Bottle World, v. 11, no. 7, July 1984, pp. 4–14+, ill. Part 2: v. 11, no. 8, Aug. 1984, pp. 10–14, ill.
Courtney collection of Midwestern glass.

FOSTER, ROBERT E.
Fostoria American Pattern
Sayre, Pa.: Murrelle Printing Co., Inc., [1984?], 43 pp., ill.

FOX, HYLA WATTS
"Carnival Glass Gets Serious"
The Carnival Pump, v. 18, no. 2, Dec. 1984, pp. 16–17.

FRANTZ, JOHN PARRIS
"Dateline: Chicago"
Home Lighting & Accessories, v. 67, no. 4, April 1984, pp. 56–58, ill.
Historical Society exhibit of Chicago furniture, including lighting: Tiffany, Art Deco, Frank Lloyd Wright.

GAMBLE, DOROTHY
and THOMSON, MADELEINE
"Centennials & Coins—Old & New"
Glasfax Newsletter, v. 16, no. 2, Spring 1984, pp. 13–15, ill.
Pressed glass patterns.

GARRETT, ELISABETH DONAGHY
"The American Home, Part IV: The Dining Room"
Antiques, v. 126, no. 4, Oct. 1984, pp. 910–921, ill.

GARRISON, MYRNA
"Cape Cod Update"
Depression Glass Daze, v. 14, no. 4, July 1, 1984, p. 7, ill.
Imperial pattern.

"Update on Imperial Cape Cod"
The Imperial Collectors Glasszette, v. 9, Feb. 1984, p. 2.

GIEROW, HERMAN P.
"A Steuben Cologne"
The Hobstar, v. 6, no. 5, Jan. 1984, p. 9, ill.
Cut glass scent bottle, attributed to Carder.

GOLDBLATT, GLORIA
"Actress Pattern Glass: Faces, Facets, and Facts"
Hobbies, v. 89, no. 7, Sept. 1984, pp. 18–22+, ill.

GOLDMAN, BERNARD
"Custard Glass . . . A Milk Glass Variation"
Renninger's Antique Guide, v. 9, no. 7, April 9–22, 1984, p. 1, ill.

GORDON, YVONNE L.
and JENKINS, SANDY
"Novelty Glass, Trademarks, and Collecting"
Heartbeat, v. 4, no. 4, Nov./Dec. 1984, pp. 1–3, ill.
20 companies currently making novelties, their products and trademarks.

GRIFFITH, SHINE and SHIRLEY
Pictorial Review of Fenton's White Hobnail Milk Glass: A Collector's Guide with Price Valuation
[Warren, Ohio]: the authors, 1984, 89 pp., ill.

HALLAM, ANGELA, ed.
"Imperial Catalogue Reprint"
Carnival Club of Great Britain Newsletter, Part 1: no. 9, Winter 1984/85, pp. 11–36, ill.
Catalog no. 200, 1914.

HANKS, DAVID A.
and PEIRCE, DONALD C.
The Virginia Carroll Crawford Collection: American Decorative Arts, 1825–1917
Atlanta, Ga.: High Museum of Art, 1983, 94 pp., ill.

Includes lamps and glass pieces from N.E. Glass Co., Mount Washington, Hobbs Brockunier, Tiffany, etc.

HANSON, LUTHER D. A.
Archaeological Data Recovery at the Williamstown Glass Works Site, New Jersey
Newark, Del.: Mid-Atlantic Archaeological Research, Inc., 1983, 300 pp., ill.
Late 19th c. furnace remains and large amounts of cullet, slag, whole and partial bottles.

HARWOOD, CONNIE
"The President's Glass"
The Hobstar, v. 6, no. 10, June 1984, pp. 5–7, ill.

HEACOCK, WILLIAM
Collecting Glass: Research, Reprints & Reviews. Vol. 1
Marietta, O.: Richardson Printing Corp., 1984, 112 pp., ill.
Mostly American: pattern glass, slag glass, opaque colored, U.S. firms such as Consolidated.
"McKee"
Glass Review (Ohio), v. 14, no. 10, Dec. 1984, pp. 10–11, ill.

HOLLISTER, PAUL
"A Bohemian-American Footnote"
The Glass Club Bulletin, no. 144, Fall 1984, pp. 12–13.
Dating of Bohemian-influenced cased and colored American glass.
"Who Knows What Lurks?"
The Glass Club Bulletin, no. 143, Spring 1984, p. 15.
Copy of Bontemps 1868 book belonging to William Leighton, Jr.

HORTON, JACK
"Dates Pertaining to American Brilliant Cut Glass"
The Hobstar, v. 6, no. 10, June 1984, p. 10.

Huntington Galleries, Biennial Report 1981–1983
Huntington, W. Va.: the galleries, 1984, u.p., ill.
Recent acquisitions, over 50 glass items.

HUNTINGTON, ROBERT
"Lighting: Wide Awakes' Torches Lit the Way to Lincoln's Presidency"
The Sandwich Collector, v. 1, no. 4, Oct. 1984, pp. 16–17, ill.
Political lanterns, 1860.

JEFFRIES, IRENE
and ANNA BELLE
"Reflections: When Duncan Went for the Gold"
Duncan Glass Journal, v. 9, no. 4, Oct./Dec. 1984, p. 17.
Ruby colored glass.

JOHNSTON, JOYCE
"Collecting Bellflower"
Glass Review (Ohio), Six-part series: v. 14, no. 3, April 1984—v. 14, no. 8, Oct. 1984.
"Glass Research"
Miniature News, series 8, no. 3, April 1984, pp. 16–20, ill.
Acorn toy glassware set, miniature hanging lamp, Tarentum pattern glass.

KERCHEVAL, KEN and others
"The Monkey Pattern"
Duncan Glass Journal, v. 9, no. 1, Jan./March 1984, pp. 9–17, ill.

KIBBLE, EDWARD
"Teague & Steuben Revised"
Industrial Design, v. 30, no. 6, Nov./Dec. 1983, p. 72, ill.
Letter regarding 1930s designs for Steuben.

KIER, C. F., JR.
"Batsto Library Aided by J. E. Pfeiffer Bequest"
The Heritage Newsletter, v. 15, no. 4, April 1984, p. 8, ill.
Research files, documents, journals, books on South Jersey factories.

KNOTTS, PHIL
"I Have Designs For You"
National Greentown Glass Association Newsletter, v. 11, no. 4, Oct. 1984, pp. 3–5, ill.
12 engraving patterns used by Greentown manufacturers.

KOVEL, RALPH and TERRY
"Glass-Globed Lamps Made During Late 1800s"
Collectors News, v. 25, no. 7, Nov. 1984, p. 4, ill.

KRAUSE, GAIL
"Delightfully Duncan"
Glass Review (Ohio), continuing series: v. 14, no. 1, Jan./Feb. 1984—v. 14, no. 10, Dec. 1984.
"Duncan American Way"
Duncan Glass Journal, v. 9, no. 2, April/June 1984, pp. 9–11, ill.
Pattern of early 1940s.
"Photos of Duncan Miller Workers"

Duncan Glass Journal, v. 9, no. 1, Jan./March 1984, pp. 18–20, ill.
"Three Patterns: Quarter Block, Chanticleer 1934, Ribbed Droplet Band"
Duncan Glass Journal, v. 9, no. 3, July/Sept. 1984, pp. 8–9, ill.

KRUMME, MICHAEL
"Collecting Liquor Services"
Depression Glass Daze, v. 14, no. 1, March 1984, p. 46.

Lackawanna Cut Glass Co., Scranton, Pa.
[catalog reprint, 1903–1905]
Shreveport, La.: American Cut Glass Association, 1983, 84 pp., ill.

Laurel Cut Glass Company, Jermyn, Pa.
[catalog reprint, 1907]
Shreveport, La.: American Cut Glass Association, 1983, 33 pp., ill.

LECHLER, DORIS ANDERSON
"American Toy Miniatures: Mislaid Jewels of Our Time"
The Doll & Toy Collector, v. 1, no. 3, Jan./Feb. 1984, pp. 37–39, ill.
Toy punch, table, and lemonade sets, 1850s–1910.
"Collecting Miniatures"
Glass Review (Ohio), v. 14, no. 1, Jan./Feb. 1984, pp. 8–9.
"Toy Glass: Pockets of Pleasure"
The Doll & Toy Collector, v. 1, no. 5, May/June 1984, pp. 43–48, ill.
Pressed glass sets from various factories.

LECHNER, MILDRED and RALPH
"Attribution of C. F. Monroe Wave Crest Salts"
Salt Shaker Collectors Newsletter, v. 2, no. 2, Sept. 1984, p. 3, ill.

LEE, RUTH WEBB
"The Little Pigs That Went to Market"
Bulletin of the Paperweight Collectors' Association, v. 1, no. 3, April 1955, pp. 3–6, ill.
Novelty paperweights, incorporating birds, flowers, and piglets, made in the late 1930s and sold as antiques.

LEE, SHIRLEY
"Celebrity Collectors: 'These Are a Few of My Favorite Things' "
Collectibles Illustrated, v. 3, no. 2, March/April 1984, pp. 39–40, ill.
Ken Kercheval, pressed glass collector.
"Stalking the Elusive Celery Vase"
Collectibles Illustrated, v. 3, no. 4, July/Aug. 1984, pp. 54–55, ill.

LEVY, BERNARD
"Pharmacy Graduates in Use from 1880 to 1920"
Pharmacy in History, v. 26, no. 3, 1984, pp. 150–154, ill.
Made by Whitall, Tatum & Co. and other firms.

LINDSEY, BESSIE M.
"Hayes-Wheeler Mug"
Miniature News, series 8, no. 4, May 1984, p. 4, ill.

LONG, MILBRA
"Cathay in Black"
Glass Review (Ohio), v. 14, no. 2, March 1984, pp. 13–15, ill.
Imperial Glass Corp. pattern, 1949–1950s.

LYDICK, HOWARD
"Historical Glass"
Glass Review (Ohio), irregular series: v. 14, no. 1, Jan./Feb. 1984—v. 14, no. 10, Dec. 1984.

LYON, SYLVIA APPLEBEE
"Glass Tableware from Nineteenth Century American Factories: NEAGC 50th Anniversary Exhibition"
The Glass Club Bulletin, no. 143, Spring 1984, pp. 3–8, ill.
National Early American Glass Club show at The Boston Atheneum.

MAGUIRE, BETTY
"Duncan's 44-Button Panel"
Toothpick Bulletin, v. 10, no. 1, Jan. 1984, p. 5, ill.

MARBUTT, KEITH and UNI
"Anchor Hocking"
Depression Glass Daze, v. 13, no. 12, Feb. 1984, p. 56, ill. Part 2: "Jeannette Jadites," v. 14, no. 2, April 1984, p. 45, ill.
Jade-ite ware of the 1940s.

"Just Jadite: Westmoreland's Green Milk Glass"
Depression Glass Daze, v. 14, no. 7, Oct. 1984, p. 6.

MARSH, MRS. WILLIAM R.
"Zachary Taylor Sulphide Paperweight"
Bulletin of the Paperweight Collectors' Association, v. 1, no. 3, April 1955, p. 23, ill.

MAWSON, RON
"Alox Marbles"
Marble-Mania, v. 36, Oct. 1984, p. 4.
St. Louis marble manufacturer, 1930s–1950.

MAY, LELAND C.
"Figural Glass Toys"
Hobbies, v. 88, no. 12, Feb. 1984, pp. 28–30, ill.

McCARL, WILSON
"Etching Department"
Duncan Glass Journal, v. 9, no. 3, July/Sept. 1984, pp. 12–13, ill.
Author's memoirs, year unknown.

McCLINTON, KATHARINE MORRISON
"American Federal Looking Glasses"
Hobbies, v. 89, no. 3, May 1984, pp. 26–28, ill.
Some with églomisé panels.

McDONALD, ANN GILBERT
"The Lamps of Westmoreland, New Martinsville, & Gillinder Glass Companies"
The Antique Trader Weekly, Annual of Articles on Antiques, v. 15, 1983, pp. 228–231, ill.

"Night Lamps in the Kerosene Era"
The Rushlight, v. 50, no. 2, June 1984, pp. 14–15, ill.

McKEARIN, HELEN A.
"Early American Glass"
Art Center Bulletin, v. 9, no. 2, Nov. 1930, pp. 19–20.

McKINLEY, CAROLYN
Goofus Glass
Paducah, Ky.: Collector Books, 1984, 128 pp., ill.

McKINSTRY, E. RICHARD
Trade Catalogs at Winterthur: A Guide to the Literature of Merchandising 1750 to 1980
New York: Garland Publishing, Inc., 1984, 438 pp., ill. [Includes 3 indexes]
General tableware, art glass, cut glass, silver mounted sets, bottles, stained and leaded glass, lighting fixtures, etc.

McNAMARA, BOB
"A Shattered Myth"
Toothpick Bulletin, v. 10, no. 6, June 1984, pp. 4–5, ill.
Mary Gregory-type glass.

MEADOR, ROY
"Benjamin Franklin and His Musical Glasses"
Glass Studio, no. 42, March 1984, pp. 34–39, ill.

MEASELL, JAMES S.
"Chocolate Syrup Found"

National Greentown Glass Association Newsletter, v. 10, no. 3, July 1983, p. 2, ill.

"D. C. Jenkins, Jr.: 1854–1930"
Glass Review (Ohio), v. 14, no. 3, April 1984, p. 19+.
D. C. Jenkins Glass Co.

"The Findlay Connection"
National Greentown Glass Association Newsletter, v. 10, no. 3, July 1983, p. 6.
Founder of Indiana Tumbler and Goblet Co. also associated with Columbia Glass Co. of Findlay, Ohio, 1886–1892.

"The Indiana Tumbler and Goblet Company, 1894–1903"
Indiana Magazine of History, v. 76, no. 4, Dec. 1980, pp. 319–333, ill.

"Natural Gas Boom"
National Greentown Glass Association Newsletter, v. 11, no. 1, Jan. 1984, pp. 3–5.
Indiana Tumbler and Goblet Co. history.

"Patented by Chas. E. Beam"
National Greentown Glass Association Newsletter, v. 10, no. 4, Oct. 1983, pp. 3–6, ill.
Patent by designer and mold-maker for Indiana Tumbler and Goblet Co., 1890.

"Pioneer's Victoria"
National Greentown Glass Association Newsletter, v. 11, no. 3, July 1984, pp. 4–6, ill.
1891 patent by J. Proeger.

"Twenty Questions about Greentown Glass"
Ohio Antique Review, v. 10, no. 3, March 1984, Section 4, pp. 7–10, ill.

"The Western Flint and Lime Glass Protective Association, 1874–1887"
The Western Pennsylvania Historical Magazine, v. 66, no. 4, Oct. 1983, pp. 313–334.

"Work/Wages at Greentown"
National Greentown Glass Association Newsletter, v. 10, no. 3, July 1983, pp. 3–5.
Conditions at the Indiana Tumbler and Goblet Co. plant from 1894 to 1903.

MICHAEL, GEORGE
"Antiques & Americana: Caster Sets"
The Antique Trader Weekly, Annual of Articles on Antiques, v. 15, 1983, p. 362, ill.

"Antiques & Americana: Gone with the Wind Lamps"
The Antique Trader Weekly, Annual of Articles on Antiques, v. 15, 1983, p. 365, ill.

"Antiques & Americana: Silver Overlay Glass"
The Antique Trader Weekly, Annual of Articles on Antiques, v. 15, 1983, p. 363, ill.
[Brief article].

MICHIE, THOMAS S.
Festivities of Form: Historical American Crafts from New England Collections
South Hadley, Mass.: Mount Holyoke College Art Museum, 1984, 22 pp., ill.
Includes South Jersey type pitcher, lamps, rolling pins.

MIDLAND, MICHIGAN. CENTER FOR THE ARTS
Midland County Historical Society's Glass Collection
Midland, Mich.: Midland County Historical Society, 1984, [9] pp.

MILLER, EVERETTE
"Imperial Free Hand: 1922–1926"
Glass Review (Ohio), v. 14, no. 2, March 1984, pp. 5–6, ill.

MITCHELL, IVAN and BETTY
"Rarities and Seldom Seen"
Heart of America Carnival Glass Association Bulletin, continuing series: Jan.–Nov. 1984.

MOORE, DONALD
"Cambridge Carnival Glass"
The Antique Trader Weekly, Annual of Articles on Antiques, v. 15, 1983, pp. 162–165, ill.
"Carnival Cameos"
Glass Review (Ohio), continuing series: v. 14, no. 1, Jan./Feb. 1984—v. 14, no. 10, Dec. 1984.
"Carnival Cameos"
Heart of America Carnival Glass Association Bulletin, irregular series: Jan.–Nov. 1984.
"Carnival Cameos"
The Keystoner, continuing series: v. 1, no. 1, Aug. 1984—v. 1, no. 3, Dec. 1984.
"Imperial—A Fresh Look"
The Carnival Pump, v. 17, no. 2, Dec. 1983, pp. 6–7, ill.
"The Jeweled Heart Connection"
American Carnival Glass News, v. 19, no. 2, March 1984, pp. 12–14, ill.
Dugan pattern.
"Meet Two Stars From the U.S. Glass Company"
The Carnival Pump, v. 17, no. 3, March 1984, pp. 8–9, ill.
Two patterns.
"Millersburg's Multi-purpose Molds"

Heart of America Carnival Glass Association Bulletin, July 1984, pp. 12–14, ill.
"Pastel Water Pitchers: The Top Ten"
Heart of America Carnival Glass Association Bulletin, Nov. 1984, pp. 5–10, ill.
"Patterns That Whirl"
Heart of America Carnival Glass Association Bulletin, April 1984, pp. 17–21, ill.
"Ten Rare Plates—Ten Common Patterns"
Heart of America Carnival Glass Association Bulletin, March 1984, pp. 11–16, ill.

MUCHA, MIRIAM E.
"Solving the Mystery of Two Altered American Bottle Molds"
Journal of Glass Studies, v. 26, 1984, pp. 111–119, ill.
19th c. molds in the Philadelphia Museum of Art.

MURSCHELL, DALE
"Darning Eggs"
The Heritage Newsletter, v. 15, no. 8, Oct. 1984, p. 5, ill.

NELSON, RICHARD
"The Secret of a Rose"
The National Button Bulletin, v. 43, no. 1, Feb. 1984, pp. 8–9, ill.
Standing rose paperweights by Ralph Barber and Emil Larson, and similar buttons by Charles Kaziun.

NEW YORK, N.Y.
STEUBEN GLASS
50 Years on 5th: A Retrospective Exhibition of Steuben Glass (Text by Brendan Gill)
New York: Steuben Glass, 1984, [32] pp., ill.

NOTLEY, RAY
"Showcase: the Unknown Northwood"
The Glass Cone (U.K.: The Glass Association), no. 2, June 1984, pp. 3–5, ill.
Harry Northwood's glassmaking career in the U.S.

NOYES, EDWARD
"Thoughts on Heisey's No. 4220 Vase"
Heisey News, v. 13, no. 4, April 1984, p. 5, ill.

NYE, MARK
"Betty, Another Cambridge Girl"
Cambridge Crystal Ball, no. 131, March 1984, pp. 4–5, ill.

"Blossom Time"
Cambridge Crystal Ball, no. 132, April 1984, pp. 6–7, ill.
"Cambridge Jugs"
Cambridge Crystal Ball, 4 parts: no. 137, Sept. 1984—no. 140, Dec. 1984.
"Caprice Update"
Cambridge Crystal Ball, no. 129, Jan. 1984, p. 13.
"Cleo"
Cambridge Crystal Ball, no. 129, Jan. 1984, pp. 4–8, ill.
"Punch Bowls and Sets 1940–58"
Cambridge Crystal Ball, Part 1: no. 133, May 1984, pp. 6–9, ill. Part 2: no. 134, June 1984, pp. 4–6, ill. Part 3: no. 135, July 1984, pp. 4–5, ill. Part 4: no. 136, Aug. 1984, pp. 4–5, ill.
"Sweetheart and Allegro Stems"
Cambridge Crystal Ball, no. 130, Feb. 1984, pp. 4–6, ill.

O'BRIAN, PAT and
DICKSON, MARY JANE
"Duncan Crucifix Candlesticks"
Duncan Glass Journal, v. 9, no. 3, July/Sept. 1984, p. 4, ill.

O'GRADY, BOB
"Heisey Candlesticks"
Heisey News, continuing series: v. 13, no. 1, Jan. 1984,—v. 13, no. 12, Dec. 1984.

OLMERT, MICHAEL
"In Steuben Show, the Art of Glass Is Clear as Crystal"
Smithsonian, v. 15, no. 7, Oct. 1984, pp. 140–147, ill.
"Fifty Years on Fifth" exhibition.

PADGETT, LEONARD E.
"A Cup Plate Refresher Course"
The Thistle, v. 5, no. 3, Summer 1984, pp. 5–6.
Cup plate history, how they are made today and companies that produce them.

PULOS, ARTHUR J.
American Design Ethic: A History of Industrial Design to 1940
Cambridge, Mass.: the MIT Press, 1983, 441 pp., ill.
Includes pressed glass, Crystal Palace, Tiffany, lighting and lamps, Teague, bottles, etc.

RAKOW, LEONARD S.
and JULIETTE K.
"American Cameo Glass"
Glass Art Society Journal 1983–1984, pp. 24–31, ill.

REAM, LOUISE
"Heisey Amber"
Heisey News, v. 13, no. 10, Oct. 1984, p. 4.
"Heisey Glassware"
Glass Review (Ohio), continuing series: v. 14, no. 1, Jan./Feb. 1984—v. 14, no. 10, Dec. 1984.
"Heisey's Little Things"
Heisey News, irregular series: v. 13, no. 1, Jan. 1984—v. 13, no. 12, Dec. 1984.
"Verlys Decorative Glass by Heisey"
Glass Review (Ohio), v. 14, no. 10, Dec. 1984, pp. 5–7, ill.

RETTKE, AL and WENDY
"Harry's Birds: Northwood's Peacock"
Heart of America Carnival Glass Association Bulletin, Jan. 1984, pp. 19–21, ill.

REVI, ALBERT CHRISTIAN
"Modern Glass Paperweights"
Bulletin of the Paperweight Collectors' Association, June 1961, [8 pp.], ill.
Work of H. E. Geron, J. Funfrock; also the Gentile Glass Co. in 1940s–1950s.

RICE, FERILL J.
"More Burmese by Fenton"
Glass Review (Ohio), v. 14, no. 10, Dec. 1984, pp. 14–15, ill.
"New Finds"
Butterfly Net, v. 7, no. 5, May 1984, pp. 7–9, ill. and v. 7, no. 6, July 1984, p. 7, ill.
Fenton glass.

RIEGEL, RICHARD
"The Industrial Side of DG"
Depression Glass Daze, v. 14, no. 2, April 1984, p. 8.
Glass businesses in the 1930s and 1940s, from *American Glass Review* trade journal.

ROCKMAN, DIANA DIZ.
and ROTHSCHILD, NAN A.
"City Tavern, Country Tavern: An Analysis of Four Colonial Sites"
Historical Archaeology, v. 18, no. 2, 1984, pp. 112–121, ill.
Comparative study of urban and rural taverns, including bottle and drinking glass artifacts.

ROESEL, JOHN C.
"Atlanta Museum to Stage Brilliant Cut Glass Exhibit"
The Hobstar, v. 6, no. 10, June 1984, p. 2+.
In Feb., 1985.

RUSSELL, WOODY
"Glass Industry Began in the 17th Century . . ."
National Opportunities Classified Combined with The Hobby Horse, v. 8, no. 2, April/June 1984, p. 1+, ill.

SAARINEN, RALPH U.
"Mt. Washington Glass Co. Salt Shakers"
Salt Shaker Collectors Newsletter, no. 4, Dec. 1983, p. 2.

SACHNOFF, MARC
"Collecting Neon Signs"
The Antique Trader Weekly, Annual of Articles on Antiques, v. 15, 1983, pp. 45–47, ill.

SCHLIESMANN, MARK
Price Survey, 2nd Edition. Includes Depression Era Glass, Pottery and China
Racine, Wis.: Park Avenue Publications, Ltd., 1984, 137 pp., ill.

SCHWARTZ, MARVIN D.
"Stiegel Glass—Another Consideration of the Problem of Attributions"
The Glass Club Bulletin, Winter 1984, pp. 14–16, ill.

SCHWIND, ARLENE PALMER
"Joseph Baggott, New York Glasscutter"
The Glass Club Bulletin, Winter 1984, pp. 9–13.

SCOTT, VIRGINIA R.
The Candlewick Collector, 4 newsletters: no. 35, Feb. 1984—no. 39, Dec. 1984.
"Looking Through the Ads"
Glass Review (Ohio), continuing series: v. 14, no. 1, Jan./Feb. 1984—v. 14, no. 10, Dec. 1984.

SERRA, ANNE
" 'Once in a Lifetime' Auction of Early Midwestern Glass"
The New York-Pennsylvania Collector, v. 9, no. 3, May 1984, p. 1+, ill.

SHAEFFER, BARBARA
"Cambridge Corner"
Glass Review (Ohio), v. 14, no. 9, Nov. 1984, pp. 13–15, ill.

SHERRILL, SARAH B.
"Current and Coming: Glass"
Antiques, v. 125, no. 4, 1984, p. 762+.
Bennington Museum displays.

SHIRLEY, G. E.
"Early Electric Christmas Tree Lights"
The Antique Trader Weekly, Annual of Articles on Antiques, v. 15, 1983, pp. 76–79, ill.

SHIRLEY, GLYNDON
"A New Frontier: Heat Resistant Glass"
Depression Glass Daze, v. 14, no. 2, April 1984, pp. 46–47, ill.
Anchor Hocking, 1940s.

SHOMETTE, DONALD G.
"The Pitcher Wreck" [in]
Shipwrecks on the Chesapeake, by D. G. Shomette. Centreville, Md.: Tidewater Publishers, 1982, pp. 181–188, ill.
1869 Hobbs and Co. molasses pitchers, both plain and hobnail.

SHUMPERT, GWEN
"Gwen's Glassline"
Glass Review (Ohio), continuing series: v. 14, no. 1, Jan./Feb. 1984—v. 14, no. 10, Dec. 1984.

SINCLAIRE, ESTELLE
"Fine Glass at the Great World's Fairs (Part 1)"
The Hobstar, v. 6, no. 7, March 1984, pp. 2–4, ill.

SIONAKIDES, GEORGE
"Glass Trends—1984"
Depression Glass Daze, v. 13, no. 11, Jan. 1984, p. 6.
Collecting market, 1983–1984.

SIONAKIDES, RONI
"Akro Agate"
Depression Glass Daze, v. 13, no. 11, Jan. 1984, p. 8, ill.

SISSON, MRS. F. J.
"Modern American Paperweights"
Bulletin of the Paperweight Collectors' Association, June 1961, [3 pp.], ill.
Degenhart, Gentile, St. Clair weights, 1940s–1950s.

SMITH, PHYLLIS
"Cambridge Sonata . . . the Oval Line"
Cambridge Crystal Ball, no. 132, April 1984, pp. 2–4, ill.
"Recent Reissues"
Cambridge Crystal Ball, no. 139, Nov. 1984, p. 3, ill.
" 'Yukon' Decoration"
Cambridge Crystal Ball, no. 139, Nov. 1984, p. 13, ill.

SPILLMAN, JANE SHADEL
"Egginton Patterns—Some New Identifications"

The Hobstar, v. 6, no. 6, Feb. 1984, pp. 2–3, ill.

"Little Known Treasures from The Corning Museum of Glass"
The Hobstar, v. 6, no. 7, April 1984, pp. 3–5, ill.
8 cut glass items.

SPRAIN, TOM
"How Do You Tell Old Carnival Tumblers from the New Carnival Tumblers?"
The Carnival Pump, v. 18, no. 2, Dec. 1984, pp. 7–9, ill.

ST. PETERSBURG, FLORIDA. MUSEUM OF FINE ARTS
Steuben Glass: The Carder Years
St. Petersburg, Fla.: the museum, 1984, [16] pp., ill.

STARBUCK, DAVID R.
"The New England Glassworks in Temple, New Hampshire"
The Journal of the Society for Industrial Archeology, v. 9, no. 1, 1983, pp. 45–64, ill.

STEARNS, GLENITA
"Fostoria from the Fifties"
Glass Review (Ohio), v. 14, no. 10, Dec. 1984, pp. 4–5, ill.

"Glancing Back"
Glass Review (Ohio), v. 14, no. 4, May 1984, p. 30, ill.
Reprint of Aug. 1979 article on a Fostoria pattern.

Sterling and Francine Clark Art Institute Annual Report 1983
Williamstown, Mass.: the institute, 1983, 48 pp., ill.
Acquisitions of nine donated items, Sandwich and other.

STOUT, VELMA
"The Art of Lighting"
Art in America, v. 47, no. 3, 1959, pp. 76–79, ill.
Brief article; includes Steuben cascade pool wall divider by George Thompson.

SWAN, LOUISE
"Collecting Cabinet Pieces"
The Hobstar, v. 6, no. 7, March 1984, p. 7+, ill.
Miniatures and small cut glass pieces.

"Cut Glass for Invalids in the Brilliant Period, 1876–1916"
Hobbies, v. 89, no. 8, Oct. 1984, pp. 18–22, ill.

"Engraved Glassware of the American Brilliant Period"
Hobbies, v. 89, no. 1, March 1984, pp. 16–20, ill.

"Nomenclature for Diamond Motifs"
The Hobstar, v. 6, no. 5, Jan. 1984, p. 2, ill.

SWANK, SCOTT T.
Arts of the Pennsylvania Germans (Ed. by Catherine E. Hutchins)
New York, N.Y.: W. W. Norton & Co. for The Henry Francis du Pont Winterthur Museum, 1983, 309 pp., ill.
Glass, pp. 200–210, by Arlene Palmer Schwind.

TARTER, JABE
"Definition of Stretch Glass"
Stretch Glass Society Newsletter, v. 11, no. 2, July 1984, p. 8.

"On Research and Its Chuckholes"
American Carnival Glass News, v. 19, no. 1, Jan. 1984, pp. 12–13, ill.
Lamp made by both Riverside and Millersburg glass companies.

TAYLOR, DOROTHY
"Recap of Years Gone By"
Carnival Glass Encore, v. 10, no. 1, Feb. 1984, pp. [9–14].
New carnival glass happenings since 1975.

TAYLOR, GAY LeCLEIRE
"Farber Donations Added to Museum Collection"
The Journal, A Newsletter for Friends of Wheaton Village, v. 7, no. 3, 1984, p. 1, ill.
Wheeling pieces.

"The Husted Mold Drawings"
The Glass Club Bulletin, no. 144, Fall 1984, pp. 3–5, ill.
Pittsburgh, Pa. and Bridgeton, N.J. mold maker, Monroe Husted, 1882–1924.

"Millville Mantel Ornament Identified"
The Glass Club Bulletin, no. 143, Spring 1984, pp. 9–10, ill.
Wheaton Museum piece made by Whitall Tatum Co., about 1900.

"New Additions to Museum Collection"
The Journal, A Newsletter for Friends of Wheaton Village, v. 7, no. 4, Oct./Dec. 1984, p. 1+, ill.
Paperweights, decanter by Carl Erickson, bottle.

TAYLOR, MABEL
"Collectors Who Love Color Should Consider Carnival Glass"
Collectors News, v. 25, no. 3, July 1984, p. 46, ill.

TEAGUE, WALTER DORWIN
"Glass Blown to New Design"
Arts and Decoration, v. 40, March 1934, p. 18, ill.
Steuben designs.

THARP, MEL
"What Iridescent Glassware Was Popular in the Early 1900s?"
Collectors News, v. 25, no. 6, Oct. 1984, p. 10.
Carnival.

TOMAZIN, ANTHONY
"Continuing Information on Sculptured Glass"
Duncan Glass Journal, v. 9, no. 1, Jan./March 1984, pp. 21–27, ill.
Fenton's Atlantis pattern a reproduction of a Duncan original.

"Perfection Glass Co."
Duncan Glass Journal, v. 9, no. 4, Oct./Dec. 1984, pp. 6–7, ill.
1902–1906, Washington, Pa.

"The Phoenix Glass Company"
Duncan Glass Journal, v. 9, no. 3, July/Sept. 1984, pp. 22–23, ill.

"Pittsburg Window Glass Co."
Duncan Glass Journal, v. 9, no. 2, April/June 1984, p. 17, ill.
Washington, Pa. 1901–1920s.

TRUMBOLD, AUDREY
"The States Series"
Toothpick Bulletin, v. 10, no. 2, Feb. 1984, p. 5+, ill.
U.S. Glass Co. patterns.

VAY, FLORENCE TAYLOR
"Taylor Bros. & Co. Cut Glass"
The Hobstar, v. 7, no. 3, Nov. 1984, p. 2+.
Philadelphia firm, 1902–1910.

VOGEL, CLARENCE W., ed.
Heisey Glass Newscaster
(Plymouth, O.: Heisey Publications), quarterly newsletter, v. 14, no. 1, Jan. 1984–v. 14, no. 4, Dec. 1984.

WAHER, BETTYE W.
The Hawkes Hunter. T. G. Hawkes & Co. 1880–1962
[Jupiter, Fla.]: Bettye W. Waher, 1984, 151 pp., ill.

"Just What Is Cut Glass? Part 2"
The Hobstar, v. 6, no. 5, Jan. 1984, p. 4, ill. Part 3: v. 6, no. 6, Feb. 1984, pp. 8–9, ill. Part 4: v. 7, no. 2, Oct. 1984, pp. 5–6, ill.
Techniques, materials, motifs on American brilliant cut glass.

WALKER, MARY
More Reamers (200 Years)

Los Angeles, Cal.: Muski Publishers, 1983, 156 pp., ill.

WANSER, BETTY
"Heisey No. 1401 Empress/No. 1509 Queen Ann"
Pony Express, v. 11, no. 11, Nov. 1984, pp. 4–5, ill.

Warman's Americana & Collectibles (Ed. by Harry L. Rinker)
Elkins Park, Pa.: Warman Publishing Co., Inc., 1984, 550 pp., ill.

WEBB, DENNIS
and RANDALL, MARK
"The Men and Machines That Make the Marbles"
Marble-Mania, v. 33, Jan. 1984, p. 2.
How factory marbles are formed.

The Welsbach Light or The Evening Beautiful. By the Welsbach Commercial Company, Philadelphia (catalog reprint, 1896)
[Talcottville, Ct.]: The Rushlight Club, 1984, [14] pp., ill.
An "improved" gas light.

WENRICH, JEANNE P.
"Lamp and Lantern Manufacturing Companies in Rochester, N.Y."
New York–Pennsylvania Collector, v. 9, no. 7, Sept. 1984, pp. 22B–26B, ill.

WERTZBERGER, DALLAS
"Silver Threads—Pattern of the Month"
The Hobstar, v. 7, no. 4, Dec. 1984, p. 9, ill.

WESLEY, CHARLES
"Handel Floor-Type Reading Lamps"
Hobbies, v. 89, no. 5, June 1984, pp. 29–34, ill.

Westmoreland Specialty Co., Grapeville, Pa., Manufacturers of Cut Glassware, Fine Pressed Table & Bar Glassware, Opal Novelties . . . Catalogue 1912 [reprint]
Newark, Ohio: Glass Research Press and the Heisey Collectors of America, [1984], [57] pp., ill.

WETZ, JON H.
"Edward Haines, Sandwich Gaffer"
The Sandwich Collector, v. 1, no. 1, Jan. 1984, pp. 3–19, ill. (Part 1: "The Early Years, 1828–1849"; Part 2: "Glassmaking in Falmouth, Mass., 1849–1854"; Part 3: "The Later Years, 1854–1891").
"Identifying Sandwich Glass: How Museums Do It"
The Sandwich Collector, v. 1, no. 2, April 1984, pp. 3–15, ill.

"Ring Vases—Sandwich or New Bedford"
The Sandwich Collector, v. 1, no. 3, July 1984, pp. 3–15, ill.
Blown-molded cylinder vases with hand painted decoration, 1870–1890.
"Sandwich Whale Oil Lamps"
The Sandwich Collector, v. 1, no. 4, Oct. 1984, pp. 3–12, ill.
"Whale Oil Lamp Burners"
The Sandwich Collector, v. 1, no. 4, Oct. 1984, pp. 13–16, ill.

WHITMYER, MARGARET
and KENN
Children's Dishes
Paducah, Ky.: Collector Books, 1984, 175 pp., ill.
Akro Agate, Depression era, pattern glass sets; full-size children's dishes.

WIENER, H. H.
"Stark Museum"
The Hobstar, v. 9, no. 8, May 1984, pp. 1–3, ill.
Texas restored home contains large collection of cut glass.

WOLLETT, MARY and BILL
"American Historical Glass"
Hobbies, continuing series: v. 88, no. 11, Jan. 1984—v. 89, no. 10, Dec. 1984.

YOUNG, ELLSWORTH
"Has It Been Repaired?"
The Hobstar, v. 6, no. 7, April 1984, p. 6+.
Cut glass.
"To Repair or Not to Repair"
The Hobstar, v. 6, no. 5, Jan. 1984, pp. 8–9.
Cut glass.

ZIEGLER, ROSERITA
"Imperial Art Glass Company, Irving W. Rice Account 1941–1945"
The Imperial Collectors Glasszette, v. 9, Feb. 1984, pp. 5–7, ill. Part 2: "Perfume Stoppers," v. 9, May 1984, pp. 4–5, ill. [This part also appeared in *Glass Review*, v. 14, no. 9, Nov. 1984, pp. 4–7, ill.].

BOTTLES, FLASKS, INSULATORS, JARS

ANONYMOUS
"Arman Absentee Auction Features Bottle-Flask Collection"
Antiques & The Arts Weekly, v. 12, no. 42, Oct. 19, 1984, p. 79, ill.
"Back to Basics"
The Milk Route, v. 50, Nov. 1984, p. 2. Part 2: v. 51, Dec. 1984, p. 8, ill.
Descriptive terminology used by milk bottle collectors.
"Bitters, Anyone?"
The Corning Museum of Glass Newsletter, Autumn 1984, p. [3], ill.
Carlyn Ring gift to museum.
"Burr's Laforme Nurser"
Keeping Abreast, v. 11, no. 2/3, Dec./March 1984, pp. 4–5, ill. Part 2: v. 11, no. 4, June 1984, pp. 13–15, ill.
Boston nursing bottle, 1860s.
"Evenflo Nursers"
Keeping Abreast, v. 12, no. 2, Dec. 1984, pp. 31–35, ill.
"Friendly Competitors"
The Heritage Newsletter, v. 15, no. 9, Nov. 1984, p. 4.
Correspondence between Whitney Glass Works and Clayton Bottle Works, 1887.
"Glass Ball and Gyro Pigeon Shooting"
Antique Bottle World, v. 11, no. 4, April 1984, pp. 7–12, ill.
[Reprinted from *Trapshooting—the Patriotic Sport*, s.l., s.n., 1920].
"Heritage Glass Museum"
The Heritage Newsletter, v. 15, no. 3, March 1984, p. 6, ill.
Glass and bottle museum recently established in Glassboro, N.J.
"Investing in Bottles"
Old Bottle Magazine, v. 17, no. 12, Dec. 1984, pp. 5–8.
"Pitkin Glassworks Had Octagonal Roof"
Somers Antique Bottle Club News & Views, v. 13, no. 8, Jan./Feb. 1984, p. 5.
Hartford, Conn. newspaper article, 1923, on Pitkin factory.
"Vitaflo—The Other Pyramid Nurser"
Keeping Abreast, v. 12, no. 2, Dec. 1984, pp. 36–39, ill.
"What Is That Bottle Used For?"
Australian Antique Bottle Collector, v. 3, no. 1, June/July 1984, p. 26, ill.
70 types of bottles illustrated.
"Wheaton Tour: 'Blow and Blow' Bottle Operation"

Glasfax Newsletter, v. 16, no. 2, Spring 1984, pp. 10–12, ill.
How bottles are made at Wheaton Glass Co., N.J.
"1983 Figured Flasks Exhibit"
Verbeck Views, Feb. 1984, pp. 5–6, ill.
At National Bottle Museum, Ballston Spa.

ACKERMAN, DAVE D.
"I'll Have a Moxie, Please!"
American Carnival Glass News, v. 19, no. 2, March 1984, p. 16, ill.

ALBERS, MARILYN
"Foreign Insulators"
Insulators, continuing series: v. 15, no. 11, Jan. 1984—v. 16, no. 10, Dec. 1984.

A. V. Whiteman, N.Y., Flint Glass Milk Jars
[New York, N.Y.: the company, n.d.], 1 leaf, ill.
Urges farmers to begin using bottles for milk distribution.

BEATTY, GARY
"Those Fabulous Flasks"
Antique Bottle & Glass Collector, irregular series: v. 1, no. 1, May 1984—v. 1, no. 8, Dec. 1984.
"Those Fabulous Flasks: G IV–32, J. Shepard & Co."
Verbeck Views, April 1984, p. 7, ill.

BENDER, GEORGE A. and PARASCANDOLA, JOHN, eds.
American Pharmacy in the Colonial and Revolutionary Periods
Madison, Wis.: American Institute of the History of Pharmacy, 1977, 48 pp., ill.
Mentions medicine bottles and vials.

BERMAN, ROS and DICK
"Nursing Bottles: Feeding Baby Through the Ages"
The Heritage Newsletter, v. 25, no. 6, June 1984, p. 4, ill.

Beverage World: 100 Year History 1882–1982 and Future Probe
Great Neck, N.Y.: Beverage World; East Stroudsburg, Pa.: Keller International Publishing Corp., 1982, 606 pp., ill.

BINDSCHEATTLE, LLOYD
"Creamer Corner"
The Milk Route, continuing series: v. 42, March 1984—v. 51, Dec. 1984.

BOGARD, MARY O.
"Colored Glass in Pharmacy"

Pharmacy in History, v. 26, no. 1, 1984, pp. 20–27, ill.
Bottles and the U.S. companies that made them.

BOWDITCH, BARBARA
"Early Jelly Glasses"
The New York–Pennsylvania Collector, v. 9, no. 8, Nov. 1984, pp. 1–5B, ill.

BOWEN, THOMAS H.
"Glass Provided Quinton's Golden Age. Part 1"
The Heritage Newsletter, v. 15, no. 1, Jan. 1984, p. 4, ill. Part 2: v. 15, no. 2, Feb. 1984, pp. 5–6. Part 3: v. 15, no. 3, March 1984, pp. 5–6.
South Jersey glasshouse.

BOWERS, DAVID
"Drake's Plantation Bitters, the Product and the Bottles"
Antique Bottle World, Part 1: v. 11, no. 3, March 1984, pp. 21–29, ill. Part 2: v. 11, no. 4, April 1984, pp. 21–28, ill. Part 3: v. 11, no. 5, May 1984, pp. 21–23, ill.
"An Early Bitters Guide"
Old Bottle Magazine, v. 17, no. 7, July 1984, pp. 6–7.
"I Don't Touch the Hard Stuff—I Only Drink Drake's Plantation Bitters!"
Rare Coin Review (Wolfeboro, N.H.) no. 50, Jan./March 1984, pp. 71–76, ill.
"An Important Offering of Bitters Bottles"
Old Bottle Magazine, v. 17, no. 4, April 1984, pp. 8–32, ill.
Includes history of the bottles, types, names, etc.
"Moxie for Me!"
Old Bottle Magazine, v. 17, no. 5, May 1984, pp. 4–10, ill.

BROOKMAN, JOHN F.
"Happy 100th Birthday to the Glass Milk Bottle!"
The Milk Route, v. 49, Oct. 1984, pp. 8–9.

BULL, DONALD; FRIEDRICH, MANFRED; and GOTTSCHALK, ROBERT
American Breweries
Trumbull, Conn.: Bullworks, 1984, 400 pp.

BURDEN, CHARLES E.
"Potter's Patent Nursing Bottle"
Keeping Abreast, v. 11, no. 2/3, Dec./March 1984, pp. 6–9, ill.

CABLE, CHIP and MURRAY, WALT
"J. C. Buffum, Pittsburgh's Bottling Pioneer"
Antique Bottle & Glass Collector, v. 1, no. 5, Sept. 1984, pp. 5–14, ill.

California Perfume Company [sales catalog]
[New York, N.Y.: the company, 1920s?], 32 pp., ill.

CANIFF, TOM
"'Exwaco'—More Than Just Another Pretty Mustard Jar"
Antique Bottle World, v. 11, no. 2, Feb. 1984, pp. 8–11, ill.
Food packing bottles, Wheeling, W.Va. area.

CANNON, RICHARD A.
"The I.X.L. Brand from Houston"
Antique Bottle & Glass Collector, v. 1, no. 4, Aug. 1984, pp. 27–29, ill.
Medicines.

CHRISTIAN, DONNA ALLGAIER
"Michigan's Kalamazoo Brewing Company"
The Antique Trader Weekly, Annual of Articles on Antiques, v. 15, 1983, pp. 21–23, ill.

CLAXTON, CAMILLE
"Digging Up Bottles"
Antiques Dealer, v. 36, no. 11, Nov. 1984, pp. 27–28, ill.

CORBETT, PATRICIA
"All the Perfumes of Arabia"
Art & Antiques, Premiere Issue, March 1984, p. 14, ill.
Vial designed by Dali.

EASTIN, JUNE
"History of the Common Bottles"
Old Bottle Magazine, v. 17, no. 12, Dec. 1984, pp. 9–14+, ill.
Lydia Pinkham's and others.

FINCH, RALPH
"Another Great Page in the Blaske Family Album"
Antique Bottle World, v. 11, no. 1, Jan. 1984, pp. 4–12+, ill.
"Heaven Preserved Us!"
Maine Antique Digest, v. 12, no. 3, March 1984, p. 32A, ill.
Fruit jar show.

FOWLER, RON
Ice-Cold Soda Pop 5: An Illustrated History of Oregon Soda Pop Bottles
Seattle, Wash.: Ron Fowler, 1981, 78 pp., ill.

"Speaking Soda Confidentially"
Old Bottle Magazine, continuing series: v. 17, no. 1, Jan. 1984—v. 17, no. 12, Dec. 1984.

FREDGANT, DON
"Antique Pharmacy Bottles: Sources and Pricing"
Pharmacy in History, v. 26, no. 1, 1984, pp. 46–49.

GABELMANN, HENRY
"A. M. Bininger & Co."
Somers Antique Bottle Club News & Views, v. 13, no. 8, Jan./Feb. 1984, p. 6, ill.

GALLAGHER, TOM
"The Whole Thatcher Story—Yet Another Chapter"
The Milk Route, v. 42, March 1984, pp. 6–7, ill.

Glassware for Packers and Preservers: Bottles, Jars, Jugs, Tumblers. Hazel-Atlas Glass Company, 1930 Catalog
Wheeling, W.Va.: the company, 1929, 257 pp., ill.

GUSTAFSON, ELEANOR H.
"Museum Accessions"
Antiques, v. 125, no. 6, June 1984, p. 1298, ill.
"Log Cabin and Hard Cider" flask, Old Sturbridge Village.

HAGENBUCH, JIM
"Courtney Collection"
Antique Bottle & Glass Collector, v. 1, no. 3, July 1984, pp. 6–16, ill.
"National Bottle Museum 5 Years Old"
Antique Bottle & Glass Collector, v. 1, no. 7, Nov. 1984, pp. 17–20, ill.

HAGENBUCH, JIM and STURM, J. CARL
"Hermanus"
Antique Bottle & Glass Collector, v. 1, no. 8, Dec. 1984, pp. 6–13, ill.
Cures from Reading, Pa.

HALLMAN, TOM
"The Art of Glassblowing? Maybe It's All in the Mold"
Antique Bottle World, v. 11, no. 2, Feb. 1984, pp. 28–29, ill.
Bottle molds.

HAM, BILL
"The Keen Embossed and Similar Sunburst Flasks"
Antique Bottle and Glass Collector, v. 1, no. 4, Aug. 1984, pp. 5–14, ill.

Hazel-Atlas Glass Co., Wheeling, W.Va. Glassware for Packers. Catalog no. 2
Wheeling, W.Va.: the company, [about 1900], 23 pp., ill.
Canning jars.

HEATHMAN, ELIZABETH
"Maw's Feeding Bottles"
Keeping Abreast, v. 12, no. 1, Sept. 1984, p. 15, ill.

HERBERTA, VICTORIA
"Charles A. Fuelscher's East Side Bottling Works, Cheyenne, Wyoming"
Old Bottle Magazine, v. 17, no. 9, Sept. 1984, pp. 6–7, ill.
"Enterprise Bottling Works"
Old Bottle Magazine, v. 17, no. 6, June 1984, p. 31, ill.
Iowa, 1886–1896.
"Pompeian Clean Before Being Seen"
Old Bottle Magazine, v. 17, no. 5, May 1984, p. 32, ill.
Cosmetic bottle, 1909–1910.

HILL, BRIAN
"Back to the Nursery"
Australian Antique Bottle Collector, v. 3, no. 2, Aug./Sept. 1984, pp. 22–26, ill.

HOVIOUS, JIM
"Bennett Bottling Works, Pioneer Kansas Bottler"
Antique Bottle World, v. 11, no. 9, Sept. 1984, pp. 10–13, ill.

JACKSON, DONALD DALE
"If Women Needed a Quick Pick-me-Up, Lydia Provided One"
Smithsonian, v. 15, no. 4, July 1984, pp. 107–108+, ill.

JANEWAY, PATRICIA A.
"Owens Machine—an Engineering Landmark"
Ceramic Industry, v. 122, no. 3, March 1983, pp. 30–31, ill.

JEWELL, DOROTHY
"When Moxie Came in a Bottle"
The Heritage Newsletter, v. 15, no. 2, Feb. 1984, p. 6, ill.

JONES, FRANK
"The Story of the Block Glass Insulators"
Insulators, v. 15, no. 11, Jan. 1984, pp. 9–18, ill.

KATH, VIVIAN S.
"Granny Kath's Kitchen"
Antique Bottle & Glass Collector, continuing series: v. 1, no. 1, May 1984—v. 1, no. 8, Dec. 1984.

KLINGENSMITH, RAY
"Insulator News"
Antique Bottle & Glass Collector, irregular series: v. 1, no. 1, May 1984—v. 1, no. 8, Dec. 1984.
"The Sterling Glass Company"
Insulators, v. 15, no. 11, Jan. 1984, pp. 19–23, ill.

KNEELAND, C.
"Bottle of the Month: Deposit Bottles"
The Milk Route, v. 51, Dec. 1984, p. 7.

KNIPP, TONY
"All Aboard—Part 2"
The Milk Route, v. 50, Nov. 1984, pp. 5–6, ill.
Milks embossed with railroad logos.

KOVEL, RALPH and TERRY
"Bottle Buffs Search for Shapes, Colors, Names"
Collectors News, v. 24, no. 9, Jan. 1984, p. 12, ill.
The Kovels' Bottle Price List. Seventh Edition
New York, N.Y.: Crown Publishers, Inc., 1984, 194 pp., ill.

LEVIN, BEATRICE
"Bottle Collecting: From the Common to the Unusual"
Collectors News, v. 24, no. 11, March 1984, p. 13, ill.

LEVITT, VICTORIA and WYANT, ROBERT
"The Man Who Made Milk 'Modern'"
The New York-Pennsylvania Collector, v. 9, no. 3, May 1984, pp. 10–11B, ill.
Dr. Thatcher.

LOCKMILLER, JIM
"A Bit About Candy Bottles"
Federation Letter, v. 14, no. 11, Nov. 1984, pp. 14–15.

LORD, DONALD E.
California Milks. A Collectors Guide to California & Other Unique Milk Bottles
[s.l.]: Donald E. Lord, (Sacramento, Cal.: Dome Printing), 1984, 302 pp., ill.

MARGULIES, J. A.
"Maw's Dinky Feeder"
Keeping Abreast, v. 11, no. 2/3, Dec./March 1984, p. 26, ill.

MASSENGALE, OLIVER
"The Common Sense Nursing Bottle"
Keeping Abreast, v. 12, no. 1, Sept. 1984, pp. 12–13, ill.

MICHAEL, GEORGE
"'Medicine' Bottles Found from Coast to Coast"
Collectors News, v. 25, no. 1, May 1984, p. 11, ill.

MILLER, GEORGE L. and SULLIVAN, CATHERINE
"Machine-Made Glass Containers and the End of Production for Mouth-Blown Bottles"
Historical Archaeology, v. 18, no. 2, 1984, pp. 83–96, ill.
Chronological developments in bottle blowing machinery.

MOORE, ROGER and ANDERSON, TEXAS
"Gilded Age Archaeology: The Ashton Villa"
Archaeology, v. 37, no. 3, May/June 1984, pp. 44–50, ill.
Late 19th/early 20th c. medicines from Galveston, Texas.

MORGAN, ROY
"The Genius Behind the Marble Stoppered 'Pop' Bottle"
Marble-Mania, v. 34, April 1984, p. 2.
Hiram Codd.

MURRAY, EDWARD H.
Canadian Fruit Jar Collector No. 1–7, January 1973–May 1976
Paris, Ill.: Acorn Press, 1984, 178 pp., ill.
Reprint, with index, of articles from an old publication.

O'CONNELL, ANNETTE
"Relic Hunt, U.S.A.: Say 'Gear-ar-delli' "
Old Bottle Magazine, v. 17, no. 8, Aug. 1984, pp. 11–16+, ill.
Ghirardelli bottles.

OSTRANDER, DIANE ROUSE
A Guide to American Nursing Bottles
Willoughby, Ohio: Will-O-Graf Publications of Ohio, 1984, [96] pp., ill.

PATTERSON, EARL
"Rare Waterford Flask Found in Conn."
The Heritage Newsletter, v. 15, no. 5, May 1984, p. 6.
Pontiled flask: Waterford, N.J., before 1863.

PETSCHE, JEROME E.
Uncovering the Steamboat Bertrand
(Reprint from *Nebraska History*, v. 51, no. 1, Spring 1970)
Lincoln, Neb.: Nebraska State His-

torical Society, n.d., 23 pp., ill.
Bitters, wines, and preserve bottles; lamps and chimneys, from 1865 wreck on Missouri River, Iowa.

PIATTI, MARY JANE and JAMES
"Fire-Related Advertising Collectibles, Part 1"
The Antique Trader Weekly, Annual of Articles on Antiques, v. 15, 1983, pp. 274–276, ill.
Avon bottles.

POTTER, FRANK N.
The Moxie Mystique: the Word, the Drink, the Collectibles
Virginia Beach/Norfolk, Va.: Donning Co. Publishers, 1981, 147 pp., ill.

PRICE, MORRIS
"McKee Nursers"
Keeping Abreast, v. 11, no. 2/3, Dec./March 1984, pp. 55–58, ill.
"Nursers Advertising Dairies"
Keeping Abreast, v. 11, no. 4, June 1984, pp. 31–35.

PUCKHABER, BERNHARD C.
Saratogas. A History of the Springs, Mineral Water Bottles . . . , Bottling Plants and Glass Works of Saratoga County, N.Y. from 1823–1889
Ballston Spa, N.Y.: Journal Press, 1976, 91 pp., ill.

REVI, ALBERT CHRISTIAN
"A New View of Pepper Sauce Bottles"
The Glass Club Bulletin, no. 144, Fall 1984, pp. 10–11, ill.
Catalog pages of the Kearns-Gorsuch Bottle Co. of Zanesville, O., ca. 1880.

RING, CARLYN and RAY, SHELDON, JR.
For Bitters Only Up-Date and Price Guide
[Portsmouth, N.H.]: Carlyn Ring, 1984, 116 pp.

ROLLER, DICK
"The Adler Jars"
Fruit Jar Newsletter, Dec. 1984, p. 247, ill.
"A Ball Wide-Mouth Half-Pint Jar"
Fruit Jar Newsletter, April 1984, pp. 215–216, ill.
"The Banner Half-Pint Jars"
Fruit Jar Newsletter, Oct. 1984, p. 240, ill.
"A Different Type of Crystal Jar"
Fruit Jar Newsletter, Dec. 1984, p. 248, ill.

"The French Jelly Glass"
Fruit Jar Newsletter, Nov. 1984, p. 243, ill.
Made by Missouri Glass Co., 1887.
"The German Kieffer Jars"
Fruit Jar Newsletter, June 1984, pp. 223–224, ill.
"The Heroine Jar Base Embossings"
Fruit Jar Newsletter, July 1984, p. 227, ill.
"The Maker of the National Super Mason Jars?"
Fruit Jar Newsletter, Sept. 1984, p. 235, ill.
"A Mason's (Keystone) Keystone Jar Variation"
Fruit Jar Newsletter, Oct. 1984, p. 239, ill.
"More Older Ball Commemorative Jars"
Fruit Jar Newsletter, Nov. 1984, p. 245, ill.
"More on the Atlas Junior Mason Jars"
Fruit Jar Newsletter, Jan. 1984, p. 205, ill.
"More on the Heroine Jars"
Fruit Jar Newsletter, Aug. 1984, p. 233, ill.
"The Norge Jars"
Fruit Jar Newsletter, Feb. 1984, pp. 207–208, ill. Part 2: June 1984, p. 225.
"Notes & News"
Fruit Jar Newsletter, continuing series: Jan.—Dec. 1984.
"The Paragon Valve Jar"
Fruit Jar Newsletter, March 1984, pp. 211–212, ill.
"Presto Jar Glass Lids"
Fruit Jar Newsletter, July 1984, p. 228, ill.
The Standard Fruit Jar Reference
Paris, Ill.: Acorn Press, 1983, 475 pp., ill.
"Standard Fruit Jar Reference Additions & Corrections"
Fruit Jar Newsletter, July 1984, p. 230, ill. Sept. 1984, p. 237. Oct. 1984, p. 242. Nov. 1984, p. 246.
"Unlisted Haines Jar Discovered"
Fruit Jar Newsletter, Aug. 1984, p. 231, ill.
"The Vacu-Top Jars"
Fruit Jar Newsletter, Dec. 1984, p. 249, ill.
"The 'Weck' Jars"
Fruit Jar Newsletter, Jan. 1984, pp. 203–204, ill. Part 2: March 1984, pp. 213–214, ill.

ROSENTHAL, JEFF and
SWEETLAND, RODGER
"The Little Known Facts Behind One of Buffalo, N.Y.'s Rarest, Most Unusual Bottles"
Antique Bottle & Glass Collector, v. 1, no. 2, June 1984, pp. 5–16, ill.
Dingens Brothers bitters.

SHERWOOD, ISABEL
"State Bottles"
Verbeck Views (National Bottle Museum), continuing series: Jan.—Dec. 1984. [Also in *The Federation Letter*, v. 14, no. 1, Jan. 1984—v. 14, no. 9, Sept. 1984.

SLOWIAK, JOHN
"A Star Was Born—100 Years Ago, August 1, 1884"
Antique Bottle World, v. 11, no. 8, Aug. 1984, pp. 4–8, ill.
Harden Star fire grenade.

STASKI, EDWARD
"Just What Can a 19th Century Bottle Tell Us?"
Historical Archaeology, v. 18, no. 1, 1984, pp. 38–51, ill.
Patterns of alcohol consumption.

STOWE, ROSEMARY M.
"Rosemary's Figurals: Elephant Bottles"
Old Bottle Magazine, v. 17, no. 11, Nov. 1984, pp. 29–33, ill.
"Rosemary's Figurals: Memorable Monks"
Old Bottle Magazine, v. 17, no. 12, Dec. 1984, pp. 15–16+, ill.

SULLIVAN, CATHERINE
"Perry Davis: King of the Wild Frontier"
Canadian Collector, v. 19, no. 2, March/April 1984, pp. 45–48, ill.
Davis' Vegetable Pain Killer bottles.

TRIFFON, JIM
"Wonderful Whiskies"
Miniature Bottle Mart, v. 15, no. 1, Jan. 1984, p. 3, ill.
From the 1930s.

TYLER, VARRO E.
"Three Proprietaries and Their Claim as American 'Indian' Remedies"
Pharmacy in History, v. 26, no. 3, 1984, pp. 146–149, ill.

VANDERLAAN, RICHARD
"Some Rochester Fruit Jars"
Applied Seals, v. 16, no. 2, April 1984, pp. 13–14, ill.

VOGELZANG, VERNAGENE
"The Uncommon H. J. Heinz. Part 1"
Collectors' Showcase, v. 4, no. 2, Nov./ Dec. 1984, pp. 23–29, ill.

VON MECHOW, TOD
"Eugene Roussel, Perfumer & Bottler"
Antique Bottle & Glass Collector, v. 1, no. 7, Nov. 1984, pp. 39–44, ill.
"Evolution of the Squat Beer Bottle"
The Federation Letter, Part 5: v. 14, no. 2, Feb. 1984, pp. 11–13, ill. Part 6: v. 14, no. 3, March 1984, pp. 12–15, ill.
Eastern Pennsylvania brewers and bottlers.

WADDY, GEORGE
"Mineral Waters from Yankee Country"
Antique Bottle & Glass Collector, v. 1, no. 7, Nov. 1984, pp. 4–13, ill. Part 2: v. 1, no. 8, Dec. 1984, pp. 64–68, ill.

ORIENTAL

ANONYMOUS
"Chinese & Japanese Art at Holyoke Museum"
Antiques & The Arts Weekly, v. 12, no. 5, Feb. 3, 1984, p. 31, ill.
Includes paintings on glass.
"Museum Acquires Ancient Glass"
The Toledo Museum of Art Calendar, April 1984, p. [3], ill.
Four pieces from Egypt, India, and China, 10th–18th c.

BLAIR, DOROTHY
"An Exhibition of East Asiatic Glass"
Artibus Asiae, v. 11, no. 3, 1948, pp. 195–205, ill.
Held at Toledo Museum, Oct. 1948.
"A Very Brief Outline of the Long History of Glass in Japan"
K.B.S. Bulletin (Kokusai Bunka Shinkokai, Society for International Cultural Relations, Tokyo). no. 47, May/June 1961, pp. 1–5, ill.

CURTIS, EMILY BYRNE
"The Impact of the West—Part Two. Snuff and the Church"
Journal of the International Chinese Snuff Bottle Society, v. 15, no. 4, Winter 1983, pp. 8–15+, ill.

FINCH, RALPH
"A Little Bottle Brings a Big Price"
The New York-Pennsylvania Collector, v. 9, no. 3, May 1984, p. 9, ill.
18th c. "famille rose" snuff bottle.

GRAHAM, VICTOR E.
"Chinese Snuff Bottle Lore"
Journal of the International Chinese Snuff Bottle Society, v. 16, no. 2, Summer 1984, pp. 7–15+, ill.
"The Fred S. Haines Snuff Bottle Album"
Journal of the International Chinese Snuff Bottle Society, v. 16, no. 1, Spring 1984, pp. 73–74, ill.
Hand-painted album of 1930s illustrating 300 snuff bottles.

HAYWARD, HELENA
"Enterprising Craftsmen"
Country Life, v. 175, no. 4530, June 14, 1984, pp. 1678–1679, ill.
Includes an 18th c. Chinese mirror picture.

INOUE, AKIKO
Satsuma kiriko
Kobe: Biidoro Shiryōko, 1982, 69 pp., ill. [In Japanese only].
History and development of Satsuma cut glass.

IRWIN, SARA
"Tobacco in China: Golden-thread-smoke and Bottles of Snuff"
Rotunda, v. 17, no. 1, Spring 1984, pp. 34–39, ill.

JIANMING, ZHU
"Wang Xisan: One Bottle Fu Zi"
Journal of the International Chinese Snuff Bottle Society, v. 16, no. 2, Summer 1984, pp. 16–20+, ill.

KEVERNE, ROGER
"Chinese Glass Painting"
The Antique Dealer & Collectors Guide, Oct. 1984, pp. 48–50, ill.

KLEINER, ROBERT
"Chinese Snuff Bottles in London"
Arts of Asia, v. 14, no. 3, May/June 1984, p. 102, ill.
Smith collection.

LAVERLOCHÈRE, GAYLE GRAY
"Chinese Snuff Bottles in Paris"
Arts of Asia, v. 14, no. 2, March/April 1984, pp. 114–115, ill.
Jutheau sale.

LONDON. THE ARTS COUNCIL GALLERY
The Arts of the T'ang Dynasty
London: The Oriental Ceramic Society, 1955, 38 pp., ill.
Exhibition catalog includes glass bracelets, hairpins, cups, jars, Buddha and animal figures.

MCCLINTICK, CHARLES
"Report from Japan"
Oriental Art, v. 29, no. 4, Winter 1983/84, pp. 401–403, ill.
Suntory Museum exhibition, "Ch'ien Lung Glass and Art Nouveau."

MOSS, HUGH M.
"The Apricot Grove Studio, Part II: The Artists, 1912–1929"
Journal of the International Chinese Snuff Bottle Society, v. 16, no. 1, Spring 1984, pp. 48–72, ill. "Part II: The Artists, 1930–1949," v. 16, no. 3, Autumn 1984, pp. 73–98, ill.
Continuation of two previous articles on the Ye family, 1982.
"Chinese Snuff Bottles: Toward a Better Understanding"
Journal of the International Chinese Snuff Bottle Society, v. 16, no. 4, Winter 1984, pp. 4–16, ill.

NGUYET, TUYET
"Editorial"
Arts of Asia, v. 14, no. 5, Sept./Oct. 1984, pp. 4–7, ill.
Recent work of Wang Hsi-san: interior painted snuff bottle series of American presidents.

RENK, MARTHA M.
"A Plique-à-jour Bottle"
Journal of the International Chinese Snuff Bottle Society, v. 16, no. 3, Autumn 1984, p. iv+, ill.

ROBERTS, ELLEN
"A Few Sparkling Facets"
The National Early American Glass Club, v. 8, no. 2, May 1984, pp. 8–9.
Snuff bottles and other glass from Poshan factory in Shantung on display at Hong Kong store.

SPEEL, ERIKA
"Japanese Enamel Variations"
Antique Collector, v. 54, no. 11, Nov. 1983, pp. 80–85, ill.

STUPLER, HARVEY
"Peking Glass in Jewel-Toned Radiance: Enduring Chinese Designs"
Architectural Digest. The 1984 Art and Antiques Annual, pp. 140–145, ill.

TOLEDO, OHIO. THE TOLEDO MUSEUM OF ART
Exhibition of East Asiatic Glass (Text by Dorothy Blair)
Toledo: the museum, 1948, 26 pp., ill.
1948 show of Korean, Japanese, and Chinese glass.

TSUCHIYA, YOSHIO
"Satsuma Kiriko. Japan's First Artistic Cut Glass"
Journal of Glass Studies, v. 26, 1984, pp. 102–110, ill.

XISAN, WANG
"Wang Xisan Speaks"
Journal of the International Chinese Snuff Bottle Society, v. 16, no. 2, Summer 1984, pp. 21–25, ill.

ZHANG, FUKANG; CHENG, ZHUHAI; and ZHANG, ZHIGANG
"An Investigation of Ancient Chinese 'Liuli'"
Guisuanyan Xuebao (Journal of the Chinese Silicate Society) v. 11, no. 1, March 1983, pp. 67–76, ill. English summary.
Analysis of beads from tombs of the Western Zhou dynasty.

RUSSIAN

ASHARINA, NINA
Russian Art Glass from the History Museum, Moscow/Russkoe Khudozhestvennoe Steklo iz Sobraniĭa Gosudarstvennogo Istoricheskogo Muzeĭa, Moskva
Leningrad: Aurora Art Publishers, 1984, folder, 16 cards.
Late 17th c.–1900.

DANTSCHENKO, LESSJA
Ukrainische Volkskunst. Keramik, Glas, Holz, Metall, Volksmalerei, Weberei, Stickerei, Teppiche
Leningrad: Aurora-Kunstverlag, 1982, 32 pp., ill.
Ukrainian beaded jewelry, reverse paintings on glass, flasks and vessels, 18th–20th c.

LANMON, DWIGHT P.
"Russian Paperweights and Letter Seals?"
Antiques, v. 126, no. 4, Oct. 1984, pp. 900–903, ill.
Group of weights, c. 1880, strongly pointing to a Russian origin.

MOSCOW. GOSUDARSTVENNYE MUZEI, MOSKOVKOGO KREMLIA
Arkheologicheskaia vystavka Muzeev Kremlia. Katalog
Moscow: Kremlin museum, 1983, 42 pp., ill.
Beads, bracelets of 12th–14th c.

SCANDINAVIAN

BERG, KERSTIN G:SON [sic]
Dryckeskärl och hällkärl
Stockholm: Nordiska Museet, 1981, 27 pp., ill.
Nomenclature of vessels for drinking and pouring.

FILLER, MARTIN
"Design: The Natural"
House & Garden, v. 156, no. 11, Nov. 1984, p. 68+, ill.
Alvar Aalto's furniture and glass exhibit at MOMA.

The Finnish Glass Museum (Text by Kaisa Koivisto)
Riihimäki: the museum, 1983, 56 pp., ill.

FREDLUND, JANE
"Sven Palmqvist—mästare i glas"
Nya Antik et Auktion, no. 4, April 1984, p. 42, ill.

HERLITZ-GEZELIUS, ANN MARIE
Orrefors: A Swedish Glassplant
Stockholm: Atlantis Publishers, 1984, 143 pp., ill.
"Tändstickstället"
Nya Antik et Auktion, no. 1, Jan. 1984, p. 40, ill.
Match holders, including glass one by Hald, about 1930.

LINKÖPING. ÖSTERGÖTLANDS LANSMUSEUM
Simon Gate, Edward Hald: Glas 1916–1973. Ur Agnes Hellners Orreforssamling (Text by Åke Livstedt, Agnes Hellner)
[Linköping: the museum], 1983; (Linköping: AB Östgöta Corresponenten), 47 pp., ill.

MEHLMAN, ROBERT
"Alvar Aalto: Furniture and Glass"
Art & Auction, v. 7, no. 4, Nov. 1984, p. 80+, ill.

MIKKELI, FINLAND. TAIDEMUSEO
Henry Ericsson 1898–1933
Mikkeli: Taidemuseo, 1983, 39 pp., ill.
Designer whose work included glass.

Nationalmuseum of Finland
[Helsinki: the museum, n.d., 33 typescript pp.]. Includes articles presented at the Meeting of the International Committee of Glass Museums and Glass Collections, Helsinki & Riihimäki, May 1984, by S. Kopisto,

C. J. Gardberg, V. Nurmi, and K. Koivisto; plus "Glassworks in Finland 1681–1982."

OSLO. KUNSTINDUSTRIMUSEET
Kunstindustrimuseet i Oslo: en kavalkade av aktuell kunstindustri gjennom hundre år
(Ed. by Inger-Marie Kvaal Lie and Lauritz Opstad)
Oslo: the museum, 1976, [216] pp., ill. English captions.
Includes the museum's glass, especially Scandinavian, 1870s to 1970s.

Prisliste over Hel-Krystals Servicer fra Holmegaards Glasvaerk, Kjøbenhavn K. (reprint, 1917)
Copenhagen: Holmegaards Glasvaerk, 1984, 4 pp., ill.

QUINTIN-BAXENDALE, MARION
"Eda Glassbruk: an Update"
American Carnival Glass News, v. 19, no. 4, Dec. 1984, pp. [16–17], ill.
"Eda Glassbruk—An Update"
The Carnival Pump, v. 18, no. 1, Sept. 1984, pp. 20–21, ill.

RØNNE, MARGRETE
"Glasmagere og arbejdsmaend. Om Kastrup Glasvaerk fra håndvaerksproduktion til automatisering"
Fabrik og Bolig (Det industrielle miljø i Danmark), no. 1, 1984, pp. 18–33, ill.
From hand production to automation at Kastrup, since 1900.

SCHLÜTER, MOGENS
"Gamle danske glas"
Glas & Mennesker (Holmegaards), continuing series: v. 1, no. 2, Aug. 1980—v. 4, no. 8, Oct. 1983.
"De grundlagde glasvaerket"
Glas & Mennesker, v. 5, no. 10, Aug. 1984, pp. 4–5, ill.
Founding of Holmegaard glassworks.

SILTAVUORI, EEVA
"The Versatile Henry Ericsson: Promise, Legend, and Shooting Star"
Form-Function-Finland, no. 1, 1984, pp. 18–23, ill.
Glassware of the 1920s and 1930s.

STAVENOW, ÅKE
and HÖRLÉN, MATTIS
Swedish Arts and Crafts: Swedish Modern—A Movement Towards Sanity in Design
[New York, N.Y.]: The Royal Swedish Commission, New York World's Fair, 1939, 95 pp.

Glass, pp. 15–25: Orrefors, Kosta, Strömbergshyttan, Åfors.

STENSMAN, MAILIS
"Edward Hald"
Form, v. 79, no. 7 (622), 1983, pp. 38–39, ill. English summary.

ART NOUVEAU AND ART DECO

ANONYMOUS
"America's Love Affair with Tiffany"
Collectors Mart, v. 7, no. 11, June 1983, pp. 5–6, ill.
Two exhibitions, 1983.
"Art Deco Glass: History and Care"
Culture and History (Dept. of Culture and History, State of West Virginia), v. 1, no. 1, July/Sept. 1984, pp. 30–31.
"Beauty Found in Automotive Mascots"
Old Cars Weekly, v. 12, no. 47, Nov. 24, 1983.
Lalique hood ornaments.
"Corning Exhibits Glass by Gallé"
Collectors News, v. 25, no. 1, May 1984, p. 39, ill.
"Corning Museum Hosts Major Exhibition of Glass by Emile Gallé"
Ohio Antique Review, v. 10, no. 5, May 1984, p. 29 Preview, ill.
"Emile Gallé: Dreams into Glass"
Antiques & The Arts Weekly, v. 12, no. 36, Sept. 7, 1984, p. 1+, ill.
Corning exhibit.
"Emile Gallé, Dreams into Glass"
The Corning Museum of Glass Newsletter, Spring 1984, pp. 2–3, ill.
"Emile Gallé's Works To Be Shown at Steuben Glass"
Antiques & The Arts Weekly, v. 12, no. 10, March 9, 1984, p. 39, ill.
"Exposition: Charles Schneider, maître-verrier"
Revue des Industries d'Art Offrir, no. 204, June 1984, pp. 55–57, ill.
"Exposition: Schneider, maître-verrier"
L'Estampille, no. 170, June 1984, pp. 56–58, ill.
"Les Expositions: Verreries Schneider au Louvre des antiquaires"
La Gazette de l'Hôtel Drouot, v. 93, no. 22, June 1, 1984, p. 55, ill.
"Fernsehen prüft Antiquitäten. Kopie wird ein 'echtes Stück'"
Antiquitäten-Zeitung, no. 17, Aug. 5–18, 1983, p. 369+, ill.

Debating the authenticity of an Art Nouveau lamp.
"Focus on Carnegie"
Southern Antiques, v. 10, no. 10, Nov. 1984, p. 1+, ill.
Auction of Lalique and Tiffany glass owned by Andrew Carnegie.
"Gallé-Deckeldose mit deutscher Inschrift"
Antiquitäten-Zeitung, no. 18, Aug. 17–30, 1984, p. 349, ill.
Auction of Gallé covered Easter egg.
"Gallé: Inspirations in Glass"
Southern Antiques, v. 10, no. 2, March 1984, p. 1+, ill.
Corning exhibit.
"Glaskunst—Ausstellungen von Daum demnächst auch in Japan"
Porzellan + Glas, no. 2, 1984, p. 239, ill.
Vases and objects from Daum on display in Japan.
"Der Kunststil einer Glasepoche"
Glaswelt, v. 36, no. 5, May 1984, p. 348+.
Jugendstil style; Gallé, Tiffany.
"Lalique Glass Exhibition at Dyansen 57 Gallery"
Antiques & The Arts Weekly, v. 12, no. 8, Feb. 24, 1984, p. 40, ill.
"Landmark Exhibit of Gallé's Glass Held"
MassBay Antiques, v. 5, no. 5, Aug. 1984, p. 28+, ill.
"Licht in eine Sammlung"
Antiquitäten-Zeitung, no. 23, Oct. 28–Nov. 10, 1983, pp. 522–523, ill.
Review of exhibit of Gruber collection at Pfalzgalerie, Kaiserslautern.
"New-York Historical Society Receives Neustadt Tiffany Collection"
Antiques & The Arts Weekly, v. 12, no. 9, March 2, 1984, p. 10.
Lamps and windows on display in 1983 presented to the society.
"Noch viele Unklarheiten zum Wiener Jugendstil"
Antiquitäten-Zeitung, no. 24, Nov. 9–22, 1984, p. 503, ill.
"Si vous aimez le verre Art Déco..."
Verres Actualités, no. 57, April 1984, pp. 27–28, ill.
Retrospective exhibition of Charles Schneider at Le Louvre des Antiquaires.
"A Touch of Glass"
Pan Am Clipper, March 1984, p. 14, ill.
Gallé exhibits at Steuben Gallery and at Corning.
"A Tribute to Tiffany... and Neustadt"
Home Lighting & Accessories, v. 67, no.

6, June 1984, pp. 62–66, ill.
Neustadt Collection.

"Turning Dreams into Glass"
Collector Editions, v. 12, no. 2, Summer 1984, p. 32, ill.
Gallé exhibit.

ADCOCK, CRAIG
"Geometrical Complication in the Art of Marcel Duchamp"
Arts Magazine, v. 58, no. 5, Jan. 1984, pp. 105–109, ill.
Duchamp's "Large Glass" sculpture.

ADLEROVÁ, ALENA
"Art Nouveau Glass from Klášterský Mlýn"
Glass Review, v. 39, no. 6, 1984, pp. 19–23, ill.
"Loetz-Gläser"
Weltkunst, v. 54, no. 7, April 1, 1984, pp. 879–882, ill.
Loetz' Witwe exhibition at Böhmerwaldmuseum, Kašperské Hory (Bergreichenstein).

Art Lamps. Combined Reprint: Jefferson Glass Company Ltd., Toronto [catalog no. 7]; Moe-Bridges Company, Milwaukee
Indian Head, Md.: Oscar and Carol Ghebelian, 1981, [42] pp., ill.
Both date from about 1924.

ASHBERY, JOHN
"Delirious Dreams Under Glass"
Newsweek, v. 103, no. 22, May 28, 1984, p. 70, ill.
Gallé show, Corning.

ASHFORD, ROGER
"Collecting Art Deco Statues"
Antiques Dealer, v. 36, no. 10, Oct. 1984, pp. 20–22, ill.
Includes lamps.

BARTEN, SIGRID
"Emile Gallé: Träume in Glas"
Sammeln Magazin, no. 10, Oct. 1984, pp. 14–23, ill.
Gallé's life and work, as well as information for the collector.

BASTARD-GRUEL, CHRISTIANE
"Verre: Décorchemont, verrier"
L'Estampille, no. 161, Sept. 1983, pp. 36–46, ill.
Stained glass, *pâte de verre*, and other glass by Décorchemont.

BAVIS, CLAIRE
"Corning Museum Announces Emile Gallé Exhibition"
Glass Review, v. 14, no. 3, April 1984, pp. 10–11, ill.

BLAKE, PETER
"Lasting Value"
Interior Design, v. 55, no. 2, Feb. 1984, pp. 234–235, ill.
Glassware designed by Josef Hoffmann, Oswald Haerdtl, and Adolf Loos for Lobmeyr.

BLOCH-DERMANT, JANINE
"Les Frères Schneider"
L'Oeil, no. 346, May 1984, pp. 60–63, ill.

BOLGER, NANCY
"Dreams Into Glass"
New York–Pennsylvania Collector, v. 9, no. 6, Aug. 1984, p. 15B, ill.
Gallé exhibition, Corning.

BORSI, FRANCO
and PERIZZI, ALESSANDRA
Josef Hoffmann, tempo e geometria
Rome: Officina Edizioni, 1982, 139 pp., ill.
Includes vessels and stained glass windows.

BOUR, EDOUARD
"Emile Gallé"
La Lorraine, Artiste et Littéraire, v. 23, Jan. 1905, pp. 3–15, ill.

BRUNHAMMER, YVONNE
The Art Deco Style
New York, N.Y.: St. Martin's Press, 1984, 176 pp., ill.
Glass, pp. 146–155 (Marinot, Décorchemont, Navarre, Lalique, and others), also Lighting, pp. 168–175.

BUDDENSIEG, TILMANN
and ROGGE, HENNING
Industriekultur: Peter Behrens and the AEG, 1907–1914
Cambridge, Mass.: The MIT Press, 1984, 520 pp., ill.
[Translation of 1979 book published in Berlin]. Designer's work includes lamps and lighting.

BUECHNER, THOMAS S.
"Emile Gallé: Dreams Into Glass"
American Craft, v. 44, no. 2, April/May 1984, pp. 32–35, ill.

CAMARD, JEAN-PIERRE
"Pioneers of Electric Lamps"
Réalités, no. 268, March 1973, pp. 60–67, ill.
Lamps by Gallé, Tiffany, and others.

CHAMBERS, KAREN S.
"Reviews: Emile Gallé: Dreams Into Glass"
New Work, no. 19/20, Summer/Fall

1984, pp. 30–31.
Corning exhibit.

CHARPENTIER, FRANCOISE-THÉRÈSE
Le Musée de l'Ecole de Nancy, s'enrichit et se renouvelle
Nancy: the museum, 1981, [11] pp., ill.
"Une oeuvre unique d'Emile Gallé: la *Vitrine aux libellules*"
La Revue du Louvre et des Musées de France, v. 33, no. 2, 1983, pp. 126–133, ill.
Dragonfly vitrine acquired by Musée d'Orsay; also other vitrines, cabinets, and glass by Gallé.

CUVELLARD, BRUNO
"Les Verreries Schneider"
La Revue de la Céramique et du Verre, no. 16, May/June 1984, pp. 11–15, ill.

DABBS, TONI
"Gallé: Creating Cameos in Glass"
Collectors News, v. 25, no. 3, July 1984, p. 45, ill.
Cameo production pieces by Gallé firm.

DARMSTADT. MATHILDENHÖHE
Charles Spindler: Jugendstil im Elsass
Darmstadt: Mathildenhöhe, 1983, 78 pp., ill.
Includes flask and drinking glass set designed by Spindler.
Joseph M. Olbrich, 1867–1908 (Ed. by Bernd Krimmel)
Darmstadt: Mathildenhöhe, 1983, 425 pp., ill.
Includes wineglasses and stained glass, pp. 340–341.

DAUM, NOËL
La Pâte de Verre
[s.l.] Editions Denoël, 1984, 188 pp., ill.
Throughout the ages, especially French 1890s–1930.

DAYTON, OHIO.
THE ART INSTITUTE
E. Colonna (Text by Martin Eidelberg)
Dayton, O.: the institute, 1983, 88 pp., ill.
Designs for stained glass, carafes, bottles, and mounts for Tiffany glassware.

DEMAY, MARIANNE
"Le Verre de la Belle Epoque"
Revue des Industries d'Art Offrir, no. 199, Jan. 1984, pp. 144–146, ill.

The market for collecting Gallé, Daum, Tiffany.

DÉZAVELLE, M. RENÉ
"L'Histoire des vases Gallé/The History of the Gallé Vases"
Glasfax Newsletter, v. 8, no. 6, Sept. 1974, pp. 1–104, ill.
Memoirs by a decorator employed by Gallé from 1919 to 1930.

EATWELL, ANN
"A Bold Experiment in Tableware Design"
Antique Collecting, v. 19, no. 6, Nov. 1984, pp. 32–35, ill.
1930s Stuart and Sons glass designs by Paul Nash, Graham Sutherland, Eric Ravilious, and others for a London exhibition.

ENGEL, VEDA, comp.
René Lalique: A Comprehensive Compilation of Articles and Illustrations on His Life, His Work, His Legacy
Rockford, Ill.: John Danis, [1984]. A looseleaf notebook of 56 xeroxed articles and illustrations.

ESCHMANN, KARL
Es war nicht alles Jugendstil zwischen 1890 und 1920
Kassel: Johannes Stauda Verlag, 1982, 268 pp., ill.
"Vasen, Gläser, Schalen," pp. 220–231: Gallé, Hoffmann, Loetz Witwe, etc.

FARLEY, KITTY
A Jean Sala Fish
New Orleans, La.: Unpublished typescript paper for the New Orleans Museum of Art, 1984, 18 pp., ill.
Made between 1925–1935.

FREDGANT, DON
"Tiffany's Touch"
Southern Antiques, v. 10, no. 8, Sept. 1984, pp. 6–7A, ill.
Desk sets with "Favrile" glass combined with other materials.

FREIBURG IM BREISGAU.
AUGUSTINERMUSEUM
Nora Ortlieb Glaskunst
Freiburg i. Br.: the museum and Hans H. Hofstätter, 1984, 48 pp., ill.
Work of German engraver and glass designer, 1924–1979.

GARNER, PHILIPPE
Glass 1900: Gallé, Tiffany, Lalique
London: Thames and Hudson, 1979, [86] pp., ill.

GARNIER, EDOUARD
"Exposition Universelle de 1889. Les industries d'art: le verre"
Gazette des Beaux-Arts, v. [1?], 1889, pp. 561–581, ill.
Gallé glass.

GLASGOW. HUNTERIAN ART GALLERY, UNIVERSITY OF GLASGOW
Margaret Macdonald Mackintosh, 1864–1933
Glasgow: the gallery, 1983, [47] pp., ill.
Includes stained glass designs and panels of painted gesso set with glass beads.

HAGEN, TED
"Residential Art Glass Windows"
Victorian Homes, v. 1, no. 2, Spring 1982, pp. 30–31, ill.

HAYOT, MONELLE
"Daum à Tokyo"
L'Oeil, no. 342–343, Jan./Feb. 1984, pp. 80–83, ill.

HINZELIN, EMILE
"Emile Gallé"
La Lorraine, Artiste et Littéraire, v. 23, Jan. 1905, pp. 16–21, ill.

HOBSON, CINDY GRAFF
"Art Glass Shown Across Country"
Antique Monthly, v. 17, no. 9, Sept. 1984, p. 8B, ill.
Special exhibitions for Fall 1984, and permanent collections.

HOLEŠOVSKÝ, KAREL
"Prutscherovy poháry ze sbírky uměleckoprůmyslového odboru Moravské galerie"
Bulletin Moravské Galerie v Brně, no. 33, 1982, pp. 44–45, ill.
Wiener Werkstätte designer Otto Prutscher.

HOLLISTER, PAUL
"Tiffany in New York"
The Glass Club Bulletin, no. 144, Fall 1984, pp. 14–15.
Displays at the N.Y. Historical Society and the Metropolitan Museum.

JACKSON, MISSISSIPPI.
MISSISSIPPI MUSEUM OF ART
Art Nouveau, Art Deco, and Modernism: A Guide to the Styles, 1890–1940 (Text by Tom Dewey, II)
Jackson, Miss.: the museum, 1983, 73 pp., ill.

KAŠPERSKÉ HORY.
MUZEUM ŠUMAVY
Secesní sklo z Klášterského mlýna 1895–1914 (Text by Alena Adlerová)
Kašperské Hory: Muzeum Šumavy v Sušici in cooperation with Prague: Uměleckoprůmyslové Muzeum, 1984, [80] pp., ill.
German summary. Czech Sezession firms and designers: Loetz, Moser, Bauer, Hoffmann, Powolny, and others.

LAMBOURNE, LIONEL
"Richard Redgrave, RA: Artist and Administrator"
The V & A Album (Victoria and Albert Museum), no. 2, 1983, pp. 115–122, ill.
Redgrave design for enameled and gilt pitcher, probably made by T. F. Christie & Co., 1901.

LEMPEREUR, MARTINE
Les Cristalleries du Val-Saint-Lambert. La verrerie usuelle à l'époque de l'art nouveau (1894–1914)
Gembloux: Editions J. Duculot, S.A., 1976, 64 pp., ill.

LJUBLJANA. NARODNI MUSEUM
Secesija na Slovenskem
Ljubljana: Razstavišče Arkade, 1984, 162 pp., ill.
Secession glass, pp. 36–39: Loetz, Harrachov, and other firms.

MCCLINTON, KATHARINE MORRISON
"Art Nouveau Lamps and Lighting"
Hobbies, v. 89, no. 8, Oct. 1984, pp. 36–40, ill.

"Lalique Lamps and Lighting"
The Antique Trader Weekly, Annual of Articles on Antiques, v. 15, 1983, pp. 80–82, ill.

MCNALLY, JANET
"The Corning Museum Seminar, a Review"
Stained Glass, v. 79, no. 4, Winter 1984–85, pp. 342–344, ill.

MERRILL, NANCY O.
"New Accession: A 'New' Tiffany Glass Flower Form"
The Chrysler Museum Bulletin, v. 14, no. 11, Nov. 1984, p. [6], ill.

MIAMI, FLORIDA. MIAMI-DADE COMMUNITY COLLEGE
Brave New Worlds: America's Futurist Vision. The Mitchell Wolfson Jr. Collection of Decorative and Propaganda Arts
Miami, Fla.: Mitchell Wolfson Jr.

Collection, the college, 1984, 71 pp., ill.
Nine glass examples of the 1930s: Fostoria, Teague for Steuben, Copier, etc.

MICHAEL, GEORGE
"Antiques & Americana: Tiffany Lamps"
The Antique Trader Weekly, Annual of Articles on Antiques, v. 15, 1983, p. 366, ill.
Brief article.

MOSS, DAVID
"Car Mascots"
The Antique Dealer & Collectors Guide, Jan. 1984, pp. 58–59, ill.
Lalique, 1920s and 1930s.

NEW YORK, N.Y.
DYANSEN 57 GALLERY
Lalique—Encore. March 1 thru March 31, 1984 (Text by Nicholas Dawes)
New York, N.Y.: the gallery, [1984, 50] pp., ill.
Sculpture and glass, 1920s.

O'BRIEN, TIM
"The Colorful, Unique Items of Louis Comfort Tiffany"
Victorian Homes, v. 3, no. 2, Spring 1984, pp. 11–12+, ill.

OKABE, AOMI
"Un Hôtel particuleur Art Déco s'ouvre au public"
L'Oeil, no. 342–343, Jan./Feb. 1984, pp. 52–57, ill.
Lalique door panels in 1930s Tokyo hotel.

OPIE, JENNIFER HAWKINS
"Twenty Years of Ceramic and Glass Design: The Collections of the British Institute of Industrial Art and Industry"
The V & A Album (Victoria and Albert Museum), no. 2, 1983, pp. 250–257, ill.
British glass of the 1920s and 30s now in the V & A.

PARIS. LE LOUVRE
DES ANTIQUAIRES
Charles Schneider, maître-verrier. Verreries Schneider France de 1913 à 1940
Paris: the gallery, 1984, 129 pp., ill.

PAZAUREK, GUSTAV E. and
SPIEGL, WALTER
Glas des 20. Jahrhunderts: Jugendstil und Art Déco
Munich: Klinkhardt & Biermann, 1983, 263 pp., ill.

RICOUR, MONIQUE
"Letter from Paris: Glass"
Antiques, v. 126, no. 2, Aug. 1984, p. 282+, ill.
Exhibition "Charles Schneider—Maître-Verrier."

RUTHER, ROSELINE
"Les Cristalleries de Baccarat lancent le livre de Janine Bloch Dermant: 'Le Verre en France d'Emile Gallé à nos jours'"
Revue des Industries d'Art Offrir, no. 199, Jan. 1984, pp. 260–262, ill.

SCHNEIDER-HENN, DIETRICH
"Die Enthüllung des Lichts"
Antiquitäten-Zeitung, no. 22, Oct. 12–25, 1984, pp. 461–469, ill.
Lamps and lighting from firm of Puhl & Wagner, Gottfried Heinersdorff, Berlin-Treptow, 1918–1923.

SCHÜLY, MARIA
"Nora Ortlieb Glaskunst"
Weltkunst, v. 54, no. 23, Dec. 1, 1984, p. 3666, ill.
Exhibit of engraver and designer at Augustinermuseum, Freiburg.

SCHÜLY, MARIA and
SCHMIDT, EVA
"Wilhelm von Eiff und seine Schule"
Weltkunst, v. 54, no. 10, May 15, 1984, pp. 1416–1419, ill.
Exhibition in Freiburg of the Stuttgart glass artist and engraver, 1890–1943.

SCHWEIGER, WERNER J.
Wiener Werkstätte: Design in Vienna 1903–1932
New York, N.Y.: Abbeville Press, 1984, 272 pp., ill.
Glass designs by Moser, Hoffmann, Peche, etc., pp. 192–199.

SEOUL. CHUNG ANG GALLERY
Arnubo Yuri maeng pum Jeon Chung Ang Gallery gae gwan gi neom
Seoul: the gallery, 1984, 157 pp., ill.
Exhibition to commemorate opening of new art gallery: Gallé, Daum, Art Deco, some contemporary glass.

SHERRILL, SARAH B.
"Current and Coming: Art Glass"
Antiques, v. 126, no. 2, Aug. 1984, p. 228+, ill.
St. Louis Art Museum exhibit.
"Current and Coming: The Arts and Crafts Movement"
Antiques, v. 125, no. 1, Jan. 1984, p. 50+, ill.
Art glass, leaded glass included in

exhibit of New York State work, 1890s–1920s.
"Current and Coming: Glass"
Antiques, v. 126, no. 3, Sept. 1984, p. 416+, ill.
Exhibition of Art Nouveau glass at Georgia Museum of Art.

SOBBE, W.
Die Metallplastik: Neueste effektvollste Liebhaberkunst. Anleitung und Katalog, 1911/12
Cassel: W. Sobbe, Leibhaberkünste, 1911, 236 pp., ill.
Home furnishings of many materials, including blank glass vases and photo holders for hand painting at home.

SPIELMANN, HEINZ, ed.
Jugendstil
Dortmund: Harenberg Kommunikation, 1983, 138 pp., ill.
Gallé, Daum, Tiffany, Lalique, Lötz in Museum für Kunst und Gewerbe, Hamburg.

STEEFEL, LAWRENCE D., JR.
The Position of Duchamp's "Glass" in the Development of His Art
New York, N.Y.: Garland Publishing, Inc., 1977 [thesis, 1960], 423 pp., ill.

SUWA-SHI. KITAZAWA
BIJUTSUKAN [KITAZAWA
MUSEUM OF ART]
Kōno jōjō gare to Aru Nuono garasu kōgei
Nagano-ken, Suwa-shi: the museum, [1982?], 137 pp., ill.
[In Japanese only]. Includes work of Gallé, Daum, Rousseau.

VIENNA. GALERIE
BEI DER ALBERTINA
Traum der Kinder. Wien um 1900. Kinder der Träume. Verkaufsausstellung/Art-Sale Exhibition
Vienna: the gallery, 1984, 145 pp., ill.
English summary.
Lamps and glass, pp. 59–69, 118–133: Bimini, Wiener Werkstätte, O. Prutscher, Hoffmann, Powolny, & others.

VIENNA. HOCHSCHULE FÜR
ANGEWANDTE KUNST
Koloman Moser 1868–1918. Zusammenstellung und Gestaltung der Ausstellung Oswald Oberhuber, Julius Hummel
Vienna: the college, 1979, 303 pp., ill.
Includes the designer's work in tableware, vases, stained glass.

WARMUS, WILLIAM
Emile Gallé: Dreams into Glass

Corning, N.Y.: The Corning Museum of Glass, 1984, 191 pp., ill.
Exhibition catalog.

WATTS, DAVID C.
"The Glass of Emile Gallé"
Glass Circle News, no. 28, March 1984, pp. 3–4.
Review of London lecture by T. S. Buechner.
"The Glass of Emile Gallé. Corning's 1984 Exhibition of Emile Gallé"
British Artists in Glass Newsletter, [no. 1, 1984, pp. 6–7].
Based on talk given by T. S. Buechner at The Glass Circle, London.

WEBER, WILHELM
"Erwerbungen für die Jugendstil-Glassammlung"
Mainzer Zeitschrift, v. 77/78, 1982/83, pp. 223–225, ill.
Acquisitions by Mainz museum.

WIEDERSHEIM, WILLIAM A.
"Touches of Tiffany: Louis Comfort Tiffany in New Haven"
Journal of the New Haven Colony Historical Society, v. 31, no. 1, Fall 1984, pp. 35–49, ill.

WILLIAMS, WILLIAM C.
Motoring Mascots of the World
Osceola, Wis.: Motorbooks International, 1979, 196 pp., ill.
Includes Lalique mascots.

STAINED GLASS

ANONYMOUS
"Acid Depositions Threaten Stained Glass Treasures in Europe"
Glass Studio, no. 43, April 1984, p. 37.
"Acid Rain Study Alarms Europe's Stained Glass Artists"
Stained Glass, v. 79, no. 2, Summer 1984, p. 111.
"Athenaeum Symposium to Study Architectural Stained Glass"
Antiques & The Arts Weekly1, v. 12, no. 32, Aug. 10, 1984, p. 8.
"Expositions: le vitrail en Lorraine"
Archéologia, no. 190, May 1984, pp. 12–13, ill.
12th–20th c.
"First Glass Cricket?"
Country Life, v. 176, no. 4538, Aug. 9, 1984, p. 377, ill.
Cricket players in an 1890s window, Lancashire.

"Ein Forum Art-Kalender für 1984 mit 13 farbigen Abbildungen von Tiffany-Fenstern"
Glas + Rahmen, no. 11, June 1983, p. 646+, ill.
Calendar of Tiffany windows.
"Garfield Memorial Window Restored"
Williams Alumni Review, Spring 1983, p. 8, ill.
John La Farge window, 1882.
"Glasgemälde. Neuerwerbungen 1983"
Schweizerisches Landesmuseum, no. 92, 1983, pp. 72–78, ill.
Wappenscheibe.
"[On the Exhibit of Stained Glass at the Fair]"
American Architect and Architecture (American Architect and Building News), v. 42, no. 933, Nov. 11, 1893, pp. 74–75.
Tiffany windows displayed at the Columbian Exposition.
"L'Origine et l'évolution du vitrail"
Dossiers de l'Archéologie, no. 26, Jan./Feb. 1978, pp. 8–11, ill.
Includes map of principal French sites.
"Reconditioned"
Preservation News, March 1983, p. 12, ill.
Francis Lathrop skylight, 1893–1895, in The Breakers, Newport, R.I.

ACHILLES, ROLF
"Art from the Past and 'Art from the Past': Tiffany and the Middle Ages"
Stained Glass, v. 79, no. 1, Spring 1984, pp. 22–26, ill.
Tiffany's interest in medieval art as a source for creative ideas.

ADAMS, HENRY
Mont-Saint-Michel and Chartres
New York, N.Y.: G. P. Putnam's Sons, 1980, 192 pp., ill.
"Picture Windows"
Art & Antiques, April 1984, pp. 94–103, ill.
John La Farge.

ALEX, REINHARD
Glasgemälde Gotisches Haus Wörlitz
Wörlitz: Staatliche Schlösser und Gärten, 1983, folder, 11 ill.

ARWAS, VICTOR
Berthon & Grasset
New York, N.Y.: Rizzoli International Publications, 1978, 144 pp., ill.
Grasset's stained glass, pp. 16–22.

BARNETT, JERRY
"Stained Glass Windows Are Recognized as Artistic Works"
Collectors News, v. 25, no. 3, July 1984, p. 64.

BERNARDI, CARLA
Cento acquerelli preraffaelliti e neogotici inglesi per vetrate
Milan: Gruppo Editoriale Fabbri-Bompiani, 1984, 93 pp., ill.
English watercolors of Pre-Raphaelite and neo-Gothic stained glass designs.

BEUCHER, MONIQUE
"Les Verrières du choeur d'Evreux"
Dossiers de l'Archéologie, no. 26, Jan./Feb. 1978, pp. 63–75, ill.
14th c. windows.

BLONDEL, NICOLE
"Le Vitrail lorrain et la technique" [in]
Le Vitrail en Lorraine du XIIe au XXe siècle, [Nancy?]: Inventaire Général des Monuments et des Richesses Artistiques de la France, Editions Serpenoise, Centre Culturel des Prémontrés, 1983, pp. 11–32, ill.

BOLGER, NANCY
"Old Stained Glass Finds New Market"
The New York–Pennsylvania Collector, v. 8, no. 11, Jan./Feb. 1984, p. 12, ill.

BONNENFANT, PAUL and GUILLEMETTE
"Les Artisans du plâtre à Sanaa, Yemen"
Revue des Etudes Islamiques, v. 45, no. 2, 1977, pp. 247–262, ill.
Method of making stained glass windows in Yemenite town.

BRINKMANN, ULRIKE
Das jüngere Bibelfenster
Cologne: Verlag Kölner Dom e.V., n.d. [1984?], 40 pp., ill.
Cologne cathedral windows.

BRISAC, CATHERINE
"Annonciation et anges de Saint-Jean de Lyon"
Revue de l'Art, no. 57, 1982, pp. 73–76, ill.
15th c. windows.
"La Peinture sur verre à Lyon"
Dossiers de l'Archéologie, no. 26, Jan./Feb. 1978, pp. 38–49, ill.
Late 12th–early 13th c.
"The Romanesque Window at Le Champ-près-Froges"

163

Journal of Glass Studies, v. 26, 1984, pp. 70–76, ill.
Le Vitrail
Rennes: Ouest France, 1980, 32 pp., ill.
History and techniques.

BRUSSELS. MUSÉE HORTA
À SAINT-GILLES
Jacques Gruber (1871–1936), ébéniste et maître-verrier
Brussels: Musée Horta à Saint-Gilles and l'Inventaire Général des Monuments et des Richesses artistiques de la France, [1984], 66 pp., ill.

CALLIAS-BEY, MARTINE
"Le Recensement général des vitraux de France"
Dossiers de l'Archéologie, no. 26, Jan./Feb. 1978, p. 124.
Stained glass census in France.

Catalog der reichhaltigen Glasgemälde- und Kunst-Sammlung der Herren C. und P. N. Vincent in Capitelsaal (Münsterplatz No. 4) in Constanz
Constanz: Verlag v.C. & P. N. Vincent, 1890, 104 pp., ill.
Collection especially strong in 14th–15th c. Swiss stained glass.

The Cathedral Church of St. John the Divine, New York City [calendar, 1982]
New York, N.Y.: the Cathedral Shop, [1981], [26] pp., ill.

CAVINESS, MADELINE H.
"Stained Glass"
English Romanesque Art 1066–1200 (exhibition at the Hayward Gallery, 1984), London: The Arts Council of Great Britain in association with Weidenfeld and Nicolson, 1984, pp. 135–145, ill.

CAVINESS, MADELINE; PASTAN, ELIZABETH; and BEAVEN, MARILYN
"The Gothic Window from Soissons: A Reconsideration"
Fenway Court (Isabella Stewart Gardner Museum), 1983, pp. 6–25, ill.

CHOUX, ABBÉ JACQUES
"Le Vitrail lorrain au Moyen-Age et à la Renaissance" [in]
Le Vitrail en Lorraine du XIIᵉ au XXᵉ siècle, [Nancy?]: Inventaire Général des Monuments et des Richesses Artistiques de la France, Editions Serpenoise, Centre Culturel des Prémontrés, 1983, pp. 33–57, ill.

COLLEY, CATHERINE
"Le Vitrail des années 20 et 30 en Lorraine" [in]
Le Vitrail en Lorraine du XIIᵉ au XXᵉ siècle, [Nancy?]: Inventaire Général des Monuments et des Richesses Artistiques de la France, Editions Serpenoise, Centre Cultural des Prémontrés, 1983, pp. 113–123, ill.
Lorraine stained glass of the 1920s and 30s.

COTTON, VERE E.
The Book of Liverpool Cathedral
Liverpool: Liverpool University Press for the Liverpool Cathedral Committee, 1964, 221 pp., ill.
Windows by Whitefriars Studios, 1906–1924, and later post-World War II replacements.
The Liverpool Cathedral Official Handbook
Liverpool: Littlebury Bros. for the Liverpool Cathedral Committee, 4th edition, 1924, 121 pp., ill.
Windows by Whitefriars Studios, 1906–1924.

COUNCER, C. R.
Lost Glass from Kent Churches: A Collection of Records from the Sixteenth to the Twentieth Century
Maidstone: Kent Archaeological Society, 1980, 170 pp., ill.

DONEGAN, FRANK
"In the Marketplace: Architecturals"
Americana, v. 12, no. 4, Sept./Oct. 1984, pp. 18–21+, ill.
Victorian and Prairie School leaded and stained glass windows, doors.

DOWN, GEOFFREY
"Stained Glass Windows in 19th Century Melbourne"
Studies in Australian Art (ed. by Ann Galbally and Margaret Plant), Melbourne: Dept. of Fine Arts, University of Melbourne, [1978], pp. 27–34, ill.

DRACHENBERG, ERHARD
Die mittelalterliche Glasmalerei im Erfurter Dom. Teil 2: Dom, Abbildungsband
Berlin: Akademie-Verlag; Vienna: Verlag Hermann Böhlaus Nachf., 1983, 375 pp., ill.
(Corpus Vitrearum Medii Aevi, DDR I, 2).

EDWARDS, JOHN
"Lily-Crucifixions in the Oxford District"
Oxford Art Journal, v. 2, April 1979, pp. 43–45, ill.

ELZEA, ROWLAND
"The Viking Ship Window from 'Vinland'"
Tiller, v. 2, no. 4, March/April 1984, pp. 60–63, ill.
Burne-Jones window done for a Newport, R.I. home, 1884.

EVANS, DAVID
A Bibliography of Stained Glass
Woodbridge, Suffolk: Boydell & Brewer Ltd., 1982, 200 pp.
Lists 6,000 items and includes a general and a topographical index.

FARMER, OSCAR G.
Fairford Church and Its Stained Glass Windows
Bath: Harding and Curtis, Ltd., 5th edition, 1938, 83 pp., ill.
Fairford Church and Its Stained Glass Windows
[Fairford, U.K.: s.n.], 2nd edition, 1928, 83 pp.

FARNHAM, SURREY. WEST SURREY COLLEGE OF ART AND DESIGN
William Morris & Kelmscott
London: The Design Council in association with the college, 1981, 190 pp., ill.
Includes stained glass designs by members of the Morris firm.

FOY, DANIÈLE
"Les Verres trouvés dans les fouilles archéologiques"
Dossiers de l'Archéologie, no. 26, Jan./Feb. 1978, pp. 114–122, ill.
Stained glass production in southern France.

FREEMAN, JOHN CROSBY
"Elbert Hubbard and the Roycroft Community"
Victorian Homes, v. 1, no. 2, Spring 1982, pp. 55–58, ill.
Stained glass lamps and lighting fixtures by Dard Hunter.

Galerie für Glasmalerei und Hinterglas, Sibyll Kummer-Rothenhäusler, Zürich [sales catalog for Kunst und Antiquitätenmesse, Basel]
[Zurich: the gallery, 1984], 19 pp., ill.

GANDIOL-COPPIN, BRIGITTE
"Dossier d'initiation: le vitrail roman"
Archéologia, no. 187, Feb. 1984, pp. 54–66, ill.
Introduction to medieval stained glass in France.

GATOUILLAT, FRANÇOISE
"Saint-Sulpice-de-Favières: des vi-

traux témoins de l'art parisien au temps de saint Louis"
Dossiers de l'Archéologie, no. 26, Jan./Feb. 1978, pp. 50–62, ill.

GILMORE-HOUSE, GLORIA
"Angers Cathedral: An Early Twentieth-Century Restoration of Mid Fifteenth-century Glass"
Journal of Glass Studies, v. 26, 1984, pp. 77–85, ill.

GOLDICH, LOUIS MYRON
An Examination of the Italian Glass Industry and Its Influence on Native Stained and Painted Glass
[Victoria, British Columbia]: thesis, Master of Arts in the Department of History in Art, University of Victoria, June 1977, 136 pp., ill.

GRODECKI, LOUIS
"Une grande entreprise internationale: Le Corpus Vitrearum Medii Aevi"
Dossiers de l'Archéologie, no. 26, Jan./Feb. 1978, pp. 124–125.

GUTSCHER, DANIEL
"Karolingische Holzbauten im Norden der Fraumünsterabtei"
Zeitschrift für Schweizerische Archäologie und Kunstgeschichte, v. 41, no. 3, 1984, pp. 207–224, ill. English summary. Fragments of 9th–10th c. painted stained glass from Zurich excavations.

HAMY-LONGUESP, NICOLE
"Troyes, haut-lieu du vitrail"
Dossiers de l'Archéologie, no. 26, Jan./Feb. 1978, pp. 86–101, ill.
16th–17th c. windows, including work of Gontier workshop.

HANY, NICOLE
"Un Peintre-verrier troyen de la Renaissance: Jean Soudain"
Revue de l'Art, no. 63, 1984, pp. 17–34, ill.

HARPER-HINTON, REGINALD
"Update on the New Zealand Stained Glass Research Project"
Stained Glass 1984 (The Magazine of the British Society of Master Glass-Painters), Autumn 1984, p. 14.
Recording and preserving 19th and 20th c. windows.

HARRISON, MARTIN
"Stained Glass: Windows on Another World" [in]
By Hammer and Hand: The Arts and Crafts Movement in Birmingham (Ed. by Alan Crawford), Birmingham: Birmingham Museums and Art Gallery, 1984, pp. 119–128, ill.

HAWARD, BIRKIN
Nineteenth Century Norfolk Stained Glass: Gazetteer, Directory, An Account of Norfolk Stained Glass Painters
Norwich: Geo Books and Centre of East Anglian Studies, 1984, 302 pp., ill.

HEATON, MAURICE
"Progressive Steps in the Making of Stained Glass Windows"
The American Architect, Jan. 20, 1929, pp. 97–103, ill.

HÉROLD, MICHEL
"Les Vitraux anciens de l'église Saint-Côme-et-Saint-Damien à Vézelise"
Le Pays Lorrain, v. 62, no. 3, 1981, pp. 177–193, ill.
"Les Vitraux anciens de Lorraine: richesse et originalité"
Le Vitrail en Lorraine du XIIᵉ au XXᵉ siècle, [Nancy?]: Inventaire Général des Monuments et des Richesses Artistiques de la France, Editions Serpenoise, Centre Culturel des Prémontrés, 1983, pp. 59–72, ill.

HUBEL, ACHIM
Die Glasmalereien des Regensburger Domes
Munich: Verlag Schnell & Steiner, 1981, 155 pp., ill.

HUSCH, GAIL E.
"David Maitland Armstrong"
Antiques, v. 126, no. 5, Nov. 1984, pp. 1175–1185, ill.
Painter who became a stained glass designer, 1880s–1930s.

International Correspondence Schools Ltd. Stained Glass and Mosaic [Instruction paper with examination questions]
London: International Correspondence Schools, Ltd., (Reading and London: Wyman & Sons, Ltd.), n.d., 102 pp., ill.
Description of techniques and methods.

KALINOWSKI, LECH
"'Virga versatur.' Remarques sur l'iconographie des vitraux romans d'Arnstein-sur-la-Lahn"
Revue de l'Art, no. 62, 1983, pp. 9–20, ill.

KENNEDY, PAUL E.
Stained Glass Windows Coloring Book
New York, N.Y.: Dover Publications, Inc., 1972, [16] pp., ill.

KJELLBERG, PIERRE
"Les premiers vitraux gothiques"
Connaissance des Arts, no. 394, Dec. 1984, pp. 80–87, ill.
Early 13th c. windows from Soissons, Bourges, Notre-Dame de Paris.

LA FARGE, HENRY A.
"The Early Drawings of John La Farge"
The American Art Journal, v. 16, no. 2, Spring 1984, pp. 4–37, ill.
Artist used *cliché verre* technique in making prints. [No reference to stained glass].
"John La Farge's Work in the Vanderbilt Houses"
The American Art Journal, v. 16, no. 4, Autumn 1984, pp. 30–70, ill.

LADIS, ANDREW
"The Velluti Chapel in Santa Croce, Florence"
Apollo, v. 120, no. 272, Oct. 1984, pp. 238–245, ill.
Windows attributed to Jacopo del Casentino, 1320s.

LARKWORTHY, PETER
Clayton and Bell, Stained Glass Artists and Decorators
London: The Ecclesiological Society, 1984, 25 pp., ill.

LAUTIER, CLAUDINE
"La Technique du vitrail"
Dossiers de l'Archéologie, no. 26, Jan./Feb. 1978, pp. 26–37, ill.

LAWRENCE, WADE ALAN
Tiffanys in Duluth: The Anne Weston Connection
[Duluth, Minn.?]: Thesis for B.A. in Art History, University of Minnesota, Oct. 1984, 79 pp., ill.
Life and work of a Tiffany Studio designer.

LEGGET, J. A.
"Bede Monastery Museum, A Review of the Permanent Exhibition"
Museums Journal, v. 82, no. 4, March 1983, pp. 229–231, ill.
Saxon window glass, releaded for display purposes.

LENNOX, JUNE
"Saving Stained Glass"
The V & A Album (Victoria and Albert Museum), no. 2, 1983, pp. 240–245, ill.

LOBRI, FANTA
Féeries lumineuses sur verre ou néo-vitrail

165

Annecy: Gardet Editeur, 1973, 31 pp., ill.
Hobby book, imitation stained glass.

LONDON. VICTORIA and ALBERT MUSEUM
Pattern and Design: Designs for the Decorative Arts 1480–1980 (Ed. by Susan Lambert)
London: the museum, 1983, 196 pp., ill.
Designs for stained glass by Christoph Murer (or Maurer) about 1600, and Charles F. A. Voysey, 1907.

LUCHS, ALISON
"Origins of the Widener Annunciation Windows"
National Gallery of Art Bulletin, v. 7, 1975, pp. 81–89, ill.

MALONE, WILLIAM R.
"Making Kokomo Colors for a Century"
Stained Glass, v. 79, no. 1, Spring 1984, pp. 34–35, ill.
History of firm making opalescent sheet glass.

McNALLY, SEAN M.
"The Deep Sea"
Stained Glass, v. 79, no. 3, Fall 1984, pp. 244–245, ill.
Rediscovered Tiffany window, c. 1882.

MÉRAS, MATHIEU
"Le Trésor de la cathédrale Saint-Jean"
Monuments Historiques, no. 116, Sept./Oct. 1981, pp. 74–77, ill.
At Lyon.

MILLARD, RICHARD
"Hiemer & Company"
Stained Glass, v. 79, no. 3, Fall 1984, pp. 252–257, ill.
History of the N.J. firm since 1931.

MURRAY, MEGAN
"Census on Glass"
Americana, v. 12, no. 1, March/April 1984, p. 30.

Musée de l'Ecole de Nancy: le vitrail
Nancy: the museum, 1981, 28 pp., ill.
Biographies of Nancy stained glass artists and catalog of the collection.

PARRY, T. GAMBIER
The Ministry of Fine Art to the Happiness of Life. Essays on Various Arts
London: John Murray, 1887, 387 pp.
Includes "Art and Artists of Glass Painting, Ancient and Medieval," pp. 211–262.

PATTYN, CHRISTIAN
"L'Apport des métiers d'art à la restauration du patrimoine"
Métiers d'Art, no. 24, Nov. 1983, pp. 96–101, ill.
Includes current restoration efforts of French stained glass.

PEACE, DAVID
"Traditional Clear Glass in Churches, Or, 'Keep the Crown'"
Association for Studies in the Conservation of Historic Buildings Transactions, v. 7, 1982, pp. 17–18.

PERROT, FRANÇOISE
"Les Verrières de Saint-Vincent place du Vieux-marché à Rouen"
Monuments Historiques de la France, no. 103, June 1979, pp. 53–61, ill.
16th c. windows installed in new Rouen church.
"Le Vitrail légendaire à Saint-Ouen de Rouen"
Monuments Historiques de la France, no. 103, June 1979, pp. 27–32, ill.
"Les Vitraux d'Ecouen"
Dossiers de l'Archéologie, no. 26, Jan./Feb. 1978, pp. 76–85, ill.
16th c. windows.

PILGRIM, DIANNE H.
"'Lost' Window Rediscovered"
The Brooklyn Museum Newsletter, Oct. 1984, p. 7, ill.
Lamb Studios window.
"'Lost' Window Rediscovered at the Brooklyn Museum"
New York-Pennsylvania Collector, v. 9, no. 7, Sept. 1984, p. 19, ill. [Also in *Ohio Antique Review*, v. 10, no. 10, Oct. 1984, p. 40, ill.].
Frederick Lamb window, "Religion Enthroned," 1899.

PIRINA, CATHERINE
"Stained Glass from Milan Cathedral at Fenway Court"
Fenway Court (Isabella Stewart Gardner Museum), 1983, pp. 26–37, ill.

POLAK, ADA
"Glassmalerier fra Agder i 1600-årene"
Aust-Agder-Arv. Årbok for Aust-Agder-Museet og Aust-Agder-Arkivet 1981–1982, Arendal, Norway: the museum, 1983, pp. 7–42, ill. English summary.
17th c. painted panes in Arendel museum.

RAGUIN, VIRGINIA CHIEFFO
"The Jesse Tree Prophet: In the

Workshop Tradition of the Sainte-Chapelle"
Journal of the Worcester, Mass. Art Museum, v. 3, 1979–1980, pp. 28–35, ill.

RODA, BURKARD VON
"Nach 40 Jahren wieder ausgestellt"
Kunst & Antiquitäten, no. 1, Jan./Feb. 1984, p. 45, ill.
Armorial panel in Aschaffenburg by Zurich glass painters C. and J. Murer, 1609–10.

ROUSSEL, FRANCIS
"Renaissance et développement du vitrail lorrain au XIXe siècle; Le vitrail Art Nouveau en Lorraine; Les vitraux de la première reconstruction" [in]
Le Vitrail en Lorraine du XIIe au XXe siècle, [Nancy?]: Inventaire Général des Monuments et des Richesses Artistiques de la France, Editions Serpenoise, Centre Culturel des Prémontrés, 1983, pp. 73–112, ill.

SIBBETT, ED, JR.
Cathedral Stained Glass Coloring Book
New York, N.Y.: Dover Publications, 1980, [32] pp., ill.

SLOAN, JULIE L.
"A Stained Glass Primer"
Historic Preservation, v. 35, no. 6, Nov./Dec. 1983, pp. 14–17, ill.

STATZ, VINCENZ
Details gothiques/Gothische Einzelheiten 1867. 7me Ptie Modèles pour vitraux
Liège and Leipzig: En, Elaesen Editeur, 1867, 7 pp., ill.
19 plates of stained glass designs, mostly geometric patterns.

The Story of Stained Glass
[St. Louis, Mo.]: The Stained Glass Association of America, 7th edition, revised 1984, 24 pp., ill.

STUTTGART. ALTES SCHLOSS SCHILLERPLATZ UND KUNSTGEBÄUDE SCHLOSSPLATZ
Die Zeit der Staufer: Geschichte—Kunst—Kultur [3 vols. Band 1: Katalog, Band 2: Abbildungen, Band 3: Aufsätze]
Stuttgart: Württembergisches Landesmuseum, 1977.
12th–13th c. German windows.

TEAGUE, WALTER DORWIN
"The Future of Stained Glass"
The Architectural Forum, v. 73, Aug. 1940, pp. 99–100.
Summary of an address given to the SGAA, 1940.

TEMME, NORMAN
"Christopher Whall Plaque Dedicated"
Stained Glass, v. 79, no. 1, Spring 1984, p. 3.

THOMPSON, B. L.
The Parish Church of St. Martin Windermere. [Bowness-on-Windermere]: A History and Guide
Leeds: Parochial Church Council, 1978, 24 pp., ill.

THOMPSON, POLLY POVEY
"Povey Brothers"
Stained Glass, v. 79, no. 4, Winter 1984–85, pp. 331–337, ill.

THORP, GREGORY
"Sporting Glass"
American Heritage, v. 35, no. 2, Feb./March 1984, pp. 60–63, ill.
Windows with sports subjects, designed in the 1920s, cathedral St. John the Divine.

Tiffany Windows [1984 calendar]
Steinheim: Forum Bildkunstverlag and Munich: Verlag L. Däbritz, 1983, 13 leaves, ill. English summary.
"Windows made between 1893 and 1923 and mostly commissioned privately."

TÖRÖK, GYÖNGYI
"Die Motive vom Marientod auf slowenischen Fresken im Lichte der mitteleuropäischen Ikonographie"
Zbornik za Umetnostno Zgodovino, v. 16, 1980, pp. 75–82.
Death of the Virgin motif in some Slovenian churches.

TROY, NANCY J.
"Figures of the Dance in De Stijl"
The Art Bulletin, v. 66, no. 4, Dec. 1984, pp. 645–656, ill.
Pair of stained glass windows by Van Doesburg, 1917.

TUARZE, PIERRE
Voie de lumière
Brest: Imprimerie Commerciale et Administrative, 1979, 117 pp., ill.
Monograph on d'Auguste Labouret, 1871–1964, a French *maître-verrier*.

VAASSEN, ELGIN
"Die ersten Fenster für den Regensburger Dom aus der königlichen Glasmalereianstalt, Gründung König Ludwigs I., aus dem Jahre 1828"
Diversarum Artium Studia. Beiträge zu Kunstwissenschaft, Kunsttechnologie, und

ihren Randgebieten. Festschrift für Heinz Roosen Runge (Ed. by H. Engelhart and G. Kempter, Weisbaden: Reichert), 1982, pp. 165–184, ill.
Early 19th c. stained glass workshops at Nuremburg and Benediktbeuren where Regensburg Cathedral windows were made.

Le Vitrail en Lorraine du XIIe au XXe siècle
[Nancy?]: Inventaire Général des Monuments et des Richesses Artistiques de la France, Editions Serpenoise, Centre Culturel des Prémontrés, 1983, 439 pp., ill.
Exhibition catalog as well as inventory of stained glass in Lorraine; articles on history of the area windows.

WALTER, ELISABETH
"Invitation au voyage: le décor"
Monuments Historiques de la France, no. 6(?), 1978, pp. 35–44, ill.
Includes mosaics and stained glass, 1920s, in French railroad stations.

WATERSON, JOHN
"From Cologne to Cassiobury: Provenance of the Stoke D'Abernon Glass"
Country Life, v. 175, no. 4527, May 24, 1984, pp. 1504–1506, ill.
15th c. panels.

WAYMENT, HILARY G.
"Six Netherlandish Roundels from the Collection of Dr. C. A. Ralegh Radford, F.S.A."
The Antiquaries Journal, v. 63, Part 2, 1983, pp. 387–388, ill.
First half of the 16th c.
"Stained Glass for the Private Collector"
Antique Collecting, v. 19, no. 1, May 1984, pp. 32–35, ill.

WHITE, CLAIRE NICOLAS
"Joep Nicolas"
New Work, no. 17/18, Winter/Spring 1984, pp. 10–13, ill.

WHITEHOUSE, DAVID B.
"Fire at York"
The Corning Museum of Glass Newsletter, Autumn 1984, pp. 1–2, ill.
Damage to the windows and the plans to restore.

WYNNE, MICHAEL
"A Life Concerned with Glass"
Country Life, v. 175, no. 4530, June 14, 1984, pp. 1740–1742, ill.
Evie Hone, 1894–1955.

BEADS

ANONYMOUS
"Important Late 19th-Century Venetian Bead Collection"
The Bead Forum, no. 5, Oct. 1984, pp. 5–7.
Sample book found in Scottsdale, Arizona.
"Manufacturing Techniques"
The Bead Society Newsletter, v. 9, no. 5, April/May 1984, p. 7.
Two bead making processes briefly described.
"Patterns of Power: The Symbols of Great Lakes Indian Art"
Canadian Collector, v. 19, no. 6, Nov. 1984, pp. 20–24, ill.
Exhibition of beadwork in the McMichael Canadian Collection, Kleinburg, Ontario.
"Woher kommen die vielen kleinen Perlen aus buntem Glas?"
Antiquitäten-Zeitung, no. 5, Feb. 17–March 1, 1984, pp. 90–91+, ill.
Auction of 19th c. items, including a Biedermeier beaker with a beaded band.

ALLEN, JAMEY D.
"Chevron-Star-Rosetta Beads: Part 1"
Ornament, v. 7, no. 1, Sept. 1983, pp. 19–24+, ill.
[Offprint: a corrected version of original in *Ornament* which had typesetting errors].
Part 2: v. 7, no. 2, Dec. 1983, pp. 24–29, ill. Part 3: v. 7, no. 3, March 1984, pp. 24–27, ill. Part 4: v. 7, no. 4, Summer 1984, pp. 24–26, ill.

BAKER, STANLEY L.
"Collecting Artifacts and Beadwork of the Plains Indians"
The Antique Trader Weekly, Annual of Articles on Antiques, v. 15, 1983, pp. 24–27, ill.

DRISCOLL, BERNADETTE
"Sapangat: Inuit Beadwork in the Canadian Arctic"
Expedition, v. 26, no. 2, Winter 1984, pp. 40–47, ill.

FRANCIS, PETER, JR.
"Bead News Roundup"
The Bead Study Trust Newsletter, no. 4, Oct. 1984, pp. 3–6.
Reports on Korean beads; beads from an early Spanish/Arawak Indian encounter, possibly connected with Columbus' landing.

"Bead Report X: Part II. A Bead Pot-pourri"
Ornament, v. 7, no. 3, March 1984, p. 29+.

"Bead Report XI: Beads and the Discovery of America, Part 1. Beads of the Native Americans"
Ornament, v. 7, no. 4, Summer 1984, pp. 16–19+, ill.

"Beadmakers' Strike in India"
The Bead Forum, no. 5, Oct. 1984, pp. 7–8.
Beadmaking processes and working conditions in a village in Andhra Pradesh.

"Early Post-Contact Native-Made Glass Beads in America?"
The Bead Forum, no. 2, May 1983, pp. 5–7.

"Letter from Peter Francis"
The Bead Society Newsletter, v. 10, no. 1, Aug./Sept. 1984, p. 14.
Korean bead history.

GILBERT, JANE C.
A Book of Crocheted and Knitted Bags [Book of Bags no. 2]
New York, N.Y.: H.K.H. Silk Co. of New York, Inc., 1923, 36 pp., ill.
"The models . . . represent exclusive creations in 1923–24 hand-worked bags."

GUMPERT, ANITA
"Special Beads from Mauritania"
Washington Bead Society Newsletter, v. 1, no. 4, Sept. 1984, pp. 1–3, ill.

HARRIS, ELIZABETH
"Bead Detective"
The Bead Society Newsletter, v. 10, no. 1, Aug./Sept. 1984, p. 5.
Glasses (and beads) with special refractive properties: opal, dichroic, chatoyance.

Late Beads in the African Trade
Lancaster, Pa.: G. B. Fenstermaker, 1984, 16 pp., ill.

"A Rare Find"
The Bead Society Newsletter, v. 10, no. 1, Aug./Sept. 1984, p. 6.
19th c. Venetian bead sample book.

HAYES, CHARLES F., III, ed.
Proceedings of the 1982 Glass Trade Bead Conference Sponsored by the Arthur C. Parker Fund for Iroquois Research
Rochester, N.Y.: Research Division, Rochester Museum & Science Center, 1983, 284 pp., ill.

HOPEWELL, JEFFERY
Pillow Lace and Bobbins
Aylesbury, Bucks: Shire Publications Ltd., 3rd edition, 1984, 32 pp., ill.
Ring of beads attached to many bobbins.

KARKLINS, KARLIS
Glass Beads
Ottawa: National Historic Parks and Sites Branch, Parks Canada (History and Archaeology no. 59), 1982, 117 pp., ill.
Book review by Peter Francis, Jr. in *Historical Archaeology*, v. 18, no. 2, 1984, pp. 130–132.

KENNEDY, S. S. J.
"Juxtaposition: Beaded Belts"
Ornament, v. 7, no. 2, 1983, p. 58, ill.

LAMOTHE, EVA S.
"The Art of Cameroon"
Arts Quarterly (New Orleans Museum of Art), v. 6, no. 4, Oct./Dec. 1984, pp. 12–17, ill.
Exhibition at the museum includes beadwork.

LIESE, GABRIELLE
"The Bead Museum"
The Bead Society Newsletter, v. 9, no. 5, April/May 1984, p. 5.
In Prescott, Arizona.

LIU, ROBERT K.
"Follow Up: Dzi Beads"
Ornament, v. 7, no. 4, Summer 1984, p. 29, ill.

"Imported Chinese Jewelry"
Ornament, v. 7, no. 4, Summer 1984, pp. 56–61, ill.

LIZÉ, PATRICK
"The Wreck of the Pirate Ship 'Speaker' on Mauritius in 1702"
The International Journal of Nautical Archaeology and Underwater Exploration, v. 13, no. 2, May 1984, pp. 121–132, ill.
Trade beads, pp. 126–127.

MUNAN-OETTLI, ADELHEID
"Bead Cap 64/88 in the Sarawak Museum Collection"
The Sarawak Museum Journal, v. 32, no. 53 (New Series), Aug. 1983, pp. 89–96, ill.

OSWALT, WENDELL H.
Kolmakovskiy Redoubt: The Ethnoarchaeology of a Russian Fort in Alaska
Los Angeles, Cal.: Institute of Archaeology, The University of California, 1980, 212 pp., ill.
Bottles and a quantity of beads, 1841–1917.

PADDOCK, FRANK K.
"The Intrigue of Glass Beads"
Antiques Dealer, v. 36, no. 2, Feb. 1984, pp. 14–16, ill.
Tribal and trade beads.

PASQUATO, MICHELANGELO
"Conterie e Cristallerie a Murano"
Il Vetro, v. 17, no. 8, Aug. 1939, pp. 288–289, ill.
Bead production, Murano.

REITBERGER, DIANA
"Luminous Seeds: The Beadweaving of Lee Dickson"
Ontario Craft, v. 9, no. 1, Spring 1984, pp. 12–13, ill.

SMITH, MARVIN
"An Unusual Glass Bead from Southern Florida"
The Bead Forum, no. 2, May 1983, pp. 3–4.

SMITH, MONTE
The Technique of North American Indian Beadwork
Ogden, Utah: Eagle's View Publishing Co., 1983, 102 pp., ill.

Trade Bead Catalog [reprint]
Lancaster, Pa.: G. B. Fenstermaker, [1984], 14 pp., ill.
[Originally published by George Shumway, York Bead Co., 1973].

UKAI, NANCY
"Kyoyo Asao: Glass Bead Master, New Work"
Ornament, v. 7, no. 3, March 1984, pp. 2–5, ill.

WESTLAKE, FLORA
"Work on the Beck Collection"
The Bead Study Trust Newsletter, no. 1, March 1983, p. 1. Part 2: no. 2, Oct. 1983, p. 1. Part 3: no. 4, Oct. 1984, p. 1.

WINDISCH-GRAETZ, STEPHANIE zu and WINDISCH-GRAETZ, GHISLAINE zu
Juwelen des Himalaja: Götter, Völker und Kleinodien
Lucerne: Reich Verlag AG, 1981, 192 pp., ill.
Includes beads.

CONTRIBUTORS

GEORGE C. BOON, Keeper of Archaeology & Numismatics, National Museum of Wales, Cathays Park, Cardiff, Wales.

ROBERT H. BRILL, Research Scientist, The Corning Museum of Glass.

DANIÈLE FOY, Chargée de Recherches, Centre National de la Recherche Scientifique, Laboratoire d'Archéologie Médiévale Méditerranéenne, Université de Provence, France.

MEREDITH PARSONS LILLICH, Professor, Department of Fine Arts, College of Arts and Sciences, Syracuse University, Syracuse, New York.

ROY NEWTON, Honorary Visiting Professor, University of York, England; formerly Director of Research, British Glass Industry Research Association.

PUBLICATIONS

THE CORNING MUSEUM OF GLASS

		Postage/Handling	
EXHIBITION CATALOGS	Price	Domestic	Foreign
Cameo Glass, Masterpieces from 2000 Years of Glassmaking Sidney M. Goldstein, Leonard S. and Juliette K. Rakow, 144 pp., 193 illus.: 41 color, 152 b/w, 1982	$15.00	1.25	1.75
The Cut and Engraved Glass of Corning, 1868–1940 Jane Shadel Spillman and Estelle Sinclaire Farrar, 101 pp., 112 illus., 1977	5.00	1.25	1.50
Czechoslovakian Glass: 1350–1980 176 pp., 108 objects illus.: 69 color, 39 b/w, 1981	15.00	1.25	1.75
Emile Gallé: Dreams into Glass William Warmus, 191 pp., 123 illus.: 117 color, 6 b/w, 1984	25.00	1.75	2.25
Frederick Carder: Portrait of a Glassmaker Paul V. Gardner, 120 pp., 86 illus.: 79 color, 7 b/w, 1985	25.00	1.75	2.00
Pressed Glass: 1825–1925 48 pp., 30 color illus., 1983	6.00	1.00	1.25
MUSEUM COLLECTIONS CATALOG SERIES			
American and European Pressed Glass *in The Corning Museum of Glass*	25.00 (softcover)	2.50	3.50
Jane Shadel Spillman, 404 pp., more than 1500 illus., 16 color plates, 1981	30.00 (hardcover)	3.00	4.00
English and Irish Glass in The Corning Museum of Glass (in preparation)			
Pre-Roman and Early Roman Glass in The Corning Museum *of Glass* Sidney M. Goldstein, 312 pp., 919 illus. including 36 color plates, 144 profile drawings, 1979	40.00	2.50	3.50
Roman Glass in The Corning Museum of Glass (in preparation)			
Venetian Glass in The Corning Museum of Glass (in preparation)			
JOURNAL OF GLASS STUDIES			
Journal of Glass Studies Vol. 27, 1985	20.00	1.85	2.50
Journal of Glass Studies Vol. 26, 1984	20.00	1.85	2.50
Journal of Glass Studies Vol. 25, 1983	30.00	1.85	2.50
Journal of Glass Studies Vol. 24, 1982	20.00	1.35	1.85

	Price	Postage/Handling Domestic	Foreign
Journal of Glass Studies Vols. 14–23 (1972–1981)	15.00/vol.	1.35	1.85

Journal of Glass Studies
    Vols. 1–13 (1959–1971)
    Out of print (available in microfiche)			

Index—Journal of Glass Studies Vols. 1–15 (1959–1973) 1976	8.00	.75	1.00

NEW GLASS REVIEW

	Price	Domestic	Foreign

New Glass Review 6
    Annual photographic survey of glass objects made
    in 1984. 58 pp., 100 color illus., bibliography of
    articles and books on Contemporary Glass, Flat Glass,
    and Glass Technology, list of galleries exhibiting
    Contemporary Glass, 1985
	5.00	1.50	1.50

New Glass Review 5
    48 pp., 100 color illus. of objects made in 1983,
    bibliography of articles and books, list of galleries
    exhibiting Contemporary Glass, 1984
	2.50	1.25	1.50

New Glass Review 4 48 pp., 100 color illus., objects made in 1982; check list	2.50	1.25	1.50
New Glass Review 3 32 pp., 100 color illus., objects made in 1981; check list	2.50	1.00	1.25

SURVEYS OF GLASS

	Price	Domestic	Foreign

Glass Collections in Museums in the United States and Canada
    Survey of 205 U.S., 27 Canadian museums,
    224 pp., 141 illus., 1982
	6.00	1.00	1.25

Glassmaking: America's First Industry
    Jane Shadel Spillman, 35 pp., 34 illus.,
    six in color, 1976
	1.40	.75	1.00

A History of Glass in Japan Dorothy Blair, 479 pp., maps, plates, 1973	60.00	2.50	3.25

Masterpieces of Glass: A World History
from The Corning Museum of Glass
    Robert J. Charleston; Harry N. Abrams, Inc.
    240 pp., 102 color plates, 1980
	40.00	2.75	3.50

A Short History of Glass Chloe Zerwick, 96 pp., 94 illus.: 29 color, 65 b/w, 1980	5.00	1.00	1.25

GENERAL TITLES

	Price	Domestic	Foreign
The Corning Flood: Museum Under Water ed. John Martin, 72 pp., 120 illus., 1977	6.00	1.25	1.50

Czechoslovakian Diary: 1980
    Thomas S. Buechner and William Warmus,
    16 pp., 52 b/w illus., 1981
	.50	.75	1.00

	Price	Postage/Handling Domestic	Foreign
Decorative Glass Processes: Cutting, Etching, Staining and Other Traditional Techniques (1911) Arthur Louis Duthie, Reprint, The Corning Museum of Glass/Dover Publications, Inc., 267 pp., 88 illus., 1982	4.50	1.00	1.25
Frederick Carder, His Life and Work Thomas S. Buechner, 23 pp., 4 b/w illus., 1952 (reprinted 1985)	2.50	.50	.75
M'Kee Brothers-M'Kee & Bros. Victorian Glass; *Five Complete Catalogues from 1859/60–71* Reprint, The Corning Museum of Glass/Dover Publications, Inc., 160 pp., 1981	5.00	1.00	1.25
René Lalique et Cie. Lalique Glass. *The Complete Illustrated Catalogue for 1932* Reprint. The Corning Museum of Glass/Dover Publications, Inc., 149 pp., 1981	8.95	1.25	1.50
Tools of the Glassmaker 16 pp., 26 b/w illus., 1981	.50	.50	.75

FICHE

	Price	Postage/Handling Domestic	Foreign
Contemporary Glass 1976 Set of 2 color microfiche of 120 outstanding contemporary glass objects made in 1976 (with descriptive booklet), 1977	2.50	.75	1.00
Contemporary Glass 1977 Set of 2 color microfiche of 120 outstanding glass objects made in 1977 (with descriptive booklet), 1978	2.50	.75	1.00
Journal of Glass Studies Vols. 1–27 (1959–1985)	10.00/vol.	.50	.75

POSTERS (22½″ x 33″)

	Price	Postage/Handling Domestic	Foreign
Aphrodite, from Cameo Glass Exhibition (21¼″ x 28″)	1.50	1.25	1.50
The Colossi of Aboo Simbel c. 1854 (17½″ x 23″)	1.50	1.25	1.50
The Cut and Engraved Glass of Corning, 1868–1940	2.50	1.25	1.50
Czechoslovakian Glass: 1350–1980	1.50	1.25	1.50
Paperweights: "Flowers which clothe the meadows"	4.50	1.25	1.50
35 Centuries of Glassmaking	2.50	1.25	1.50
Glass Snuff Bottles of China	1.50	1.25	1.50
Tiffany's Tiffany (19½″ x 36″)	4.50	1.25	1.50

POSTCARDS

	Price		
56 different postcards of objects in The Corning Museum of Glass Collection	.15 each		

	Price	Postage/Handling	
		Domestic	Foreign

SLIDES

Slide catalog of 1,825 slides	5.00	1.00	1.25
(temporarily out of print)			
Slides of objects in The Corning Museum of Glass:	.75 each (see chart)		
Ancient to Contemporary, including selected			
paperweights, New Glass, Cameo, Czech,			
Pressed Glass, and Gallé objects from 1978–1984			
Frederick Carder: Portrait of a Glassmaker exhibition, 1985			
77 slides @ $.75 each			
12 postcards @ $.15 each			

Postage Chart for Slide Orders

1–5	$ .30
5–15	.70
15–20	.85
20–40	1.10
40–60	1.60
75–over 100	2.10

NOTECARDS AND PRINTS

Museum Notecards

The new Corning Museum of Glass, designed by
Gunnar Birkerts and opened in 1980, part of The
Corning Glass Center complex with the Hall of
Science and Industry and the Steuben Glass Factory.

	Price	Domestic	Foreign
10 notes and envelopes (8½" x 3¾")	3.00	.50	.75
ink sketch on ivory stock			
Print of The Corning Museum of Glass (9" x 20")	1.25	1.50	1.75

Glassmaker Notecards

A series of 18th-century glassmakers and glaziers
dressed in samples of their wares from a set of
engravings in The Corning Museum of Glass
print collection.

	Price	Domestic	Foreign
6 notes and envelopes (4¾" x 4½")	2.75	.50	.75
Subtle colors on ivory stock			

Note: New York State residents please add appropriate sales tax.
Postage charges may be subject to change without notification.

Bibliographies are available. Inquiries are invited.
ORDER FROM: The Corning Museum of Glass
Sales Department
Corning, New York 14831

Museum Members receive a 10% discount on orders of $5.00 or more.
MasterCard and Visa accepted.

THE FELLOWS OF THE CORNING MUSEUM OF GLASS

The design, composition, printing, and binding of
this publication are by Meriden-Stinehour Press,
Meriden, Connecticut and Lunenburg, Vermont.